Unhomed

*The publisher and the University of California Press
Foundation gratefully acknowledge the generous support of the
Fletcher Jones Foundation Imprint in Humanities.*

Unhomed

CYCLES OF MOBILITY AND
PLACELESSNESS IN AMERICAN CINEMA

Pamela Robertson Wojcik

UNIVERSITY OF CALIFORNIA PRESS

University of California Press
Oakland, California

© 2024 by Pamela Robertson Wojcik

Library of Congress Cataloging-in-Publication Data

Names: Wojcik, Pamela Robertson, 1964- author.
Title: Unhomed : cycles of mobility and placelessness in American cinema / Pamela Robertson Wojcik.
Description: Oakland, California : University of California Press, [2024] | Includes bibliographical references and index.
Identifiers: LCCN 2023040999 (print) | LCCN 2023041000 (ebook) | ISBN 9780520390355 (cloth) | ISBN 9780520390362 (paperback) | ISBN 9780520390379 (ebook)
Subjects: LCSH: Homeless persons in motion pictures. | Tramps in motion pictures. | Motion pictures—United States—History. | Place (Philosophy) in motion pictures.
Classification: LCC PN1995.9.H545 W65 2024 (print) | LCC PN1995.9.H545 (ebook) | DDC 791.43/6526942—dc23/eng/20231206
LC record available at https://lccn.loc.gov/2023040999
LC ebook record available at https://lccn.loc.gov/2023041000

33 32 31 30 29 28 27 26 25 24
10 9 8 7 6 5 4 3 2 1

CONTENTS

List of Illustrations vii
Acknowledgments ix

Introduction. All Over the Map: Figurations of Mobility and Placelessness 1

1 · Ubiquitous: The Tramp's Mobile Masculinity 19

2 · Uncivilized: World War II Mobilization and Homecoming as Social Problem 64

3 · Adrift: The Ambivalent Freedom of the Female Hitchhiker 111

4 · Trash: The Homeless as Urban Waste 158

Epilogue. Stuck: Precarity and Perpetual Motion as Slow Death 204

Notes 221
Works Cited 253
Index 269

ILLUSTRATIONS

I.1. Fern and Linda get a safety lesson in *Nomadland* 3
I.2. Instagram post about monetizing #vanlife 6
1.1. Whiteface in *Tramp Strategy* 37
1.2. Acorn authenticates Bumper in *Hallelujah I'm a Bum* 39
1.3. Black Mose tends to an injured white tramp in *Beggars of Life* 40
1.4. Sally disguised as a boy tramp in *Wild Boys of the Road* 44
1.5. Chaplin's Tramp as a masher in *Twenty Minutes of Love* 49
1.6. The Tramp's invasion of domestic—and screen—space in *Suspense* 51
1.7. A queer romance emerges from under the train in *A Romance of the Rails* 56
1.8. A queer embrace in *Clubs Are Trump* 58
2.1. Lovers say goodbye at the train station in *Since You Went Away* 73
2.2. Hildy shows unrestrained desire as she urges Chip to come to "My Place" in *On the Town* 79
2.3. Making Trudy's quickie marriage to Ratzkiwatzki official in *The Miracle of Morgan's Creek* 81
2.4. The "ugly" quickie wedding between Joe and Alice in *The Clock* 83
2.5. Everybody pitches in to build housing for veterans in *Living in a Big Way* 90
2.6. Women drive returning veterans in *The Impatient Years* and *The Best Years of Our Lives* 93
2.7. The Black soldier (Caleb Peterson) in the background in *Till the End of Time* 103
3.1. Hitchhiking as prostitution in *Highway Hell* 120

3.2. Al Roberts, an unreliable and wayward hitchhiker in *Detour* *127*

3.3. The sociopathic hitchhiker in *The Hitchhiker* *131*

3.4. Titillating shot of Maggie hitchhiking in *The Hitchhikers* *152*

3.5. Mouse and Bird try to get a ride in *Teenage Hitchhikers* *153*

4.1. Homeless woman in the music video for "Gypsy Woman (She's Homeless)" *160*

4.2. Punk "Sleez Bags" throng to see Nicky in concert in *Times Square* *183*

4.3. Matthew and Jerry seek shelter in *The Saint of Fort Washington* *188*

4.4. Flora emerges from a trash bag in *Stone Pillow* *189*

4.5. Bolt is stripped of his phallic power and becomes "trash" in *Life Stinks* *193*

4.6. From homeless hustler to Wall Street tycoon via bromance in *Trading Places* *197*

4.7. The Artist and Young Woman in *Sidewalk Stories* *202*

E.1. Ale hustles for an auto repair shop at Willet's Point, Queens, in *Chop Shop* *211*

E.2. Mont and Jimmie skateboard past new construction in *The Last Black Man in San Francisco* *214*

E.3. *Heaven Knows What* and the refusal of closure *217*

ACKNOWLEDGMENTS

This book, like its subject, has gone through many cycles, each chapter leading me down a different pathway of research and film viewing, each one teaching me a great deal about American history and film history, each one introducing me to different characters and variations of mobility and placelessness. Working on this book has sometimes been difficult, but the pleasure of discovering aspects of United States history and films that I did not previously know, or had not previously known much about, has been a joy and a privilege.

This project was conceived in 2018 when Yannis Tzioumakis invited me to deliver a keynote lecture at the conference "Retrenching/Entrenching Youth: Mobility and Stasis in Youth Culture Representation on Screen" at the University of Liverpool. That keynote, "Perpetual Motion: Mobility, Precarity, and Slow Death Cinema," compared contemporary films about the youthful precariat to Depression-era tramp films. It inspired me to work backward to consider the long arc of precarity, mobility, and placelessness in cinema, ultimately arriving at this project. I am very grateful to Yannis for the generative opportunity. In October 2020, I presented a version of that talk online for the Columbia Film Seminar with Dana Polan as respondent, and the paper was revised for publication in the volume I coedited with Paula Massood and Angel Daniel Matos, *Media Crossroads: Intersections of Space and Identity in Screen Cultures* (2021). Thanks to Dana, members of the seminar, and especially Paula and Angel, for their astute comments and questions. The essay, now my epilogue, leans heavily on the late Lauren Berlant's work, and I was honored to have them read and respond positively to it and to have them teach it in their seminar.

Portions of chapter 1 were presented at the Society for Cinema and Media Studies (SCMS) online conference in 2021 and the "Space Between:

Literature and Culture, 1914–1945" conference in Cleveland in 2022. Portions of chapter 2 were presented at SCMS online in 2022 and in person in Denver in 2023. Chapter 3 was presented at the "Chicago Seminar on Media and the Moving Image" in November 2021. Chapters 1 and 3 were presented at the "Visual Culture Workshop" at Notre Dame in fall 2020 and fall 2022. In 2023, Yannis Tzioumakis invited me back to Liverpool for the "New Directions in the Cinema and Youth Cultures Research Symposium," where I presented part of chapter 3. I was fortunate to present an overview of the project for the online "Mobility Roundtable" in January 2021. I participated in another online roundtable, "Media, Precarity, and Home," organized by Anna Viola Sborgi and published in the online journal *Mediapolis* in 2021. I am grateful to the attendees and interlocutors at each presentation, all of whom helped shape my thinking.

Many smart friends and colleagues read or heard portions of this project and provided essential feedback, including Chris Becker, Don Crafton, Michael DeAngelis, Eva Fernandez, Barbara Green, Michael Kackman, Mary Celeste Kearney, Priya Jaikumar, Barbara Klinger, Paula Massood, Angel Matos, Dan Morgan, Susan Ohmer, Matthew Payne, Dana Polan, Ariel Rogers, Lynn Spigel, Neil Verma, and especially Jim Collins, who kindly read and commented attentively on every chapter with incredibly helpful feedback. Rick Wojcik and Joe Bryl provided crucial pop cultural resources, Benjamin D. Brazil graciously shared his dissertation, and Sam Wojcik provided helpful references.

Chase Cummings and Shea Murphy served as extremely useful and energetic research assistants. Chase especially helped me locate hundreds of tramp films. Shea's impeccable historical research on World War II and hitchhiking deepened and expanded the project. Jakim Aaron also produced helpful research and performed yeoman's work copyediting, changing all my citations from parenthetical style to endnotes.

Thanks to Raina Polivka for being such a welcoming and astute editor and to everyone at the University of California Press, including the thoughtful anonymous readers and the very patient and helpful editorial assistant Sam Warren, for shepherding this book to completion.

I was extremely honored and fortunate to receive a Guggenheim Fellowship in 2020 that made work on this book possible. Ironically, for a book about various forms of homelessness, I was largely ensconced at home in the spring of 2021 and again in spring 2022, taking two semester-long leaves from my position at the University of Notre Dame to research and write. I would not have had these leaves without generous financial support from the Guggenheim, and I could not have taken them if Kevin Dreyer had not graciously stepped in to serve as acting chair of my department during those semesters. Thanks to Rick Wojcik, Sam Wojcik, and Ned Wojcik, who were each trapped at home with me for portions of that time and proved to be lovely cellmates, despite all of us being a bit stir-crazy.

This book is dedicated to those without any such agreeable homes and to the many activists and volunteers who work tirelessly to help the unhoused and unhomed.

INTRODUCTION

All Over the Map

FIGURATIONS OF MOBILITY AND PLACELESSNESS

IN 2021, CHLOÉ ZHAO'S FILM *Nomadland* won the Golden Lion at the Venice Film Festival, the Academy Award, Golden Globe, the British Academy Film Award (BAFTA), and many other awards for Best Picture, as well as numerous Best Directing awards for Zhao and Best Actress awards for Frances McDormand. *Nomadland* captures aspects of a hitherto ignored subculture of transient houseless older Americans who have taken to the road in RVs and vans, seeking itinerant jobs rather than experiencing the promised ease of retirement. The film filters our knowledge and experience of the nomads through McDormand's fictional character Fern, a widow who loses her home when the US Gypsum plant that dominates her hometown of the ironically named Empire, Nevada, shuts down and the town is abandoned.

The film is based on the nonfiction book *Nomadland: Surviving America in the Twenty-First Century*, by Jessica Bruder, and the film incorporates many of Bruder's characters, who play themselves and interact with Fern. Bruder details the economic realities that underpin the reasons why the people documented are forced to adopt nomadism: societal and economic failure that produces extreme income disparities, high medical expenses, crushing debt, inadequate Social Security payments, a reliance on itinerant workers, and lack of benefits and savings. Bruder notes that nomads often claim to be choosing their destiny, but she emphasizes how the sense of choice is kettled by economic realities. Bruder quotes one nomad who makes clear that they face, at best, a Hobson's choice: "The economy is not getting better. You have a choice—you can be free or you can be homeless."[1] With regard to female nomads, in particular, Bruder calls attention to the economic reality of older women in America: among older women living alone, more than one in six live in poverty; older women are two times more likely than older men to be poor; and, owing to the gender wage gap, wherein women earn eighty cents on the male dollar, and time out of employment because of maternity and other caregiving work, women earn significantly less than men over their lifetime and thus get fewer benefits from Social Security and accumulate less savings than men.[2] Bruder underscores how difficult the nomad lifestyle can be. She describes how these older workers are hired by Amazon for seasonal work, which specifically recruits the elderly homeless under the moniker CamperForce. These workers walk more than twenty thousand steps a day doing hard physical labor and are often injured, yet they have no benefits.

Some reviews of *Nomadland* censure the film for softening Bruder's critique. Richard Brody notes that the film shows both "the struggles of nomads of necessity, who lost their livelihoods, and those who describe their nomadism in terms of a spiritual quest, an intentional rejection of settled ways of life and what they consider more conventional and more commercial, consumerist values."[3] He argues, however, that the film tilts the balance to the latter by tying Fern's motives to a desire for independence rather than economic concerns. Joshua Keating claims, similarly, that rather than emphasize "the economic conditions that make retirement impossible for middle-class Americans," the film opts to present nomadism "as a means of personal liberation or escaping personal trauma."[4]

In many ways, the film explains Fern's nomadism as the result of a character trait. For example, given a chance to move in with fellow nomad and semiboyfriend Dave (David Straithairn), who is leaving the road for the comforts of his son's comfortable house and the ties of family, Fern opts for the road. She won't even sleep in the guest bedroom, choosing her van over a comfortable bed. When Fern visits her sister to borrow cash for van repairs, her sister asks her to move back to her childhood home, but Fern says she can't live there. Her sister identifies Fern's refusal as a long-standing character trait: "It's always what's out there that's more interesting. You left here as soon as you could." Her sister expresses her disappointment that she didn't have Fern with her when she was growing up but commends Fern for her unconventionality. Where others viewed her as "eccentric," or "weird," she says, she always saw Fern as "braver and more honest than everybody else."

Not only does the film play up Fern's choice, but it also downplays the difficulty of nomadism (the infamous scene of Fern pooping in a bucket, aside). Keating suggests that the film presents a "surprisingly benign portrayal of work at Amazon, leaving out the long hours, grueling physical demands and frequent injuries," in order, he implies, to get permission to film

FIGURE I.1. Fern (Frances McDormand) and nonactor Linda May get a safety lesson in this portrait of Amazon as a beneficent employer in *Nomadland*.

at an Amazon warehouse. Indeed, we see the CamperForce workers getting safety tips from an Amazon worker, taking a convivial lunch break, and working without any sense of strain or difficulty, all while the Amazon logo is prominently displayed on uniforms and boxes. Fern, especially, seems to be enjoying the work and smiles as she carries a bin through the Amazon warehouse wearing an Amazon hat. In addition to Amazon, Fern labors at a turnip farm, works the kitchen at Wall Drug, and serves as a cleaning lady at a campsite. None of these are made to seem terrible, and McDormand brings a degree of wonder and joy to her portrayal that makes her character seem to be enjoying even the grubbiest labor.

Other reviews read the film through a more romantic lens. Brian Tallerico calls it "a gorgeous film that's alternately dreamlike in the way it captures the beauty of this country and grounded in its story about the kind of person we don't usually see in movies."[5] Tallerico notes that "there's an interpretation of *Nomadland* that it's the story of a woman running from grief, unmoored from society after everything she knew up and vanished," but he emphasizes, on the one hand, the film's striking landscapes and beautiful cinematography and, on the other, its attention to the beauty of small things and kind gestures. Viewing the film as a balm for the multiple anxieties of 2020, he avows, "Maybe we should all hit the road." A. O. Scott notes that the film "smooths" the social criticism in Bruder's book to focus on "resilience, solidarity, [and] thrift" in a narrative that toggles the "tension between stability and uprooting, between the illusory consolations of home and the risky lure of the open road."[6] Nonetheless, he ultimately celebrates the unsettling as indicative of a "fine Emersonian spirit."

In some ways, these romantic readings of the film are inevitable. While some may have wanted the film to hew more closely to Bruder's dark portrayal of elderly itineracy, Keating suggests it may be impossible to make an anti–road movie: "Put your protagonist on the open road through a classic American landscape and it will seem appealing, no matter what the circumstance."[7] Keating may be wrong about the anti–road movie: has he seen *Detour* (Ulmer 1945), *Duel* (Spielberg 1971), or *The Road* (Hillcoat 2009)? But he is right that we have been culturally conditioned to view shots of the landscape from a moving vehicle as appealing and that we often project onto the open road what Scott refers to as a "risky lure."

When *Nomadland* screened at my university, many of these competing views of the film came into play during a panel discussion after the screening. The panel consisted of myself, a white male colleague working in labor history, and a Black British female postdoc in sociology. The labor historian and I both read the film through the lens of precarity. He came armed with statistics about the dismal financial prospects for elderly women and the horrendous working conditions at Amazon. I discussed the long arc of precarity in film, linking this film to others about tramps and the unhoused. The postdoc, however, had a different view. She saw in this film her mother's migration to the United States from England: for her, it was a story of grit, resilience, and hope. I pushed back a bit, discussing the way in which the film's aesthetics idealized Fern's experience; and I asked the audience if they would really want to see their mothers or grandmothers living like this. A white male colleague in my department responded by saying that his mom was doing just that, traveling the country in an RV. He admitted, however, that his mom was not hauling turnips or working at Amazon, and his mom still had a nice suburban house available when she wanted to return.

OTHER VANS

As these varying responses indicate, *Nomadland* conjures a spectrum of connotations of itinerant mobility as variously related to freedom, grit, resilience, escape, and tourism, on one end, and poverty and lack of stability, on the other. Amplifying the spectrum, the elderly nomads can be placed in conversation with the contemporaneous movement labeled #vanlife, which stitches nomadism to privilege more than precarity. As Chris Moody describes it, #vanlife is aimed at "how to live a counterculturallifestyle but keep making money doing it."⁸ Where *Nomadland* shows characters working itinerant jobs to survive, the ethos of #vanlife monetizes itineracy itself to escape the drudgery of work. Moody declares it "a new version of the American dream. It is no longer one of stability and rootedness but one more fit for the current age that promises you can have it all: the so-called 'dream job' can be yours, all while enjoying an endless vacation."

To be sure, elderly nomads share images and information about their van life on YouTube, Instagram, and other social media, "but vanlife, as a concept and as a self-defined community, is primarily a social-media phenomenon."⁹ As Caity Weaver describes them, the TikTok and Instagram accounts of so-called vanlifers "are an infinite reservoir of gorgeous, unpeopled scenery previously encountered only in desktop backgrounds: sunrise canyons, sunset oceans, high-noon highways that stretch on, carless, forever."¹⁰ Rachel Monroe shrugs that "the same vanlife pictures get taken over and over: the van's back doors opening onto an ocean vista; a long-exposure nighttime shot of the van, cozy and lit from within, against a backdrop of stars; a woman on the van's roof, in the middle of a sun salutation."¹¹ Open #vanlife on Instagram and you will see myriad images like this, populated especially by young white heterosexual couples, the woman frequently photographed alone and in a bikini.

More than simply documenting #vanlife, vanlifers are social media influencers who earn money as brand ambassadors and by garnering multiple sponsorships with product placements. Monroe describes one sponsored #vanlife post for the water-bottle company Hydro Flask. The Instagram image shows a gorgeous white woman "heating water in a teakettle, a light-blue thermos conspicuous in the background. 'Our bodies, the most precious vehicle for our journey here, run on water,' she wrote in the caption. 'A big thank you to @hydroflask for creating durable water bottles that help shift the bottled/privatization of [the] water paradigm.'"¹² A recent Instagram post under the moniker through.the.llyns shows a beautiful white woman lounging on top of her van. The posts respond to the seemingly annual declaration by through.the.llyns, "I'm not doing that for free," with commenters referring to "the industry" (presumably that of influencers?), proclaiming "know your worth" and "don't work for free" (work as lying on top of a van?), and describing themselves as wanting to work only with people who have an "abundance mindset" and "high values."

We can thicken our understanding of the connotations of mobility expressed around van living by looking back historically. In many ways, not

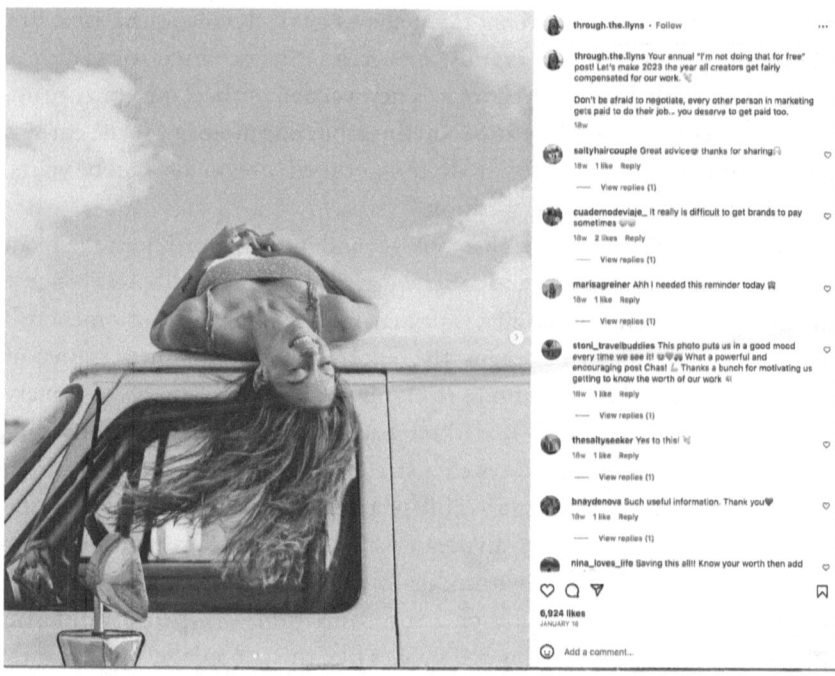

FIGURE I.2. Instagram post by through.the.llyns about monetizing #vanlife.

least in their fondness for VW vans, contemporary #vanlifers hearken back to countercultural hippie van dwellers. Celebrated in books like *Roll Your Own: The Complete Guide to Living in a Truck, Bus, Van or Camper,* hippie van or "truckee" life dovetailed with the larger movement of youth travel in the 1960s and 1970s.[13] Truckee Rob McGraw declared of two buses he shared with friends, "They were our houses, our homes, and we were on the move, looking for America and ourselves, too, I suppose."[14] The TV movie *In Search of America* (Bogart 1971), a pilot for a never-made TV series, echoes this view of truckee life, as a college dropout (Jeff Bridges) convinces his entire family, including his grandmother, to reexamine their life goals and leave it all for a cross-country trip on a renovated 1920s bus across America.

While #vanlifers borrow some of the language of the counterculture, they differ from hippie truckees in crucial ways. For one thing, #vanlife seems to be primarily populated by young, white heterosexual couples—as opposed to elderly nomads who seem to be mainly single—whereas truckee life carries the ethos of the commune and cooperative living. Most important, #vanlife differs from truckee life in the attitude toward work and money.

Certainly, truckees need to earn money, and *Roll Your Own* includes information about selling crafts or doing itinerant handyman work on the road; but the overall ethos of truckee culture is anticapitalist, aiming to escape the grind and tension of "the vicious earning-paying-for-the-right-to-live-and-eat cycle."[15]

If we consider van dwelling in the 1940s, a very different ethos motivates it, as it serves as a form of government housing. As Richard Foster details, trailers and trailer parks that had emerged in the 1930s "to satisfy the needs of vacationing motorists... lost their primary association with travel" in the 1940s and were, in effect, demobilized to serve as residences in areas suffering acute housing shortages during World War II.[16] Some thirty-six thousand trailers were purchased by the federal government for residential use and placed near defense plants and other wartime employment. Here, rather than mobility—whether perceived as freedom or precarity—the trailers provided stability in an insecure housing market. This can be seen in the film *Apartment for Peggy* (Seaton 1948), in which a young couple lives in a trailer allocated for GI housing as the husband attends college.

I begin with these variations on van, bus, and RV living as examples of the way in which even the same form of mobility—here, living in a vehicle—can carry multiple and competing meanings. Some of these differences depend on historical context—the difference between 1970s hippie culture and World War II, for instance—and others relate to cultural connotations—the lure of the open road or the image of a sunset, for example—that have accumulated over time. They variously characterize mobility as freedom and authenticity or as poverty and necessity—privilege or precarity. Where some are escaping the trappings of home for the pleasures of the open road, but have the option of returning to a more traditional home, others are uprooted and houseless but for their vehicle. These depictions also reflect different relations to work, as elderly nomads extend their working years past the age of retirement to work in temporary and seasonal jobs that are necessary for their survival; #vanlife influencers monetize their lifestyle to be free from the constraints of nine-to-five work; hippies work only enough to enable their lifestyle on the road; and World War II veterans and defense workers live in an RV in order to be proximate to their jobs. Each of these modes of van living is mediated through films, television, social media, and books, and those mediations shape our understanding of the differences among modes at the same time that they become part of the larger discourse about mobility.

THE TERRAIN

This book examines America's ambivalent and shifting attitude toward placelessness through marginalized figures of mobility in film. It examines films that show characters as unhomed and placeless, mobile rather than fixed: failing, resisting, or opting out of the mandate for a home of one's own. These narratives suggest the degree to which ideas of home and fixity in America depend on othering certain modes of mobility while promulgating others. They reveal a tension in the American imaginary between viewing homelessness as, on the one hand, deviance or threat and, on the other, as freedom and independence. This study points to changing ideals in America regarding the status of home, poverty, the ethics of care, class, and social mobility. It provides ways to think about what it means to be domiciled, who can choose to be unhomed, and how mobility is defined through privilege and precarity.

At the same time, the book provides a new way to view American film history. While these stories may seem to be insignificant trend-driven narratives of people on the fringe, they are in conversation with more conventional narratives of success, social mobility, and home: they are the flip side. Rather than marginal, these cycles of films about unhomed figures remind us that genres of precarity have been central to the American cinema (and American story) all along. These precarious narratives, in effect, unhome dominant narratives about American cinema as a cinema focused on ideologies of success and social mobility.

This project connects to my earlier work *The Apartment Plot: Urban Living in American Film and Popular Culture, 1945 to 1975* in thinking about the apartment as offering a vision of home centered on values of community, visibility, contact, density, friendship, mobility, impermanence, and porousness that contrasts sharply with more traditional views of home as private, stable, and family-based. It also connects to my work in *Fantasies of Neglect: Imagining the Urban Child in American Film and Fiction*, about the mobility of the urban child and two different senses of neglect: on the one hand, the view that the child appears to be neglected and thus unmoored, unsupervised, and unprotected; and, on the other hand, a more benign sense of neglect that points to the positive thrill and possible risk of the child's freedom, independence, and movement. *Unhomed* also considers alternatives to dominant narratives of home and competing views of mobility but hitches those concerns to notions of being unhomed, mobile, and placeless.

LEXICON

Let me start by considering my terms.

Unhomed

First, what do I mean by *unhomed*? Most people will hear that word and think of Homi Bhabha's famous formulation of the "unhomely" as "a paradigmatic post-colonial experience" that "has a resonance that can be heard distinctly, if erratically, in fictions that negotiate the powers of cultural difference in a range of historical conditions and social contradictions."[17] As Elisenda Masgrau-Peya suggests, Bhabha's conception of the unhomely is not "a question of being 'homeless,' . . . but a question of being outside of 'home,' of being forced to negotiate one's place in the world."[18] This condition of unhomeliness is not limited to, but is most clearly related to, the experience of migrants, postcolonials, and culturally hybrid people "for whom geographic or cultural dislocations are defining traits, either because they have been uprooted from former places of identification or because a familiar place has undergone radical change as a result of its colonial past or present."[19]

Of course, Bhabha's notion of the unhomely deliberately echoes Freud's conception of the *unheimlich,* or the uncanny, which blurs the line between home (*heimat, heimlich*) and its other. Bhabha describes "uncanny literary and social effects of enforced social accommodation, or historical migrations and cultural relocations."[20] For Freud, the *unheimlich* is "that class of the frightening which leads back to what is known of old and long familiar."[21] It is something familiar but repressed: it is the *un* or repressed of home. Thus, Dwayne Avery's book *Unhomely Cinema: Home and Place in Global Cinema* takes up Bhabha's notion with a strong emphasis on the uncanny to focus on films in which "dislocation and homesickness are ever present" and "the familiarity of home can quickly become alien, precarious and foreboding."[22] For Avery, unhomeliness describes "the shared anxieties that arise from living in a borderless world," as well as "the disappearance of the body in the fleshless spaces of information." He continues: "To encounter the unhomely is to witness the proper space of the nation unravel into the multilateral flows of network society."[23] For him, unhomely cinema relates to the conditions of globalization, the gig economy, social media, and technological mobility.

My use of the term *unhomed* intersects with these understandings of the unhomely but differs in fundamental ways. Bhabha's *unhomely* correlates being physically unhomed—moved—with a sense of what Edward Relph describes as "existential outsideness,"[24] in which one resides in a location but experiences feelings of alienation and not belonging. I am more interested in the physical dislocation and the condition of being unhomed prior to, or instead of, finding a new location—more in the space between homes than the uncanniness of home, more in the journey or movement than the destination. While mobility and placelessness exist in many different contexts and certainly apply to immigrants, postcolonials, refugees, or figures in exile—and my work is partly in conversation with those discourses—I am interested in quotidian forms of placelessness, the taken-for-granted forms of mobility and homelessness that exist alongside normative home life in America.[25]

Home is the structuring absence that shapes the sense of being unhomed. Elisabeth Bronfen works in the opposite direction from my interest in mobility, examining the meaning of home in Hollywood film, but her work also seeks to trouble the "opposition between home and dislocation." She writes that "stories about the successful achievement of a sense of being at home... at the same time articulate that even while their fantasy scenarios fill an originary sense of lack in plenitude, the traumatic core of dislocation can never be fully erased."[26] Reversing this idea, I suggest that stories of mobility and dislocation, even when they do not explicitly invoke, represent, or mention home, point to "the ambivalences and unresolvable antagonism written into any conception of home."[27] If, as John David Rhodes argues, "the detached single family home is one of the most powerful metonymic signifiers of American cultural life—of the dreams of privacy, enclosure, freedom, autonomy, independence, stability, and prosperity that animate national life in the United States"[28]—that is not to say that the home in American cinema is a simple or stable construct. If anything, it is represented most often as troubled, precarious, invaded, porous, or otherwise unstable. Indeed, across various genres, in narratives of home, "we are confronted immediately with the problem of how one is to live in a house, whether one is to live in a house—in one house or another, or even whether to live in a house at all."[29] In attending to narratives of mobility, I aim to unsettle narratives of home.

This book thus considers different ways of being unhomed—both by those who choose to be uprooted and mobile and those who have no choice; those who resist the trappings of home and those who desire them; those who perceive themselves as free and those who perceive themselves as unmoored or homeless.

Mobility

My second term is *mobility*. At base, mobility "encompasses both the large-scale movements of people, objects, capital and information across the world, as well as the more local processes of daily transportation, movement through public space and the travel of material things within everyday life."[30] Mobility is movement or the capacity for movement. It can mean simple movement, such as that of one's limbs or walking or riding in a car or bus, or it can mean large-scale migration. It may be bodily or geographic, relatively easy, complex, or constrained. The term can also be used to refer to the ability or capacity to move between social levels or classes, commonly referred to as "social mobility," or to move between occupations. My analysis does not take up questions of physical ability but considers the intersection between and among other forms, such as geographic mobility and social mobility or occupation.

While *mobility* can refer to different forms of literal or metaphoric movement, it also carries varying ideological meanings, depending on context. Tim Cresswell writes that mobility is "a kind of blank space that stands as an alternative to place, boundedness, foundations and stability."[31] As this suggests, the meanings of mobility can vary dramatically, depending on how place, stability, and fixity are defined. As Cresswell notes, "Mobility as progress, as freedom, as opportunity, and as modernity, sit [sic] side by side with mobility as shiftlessness, as deviance, and as resistance."[32] Forms of mobility usually associated with freedom include tropes of modernity such as the flaneur's aimless strolling, train travel, tourism, voluntary migration, and geographic mobility for jobs, better housing, and other forms of social mobility. These models of mobility are viewed as positive and progressive; they are opposed to things viewed as rooted, static, and bounded, which are seen to be reactionary and dull. Under the often more negatively viewed modes of mobility—those represented by the homeless, nomads, gypsies, refugees, exiles—fixity becomes an ideal, not reactionary or dull but grounding. Mobility, in this sense, looks like rootlessness.

Of course, neither the freedom to be mobile nor the ability to be rooted is ever accorded equally. We can think of *mobility* as defined not only in terms of freedom vs. rootlessness but via privilege and precarity. As sociologists Timothy Shortell and Evrick Brown note, "For the powerful, mobility is a lifestyle choice.... For the powerless, mobility is often forced—by the state, by the threat of violence, or impoverishment. And for some, mobility is denied entirely—by imprisonment or segregation."[33] Thus, ideas of mobility not only vary according to which kind of mobility one discusses—travel vs. migration, voluntary migration vs. involuntary, the figure of the flaneur vs. the homeless individual, etc.—but also in relation to which community, at which historical moment in time. This became very clear when the COVID-19 pandemic rendered questions of mobility and immobility—who could stay in place and who had to be mobile for work, for example—life-and-death questions of privilege and precarity.[34]

In thinking about mobility, I am also thinking about the centrality of movement to cinema. In Siegfried Kracauer's famous formulation, "movement is the alpha and omega of the medium."[35] Furthermore, Kracauer claims that cinema is concerned with the "flow of life," which entails, on the one hand, a sense of life's "haphazard contingencies" and, on the other, life's open-endedness. Movement, the flow of life, and contingency all come together, for Kracauer, in the *street*, "a term designed to cover not only the streets, particularly the city street, in the literal sense, but also its various extensions, such as railway stations, dance and assembly halls, bars, hotel lobbies, airports, etc."[36] These are spaces of mobility, spaces marked by transience.

Unhomed considers different kinds of mobility—including walking, train travel, public transit, and hitchhiking—and different scales of mobility, ranging from travel across the country and overseas to small circuits of movement within a city or neighborhood. These include the tramp's movement on foot and by rail, governmental movement of troops by train during World War II, young women hitchhiking, the wanderings of homeless people in urban centers, and the constant movement of workers in a gig economy. I am thinking about those modes of mobility in and through film, partly through a consideration of the aesthetics of mobility in tracking shots, for example, and more so in cinema's attention to movement, the contingency of encounter, and transient spaces of mobility, such as train stations, hobo camps, and sidewalks.

Placelessness

My third term is *placelessness*. For human geographers, the transient sites Kracauer lists as emblematic of the flow of life engender what Relph characterizes as placelessness. For Relph, placelessness is partly about the rapidly accelerating homogenization of places, "spaces that seem detached from the local environment and tell us nothing about the particular locality in which they are located."[37] But Relph also connects placelessness to increased mobility, as people are less anchored to any one place and as places are constructed to be transient and made for outsiders rather than to enable people to be inside a place and identify with it. Rather than placelessness, Marc Augé identifies transient spaces, such as Kracauer's street, as nonplaces. Such nonplaces are marked by "the fleeting, the temporary and the ephemeral"; they are "unrooted places marked by mobility and travel."[38]

While Relph, Augé, and others view placelessness as absence, Lucy Lippard considers nonplaces spaces of encounter and contact: "Most of us move around a lot, but when we move we often come into contact with those who haven't moved around, or have come from different places."[39] Thus, she argues, placelessness does not so much erase identity as stimulate hybridity, consisting of multiple influences and encounters. Not only do we bring ourselves and interact with others in nonplaces, but also, Lippard suggests, the "pull of place" never disappears: "Even as the power of place is diminished and often lost, it continues—as an absence—to define culture and identity."[40] Thus, we can think of placelessness as a condition of being mobile, of moving through transient spaces without inhabiting them as place or without being anchored to them; but we can also think of placelessness as lacking place, the lack creating a desire for place. The chapters that follow will take up these different meanings, often simultaneously, to capture the feeling of placelessness, as well as the movement inherent to it.

I consider placelessness as being without anchor and moving through transient nonplaces; as not confined to place, not bounded or defined; and as having no place in the social fabric, being marginal or even disposable. I consider how mobile and placeless figures interact with those who are housed and in places. I consider the desire and envy, as well as the fear and distrust, that figures of mobility engender.

Cycles

The fourth major term in my title is *cycles*. *Unhomed* considers mobility and placelessness in five different historical moments and distinct film cycles. I have chosen to look at film cycles in a distinct and intentional departure from genre studies—such as the road movie, one-off films like *Wanda* (Loden 1970), or more timeless figures, such as the drifter, for example—because I am interested in historical moments of heightened attention to homelessness, mobility, and placelessness.[41] Film cycles are, according to Amanda Klein, often neglected in film studies because they are associated with "commercialism and artlessness," providing audiences with "the same images, characters, and plots that they enjoyed in previous films."[42] As "cultural ephemera cranked out to capitalize on current trends, fads, and the success of other films," however, film cycles offer an incredibly useful lens on the complex and contradictory cultural discourse of a historical moment, particularly when the cycle emerges as the "result of some sociocultural cue" such as a social problem.[43] As short-term, market-driven clusters of films, film cycles, as Klein demonstrates, retain the marks of their historical, economic, and generic contexts and therefore can reveal much about the state of contemporary politics, prevalent social ideologies, aesthetic trends, popular desires, and collective anxieties.

Often, film cycles emanate from moral panics about a perceived threat to societal values or interests. Here, I chart moral panics about mobile and placeless figures and examine the film cycles generated in response to those panics. These panics are media-driven projections of an alleged social threat onto figures whose behavior—and, here, specifically, their status as unhomed, mobile, and placeless—is perceived as deviant and dangerous. Film cycles both exploit and fuel moral panics, ginning up concern about the threat. But film cycles are not mere megaphones for the panic. Instead, as works of art that aim to entertain as well as edify, and as commercial products that aim to compete with other films and thus cannot simply duplicate the narrative, aesthetics, or message of other films, film cycles can and must present multiple and varied approaches to a moral panic. Borrowing from John Ellis, I will consider film cycles as "working through" moral panics by compiling "multiple stories and frameworks of explanation which . . . enable viewers to work through the major public and private concerns of their society."[44] Since film cycles tend to occur in the midst of a moral panic, rather than reflect on an earlier time from the vantage point of the present, the narrative about a certain form of mobility (e.g., tramping) has not yet cohered and settled; therefore, the cycle is a multiplicity, not a monolith. Thus, rather than think of film cycles as merely reflecting a moral panic, we can think of them as refracting and transmuting moral panics. This means they often marshal potentially contradictory discourses and create sympathy for the supposedly deviant or troublesome figures rather than support the moral panic's attack on them.

Klein argues that film cycles have been marginalized both because they represent "deviant" subject matter and because they do so in "low culture" forms.[45] I make a case for both marginal "deviant" figures and marginal "low" films. This is a story of people on the margins, but being marginal does not mean insignificant; it means adjacent to the dominant, existing alongside it, commenting on it.[46] Stories of the marginal not only help us to revise our understanding of the dominant; they can be viewed as important in their own right. *Unhomed* asserts the importance of marginal figures such as the tramp, the veteran, the hitchhiker, and the unhoused. Some chapters find stories of these characters in mainstream and even canonical films that participate in a broader film cycle. But much of the book examines films that are largely forgotten, including exploitation films, B movies, made-for-TV movies, drive-in movies, and middlebrow Hollywood films that are no worse, really, than many we remember but that do not usually appear in academic classrooms or books. These films are crucial to the broader commercial cinema culture but have been consigned to the dust heap or circulate on the margins of film culture in alternative online video sites, YouTube, and streaming services, where they often serve marginal audiences such as youth or consumers of paracinema.

In attending to cycles of films, I hope to generate a thicker description of cultural discourse and a sense of the plurality of views and emotions generated by figures of mobility at any given time. In looking at film cycles, and especially by considering films not usually discussed as great works of art or even as historically significant, I aim to capture what often gets lost from our understanding of history as time slips away. By looking at distinct film cycles, this book seeks to explore why and how ideas about mobility and placelessness come to the fore at certain points in time, what anxieties or fantasies they manifest, and how they change over time. Throughout the book, each cycle of films will be read in context, in conversation with economic, social, and political discourses of the time, to situate the interest in mobility within its historical moment. Across each chapter, I will explore attitudes toward figures of mobility in relation to gender, race, and sexuality, as well as class.

ROADMAP

Each chapter is organized around a word that aims to capture the dominant discourse around an unhomed, mobile, and placeless figure, and each one has a defining cinematic mode.

Chapter 1, "Ubiquitous: The Tramp's Mobile Masculinity," examines a lengthy cycle of tramp films that extends from the beginning of cinema until World War II. This chapter hangs on the word *ubiquitous* because the tramp is an inescapable and intrusive presence in the cultural imaginary. Tramp films are as pervasive as tramps themselves, traversing multiple genres. While film cycles are normally shorter than this decades-long one, I consider tramp films a cycle because they relate to a wave of moral panics about tramps from the 1870s to the 1940s and because the figure of the tramp, so ubiquitous during this decades-long cycle, disappears suddenly and almost entirely from the cultural landscape.

Chapter 2, "Uncivilized: World War II Mobilization and Homecoming as Social Problem," considers the wholesale crisis in domesticity engendered by World War II, impacting not only servicemen and -women uprooted from home but also civilians who moved to be near defense plants and bases, and the years-long housing crisis that followed. This chapter is called "uncivilized" to indicate the tension between a return to civilian life for soldiers and their having become uncivilized while in the service, a concern that produced a moral panic about "the veteran problem." The temporary unhoming of soldiers and the movement of soldiers and civilians alike are seen to be life-changing as citizens are liberated from conventions associated with civilized life and unmoored from the norms of society related to sex, marriage, race relations, and more. This chapter considers a range of films, including comedies, musicals, and melodramas, under the broad rubric of social problem films.

Chapter 3, "Adrift: The Freedom of the Female Hitchhiker," examines the figure of the female hitchhiker in early 1970s films, with attention to earlier representations, especially male hitchhikers in midcentury film noir. While the film noir hitchhiker speaks to a moral panic created by the FBI as it demonized the formerly popular and acceptable practice of hitching a ride and rendered male hitchhikers, especially, as sociopaths, the female hitchhiking films address a moral panic about young countercultural runaways who seem to be abandoning not only their homes but also traditional gender roles and conceptions of family. The female hitchhiker is "adrift" both in the sense of wandering and in being perceived as sexually loose. Her voluntary countercultural precarity and mobility threaten ideals of home and family and challenge conceptions of youth. These films are mainly in the realm of exploitation and aim to titillate while they moralize.

Chapter 4, "Trash: The Homeless as Urban Waste," considers the 1980s cycle of films about the unhoused that appeared as the new category of "homeless" was just emerging and produced a moral panic that denigrated the unhoused as a scourge on the gentrifying city. These films oscillate between, on the one hand, demonizing the homeless as "trash," or urban waste that needs to be eradicated, and, on the other, fetishizing them as having transformative, even magical, powers. In these films, the unhoused are paired with the figure of the yuppie as distinct representatives of urban life in the context of gentrification. This chapter consists of an uneasy mix of social problem films and bromances that emphasize free-market capitalism and even a form of trickle-down economics in narratives of private benevolence and individual transformation.

The epilogue, "Stuck: Precarity and Perpetual Motion as Slow Death," focuses on a recent cycle of films that show figures associated with the precariat in a kind of hypermobility or perpetual motion in place. These films disclose an anxiety about mobility that is not yet a moral panic. As the certainty of moving up has diminished, these resolutely realist films reveal the normative orientation itself—the assumptions about social mobility and the ability to successfully enter adulthood (i.e., having a home, family)—as having been bent, distorted, or derailed. These characters are "stuck," constantly moving but going nowhere. Sometimes branded as neo-neorealism, I characterize these films as slow death cinema as they embody what Lauren Berlant describes as "the physical wearing out of a population and the deterioration of people in a population that is very nearly a defining condition of their experience and historical existence."[47] This chapter examines that physical wearing out via tropes of physical mobility that trap characters in an unending circuit of precarious movement and underscore the lack of social mobility.

While I consider each film cycle on its own, I also aim to make connections among the cycles, to consider these cycles as a series. Each individual cycle functions as an episode, but in aggregate, they tell a story about recurrent panics and fascination with precarity, mobility, and placelessness. The individual cycle drills down synchronically into a cultural moment, whereas the flow of cycles provides a diachronic view of changing characterizations of the unhomed and attitudes toward them.

Across *Unhomed,* I discuss a great many films, likely introducing readers to new ones. This large corpus means that I do not attend to the production, narrative, thematic, or aesthetic analysis each film may deserve. Still, the book is not intended to be a comprehensive compilation of films about mobility. Indeed, readers will think of relevant films I have not discussed. Instead, in looking at large numbers of films, I endeavor to recover the density of representation, to chart patterns, and to uncover themes, aesthetics, and plots. Rather than claim a fully unified response to any figure of mobility, however, I aim to map contradictions, fissures, and nuance in the modes of representation. I am not claiming that films merely reflect society or are themselves simply products of the zeitgeist, nor am I claiming that filmmakers are engaged in actively or even knowingly commenting on social problems. More accurately, I am considering the films as reflecting *upon* society; negotiating discourse; responding to other films; inventing, repeating, and revising tropes; and speaking from within and in conversation with contemporary affects and ideologies. This is a situated reading of films *in* and *as* history, a cultural history.

In showing the broad investment in the unhomed across historical cycles with a vast number of film examples, I hope to show a different side of American cinema and to underscore its affective and ideological investment in precarity. *Unhomed* is about a curiously neglected dominant in American culture: mobility without Manifest Destiny, movement without terminus, geographic mobility that does not produce hope of social mobility. *Unhomed* is also about the panics, anxieties, desires, and envies projected into figures who are unhomed, mobile, and placeless. In thinking through film about the various ways in which we imagine the unhomed, I am hoping that this project makes us see the unhomed and see them differently.

ONE

Ubiquitous

THE TRAMP'S MOBILE MASCULINITY

IN 1913, EPES WINTHROP SARGENT published a filmmaking manual, *The Technique of the Photoplay*. In a section on "putting in the punch," which he describes as the "heart interest, grip, suspense, and a dozen other things rolled into one," Sargent provides various scenarios about a tramp.[1] In one, the tramp dies in a workhouse, and, Sargent says, the story is of interest to no one. In another, he dies in a vacant lot, which creates a slight mystery.[2] In variations, the tramp dies gallantly trying to rescue someone from a fire; or he dies in a cellar, just a few feet from food but too weak to eat it; and, finally, "putting in the punch," Sargent augments the story with a child whom the tramp saves by letting himself starve so the child can eat. Sargent sums up: "The tramp dead in a workhouse is commonplace. The tramp dead in a vacant lot is unusual, the tramp saving the life of another at the cost of his own is heroic, the tramp dying of starvation in the sight of food is dramatic, the tramp dying that a little life may be spared is pathetic. In each story there is an increasing punch."[3] Here, Sargent builds an increasingly dramatic and sentimental narrative. It could be about any kind of character, but this early filmmaking manual uses the tramp, a figure it treats as absolutely conventional and accessible, as an example.

In the 1922 *Palmer Handbook of Scenario Construction*, in a chapter on plot, the author, Frederick Palmer, similarly imagines a scenario organized around a tramp: "Two lovers are riding on horseback on the highway. The sudden appearance of a tramp from behind some wayside bushes frightens the horse the young woman is riding. It jumps and throws its rider. The tramp catches her in the fall and saves her from being hurt."[4] Later, the author extends this scenario so that the tramp appears at the office of the woman's lover. It turns out that the two have been friends and the tramp went to jail for a crime committed by the lover. This turns to blackmail.

Finally, a 1933 volume titled *The Home Cinema* uses the figure of the tramp as a commonplace cinematic subject, even for home movies. *The Home Cinema* provides specific and practical advice both for setting up home screenings and for making home movies. In a section on writing the script for home movies, it presents what it claims is a reprint of a script provided by the Kodak company.[5] The script has a cast of four: two kids, a cook, and a tramp. The kids make mud pies and swap a mud pie for a pie cooling on a windowsill. The tramp eats the mud pie. Hilarity ensues.

In using the figure of the tramp to construct cinematic scenarios, each of these filmmaking manuals, spanning three decades, point to the pervasiveness of the tramp both as a filmic character and as a participant in imagined versions of everyday life.[6] In teaching people how to construct film narratives using the figure of the tramp, the manuals assume a familiarity with the figure of the tramp as a stock character. Moreover, in each scenario, the tramp is imagined as readily at hand within the film's diegesis. Indeed, for Sargent's *Technique of the Photoplay,* the tramp is so ever-present that even his dead body in a workhouse is "commonplace": it requires his starving to death to save a child to make his situation vaguely interesting. In the *Palmer Handbook of Scenario Construction,* the tramp is so ubiquitous that he appears from nowhere just as the lovers ride by, a figure of chance and contingency. Similarly, *The Home Cinema* suggests that a tramp would automatically appear as soon as a pie was set to cool on a windowsill: the gag depends on the tramp's proximity, his presence near the home unquestioned. Additionally, the narratives suggested by these filmmaking manuals provide a decent encapsulation of how the tramp will be variously mobilized in cinema: as a figure of tragedy and ultimately pathos, as a triangulating figure in a romance, as menacing criminal, and as a slapstick comedic figure.

I begin with these filmmaking manuals not only to underscore the availability of the tramp as a stock character in film but also to launch a consideration of the tramp as a figure central to the American cultural imagination from the late nineteenth century through almost the first half of the twentieth. While the tramp has been well documented in histories and analyses concerned with poverty and homelessness, within cultural and film studies the tramp is now recollected only as a residual minor figure in American culture—memorable and interesting, perhaps, but not important to the story. But while the tramp may have been marginalized in society, the *story* of the tramp was, for a long time, not marginal at all. The tramp deserves to be recalled as a curiously underacknowledged but conspicuous figure that not only shaped a multitude of individual stories but also traversed key decades for thinking through modernity, from the 1870s to World War II.[7] In claiming Hollywood cinema as a kind of vernacular modernism, Miriam Hansen writes: "The question was, and continues to be, how particular film practices can be productively understood as *responding*—and making sensually graspable our responses—to the set of technological, economic, social and perceptual transformations associated with the term modernity."[8] One way that film makes modernity "sensually graspable" is through the figure of the tramp, who functions as a palimpsest for a host of issues related to modernity, particularly industrialization, immigration, race, and changing gender roles.

In *The One vs. the Many: Minor Characters and the Space of the Protagonist in the Novel*, Alex Woloch investigates the question, "How can many people be contained within a single narrative?"[9] If we extend the question from concerns about the novel to the larger narrative of modernity, we can think of the typical characters who are invoked to tell the story of modernity—the *flaneur* and *flaneuse*, for example, or the tourist, detective, prostitute, shopgirl, New Woman, sapphist, suffragette, flapper, or the New Negro—and rather than ask if those characters can all be contained, or are too many, we could ask instead if they are *sufficient* to tell the story. The stories organized around each figure are different, and each figure provides a different and contested point of view on modernity related to mobility and the gaze, for example, or the power of technologized vision, or the role of women in the public sphere, or consumption, or sexual freedom, or race, and so on. The tramp exists alongside these other characters as a neighboring character in literature, film, and popular culture and offers an alternative perspective on modernity formed in relation to mobility, placelessness, and poverty—as well as race, class, immigration, and gender—that intersects with but is not identical to the stories told by and through these other figures.

As Tim Cresswell argues, the tramp was brought into being as an always already marginal figure. "In the process," he argues, "marginality itself was being constituted in relation to deeply held notions of what constitutes normality."[10] Complicating Cresswell's assumption of "deeply held" notions of normality, however, I suggest that the figure of the tramp materializes precisely at the moment when what counts as normal is up for grabs. Different aspects of modernity—including new forms of mobility, industrialization, mass communication, mass amusements, changing gender roles, changing race roles, urbanization, bureaucratization, and shifts in both the private and public sphere—all destabilized "deeply held" norms because they created a sense of fragmentation, alienation, and intense sensory stimulation and changed accepted ways of seeing, hearing, and experiencing the world. Certainly, in the sociological sense of "marginality" that Cresswell implies, the tramp can be seen as isolated from or not conforming to the dominant. But being marginal also means existing on the edge, being proximate, affecting or commenting on the main text.

As Woloch suggests, there are two extremes of "minorness" in the nineteenth-century novel, and they relate to the main narrative differently: "the *worker* and the *eccentric,* the flat character who is reduced to a single functional use within the narrative and the fragmentary character who plays a disruptive oppositional role within the plot. . . . In one case, the character is smoothly absorbed as a gear within the narrative machine. In the other case, the minor character grates against his or her position and is usually, as a consequence, wounded, exiled, expelled, ejected, imprisoned, or killed (within the *discourse* if not the *story)*."[11] In Woloch's terms, the tramp is not a flat *worker* in the discourse on modernity, reduced to a single function, as is typical for stock characters, but an *eccentric* who plays an oppositional role in the context of modernity, even if he has been so far expelled or exiled from the *discourse* about modernity. The tramp is not simply constituted in relation to clearly defined norms, or "absorbed as a gear" in the machinations of modernity, but "plays a disruptive oppositional role" that shapes and comments on what counts as normality and how the dominant is perceived.

My argument hinges on the tension between the tramp as simultaneously marginal and ubiquitous. Michelle Granshaw suggests that "a key aspect of the tramp figure in the dominant imagination" is that he has "no place in contemporary society."[12] This means, on the one hand, that tramps are homeless and thus have no fixed place or abode, no place to live, and, as a result, no place in the social fabric: they are marginal. But, on the other hand, being placeless also means that tramps are not confined to any one space, not bounded or defined: they are ubiquitous. Ubiquity is a defining feature of the tramp; he is an inescapable and intrusive presence in the cultural imaginary and across decades through newspaper accounts, sociological studies, novels, autobiographies, legal discourse, popular culture, and especially film.

THE TRAMP AS UBIQUITOUS

The tramp emerged specifically as a ubiquitous presence, and his seeming pervasiveness produced a need to name, analyze, and control him. As key historians of tramping and poverty Cresswell, Kenneth Kusmer, Todd DePastino, and others have detailed, the figure of the tramp, as opposed to the vagrant or beggar, emerges between 1865 and 1880, with the term *tramp* first used to describe a person in 1875. As DePastino indicates, besides his "stunning mobility," the new word *tramp* "also signified a sense of novelty, as if older terms such as 'vagrant' or 'vagabond' were somehow inappropriate to the moment."[13] Kusmer links the tramp's mobility to a perceived ubiquity that differentiated him from previous generations of the poor, noting that as the homeless began traveling by train rather than by foot, they extended their reach into rural, as well as urban, communities and "brought the specter of homelessness to the doorstep of every family in the country": put bluntly, "prior to World War II, tramps and beggars could scarcely be avoided."[14]

The seeming ubiquity of tramps led to the "tramp scares" that began in the 1870s, reached their pinnacle in the 1880s and 1890s, and didn't really disappear until the 1940s.[15] During these scares, tramps were insulted by the public, gibbetted by the press, compared to invasive pests and contagious diseases, and arrested under new laws designed to control their movements. The first of many tramp laws were passed in 1876, superseding vagrancy laws, as the tramp was perceived as a mobile figure whose mobility carried him over large distances, often traversing the country, whereas vagrancy was more localized.[16] Between the 1870s and 1940s, tramps were constantly policed, subjected to laws aimed at curtailing their movements, chased off boxcars by railroad police, shepherded into police overnight "tramp rooms"[17] and, later, wayfarer lodges and municipal lodges, and considered criminals just for being homeless. But, as their persistent and pervasive presence suggests, tramps were never fully contained.

The figure of the tramp emerges as the result of a perfect confluence of events and developments. As Cresswell notes, it only becomes possible to be a tramp in the 1870s, owing to the increased mobility of the late nineteenth century enabled by the advent of a national rail system, economic downturns that led to mass unemployment across the country, and the new mobility of capital and labor.[18] The Civil War helped "shape the contours of the tramp crisis" as the word *tramp* was used to describe the exhausting marches soldiers undertook; the railroad was expanded to facilitate troop movements;

men had learned to ride the rails as soldiers and forage for food on farms, establishing habits of "marauding" and "roving" that served them well as tramps; and the experience of war loosed men from domesticity, either owing to a kind of post-traumatic stress disorder that made it hard for them to settle down or because the excitement of war made them chafe against the boredom of domesticity.[19]

In addition, the tramp needs to be understood in the context of modernity. Tramping "represented a respite from—and often a reaction against—many of the trends that were transforming the American social and economic system in the decades after Reconstruction: the increasing power of technology, the quest for economic efficiency, and the growth of organization and bureaucratic thinking."[20] Instead of homestead or stable localized work, in which many were self-employed or, if employed by others, protected from economic downturns by their employer, new modes of industrialized work meant that unemployment surged.[21] Furthermore, modernity also meant there were an increasing number of jobs that required worker mobility, such as railroad building, crop harvesting, and lumberjacking.[22]

For most people today, references to the tramp in early twentieth-century popular culture might augur images of Charlie Chaplin's famous Little Tramp character. But the character of the tramp long precedes Chaplin and, well before Chaplin adopted his iconic hat, mustache, cane, coat and oversized shoes, the tramp was already the most popular figure in turn-of-the-century culture.[23] Popular fascination with and fear of the tramp produced a plethora of tramp accounts and representations across various popular media. For example, in the late nineteenth and early twentieth centuries, the tramp is the focus of well-known autobiographies such as Josiah Flynt's *Tramping with Tramps* (1899), Jack London's *The Road* (1907), *The Life and Adventures of A-No. 1, America's Most Celebrated Tramp* (1910),[24] W. H. Davies's *The Autobiography of a Super-Tramp* (1908), Jim Tully's *Beggars of Life: A Hobo Autobiography* (1924), Tom Kromer's *Waiting for Nothing* (1935), and *Sister of the Road: The Autobiography of Boxcar Bertha* (1937), as told to Ben L. Reitman.[25] Writers such as William Dean Howells, Stephen Crane, and Theodore Dreiser brought "the evocative symbol of the tramp"[26] into prestigious realist fiction. The tramp became a special focus of the emergent Chicago School sociology and urban theory, notably in Nels Anderson's *The Hobo: The Sociology of the Homeless Man* (1923).[27]

Beyond literary and intellectual circles, tramps were also very popular stock characters in vaudeville and comic strips.[28] For example, Lew Bloom headlined in vaudeville as "The Society *Tramp*" starting in 1888; W. C. Fields entered vaudeville as "The Tramp Juggler" in 1898; Nat Wills developed his tramp character in 1891 and was the top tramp comic in vaudeville, on Broadway, and in early comedy recordings as "The Happy Tramp." Emmet Kelley developed his famous clown as the tramp "Weary Willie" during the Depression, the name a common moniker for a tramp borrowed from Tom Brown's cartoon "Weary Willie and Tired Tim," which ran in England's *Illustrated Chips* from 1896 to 1953. Frederick Burr Opper's tramp comic strip *Happy Hooligan* debuted in March 1900 with Hearst papers and ran until 1932 as one of the first comics in the King Features Syndicate. Collected into books, *Happy Hooligan* was also made into both live-action and animated films between 1916 and 1921. James Montgomery Flagg created the character "Nervy Nat," possibly based on W. C. Fields's tramp character, for *Judge* magazine, where it ran from 1903 to 1907. It was adapted into various Broadway revues and at least a few films. *Little Orphan Annie* has stints as a tramp in her repeated unmooring from life with Daddy Warbucks.[29]

Tramp culture also entered the vernacular through hobo songs that crisscrossed folk music, country music, and the blues. Famous hobo songs include "Hallelujah I'm a Bum," said to have been written by a Kansas City hobo known as "One-Finger Ellis" on his prison wall in 1897; "The Big Rock Candy Mountain," first recorded by Harry McClintock in 1928; and "Jungle Man Blues," by Peetie Wheatstraw, released in 1936. Many hobo songs and hobo poems were collected in *The Hobo's Hornbook,* edited by George Milburn in 1930.[30]

Most important for my purposes, the tramp was a prominent figure in film from the dawn of cinema through at least World War II. The comic tramp appears as early as the recently discovered 1896 Selig film *The Tramp and the Dog,* but Rob King argues that the comic tramp receded from film in the early aughts and did not re-reemerge until the 1910s, becoming especially popular in 1915/1916, when Chaplin brought his Little Tramp character from Keystone to Essanay and then Mutual Production Company.[31] But the American Film Institute (AFI) catalogue shows 349 films with keywords *tramp* or *hobo* between 1895 and 1913, before Chaplin's Tramp appears in Keystone's 1914 *Kid Auto Races* or *Mabel's Strange Predicament* (the former the first *screening* of his new character, the latter the first *produced* and second one shown with the character). Between 1914 and 1920, the AFI catalogue shows ninety-two tramp films and from 1921 to 1929 another eighty-one. During the Depression and World War II, another 178 films with *tramp* or *hobo* as keywords appear. All told, the AFI catalogue turns up seven hundred results for films with *tramp* or *hobo* as keywords between 1895 and 1945. If we deduct the nearly fifty short films and dozen features Chaplin starred in as the Little Tramp between 1914 and 1936, that still leaves well over six hundred films with tramps as major characters. Rather than think of Chaplin as the apex of the tramp cycle, we need to acknowledge that he joined a larger trend that preceded, continued through, and endured well past his tenure.

Just as the tramp is ubiquitous, tramp films traverse genres. Early films featuring tramps include many short tramp comedies (some featuring stars Fatty Arbuckle and Harold Lloyd), animated films, and suspenseful narratives featuring menacing tramps who threaten women. Early films also tap into pathos in such films as *Only a Hobo* (Atlas Film Co. 1910), in which a hobo risks his life to save a toddler from an automobile crash, or *The Tramp's Story* (Essanay 1909), which claims in its catalogue description that "there never was a more picturesque character in all the world than the American tramp, yeggman, hobo. His mysterious comings and goings, and his occasional visits at our back doors often excites the desire to inquire of him: 'What made you a tramp?' This motion picture tells the tragic story of the making of an American tramp."[32] Feature films centered on tramps range from prestigious melodramas to B movie action films, social problem films, and musicals. Tramps also feature prominently in comedies starring Will Rogers, romantic comedies, and screwball comedies directed by Gregory La Cava, Preston Sturges, and Frank Capra. During the Depression, child actors Shirley Temple and Jane Withers each portrayed girl tramps, or what were termed "street arabs," in *Dimples* (Seiter 1936) and *This Is the Life* (Nielan 1935), respectively.[33]

The tramp in popular culture does more than merely reflect the sociohistorical fact of his emergence as a new form of traveling vagrant: representations of the tramp in popular culture negotiate aspects of modernity. Newspaper accounts, sociological studies, legal discourse, and other representations shape competing and even contradictory perceptions of both the tramp and modernity, and these perceptions are all in conversation with and being transmuted through popular culture, especially cinema. Additionally, the pop cultural forms that promulgate images of the tramp are themselves defined by and in response to modernity. For example, the tramp emerges alongside vaudeville, a parallel traveling phenomenon.[34] Vaudeville performers were, like tramps, migratory workers with "peripatetic lifestyles, seasonal unemployment, and [a] penchant for cheap lodging houses."[35] It is no accident that tramp figures are prominent in comic strips given that the modern strip was invented in the 1890s, evincing the "central place that seriality occupies as one of modernity's organizing principles."[36] In a different vein, the knowledge and circulation of hobo songs increases exponentially as they shift from folk culture to mass-produced songs available via sheet music, radio, and phonograph recordings. Additionally, tramp scares only slightly predate cinema and are at their height when cinema is first invented. Cinema is defined by modernity as a new technology, a mass-produced technology, and a new amusement; as Hansen and others have argued, cinema provided a crucial arena for the effects of modernity to be processed, represented, negotiated, and diffused.[37]

In what follows, I discuss the decades-long cycle of films that feature tramps. While cycles are normally shorter groups of film attendant to topical concerns of a particular moment or the popularity of a particular film or film style, I want to claim these films as a cycle in order to capture the degree to which they seem to capitalize on the ongoing moral panics about tramps. As Amanda Klein indicates, moral panics trigger film cycles but also associate those events with larger issues and problems in society.[38] This group of films is linked by having a shared character and some shared plots and themes, more than by other consistencies, such as visual style, music, or sound, which might define a genre.[39] These films will, however, share a particular mise-en-scène associated with the tramp. He is usually a male, dressed in a suit that is shabby or mismatched, most often wearing a hat. He is usually neither fully bearded nor clean-shaven. He carries his belongings in a bag, not a suitcase, but not the stereotypical bundle on a stick. He is often seen walking along the road, catching a ride, or traveling in freight cars and boxcars, and visiting hobo camps. Most tramp films will show the tramp begging or, in some cases, stealing. Rarely, the tramp will work for food.

Representations of the tramp sometimes support hegemonic ideals in the context of modernity and sometimes critique them. The tramp is sometimes seen as a victim of economic circumstance or societal failure and sometimes as a nonconformist who chooses tramping as a way of life. Certainly, the tramp is often demonized as dangerous, pathological, and criminal, "a metaphor for social disorder,"[40] but he can also be seen as offering an alternative view of society or reversing conventional hierarchies and priorities. The contradictions and tensions among these views persist across the decades in which the tramp is dominant, but he tends to be viewed more sympathetically during the Great Depression than previously, as large swaths of the population find themselves unemployed and homeless or have more intimate connections with people who do.

Primarily, the tramp unspools the range and variety of possibilities for what might constitute modern masculinity. Just as modernity created the horizon of possibility for the creation of the tramp, it also created a crisis of masculinity. As Michael Kimmel explains, "Rapid industrialization, technological transformation, capital concentration, urbanization and immigration—all of these created a new sense of oppressively crowded, depersonalized, and often emasculated life. Manhood had meant autonomy and self-control, but now fewer and fewer American men owned their own shops, controlled their own labor, owned their own farms. More and more men were economically dependent, subject to the regime of the time clock."[41] The tramp did not fit the paradigms of hegemonic masculinity associated with modernity, but neither did he suffer the potentially emasculating effects of such paradigms. While the tramp could be seen as failing to achieve proper stability and domesticity, he could also be seen as challenging the emasculation inherent to modern work, marriage, reproduction, and breadwinning.

If, as Steven Cohan has argued, hegemonic masculinity "articulates various social relations of power as an issue of gender normality," the tramp, defined as marginal, serves to shore up the hegemonic ideal that "underwrites positions of power and wealth."[42] At the same time, the ubiquitous figure of the tramp offers a seemingly counterhegemonic image of masculinity that flips the script to privilege unemployment over employment, begging or stealing over earning, being single over being married, mobility over home, unfettered sexuality over reproduction. But while the cinematic tramp's masculinity is defined in opposition to hegemonic masculinity, it nonetheless works *like* hegemonic masculinity to subordinate others, notably feminized elites, immigrants, nonwhites, women, and homosexuals; and it proves its power by occupying the very women's and domestic spaces it rejects.

THE TRAMP AS A HAPPY HOOLIGAN

The tramp diverges from modern hegemonic masculinity most clearly in relation to the linkage between masculinity and work. Popular culture presents competing views of the tramp as a figure who, on the one hand, disaffiliates from work and, on the other, affiliates with the working class. Of course, during the Great Depression, when work was scarce, sympathy for and identification with tramps increased, but even early on, amid the changes to work culture engendered by industrialization, the tramp's resistance to work sometimes registers as admirable defiance.

During tramp scares, commentators referred to tramps as "an army of the unemployed," and they were frequently characterized as criminal, lazy, shiftless, and depraved—failures, in other words, according to the American work ethic and ideals of social mobility.[43] This view of tramps dominates early representations. Hansen argues that the use of the tramp and other stock characters in early cinema shored up the spectator's "position of social and epistemological superiority." Viewing the tramp as a social outcast, she argues, "viewers could put a safe distance between themselves and a lower-class background from which many of them were at best one or two generations removed."[44]

Certainly, many representations of the tramp emphasize the tramp's laziness and low-level opportunistic criminality. As the film scholar Charles Musser says, "In short films, the tramp is generally portrayed as an annoying, but relatively harmless, scavenger, whose petty thievings and inevitable punishment provide numerous situations for comedy."[45] For example, the animated *Happy Hooligan: The Spider and the Fly* (Nolan 1918) shows Happy refusing to work and being beaten by a man chopping wood who tries to enlist him in the job. Slag, the tramp in *Square Shoulders* (Hopper 1929), refuses the offer of a good job and decides instead to rob the man who offers it. In *Jubilo* (Badger 1919), Will Rogers's titular tramp resists work and is clueless about how to do basic chores like milking a cow or plucking a chicken; and in its remake, *Too Busy to Work* (Blystone 1932), he Tom-Sawyers a farm handyman into doing the chores for him. In *The Scarecrow* (Birch/Bamforth 1916), a tramp labeled Weary Willy assumes the clothing and posture of a scarecrow when he realizes that two sets of lovers are using the scarecrow's pockets to exchange gifts and food and that he can be the receptacle instead. In *Nervy Nat Kisses the Bride* (Porter 1904), Nat steals a train passenger's ticket when he finds him asleep at the railway station. Across the large body of tramp films, tramps engage in such petty opportunistic theft, their energies directed more at minor criminal schemes than honest labor. Rather than condemn his actions, however, the films toggle the line between mockery and admiration.

Musser claims that the tramp's petty crimes demonize him legally and socially: "The ritual beatings he receives at the hands of the law or outraged citizenry humorously define proper society's boundaries in terms of the outcast."[46] To be sure, the police are vital to the imaginary of the tramp, but where Musser claims that the police in tramp films draw boundaries between the tramp and society, I suggest that the encounters between the police and tramps show exactly how difficult those boundaries are to maintain. The police are key signifiers of the urban landscape in cinema during the same decades when tramps were pervasive.[47] In tramp films, police are seemingly just outside the frame whenever a tramp appears: they seem to be telepathically aware of tramps and magnetically drawn into their field of action. Of course, in Keystone comedies, famous for their Keystone Kops, police proliferate, and most of those tramp films end with the tramp being chased by a slew of cops. The Mack Sennett comedy *Wandering Willies* (Lord 1926), for example, ends with the tramp Percy (Billy Bevan) pursued by two cars: one with a restaurant owner whose efforts to get a monopoly on the water supply Percy thwarts, the other a patrol car filled with numerous cops who slide around in the car, fall out, and create a daisy chain of police that whips around a street post. Outside of Keystone, Hal Roach's *Clubs Are Trump* (1917) presents cascading numbers of police chasing two tramps: Harold Lloyd's Lonesome Luke with "Snub" Pollard. Starting with one policeman, whom they kick and then manage to wedge into a tree, the duo attracts half a dozen more policemen whom they evade, but in doing so, they stumble on half a dozen more. As these dozen cops unite in a chase, the tramps run through the center of a separate formation of police practicing a march in the park. These cops join the rest and surround the tramps, but the two tramps slip out of the scrum and casually light cigarettes while pondering what to do next. When the police notice them, they run to the park boathouse and lead the police on a canoe chase, with dozens of canoes circling the pond. Returning to the dock and hiding under a boat, the two successfully evade capture. These tramp films, and I would include the many in which railroad police pursue tramps, not only show that the tramp is perceived as always already criminal but also situate viewer pleasure in the tramps' ability to outsmart or outrun the police, whom they show as largely ineffectual. These films applaud the tramp as an antiauthoritarian figure and show that he cannot be fully contained.[48]

Not only can the tramp be seen sympathetically as antiwork and antiauthoritarian but also as offering a critique of "the nature of work itself under the industrial/bureaucratic regime."[49] Viewing the tramp in this way, the International Workers of the World (IWW), or Wobblies, recruited tramps, and the hobo song "Hallelujah I'm a Bum" became a Wobblie anthem that was collected along with other songs in *The Little Red Songbook*, made especially to be portable for tramps.⁵⁰ Tramps dominated both Coxey's Army in 1894, in which groups of unemployed men marched to Washington to demand assistance following the Panic of 1893, and the Bonus Marchers of 1932, World War I veterans who marched to demand early payment of a bonus that was not due to them until 1945.⁵¹

Some tramp films specifically critique the inequities and alienating effects of modern work. In the Depression-era *Gabriel over the White House* (La Cava 1933), for example, after being concussed and receiving an angelic revelation, the president (Walter Huston) recognizes the hollowness of his previous calls of "prosperity for all" and gives support to the millions gathering as an "army of the unemployed," promising to provide them work as an "army of construction." Hoboes here are seen as lacking work not owing to laziness but to government failure. Like the Bonus Marchers, the "army" are all World War I veterans who served the nation, and their logic is that the nation should now support them. Where previously, the president put money into the military rather than helping the poor, now he makes poverty and starvation his top priorities, and he convinces multiple nations to disarm and transfer their monies to aiding the people rather than fighting wars.

While *Gabriel over the White House* is presented as a quasi-religious fantasy, Chaplin's *Modern Times* (1936) evinces more prominent social realism than earlier Chaplin films in its attention to the problems inherent to industrialization.⁵² The film begins with an Einsteinian juxtaposition of a shot of milling sheep with one of workers leaving the subway, suggesting a critique of the dehumanizing effects of modern labor. Then, dismantling the logic of industrialized labor, factory scenes show the alienating effects of technology and Taylorism. Chaplin's Tramp is brutalized by an automated "feeding machine" that turns a lunch break into a scientific management exercise. Famously, he is sucked into a factory machine of gearwheels, his body flattened and bent as he is threaded through cogs in the machine. Trying to match the increasing speed of the assembly line, urged on by the mechanized voice of the boss, he has a nervous breakdown and begins to function as an automaton who cannot stop tightening nuts—hilariously chasing a buxom woman whose buttons on her dress resemble the nuts on the assembly line. After being released from the mental hospital, Charlie walks by a shuttered factory and stumbles into a workers' protest. Even though Chaplin's Tramp is oblivious of the protest and has merely picked up a dropped red flag to return it, the police beat demonstrators with billy clubs and jail Charlie as a

Communist agitator. As in other Chaplin films, the poor are treated sympathetically, seen as deserving of care and as criminal only owing to deep need.

Most films, however, avoid direct political critique. The Jolsen musical *Hallelujah I'm a Bum* (Milestone 1933), for example, from the same year as *Gabriel over the White House,* uses the Wobblie anthem but dismisses leftist critique. When the bum Egghead (Harry Langdon) complains, in verse, of "rich idle workers who live on us shirkers," Jolsen's character, Bumper, counters, "That's just about enough of that radical stuff"; and when Egghead sings that "if a man doesn't work, he ought to be dead," Bumper, aligning himself with the tramp's aversion to work, as opposed to anxieties of unemployment, stops Egghead with, "You talk like a red." Bumper's response deflects political critique by asserting tramping as a lifestyle choice or personal temperament. He sings, "I love to breathe the air and feel I'm free. . . . I find great enjoyment in unemployment. . . . Hallelujah, I'm a bum."

Rather than engage leftist critiques, many tramp films create sympathy for the tramp as a working-class character by contrasting him with the rich, often positing the tramps' masculinity as more manly and authentic than the feminized elite. For example, in *Caught in a Cabaret* (Normand/Chaplin, 1914), Chaplin's Tramp proves himself braver and more virile than a wealthy suitor of Mabel Normand's Mabel. The film introduces Chaplin's Tramp working as a waiter in a saloon in the poor part of town. On break, he takes the bar's dog for a walk in the park. An intertitle announces, "A stick up guy holds up a stuck-up guy," and we see Mabel and her boyfriend (Harry McCoy) challenged by a mugger (William Hauber). The mugger easily bests the boyfriend and begins pawing at Mabel's dress. The Tramp arrives and trounces the assailant, knocking him to the ground a few times and then routing him from the park, while the boyfriend looks on from a distance. "How brave you are to fight that gunman," Mabel declares, and she invites the Tramp for a "tête a tête" at her house, leaving the boyfriend behind. The Tramp presents a phony card that declares him to be the Ambassador to Greece. Invited to a party that night, the Tramp initially "passes" as wealthy and successfully flirts with Mabel. But, after the Tramp makes an excuse to leave, so he can return to work, the boyfriend, who has jealously followed the Tramp and discovered his secret, shames him by bringing the partygoers on a "slumming" trip to the saloon where he works. Here, the tramp's lowly social status is countered by his physical and moral superiority to the wealthy man who seems emasculated and petty in contrast to the tramp.

In a different vein, in *Father Steps Out,* a.k.a. *City Limits* (Yarbrough 1941), the simplicity of tramp life helps an emasculated millionaire regain masculine power. J. B. Matthews (Jed Prouty) is introduced as a millionaire who has finagled the market to take control of Midland Railroad. Despite his financial and business acumen, J. B. experiences a host of ills, similar to the midcentury men Cohan describes who achieve the hegemonic ideal of masculinity but paradoxically register discontent: "High blood pressure, ulcers, alcoholism, boredom and depression, and heart disease all testified to the dangers of job-related stress or, as many writers interpreted it, to the breadwinner's debilitation caused by his pushing too hard to satisfy his wife's ambition and finance her consumerism."[53] J. B. is nagged by his assistant to take an array of pills to cure indigestion, nervousness, and other unnamed ills. At home, J. B. receives a house call from his doctor, who urges him to take more pills, follow a strict diet, and take a vacation. Unlike the 1950s version of masculine discontent that Cohan describes, J. B.'s maladies are not clearly blamed on his wife's ambition, but his wife emasculates him as she aligns with the doctor to medicalize and contain her husband's actions, denying him rich food and cigars and pushing pills. When J. B. takes the prescribed vacation—with his wife, daughter, and a conniving newsman posing as a doctor along for the ride—he accidentally falls off the train's observation deck and tumbles into a small hobo camp where two tramps are cooking Mulligan stew. When J. B. tells them that he is the railroad president, they assume he is concussed and confused, so they mockingly tell him they are the King of Siam and Napoleon. The hereinafter named King (Frank Faylen) and Nap (Charlie Hall) work on their broth, seasoning it with a garlic clove tied to a string, arguing over whether three or four dips of garlic in the broth is best. J. B., whom they nickname Pres, initially refuses to take any: "Too rich for me." He eats some bread but then can't resist and happily tastes the broth. When the tramps offer him a smoke, he surreptitiously takes one of his own from his pocket and breaks it, to match their half-smoked ones, then gleefully smokes with them. While J. B.'s family and business associates frantically search for him—the railroad deal at risk—he settles in happily with the tramps. When the tramps delegate him to beg from an ungenerous rural woman, he returns with a banquet, secretly paying for it rather than begging but wanting to join and honor the lifestyle of his new friends. He stops taking his pills, but King and Nap steal a few, thinking they are what make Pres "balmy." The pills, however, make them feel ill and miserable, underlining their lack of efficacy for Pres. Ultimately, the newspaperman finds J. B. and tries to rush him back to save the deal, but thugs hired by his business rival arrive to stop him. Protecting Pres, King and Nap beat up the bad guys while

Pres races back to save the deal. At film's end, after his daughter marries the newsman, J. B.'s wife searches for him in the house. We see him outside, with King and Nap, over a pot of stew, and, this time, J. B. takes a garlic clove out of his pocket and dips it *five* times, proving he can now digest spicy food.

In disentangling an image of authentic working-class masculinity from work and social mobility, the tramp provides a counter to hegemonic ideals of masculinity that linked manhood to economic obligation.[54] Instead of a critique of the alienating effects of industrialized and bureaucratized work, for the most part, the tramp thumbs his nose at the whole system and adopts simultaneously an antiauthoritarian and antielite posture. While some films emphasize the tramp's status as outcast, casting him as criminal as well as lazy, many films hold him up as a model of masculinity associated with physical prowess and action, on the one hand, and, increasingly in later films, imbue him with authenticity, as someone who has opted out of a civilization perceived as corrupt and femininizing.

THE TRAMP AS WHITE AMERICAN

In addition to functioning as a lightning rod for changing ideas about masculinity under conditions of industrialization, the tramp's masculinity is also infused with attitudes toward foreign-born and African American men. During the initial tramp scares, it was "a common misperception in the popular press that the population was predominantly foreign born."[55] In projecting immigrant status onto the tramp, and equating them, commentators mutually damned them as unwanted in society. But while there were immigrants among the tramp population—mainly Irish, with some Germans, Italians and English—the majority were white and born in America.[56] Remarkably, given the mass influx of immigrants between 1870 and 1890, and given the relative size of the immigrant population in cities,[57] the percentage of immigrants among tramps actually declined from their height in the 1860s whereas the Americanization of tramps increased to a very large majority, somewhere between 70 and 85 percent of all tramps.[58]

Surprisingly, although the Great Migration of African Americans from the South to the North also coincided with mass European migration and the emergence of the tramp, African Americans are not typically viewed as tramps. Scholars disagree somewhat on whether Black tramps existed and were simply ignored or whether tramping was unavailable to African

Americans, even as they were often mobile and placeless. On one side, historian Kenneth Kusmer claims that the tramp lifestyle was attractive to African Americans and that Black tramps were frequently mentioned in accounts of tramp life.[59] He claims that African Americans became mobile as runaway slaves and then, during the post–Civil War migration, Black tramps, along with white tramps, traveled illegally on the railroad to get to seasonal jobs. Kusmer claims that the tramp subculture was less segregated than the mainstream and that "the lifestyle of transients was surprisingly free of overt racism."[60] In contrast to Kusmer, DePastino argues that while geographic mobility was idealized as a crucial component of freedom for enslaved Black people, after the Civil War, Black mobility was severely restricted by "debt peonage, draconian vagrancy ordinances, and a uniform structure of low wages"[61] that barred Blacks from tramping. In the North, Black tramps couldn't count on the kindness of strangers or network of help usually available for tramps, and skid rows and lodgings were still segregated, if not off-limits altogether, to Black tramps.[62] Indicating the existence of Black tramps, but signaling that racism could certainly exist among tramps, the events of Scottsboro in 1931 started as an argument between white tramps and Black tramps on a freight train that led to an accusation that the Black tramps had tried to rape white girl tramps on the train.[63] In a different vein, Paul Garon and Gene Tomko argue that if you research seasonal workers, as opposed to tramps, the presence of African American hoboes comes to light; and the lives of these Black hoboes leave material traces in numerous hobo song lyrics and recordings.[64]

Despite historical claims that most tramps were native-born whites, within popular culture, foreign-born and Black tramps are not entirely absent, and neither the Americanness nor the whiteness of the tramp is assumed. In vaudeville, Granshaw claims that the earliest comic tramps in the 1870s performed equally in blackface or as "stage Irish," which often entailed whiteface, and that both were recognizable through similar characters, costume, and comedy, especially in a penchant for slapstick-style lack of bodily discipline linked to drunkenness.[65] In playing tramps as Black or Irish, performers conflated negative stereotypes of tramps with the racial and national stereotypes, marking the tramps' presumed reluctance to work, laziness, lack of personal hygiene, and ineptitude as racially or nationally determined.[66] Granshaw claims that as the decade progressed, however, comic tramps performed less frequently in blackface and became increasingly Irish, "turning the comic tramp into a performance of racial privilege, even for immigrant and ethnic groups who faced staunch prejudice."[67] Arguing against claims that the Irish "became" white, having been previously discriminated against in ways similar to African Americans, Granshaw emphasizes that, *legally,* the Irish were always defined as white and thus had privileges of whiteness all along, despite being subject to stereotyping and discrimination.[68]

The waning of the blackface tramp indicated the "North's limited ability to imagine freedom of mobility for black Americans."[69] Additionally, in disentangling the performance of blackness from the performance of tramping, early vaudeville also participated in the erasure of the Black tramp. Granshaw writes: "Blackface comic characters that performers, managers, newspapers and historians could reasonably call tramps continued to appear on variety and vaudeville stages, but people tended not to label them as tramps."[70] As whiteface was linked to tramps and blackface to other kinds of poor characters, vaudeville "implicitly tied whiteness to mobility"[71]

King argues that early cinema not only whitened but deethnicized the tramp. Against Hansen's claim that film audiences would respond to the tramp from a position of social superiority, King suggests that part of what makes the tramp a figure of identification for at least working-class audiences was his association with both working-class and native-born whiteness, "an image of class identity that could assuage rather than exacerbate ethnic divisions, perhaps even contributing to a sense of whiteness that cut across lines of ethnicity, mobilizing patterns of empathy and belonging." Thus, King argues, part of what differentiates Chaplin from other Keystone comics is that he "engages familiar ethnic iconographies, while stripping them of overt ethnic meaning."[72] In *The Immigrant* (Chaplin 1917), for example, whereas Albert Austin clearly plays a Russian immigrant, recognizable from his Cossack hat, tall shiny boots, and wooly beard, Chaplin's national origin is not indicated. The only indication that Chaplin is foreign-born comes when he enters a restaurant in America and cannot understand the waiter's demand that he remove his hat, but this incident is treated less as the result of a language barrier than as the Tramp's failing to understand a social cue.

Vestiges of vaudeville's tramp survive in preteens cinema. The live-action *Happy Hooligan* (American Mutoscope and Biograph 1903), for example, portrays Happy Hooligan using whiteface. The film, which runs just under a minute, shows Happy Hooligan and an organ grinder on the sidewalk. Happy encourages the organ grinder's continued playing, while a woman in an apartment looks out her window and scolds them. When, inevitably, a policeman arrives, Happy pushes the organ grinder away out of the frame. As

FIGURE 1.1. In *Tramp Strategy*, the "simian" tramp kidnapper and the foppish lover both appear in white-face.

the policeman grabs Happy and strangles him, the woman returns to her window and pours a bucket of water, intended for the organ grinder, onto the policeman, soaking him, to Happy's delight. This film points to many of the tropes that interest me here, including the proximity of the tramp to home, his threat to the woman, and the effort and failure to police him. Here, I focus on the ways this brief film marks out the tramp's position via codes of ethnicity. Happy, like his comic source, wears a tomato can on his head, signaling his lowly status as a "tomato-can vag."[73] He wears a tattered coat, vest, and pants with a T-shirt. His head is bald, except for a rim of hair around the circumference. He wears a prosthetic bulbous nose. His entire head and neck are whitened with makeup, giving him the appearance of a clown. To the degree that we can interpret him as "stage Irish," we can also construe the organ grinder, whose skin is not whitened by makeup, as another itinerant and most likely an Italian immigrant.

Alice Guy-Blaché's *The Tramp Strategy* (1911), similarly, carries over vaudevillian associations between tramping and Irishness. In this film, not only the tramp but also the main lovers have skin visibly whitened by makeup. This accords with conventions that lighten the skin of featured players to make them appear youthful and to stand out.[74] In contradistinction to the lovers, however, the tramp is coded as Irish by his curly hair and beard and his "simian" prosthetic nose, which distinguishes him clearly from the overly delicate, almost foppish appearance of the male lover.[75]

As King suggests, however, from about the midteens, tramps tend to be represented without obvious ethnic markings. Often, tramps are placed in opposition to ethnic others who help define the tramp as "real American." King notes that as the tramp assimilates into an image of deethnicized white Americanness, he is positioned between the world of the moneyed elite, above, and the world of the immigrant, below. In tandem with the manner in which the tramp is differentiated from the feminized wealthy men I discussed above, "in a kind of parsing of working-class identities, the tramp is aligned with a candor and virility set in comic juxtaposition with the flamboyance, dim-wittedness, and/or overwrought emotions of the ethnic worker."[76] King notes that in *Ham's Whirlwind Finish* (Hamilton 1916), for example, the "unpretentious strength" of the comic tramp duo Ham and Bud (Lloyd Hamilton and Bud Duncan) is pitted against the Italian immigrants' secretive treachery and reliance on bombs.[77] Many of the gags in the film rely on use of accented titles, such as "I giv-a you da job" or stem from Ham and Bud's mockery of stereotypical Italian comestibles, such as spaghetti and red wine.

As the tramp evolves, his nonethnic whiteness is increasingly taken for granted. Even Jolsen, whose major roles such as *The Jazz Singer* (Crosland 1927) mostly mark him as Jewish, is deethnicized when he plays a tramp. In *Hallelujah I'm a Bum,* class rather than ethnicity shapes his character. Although Bumper is not ethnically marked, his whiteness is accented through his friendship with a Black tramp, Acorn (Edgar Connor). The Black character authenticates Bumper by showing him as having friendship across racial boundaries but also delineates his white privilege. Acorn is with Bumper down South when the film opens, and he tramps with him all the way back to New York. Acorn considers Bumper and himself a unit. When Bumper finds a $1,000 bill in a wallet while lunching with Egghead and Acorn, Egghead wants to take half the money, but Acorn asserts, "Bumper found it: it belongs to *us!*" When Bumper takes a job at the bank, he insists that Acorn take one, too. Acorn is queerly attached to Bumper, jealous when he leaves the park to live with a woman. Moreover, Acorn is not aligned with any other Black characters and mainly acts to serve Bumper: when they get lunch at the backdoor, Acorn provides menus; when Bumper returns to the park at film's end, Acorn brushes off his old suit for him; and when they work at the bank, Bumper has a desk job and wears a suit and tie while Acorn wears a uniform and does menial labor.

While *Hallelujah I'm a Bum* uses a Black character to shore up the main character's whiteness, the Will Rogers films *Jubilo* and its remake, *Too Busy for Work,* highlight the tramp's whiteness through his appropriation of blackness—and elide Rogers's own Cherokee heritage in the process. In both films, Rogers's character is named Jubilo. In *Too Busy for Work,* he explains that his nickname comes from his constant singing of "The Year of Jubilo." Also known as "Kingdom Coming," this 1862 song by Henry C. Work is a

FIGURE 1.2. Acorn (Edgar Connor) authenticates Bumper (Al Jolsen) in *Hallelujah I'm a Bum,* here showing him a mirror image of himself.

pro-Unionist Civil War song written in an exaggerated dialect and sung from the point of view of slaves who celebrate their coming freedom as their masters flee the Union soldiers. In *Too Busy for Work,* Jubilo sings it to the young woman Rose (Marian Nixon), who, unbeknownst to her, is Jubilo's daughter, her mother having run off with another man when he was in the first World War. He sings, "De massa run, ha, ha! De darkey stay ho, ho!" Hearing the song, Rose recalls her mother singing it to her. Like many white songs that attempt to capture Black voices, "The Year of Jubilo" performs a kind of aural blackface. Even as it celebrates the end of slavery, it conjures plantation stereotypes and roles. Jubilo's attachment to the song entails a borrowing of blackness that highlights his and Rose's whiteness, even more so as Rose has a Black maid called Mammy (Louise Beavers), whose name and servile role provide a link to plantation dynamics. Interestingly, in the earlier film, the racist connotations of the song are downplayed: the lyrics are bowdlerized to match the action in the film, and the connection to both war and the plantation are removed. In the 1919 film, after Jubilo witnesses a train robbery, an intertitle reads: "De train's been robbed! Ha, Ha! / I saw the job! Ho, ho! / The sheriff will pinch somebody, / So Move on, Jubilo!" This film does not explain the tramps' nickname and seemingly assumes that audiences will be familiar enough with the song that its connotations will be clear, even as it is parodied.

To the degree that Black tramps are represented at all, similar to Acorn, they mainly serve to support the white tramp. In *American Pluck* (Stanton 1925), when playboy Blaze Derringer (George Walsh) leaves home to prove he can earn his own money, we find him among a group of tramps on a freight train. Blaze has somehow become master of sorts to two tramps: one British, named Lord Raleigh (Leo White), "the sap of an old family tree," and one

FIGURE 1.3. Black Mose (Blue Washington) tends to an injured white tramp in *Beggars of Life*.

Black, "the black sheik of his family," named Jefferson Lee, played in blackface by a white actor, Tom Wilson. The British and Black tramp carry the stereotypical associations with British butlering and Black servitude. Jefferson Lee's obsequious service to Blaze extends even to traveling with him to the fictional foreign country Bargonia, where Blaze helps a princess assert control over her dominion, and Jefferson Lee functions as his subsidiary. In a more realist vein, *Beggars of Life* (Wellman 1928) introduces a Black tramp, Black Mose (Blue Washington), in a scene at a "hobo jungle" (encampment).[78] Gently tending to an ill white tramp, Black Mose says, "Lay still white boy, you guine be ok." When the tramps are chased from the camp, he carries the white tramp to the train. Later, when the tramps are chased again, this time off a train, he carries the white man again. As Louise Brooks's female tramp is in double danger, both from the police on a murder charge and from a vicious tramp who plans to rape her, Black Mose helps her and The Boy (Richard Arlen) find a shack to hide out and then goes to forage food for the sick man. Later, after the sick white tramp dies, and the menacing tramp, Oklahoma Red (Wallace Beery), has been converted to goodness by seeing the love between the Girl and Boy, Black Mose supports Oklahoma Red. He helps him divert police attention away from the lovers and gets arrested while doing it.

The Spencer Williams picture *Marching On,* a.k.a. *Where's My Man To-nite* (1943), offers the only Black tramp in an all-Black-cast film of which I am aware. Even here, though, the Black tramp serves mainly to shore up the dominant white American ideal. As Elizabeth Reich argues, the film "addressed black anxieties about the war by employing the figure of the black soldier to deliver a pro-war message and redress the absence of black representation in nationalist narratives."[79] In *Marching On,* when a military recruiting rally comes to town, we learn that the father of Rodney Tucker Jr. (Hugo Martin) had been in the service during World War I and never returned to his family; thus, Rodney proclaims himself antimilitary. Rodney's fiancée, Martha Adams (Georgia Kelly), breaks their engagement, calling Rodney "a bragging coward" and "not a real man" who has proved himself. Despite his protestations, Rodney is drafted into the all-Black Twenty-Fifth Infantry. In the army, he's resentful, and when a Sergeant who knows Martha invites him over to watch her sing on TV, Rodney believes the gesture is intended to make him jealous. He goes AWOL. After an extended sequence at a burlesque house where we never see Rodney—but that seemingly stands in for what we may presume to have been a night of debauchery—we find Rodney surprised to wake up in a boxcar with a tramp by his side. The tramp (John Hemmings) says that Rodney crawled into the train the night before and that the tramp protected Rodney from the railroad "bulls." When the tramp, who sleepwalks, falls asleep and walks right off the moving train, Rodney tries to grab him and then jumps off the train to help him. Lying on the ground, injured, the tramp rambles, seemingly concussed, and we learn that he is a veteran of the First World War and is seeking his wife and child. As a result of injuries sustained in the war, however, he has amnesia and has not been able to find them. Sure enough, just before the tramp dies, Rodney realizes that he is his father. His death inspires Rodney to ask for another chance to prove that he is a "red-blooded American," a claim of both pride and equality that counters racialist logic of the one-drop rule for "black blood."[80] After his father dies, Rodney's grandfather appears, searching for him. He reminisces about his own military service with Teddy Roosevelt in the Spanish-American War as they search for a watering hole. Together, they stumble on a secret Japanese radio unit located in the hills. They fight two Japanese men, the film thus hailing "a viewership defined by its marginalization," Black spectators, "over and against other communities of marginalized races," the Japanese.[81] Grandpa (George Sutton) also dies "just the way I wanted to die," thanking the Lord for letting him "have one last fight for my country." Rodney then gets his second chance and rejoins the army, and Martha reclaims her engagement ring. The tramp here, then, is shown to be a "red-blooded American" who has sacrificed for his country. In stitching Rodney's personal story of loss to the tramp's story of being lost in the war, the film, as Reich claims, "structures the larger parable . . . : that blackness is already American, and the memories and histories of blackness and Americanness are inextricable."[82] Thus, speaking from within a Black perspective, the film negotiates Black disaffection to produce a patriotic resolution in which the Black soldier—and Black tramp—gain their integrity by serving the white-controlled military.

Even though the tramp represents a marginalized and subordinate masculinity, the suppression of ethnic and Black tramps locates the white tramp a step above them in the masculine hierarchy. In lifting the tramp above immigrants and African Americans, these films assert the privilege and primacy of whiteness across class boundaries and against more inclusive class affiliations, creating empathy and identification between and among white men of different classes at the exclusion of ethnic and nonwhite others.

THE "INVISIBLE" FEMALE TRAMP

The gendering of the tramp as male depended, in part, on the exclusion of female tramps. Cresswell refers to the "frequently invisible world of female tramps" and argues that one reason for their invisibility is that tramp laws specifically defined the tramp as a man, excluding women from the category.[83] Women tramps did exist, however. According to Lynn Weiner, as early as 1874, two of five police station lodging houses in New York City were designated for women, and there was a Women's Itinerant Hobo Union, as well as women's hobo conventions.[84] In the 1870s and 1880s, women's hotels and transient homes were established in most major cities.[85] But, as Elaine S. Abelson reminds us, "poverty is gendered in specific ways at different times."[86]

The slang use of *tramp* to describe a sexually promiscuous woman, as opposed to a transient, further elides the existence of female tramps.[87] According to Weiner, some women transients went on the road to seek sexual freedom; some were lesbian, and some traded sex for safety or food. Thus, because women tramps were perceived as sexually immoral, or conflated with prostitutes, *tramp* came to denote a female sexual outcast.[88]

The invisibility of female homelessness reveals deep ideological bias. As Abelson says, describing the relative invisibility of single homeless women in the Depression as opposed to single men and families, "People did not see these women because they did not expect to see them; they had not learned to see them and, in complicated ways, they did not want to see them."[89] Just as Black tramps were ignored because the power and freedom of mobility were not accorded to African Americans, women tramps were not seen because women were ideologically tied to the private sphere and not afforded the freedom to be mobile; thus, those looking for tramps "did not want to see them."⁹⁰

Although less visible than male tramps, female tramps nonetheless produced a category crisis. Female tramps frequently dressed as men, both to avoid rape and to ensure greater freedom; also, there was likely a lesbian subculture among women tramps.⁹¹ Cresswell argues that, in both their masculine appearance and their mobility, women tramps created "a fundamental crisis in the ability of onlookers to categorize them," and in this they seemed to "essentially renege on being a woman."⁹² Weiner argues that female tramps "symbolized extreme deviance from 'woman's place' in American society—a place characterized by dependency, domesticity, submission, and other prescribed female virtues."⁹³

For the most part, films tend to ignore female tramps, although there are a few incidental representations. In rare cases when female tramps are the central focus of the narrative, their situation is seen as different in kind from that of male tramps. In *Girls of the Road* (Grinde 1940), for example, the female tramp Mickey (Helen Mack)—one of a few female tramps in the film with masculine-sounding names—articulates a fundamental difference between male and female tramps. The do-gooder Kay (Ann Dvorak), the governor's daughter, embeds herself among "road girls" to learn more about them and asks Mickey why she is on the road. Mickey says it is because she has no home. When Kay presses her on why she doesn't settle down and get a job, Mickey explains that she is caught in a vicious circle: "The first thing they ask you is, 'Where'd you work last?' You can't answer. Then they ask you, 'Where do you live?' And all you can say is nowhere." Unable to find work because she has no work experience and, as a result, no home, she seems unworthy of a job: "Oh, one of those road girls, go away, no job for you today." Mickey continues, providing an analysis of the different experience of transience for men and women: "You see, when a man loses a job and he's got no home and nobody to turn to, he can still get along. He can ride the rods with the hoboes or panhandle on the streets, and anytime he gets a shave and a decent suit of clothes and a square meal under his belt, he can walk in anywhere, no marks on him. A man can beg for a job and get it. A girl can't."

In Mickey's view, the temporality of tramping is different for men and women because the shame is greater for women. In her account, the male tramp can pass through an experience of tramping and yet return to normal life, "no marks," whereas the female tramp is stigmatized and dismissed, her status as a tramp turned into permanent baggage she must carry. Against

FIGURE 1.4. "He's a she!" Sally (Dorothy Coonan Wellman) disguised as a boy tramp in *Wild Boys of the Road*.

fantasies of tramping as being about freedom, when one of the road girls dies, Mickey considers her better off since she no longer has to beg for money or rides or hide from cops. Mickey does allow, however, that "there are two kinds of girls on the road: those that like it and those that don't," suggesting a category of female tramps who may be more aligned with the more purposeful male tramps who seek out the road.

The female tramp's status requires a backstory, which is, on the whole, not true of male tramps; this marks the female tramp as a special case, her role as a tramp not able to be taken for granted. In *Wild Boys of the Road* (Wellman 1933), for example, the two main boy tramps, Eddie (Frankie Darro) and Tommy (Edwin Philips), are surprised to meet a girl dressed in male clothing riding on the boxcar: "He's a she!" (fig. 1.4). The girl, Sally (Dorothy Coonan Wellman), explains that her mother died, and her family had many kids, so she decided to unburden them, and riding the rails was the only way to travel to her aunt in Chicago. In *Girls of the Road,* Irene (Marjorie Cooley) travels by freight car to marry her fiancé, carrying a boxed wedding dress, having had money for either a dress or bus fare. In *Man's Castle* (Borzage 1933), when Bill (Spencer Tracy) meets Trina (Loretta Young) alone and hungry in a park, he tells her that no female has to starve and that the unemployment situation has nothing to do with women. In coded language, he suggests that she should be a prostitute or gold digger. She says she has "thought of that" but cannot.

The female tramp not only demarcates the tramp as, by definition, masculine; she also serves to underscore and critique male sexual violence against women. Often, the narratives of female tramps involve sexual abuse or risk as cause or consequence for being on the road. In *Beggars of Life,* for example, when the unnamed Boy approaches a kitchen back door seeking food, he finds a man slumped, dead in a chair, an uneaten breakfast on the plate. The similarly unnamed Girl emerges from upstairs dressed in a man's clothing and cap. She explains to the Boy that the man adopted her from an orphan's home two years ago and was always after her, "pawin'," but that this morning he attempted to rape her. In a dramatic flashback that maintains a shot of Brooks's face in close-up superimposed over the events recalled, we see the man grabbing her, tearing at her clothes. The battle between them is shown in close-ups of feet approaching and then hands grasping, as she finds a gun and shoots him, then retreats upstairs. The Boy takes the Girl on the road with him, and they develop an innocent romance as he protects her, helping to keep her warm while they sleep in a haystack and rubbing her weary feet. At the hobo jungle where we meet Black Mose, one of the tramps ascertains the Girl's gender. After the police come, seeking her for the murder, and all the tramps run to catch a freight, we see the men in the boxcar frozen, all staring at her. Oklahoma Red offers her a drink and tells her not to be "so exclusive," as she clings to the Boy. Asserting his masculine authority, Oklahoma Red declares himself the head of the entire gang and says that "if there is a gal in the gang, she's *my* gal." A "kangaroo court" is convened and decides that the "sheik," the Boy, "loses custody of his sweetie and gets pushed off the train." A fight ensues, and then railroad "dicks" begin searching cars, so all the hoboes run. The Girl is saved only because Oklahoma Red has a mysterious change of heart and opts to help the young lovers escape, risking his own freedom—and that of Black Mose—and giving his life to do so. Here, the Boy is differentiated from the older tramps, who all seem aggressive and uninhibited in their sexuality, where he is romantic and chivalrous. Oklahoma's reversal seems like a last lost spark of humanity.

Beggars of Life emphasizes the older male tramps' unrestrained sexuality, to show life on the road as treacherous for women, but allows that the younger man may be more sensitive. Similarly, *Wild Boys of the Road* situates the danger to women in an older man, not the teen tramps. When Eddie and Tommy meet Sally, the three quickly become friends; and as the teen tramp community grows on freight trains and then in a "sewer town," we see other girls among the boys, all part of the communal work of cooking, taking care of the lean-tos that house the community, and begging. Sally, for example, dances on the street while Tommy, having lost a leg in an accident on the rails, plays the harmonica. Sexual danger comes when the teens are chased off a freight train and one girl (Ann Hovey) lingers behind, trying to dry her soaked clothing by a fire. As she removes her wet shirt while alone in the freight car, the train brakeman (Ward Bond) enters and rapes her. When the teens return to fight the railroad men, they find the girl, traumatized, and, discovering what happened, they swarm the brakeman, who then falls off the train.

Girls of the Road shows sexual harassment to be the unconditional currency of the road. When Kay first leaves home to meet and learn about road girls, she hitchhikes. When a driver picks her up, he immediately starts commenting on her looks and asks if she has a boyfriend. Then he puts his arm around her and pulls her close. As she wrestles, he tells her to "relax and enjoy yourself." Later, when the police force all the female tramps onto a freight train to remove them from the county, we see hordes of men staring at the women. When they get in the boxcar, male tramps sidle up to the women. One girl, Irene, gets separated from the other girls. When a friendly truck driver finds her, she is battered and confused but keeps muttering about a man grabbing her and jumping off the train.

If part of the way in which tramps were masculinized was to exclude or deny female tramps, female tramps nonetheless haunt the margins of tramp films. They serve to underscore and shore up the presumptive masculinity of tramp culture, certainly. Where the sociological literature on female tramps portrayed them as sexually transgressive, films tended to show them as victims of unrestrained male sexuality. But the female tramp in film produces contradictory images of the male tramp's gendering in relation to sexuality. Narratives about female tramps highlight the aggressive sexuality of male tramps but also serve to romanticize at least some male tramps, who are elevated through codes of chivalry and romance. While the sexually aggressive tramps are aligned more with older age and seemingly choose to be tramps, the more romantic figures are younger and seem to be more sympathetic victims of circumstance.

INTRUSIVE MASCULINITY

More than just excluding female tramps, the contours of the tramp's manliness were shaped most strongly in opposition to femininity and feminine influence, which was perceived as the civilizing influence. *Hobohemia,* a term popularized in the 1920s by Anderson's book on hoboes, was identified with "absence of feminine manners, morals and domesticity."[94] Tramps privileged women as sources of charity, seeking handouts from women whose husbands were away from home and relying on help from female missionaries, social workers, innkeepers, and waitresses in the "main stem" or skid row neighborhood.[95] At the same time, tramps were often perceived as a threat to women and the home: the moment when the tramp arrived at the door of a house to beg for food or money was seen as a moment when the woman was especially vulnerable.[96] Moreover, free from the regulation of male sexuality by the bonds of domesticity and marriage, the tramp was feared as an unrestrained figure who would look to women as sources of noncommittal sex in brothels, saloons, gambling dens, and lodging houses or whose sexuality would express itself through rape.[97] Tramps, then, were viewed as living outside the bounds of domesticity and feminine influence, but tramping depended on frequent proximity to and exchanges with women, whether asking for charity or seeking sex.

The tramp stood in opposition to femininity via his mobility, which was gendered male. In the discourse around the tramp scares, the tramp was seen as a "super-mobile" masculine figure aligned with more general associations between public space, mobility, and masculinity.[98] As a figure who is unfixed, the tramp signifies a threat to rootedness, stability, fixity, and home, all associated with femininity. In his ubiquity, he can be seen as a pervasive and infiltrating figure whose movements reveal the porousness and precarity of boundaries between inside and outside, public and private, us and them. Uncontained, the tramp intrudes on feminine spaces, in particular, marking both public and private spaces inhabited by women as vulnerable.

The tramp's mobility works in tandem with his unrestrained sexuality so that in early films he is often represented as a masher who infiltrates women's personal space. Perhaps not coincidentally, the use of the word *masher* to describe a "womanizer who makes unwanted sexual advances towards women, especially in public places" emerges at the same time as the term *tramp*, suggesting both the increased appearance and vulnerability of women in public spaces and the concern over itinerant men.[99] A frequent plot in tramp films involves the tramp's efforts to seduce a woman on a park bench. These films show the tramp invading the woman's space and creating a momentary love triangle as he replaces the lover. This plot appears in AFI catalogue descriptions of the films *On the Benches in the Park* (American Mutoscope and Biograph 1901), *The Tramp's First Bath* (Lubin 1903), and *When We Were Twenty-One* (American Mutoscope and Biograph 1900). In each of these films, a woman and her beau are seated on a park bench. The man gets up and leaves for a moment, either because the couple quarrel or because the man has something to do. The tramp takes the man's seat and imitates the lover, putting his arm around the woman. She eventually notices the substitution and screams or runs away; the tramp is then punished by the returning lover. A related plotline takes place on the train or streetcar. In *Nervy Nat Kisses the Bride, Hubby to the Rescue* (Lubin 1904), and *Weary Willie Kisses the Bride* (Porter 1904), for example, the tramp sneakily steals the ticket or fare, then replaces the boyfriend or husband when he gets up, attempts to kiss the woman, and is then thrown off the vehicle.[100]

Early on, Chaplin frequently plays the role of masher. When he is at Keystone, before he refines his tramp to be what he later describes as "a gentleman, a poet, a dreamer, a lonely fellow, always hopeful of romance and adventure," the Charlie persona was often "mean, crude and brutish."[101] Rather than the tentative, tender, and vulnerable romances of his feature films, Chaplin's early Tramp is sexually aggressive and vulgar. In the first filmed appearance of the Tramp, *Mabel's Strange Predicament* (Normand 1914), Chaplin plays a drunk masher who loiters in a hotel lobby, hitting on various women and following one upstairs before he runs into Mabel, locked out of her room wearing her pajamas. In Chaplin's first directorial effort, *Twenty Minutes of Love* (Chaplin 1914), the Tramp witnesses a couple (Minta Durfee and Edgar Kennedy) embracing passionately on a park bench; giggling, he mockingly imitates them, flinging his arms around a tree and kissing it. He approaches the couple and sits on the small sliver of bench left available next to the woman (fig. 1.5). He taps her, then nudges her, and then places his hand on her hand and her lap, until the man switches places with his girlfriend and threatens the Tramp. The Tramp then taps him, just as he did the woman, and the man shoves him off the bench. The Tramp sits again, and as he and the man jostle, the man falls off and the Tramp moves closer to the woman and flirts until he is finally routed from the scene. We cut to "another case" in which a woman (Eva Nelson) tells her lover (Chester Conklin) to prove his love with a gift. As the man steals a watch from a lone man (Josef Swickard) sleeping on a bench, the Tramp meets the lady, who smiles at him before entering a wooded area. Looking for her, the Tramp stumbles on a third couple on the grass and offends them so that the man tosses him into the clearing. The Tramp meets the pickpocket and steals the watch from him, then gives it to the woman: she gives him two kisses before she slaps him, but she still allows him to bestow two more kisses on her. A melee occurs in which the Tramp and pickpocket fight and the watch's owner

FIGURE 1.5. Chaplin's Tramp as a masher in *Twenty Minutes of Love*.

brings the police. As the pickpocket and police fall into the pond with some onlookers, the Tramp walks away with the woman.

A different scenario has the tramp invade a woman's workspace. In D. W. Griffith's *The Lonedale Operator* (1911) and *A Girl and Her Trust* (1912), a tramp assays a woman's workplace as a telegraph operator in a railroad station and sets up the film's famous suspenseful parallel editing and rescue. Leana Hirschfeld-Kroen argues that just as the telephone and telegraph themselves have been recognized as crucial to the "codification of cross-cutting, one of the essential operations of classical cinematic syntax," the female telephone and telegraph operators who populate these films should also be considered "singularly legible as *demonstrators* of an emerging syntax."[102] While both the technology and the women are essential to visually imagining the narrative logic of crosscutting—with the technology operated by the women serving to provide an objective correlative for the cuts and links between disparate spaces—it is also no accident that tramps create the threat that sets in motion the triangulated action that motivates the parallel editing. In both films, a large shipment of cash arrives at the station and must be protected. In both films, the woman is left alone in the railroad office by her male coworkers. And, in both films, just as the men leave, two tramps arrive at the station on a freight train. In *The Lonedale Operator,* they hop out from the rods below the train and in *A Girl and Her Trust,* they creep out of the boxcar. The tramps approach the office, spy on the woman through a window, and then attempt to break into the office and gain access to the cash. These films could not exist without the figure of the tramp. The scenario depends on the ubiquity of the tramp, as the stations are isolated in the countryside and would not have many passers-by. Their transience makes their appearance contingent, as opposed to planned, and the films depend on an automatic assumption that the tramp would opportunistically steal money and pose a threat to the woman. *A Girl and Her Trust* even labels the tramps' appearance at the station with an intertitle declaring "The Tramps' Opportunity."

While the tramp preys on women in public, in early films he is viewed even more so as a threat to domestic space. "In the bourgeois imagination," Susan Fraiman notes, tramps "would come to represent everything at odds with stability and respectability."[103] We can see the tramp's intrusion into private space in numerous films, such as Griffith's *Lonely Villa* (1909), in which three tramps lure a father away from home, then corner the mother and her children in the home, where they hide behind a closed door until a last-minute rescue. Lois Weber and Phillips Smalley's *Suspense* (1913) adopts a triangulated structure similar to Griffith's, with the tramp threatening the female domestic space while the man is outside the home. A self-conscious reworking of Griffith's last-minute rescue, "the film's generic title," as Shelley Stamp suggests, "condenses Griffith's well-worn plotline to its elemental component—suspense—in order to investigate how tension is created in and around domestic environments and female victims."[104] Smalley and Weber's film investigates the tension created around domestic space not only by reworking Griffith's parallel editing but also by using the figure of the tramp as the threat to the home, relying on contingency enabled by the ubiquity and proximity of the tramp. The film opens in a kitchen where a female servant, Mamie (Lule Warrenton), looks through a keyhole at a woman (Lois Weber) tending to her baby, then leaves a note saying she is quitting her job because "no servant will stay in this lonesome place." She exits the house, suitcase in hand, and leaves a key under the mat, then exits the frame to the right. Belying the sense of the house as "lonesome," in the sense of being solitary or unfrequented, but underscoring the feeling of the woman's being alone and without assistance, a tramp (Sam Kaufman) immediately enters from the left of the frame and walks up the path to the house. The woman's husband (Paul Valentine) calls to say he will be late and asks his wife if she is okay. Not knowing that Mamie has left, the wife believes she will be fine. As we see the husband and wife in two triangles in a three-way split screen—the husband at the bottom, the wife at top right—the tramp enters the third triangle at top left and seemingly listens in (fig. 1.6). Finding Mamie's note, the wife secures the windows and doors and resists calling her husband. We see the tramp looking in the window, then stepping over the porch railing. The wife looks out her upstairs window, and we see the tramp in an overhead point-of-view shot, his face filling the frame in a perpendicular glance upwards. In

FIGURE 1.6. The Tramp's invasion of domestic—and screen—space in *Suspense*.

another triangulated split screen with wife, husband, and tramp each featured, we see the woman call her husband to report, "A tramp is prowling around the house!" as we see the tramp in a ground-level shot lift the key from under the mat. "Now he is opening the kitchen door," she says, as we see the tramp cautiously enter the kitchen. As she says, "Now he is in the—," we see the tramp's hand in close-up as he cuts the phone line. The husband then rushes home, stealing a car, which puts the car owner and police in pursuit of him. Indicating the abundance of tramps, along the way, the husband runs over another tramp (Lon Chaney) walking along the road, but he is unhurt. As the father and his pursuers approach the house in cars, the tramp moves farther into the house, takes a sandwich from the kitchen cupboard, where he finds a knife, then moves upstairs, breaking through the door to enter the bedroom, and approaches the woman and baby on the bed, knife in hand, until the arrival of the father and police forces him to attempt an escape down the stairs.

Home is rarely shown as desirable for tramps, and, when it is, it is seen as out of reach. In *Beggars of Life,* as the Boy and Girl settle in to sleep inside a haystack, the Girl opines that she knows what she wants: "A place to be quiet, clean, a place to call home. I never had it—that's why I want it so much." Her desire is never fulfilled, even as she escapes on a train to Canada. In *Modern Times,* Chaplin's Tramp and the Gamin (Paulette Godard) fantasize about a home. As they sit on a curb, he asks her where she lives. "No place—anywhere," she answers. Just then, a couple step out of their house, the man in neat work clothes, overalls, and a jacket, the woman in a gingham dress and crisp white apron. They hug and wave goodbye. The Tramp initially mocks them, imitating the woman's loving exclamations, then asks, "Can you imagine us in a little home like that?" A conjoined fantasy sequence follows in which we see the Tramp, wearing overalls and a neckerchief, situated in a cozy home. He plucks a grapefruit from a tree, then calls a cow to the kitchen door to fill a pitcher of milk, and eats grapes that dangle from above the door; the Gamin, wearing a pretty patterned dress and apron with a bow in her hair, cooks two enormous steaks. Their fantasy of domestic plenitude makes them conscious of their hunger, and the Tramp declares, "I'll do it. We'll get a home even if I have to work for it," as the inevitable arrival of a policeman interrupts their idyll.

But tramps can sometimes create temporary alternative homes. Chaplin's *The Kid* (Chaplin 1921) shows the single male tramp as a better parent than a biological mother. In this film, a woman (Edna Purvience) is "ruined" by a male painter (Carl Miller), who abandons her when she becomes pregnant. She leaves her baby in an expensive car, with a note pinned to it, asking whoever finds it to care for the orphan child. Unfortunately, two thieves take the car, and when they find the baby, they ditch it in an alley. The mother has a change of heart and attempts to retrieve the baby, but it is too late. The Tramp finds the baby in the alley, and after a few attempts to unload it on others, ends up caring for it, fashioning diapers and feeding apparatuses out of household items. The film cuts to five years later, and we see the Tramp and his adopted son, John (Jackie Coogan), in an impoverished but loving home. The Tramp and child engage in minor illegal schemes to get by: the kid breaks a window, for example, and the Tramp shows up as a window repairman. Eventually, social services take the child away from the Tramp, and, through a *deux ex machina* discovery, he is returned to the mother, now a rich actress. At film's end, the Tramp is brought to the mother's house and welcomed in to form, perhaps, a new family.

While the tramp sometimes presents a threat or alternative to traditional domesticity, as the tramp cycle matures, he also sometimes offers a cure for domesticity in crisis. A rare postwar tramp film, *It Happened on Fifth Avenue* (del Ruth 1947), proffers the tramp as both an intruder and a cure for domestic ills. In this film, the tramp Aloysius T. McKeever, or Mac (Victor Moore), "borrows" empty mansions when rich people are away at their vacation homes. Even though he gave up work years ago and lets "others work to satisfy his lavish tastes," he refers to himself as a "guest" in other people's homes and takes good care of the homes, clothing, and household amenities he borrows. In line with films that valorize the tramp against the millionaire, the film pits Mac's authenticity against the money-grubbing cynicism of Michael O'Connor (Charles Ruggles), a rich man who evicts poor people from buildings to tear them down and build a depot for his business. Through a complicated series of coincidences, without revealing her identity, O'Connor's daughter, Trudy (Gale Storm), ends up living in the house with Mac and an army vet, Jim (Don DeFore), who is also homeless. She convinces first her father and then her mother, Mary (Ann Harding), to join her as pretend tramps. Living with Mac and friends, Mike and Mary, who have separated as a result of Mike's focus on work and money, begin to rediscover simple values and their love for one another. Eventually, Mike helps Jim and the other vets who have moved into the house start a business building homes for returning vets in the deserted barracks he was going to use to expand his business. Without revealing their identities to Mac, Mike and Mary say goodbye to Mac as he heads to their *other* home in Virginia, and Mike asserts that next winter Mac will enter the New York home by the front door.

My Man Godfrey (LaCava 1933) brings an "imposter tramp" into the domestic space, where he both finds authenticity and provides a cure for domesticity in crisis. Godfrey (William Powell) is discovered in a shantytown at the dump by rich partygoers seeking a "forgotten man" as one of the items in a scavenger hunt. Irene Bullock (Carole Lombard) explains that a scavenger hunt is "like a treasure hunt, except in a treasure hunt you try to find something you want; in a scavenger hunt you try to find something *nobody* wants." "Like a forgotten man?" Godfrey asks. Desperate to have a "protégé," like her mother, Angelica Bullock (Alice Brady), whose protégé, Carlos (Mischa Auer), is a barely disguised gigolo, Irene hires Godfrey as a butler. Despite castigating the partygoers, as "empty headed nitwits," Godfrey accepts. Eventually, we learn that Godfrey is scion of a wealthy family, the Boston Brahmin Parks, but became a tramp after suffering a bitter breakup. Despondent and suicidal, Godfrey stumbled on the tramps at the dump and discovered "people fighting it out, not complaining," and joined them. Having discovered authenticity and grit through life among the tramps, Godfrey teaches the same to the Bullock family. He brings much-needed discipline to the screwball disorder of the household. He humbles Irene's sister, Cornelia (Gail Patrick)—a "Park Avenue brat," who had tried to frame Godfrey for theft of a pearl necklace when he spurned her romantic advances—and teaches her not to treat people as objects. Crucially, he saves the family from financial ruin. Having observed that Mr. Bullock (Eugene Pallette) was suffering financial losses, Godfrey had offered to help; but, dismissed by Bullock, who viewed Godfrey as a tramp and servant, Godfrey nonetheless took the liberty of playing the market, using the pearl necklace to buy shares of stock that Bullock dumped. Godfrey claims that in giving him work, Irene "helped me to find myself," and he now works to create something to help the poor. Restoring the money to the family, and the pearls to Cornelia, Godfrey keeps enough for himself to open a nightclub named "The Dump" on the banks of the East River, the site of the old shantytown: it provides work for forgotten men in the summer and homes and food in the winter.

If the tramp's manliness was shaped in opposition to femininity and feminine influence, the nature of his opposition took different forms. During the initial tramp scares, the tramp was often imagined as a threat to women in both public and private spaces. At the same time, however, and increasingly over the decades, the tramp's intrusion into feminine and domestic space could also be seen as beneficial. As attitudes toward the tramp shifted and he became a more sympathetic figure, the tramp seemed to offer a counter to a creeping decadence associated with wealthy homes in particular, ironically importing civil and civilizing values into homes where those values had been forgotten. If the tramp began his film career as a masher and thief, he ended as a more beneficent intruder—a caretaker, servant, and ultimately good neighbor.

QUEERING THE TRAMP

In excluding female tramps and resisting feminine influence, tramp culture could be seen not just as a male dominion but also as homosexual. In sociological accounts, homosexuality among tramps is highlighted, their deviation from normative masculinity taken as defining. As historian Peter Boag details, autobiographies, sociologies, and legal cases document widespread homosexual relations among male tramps. Some commentators, such as Nels Anderson, ascribed the rampant homosexuality among tramps to the anonymity afforded by a mobile and placeless life, an anonymity furthered by the tramp's penchant for using nicknames and refusing to give details about his pretramp life. But homosexuality was not a hidden aspect of tramp life. As Boag suggests, tramps had a fairly open same-sex sexual culture that was widely recognized and accepted and could have provided a refuge for those whose desires made them feel unwelcome in mainstream society. Homosexuality among male hoboes was one way that the tramp both troubled the boundaries of masculine behavior and asserted masculinity outside the bounds of feminine influence because it gave them access to sex while maintaining all-male communities and exploring nonheterocentrist forms of sexuality.

But if gay sex distanced tramps from certain conceptions of normative masculinity, it also asserted "normal" masculine gender roles. Although same-sex relationships between men of all ages certainly occurred, the most typical relationships were those between older males, referred to as "wolves" or "jockers," and teen males, labeled "punks," "prushuns," or "lambs."[105] Indeed, the original lyrics for "Big Rock Candy Mountain," later expunged from the popular song, included a description of a young punk being lured by a jocker with promises of "cigarette trees" and other treats.[106] Wolves and jockers were sometimes painted as predatory and penetrating, but "the jocker-punk relationship was based on more than sex, which by definition it included."[107] Rather than merely coercive, punks participated in relationships with jockers for economic rewards, protection, sexual pleasure, and romance.[108] In ways similar to the urban working-class cultures that historian George Chauncey analyzes in the same period, insofar as the adult male tramps took on the sexual role of inserter, they took on the phallic power of manliness.[109] The young men were aligned with a receptive feminine position and became desirable in part because, in their adolescence, they resembled women more than men; but the punk differed from the urban "fairy" in that he did not act effeminate via costume, posture, or other aspects of gender performance; and the punk would commonly "graduate," or mature, to become a jocker.[110] Men who participated in homosexual sex acts may not have considered themselves gay in our modern sense; they may have considered male-male sex a substitute for the absence of women, or they may have viewed homosexual sex as an activity more than an identity.

In films, not surprisingly, homosexuality among tramps is suppressed. But tramp films do allow for small queer moments that hint fleetingly at the possibility of gay tramp culture. *A Romance of the Rail* (Porter 1903), for example, inserts a male tramp couple into a film that otherwise functions as what film scholar Lynne Kirby refers to as a "honeymoon train" film. According to Kirby, the film was commissioned by the Delaware, Lackawanna and Western Railroad to advertise the cleanliness of the line.[111] In the film, a woman wearing a bright white dress, shoes, and hat is met at the station by a man, also dressed head-to-toe in white, who escorts her onto the train. Together, they stand on the observation deck and wave white handkerchiefs goodbye. Much of the film consists of a virtual Hale's Tour as we watch the

FIGURE 1.7. A queer romance emerges from under the train in *A Romance of the Rails*.

woman and her beau sit on the observation deck observing and reacting to the changing landscape, their clothes unmarked by soot. Suddenly, a cut brings us to a scene in which the train is stopped and the couple stand outside the observation deck, on the ground. A priest steps onto the observation deck and conducts a marriage ceremony. The couple exchange rings, kiss, and thank the priest. We then cut to a shot of the moving train as it enters a station and stops. After the couple—their clothes still sparkling white—exit the train, the camera lingers. To the left of the exit, we see two bald male tramps pop out from underneath the rods on the train. Attired in shabby tuxedos, they put on top hats, take each other's arms, and walk, tottering slightly, as if drunk (fig. 1.7). Another tramp materializes from the right side of the screen and tries to brush their clothes with a whisk broom, but they dismiss him and exit. As Kirby suggests, the male tramps seem to parody the heterosexual couple: "literally beneath the romance journey, buried within the narrative and functioning as an antinarrative coda, with its ending-beyond-the-ending, the ribald same-sex couple sabotages both the 'straight' couple and the 'straight' ending by repetition with a difference."[112] The male tramps not only queer the heterosexual romance through parody but also acknowledge the possibility of a parallel world beneath the surface in which same-sex couples also honeymoon, even if marginalized and riding the rods.

Other films also hint at queer tramp culture. In *Wandering Willies,* for instance, the first shot introduces us to Percy Nudge (Billy Bevan), "well-known tourist visiting at Bull Frog Lake," and we see Bevan lying down, seemingly on a park bench, just waking up. As he shifts, we cut to a long shot that shows a shelf below him on the bench, with another man (Andy Clyde) sleeping, "Dusty Duncan, playing hookey from the Hoosegow." They wander together, trying to steal food. Then, spying a policeman getting free food and chatting up a woman, they decide to steal his clothes. Percy creates a distraction by saying that the woman's baby has fallen in the lake. While the policeman chases a duck in the water that Percy has dressed in the child's blanket, Percy steals the policeman's clothing, and Dusty gets into the baby's carriage, recklessly leaving the baby on the grass. The two men then form a queer alternate family as the "policeman" takes the "baby" into a restaurant and attempts to get a free meal.

The queering of the masculine duo in *Clubs Are Trump* constantly threatens to overwhelm the nominally heterosexual narrative. The film opens with a shot of a middle-aged heterosexual couple sitting together on a park bench, then dissolves to a younger couple giggling on a bench, then a policeman and lady spooning on a bench, followed by a serious and talkative couple, and, finally, a large grumpy man who keeps turning away from a lovely attentive woman who tries to soothe him. After this parade of heterosexual couples, a title introduces us to two tramps—Harold Lloyd and Snub Pollard—labeled "two famous lascars" (sailors), possibly indicating homosexuality.[113] Squabbling over one tramp's theft of the other's snack, the two glare at each other and come close, face-to-face, almost in a kiss. A policeman approaches, and they walk away, arm in arm. The two then attempt to individually join couples on the benches, enacting the masher trope discussed above. The large grumpy man reacts jealously and beats them, then dumps them in the pond. They exit the pond holding hands. As they sit on a bench, Lloyd picks up a magazine with an illustration of cavemen. The two tramps then sit on the bench back-to-back and fall asleep. We then enter a dream sequence in which the two tramps and the park-bench couples are all cavemen and -women. In the fantasy sequence, the two tramps engage in masculine competition, ultimately beating the other men to win two women for themselves. As they wake from the seemingly shared dream, the tramps sit on the park bench locked in an embrace, petting and kissing each other (fig. 1.8), until a policeman wanders up and stops them, hitting them with a billy club. The remainder of the film entails a lengthy chase with police, abandoning in the real world the heterosexual conquest fantasized in the dream.

FIGURE 1.8. A queer embrace between "Snub" Pollard and Harold Lloyd's Lonesome Luke in *Clubs Are Trump*.

These queer narratives are exceptional in a sense, but they underscore the degree to which the tramp is always already a queer figure, in Alexander Doty's sense, in which *queer* refers to a variety of discourses that have grown up in opposition to or at variance with the dominant straight symbolic order as "non-, anti-, or contra straight."[114] As a marginal but pervasive figure, the tramp queers work, heterosexual romance, the family, public spaces, and the home. In claiming the tramp as queer, I am not claiming him as a progressive or liberatory figure; instead, I suggest that the tramp represents non-, or anti-, or contra-hegemonic masculinity. He is a figure who challenges certain precepts and hierarchies of the dominant ideal but also helps shore up dominant conceptions of manliness by participating in the dominant culture's privileging of whiteness, misogyny, and heterosexuality.

CAPRA-ING THE TRAMP CYCLE

For the most part, the tramp cycle of films ends with the onset of World War II.[115] The propaganda race picture *Marching On* and the romantic comedy *It Happened on Fifth Avenue,* both of which I discussed above, are stragglers, and both deal directly with the situation of soldiers and veterans, as well as tramps. Two of the most famous tramp films, Frank Capra's *Meet John Doe* and Preston Sturges's *Sullivan's Travels,* appear in 1941, prior to the United

States' entry into World War II, and they serve as fitting end points for the cycle. The tramp in *Meet John Doe* is seemingly, in Woloch's terms, an *eccentric* who plays "a disruptive oppositional role within the plot" and inspires a populist movement, where *Sullivan's Travels* presents the tramp as what Woloch calls a *worker*, "a flat character who is reduced to a single functional use within the narrative." Both films, however, create a narrative that ultimately embraces the status quo, and both erase the tramp's distinctive characteristics and absorb him into larger narratives about the disenfranchised.

In *Meet John Doe*, newspaper reporter Ann Mitchell (Barbara Stanwyck) is fired, part of a massive downsizing and overhauling of the paper. As her final act, a gamble aimed at keeping her job, she publishes a phony letter from a John Doe who threatens to kill himself on Christmas Eve as a protest against the state of civilization. This vague canard sets off a media frenzy, and Ann convinces the newspaper's new managing editor, Connell (James Gleason), to keep the ruse going rather than face the humiliation of admitting to a hoax. Together, they hire a tramp—a former bush-league ballplayer, "Long John" Willoughby (Gary Cooper)—to pose as their John Doe and let Ann ghostwrite weekly columns labeled "I Protest" in his name.

Meet John Doe subsumes the tramp into the larger category of "little people"—a homily slightly undercut by a gag in which the newspaper sends two Little People, or dwarves, in for publicity photos with John. The film's opening credits are superimposed over a montage of black-and-white footage depicting a broad swath of people encompassed by the film's conception of "the people": factory workers, farmers, miners, switchboard operators, urban crowds, people engaged in leisure activities, the military, and newborn babies.

In this film, John's status as a tramp makes him available to be hired but is not what powers the movement; rather, it is his ability to be subsumed into a narrative about average Joes and vague Christian platitudes. In a radio broadcast, John reads a speech written by Ann, a heartfelt but toothless call for people to "tear down all the fences" and meet their neighbors, to focus on teamwork and helping each other: this is an explicit rejection of the need for government. The speech inspires the formation of John Doe clubs across the country, where people work together to find jobs for those without and get people off relief, all without government assistance. Ann's boss, the newspaper owner D. B. Norton (Edward Arnold), plans to use John to lead the John Does to form a third party with him as leader. John refuses and, exposed as a con man and thus having punctured the momentum of the John Doe movement, he decides he will commit suicide after all. But before he does,

Ann—with both the corrupt politicians and the folks from a John Doe club as witnesses—convinces John to lead the movement instead, reminding him of "the first John Doe," Jesus. The editor Connell gets the last word: "There you are, Norton, the people. Try and lick that!"

Only John's older friend the Colonel (Walter Brennan)—whom John met on a boxcar and with whom he plays music on the mouth organ—maintains a distinctive tramp identity. When John is first hired, the Colonel warns him that the job will "wreck" him and make him soft: "When you become a guy with a bank account, they've got you!" Throughout the narrative, the Colonel nags at John: "I bet you ain't heard a train whistle in two weeks." But the Colonel is a minor character in the narrative. A seemingly outmoded figure, through his refusal, he eventually serves to mark John's ability to assimilate; and his and John's homosocial coupling is eventually displaced by the normative classical Hollywood coupling of Ann and John.

Sullivan's Travels explicitly takes aim at the "deep-dish," "artistic" films like those of Capra. John L. Sullivan (Joel McCrea) is a successful Hollywood director known for light sex comedies such as *Hey Hey in the Hayloft* who wants to make a new film, *O Brother Where Art Thou*, based on a novel by Sinclair Beckstein. This new film will be "a commentary on modern conditions ... [via] stark realism, [dramatizing] the problems that confront the average man." "But with a little sex in it?" asks his producer, hopefully. "A little, but I don't want to stress it," Sullivan asserts: "I want this picture to be a document. I want to hold a mirror up to life. I want this to be a picture of dignity, a true canvas of the suffering of humanity." Realizing that he knows nothing of "trouble," Sullivan, nicknamed Sully, sets out to find it by masquerading as a tramp. Sturges voices his critique of such "deep-dish" ambitions most forcefully through Sully's butler (Robert Grieg). As Sully's valet (Eric Blore) dresses Sully as a bindle stiff, wearing dirty, torn clothes and carrying a bundle on a stick, the butler interrupts: "I have never been sympathetic to the caricaturing of the poor and needy, sir. . . . If you will permit me to say so, sir, the subject is not an interesting one. The poor know all about poverty, and only the morbid rich would find the topic glamorous."

Despite the butler's protestations, Sully begins his "experiment." Initially, Sully finds he can't escape Hollywood, and as James Harvey explains, "He can't get out of the movies, either, it seems."[116] Sturges navigates various film genres as Sully progresses through his various travels, including a Keystone-like slapstick sequence and a small-town comedy with a man-hungry widow (Esther Howard) who gives him work chopping wood and a place to stay while she admires his torso. After he escapes her pernicious desire, Sully finds himself back in Hollywood, where he meets the unnamed Girl (Veronica Lake)—because "there's always a girl in the picture"—a would-be actress who has given up on Hollywood and is leaving but who becomes absorbed into Sully's experiment, adding the "little sex" we were promised. With her dressed as a "beazle" or "frail," in a newsboy cap and men's jacket, they hop a freight along with a multitude of other tramps, Black and white. As they awkwardly wriggle onto the boxcar, two tramps already inside call them "amateurs" and then exit the car when Sully attempts to engage them in a discussion of "labor."

Eventually, Sully finds "trouble." He and the Girl enter a new style of film: "silent, mixing comedy and pathos, looking like Griffith at times, Chaplin at others," as Harvey writes.[117] In an extended sequence, we see Sully and the Girl in a hobo shantytown filled with men and women, old and young. Then they are in a soup line, then sleeping and showering at what seems to be a wayfarer's lodge. They attend a mixed-race, mixed-gender revival meeting. They eat at long tables in another charity organization. Crammed into a tight space sleeping amid piles of tramps in a shelter, Sully wakes to find that his shoes have been stolen and a tramp's boots left behind. A close-up of Sully's feet in these boots literalizes the notion of Sully "walking in a poorer man's shoes" even as the film challenges the metaphor.[118] Finally, we see Sully and the Girl react with revulsion as they peer into a garbage can, and they run back to Hollywood.

Throughout this silent sequence, none of the tramps speak or are given individual identities. Indeed, when the tramp calls Sully an "amateur" early on, it is the only time we hear the voice of a tramp in the entire film. This lack of individuation is especially surprising in a Sturges film, since his films are generally ensemble pieces that provide every minor character with space to shine. After Sully's successful venture, he goes back to skid row to hand out five-dollar bills to tramps. There, he is knocked out and robbed by a tramp who stuffs him into a freight car and then is run over himself as he crosses the track carrying wads of cash. "We hardly know this character," Harvey acknowledges. "In fact we don't know him at all.... Neither does Sturges offer to 'know' him."[119]

The tramp who robs Sully turns out to be the very same one who stole his shoes. Because Sully's valet sewed an identification card into the sole of his shoes, when the tramp dies, people believe Sully is dead. Meanwhile suffering a bout of amnesia, Sully is sent to a hard labor camp for six years because he hits a railroad bull with a rock when he wakes up disoriented on the freight train. After working on a chain gang and being put in a sweatbox for insubordination when he is caught reading a headline about his own death, Sully, along with the other convicts, is allowed to attend the "pictures" at a rural Black church. Watching Disney's *Playful Pluto* (Gillet 1934), Sully, along with the convicts and parishioners finds himself laughing. Released from prison after he confesses to the murder of John L. Sullivan, to get his picture in the paper, Sully announces that he no longer wants to make *O Brother Where Art Thou?* With "some embarrassment," he says he wants to make a comedy. "There's a lot to be said for making people laugh," he says. "Didja know that's all some people have? It isn't much, but it's better than nothing in this cockeyed caravan. Boy!" With Tramp and the Girl superimposed at the center, the scene out-Capras Capra as it dissolves into a swirling montage of not only the convicts laughing—the Black faces now excised—but also hospital patients, children, and then various John Does, all the "people" who need laughter. Thus, Sully is authenticated through his experience of tramping, like other rich men I have described, but instead of a change in character, he realizes the value and importance of what he already does, which requires no change in station for him or for anyone else.

In subsuming the tramp into a larger narrative about "little people," both *Meet John Doe* and *Sullivan's Travels* mark the end point of the tramp's significance as a unique character. Instead of a character who challenges the dominant ideal or hegemonic masculinity, or a figure whose ubiquity threatens the status quo, the tramp in these films is neatly installed into narratives of heterosexual coupling and absorbed into a broader sentimentalized category of the humble poor.

. . .

Today, the image of the tramp exists mainly via nostalgia as a Halloween costume meant to be funny and unthreatening. The tramp became the go-to getup for those who did not want to sew or buy a costume—an easily assembled outfit made of an old borrowed coat and hat, with smudges on one's face, and a bandanna tied to a stick as a sack—that I, for one, wore at least once in the early 1970s. As offensive as it is now to think of a child dressing up as a homeless person, the tramp costume, now fading from practice, was once as ubiquitous as the tramp himself.[120]

The Halloween tramp may at one time have gestured toward menace—as with Tootie's (Margaret O'Brien) costume as a tramp in *Meet Me in St. Louis*

(Minelli 1944)—a nostalgic sense of freedom, or the adventure of riding the rails; but he seems, in the main, to function as a familiar stock character, like the pirate or princess, an evacuated signifier. The Halloween tramp does not, I think, carry connotations of being antiwork, criminal, antipolice, dangerous, sexually aggressive, or queer. Rather than recall the tramp as a figure who inspired numerous scares or hail him as the forebear for the prevalent problem of homelessness today, the tramp Halloween costume nostalgically locates the tramp as a residual reminder of the past associated with outmoded technologies, such as the train, and old-fashioned ways of being, such as finding pies on a sill to cool and seeking charity at kitchen doors. Perhaps the tramp should be remembered as a figure who migrated from the margins of society to the center of the popular imagination, a figure who provided a crucial window for looking (at times askance) at modern masculinity, to see it as not only complex and contradictory but as constantly up for grabs, contested, and intermediary.

TWO

Uncivilized

WORLD WAR II MOBILIZATION AND HOMECOMING AS SOCIAL PROBLEM

Civilian: A person who is not professionally employed in the armed forces; a nonmilitary person.

Civilize: transitive. To bring (a person, place, group of people, etc.) to a stage of social development considered to be more advanced, esp. by bringing to conformity with the social norms of a developed society; to enlighten, refine, and educate; to make more cultured and sophisticated.

Rehabilitation: The reintroduction of a serviceman or servicewoman into civilian life through the provision of training, employment, land, etc.

IN 1944, A YEAR BEFORE both V. E. (Victory in Europe) and V. J. (Victory over Japan) days and the end of World War II, Willard Walter Waller published *The Veteran Comes Back,* a sociological and historical analysis of "the veteran problem." "The veteran who comes home is a social problem, and certainly the major social problem of the next few years," Waller argued.[1] For Waller, "the veteran problem" related to the way in which soldiers had been trained as "machines" without personal or moral responsibility, their deep attachment to comrades over family, their sadistic-aggressive tendencies, their psychological damage, their hedonism, and their overall alienation from civilian—and civilized—values.[2] Waller notes that it is not only the soldier who has changed, but "the world to which he returns is not the one he left behind": its economy is different, the state controls much more of the life of the people, women have newfound freedom, and the family has been strained by separation.[3] To turn the soldier back into a civilian, he suggested, "What the times demand is a new art, the art of rehabilitation."[4] Rehabilitation—which, along with "adjustment," becomes a key buzzword of demobilization—will, in Waller's account, entail education; physical therapy; psychoneurotic therapy; economic help in the form of pensions, loans, and unemployment benefits; help with employment; and help establishing "normal and rewarding" relations with family, community and church.[5] Overall, he argues, "before the veteran can become a civilian again, he must find his place in society and settle down in it."[6]

Waller was not alone is his assessment of the difficulties facing returning veterans after World War II. Dixon Wecter's 1944 book *Johnny Comes Marching Home* similarly analyzed the veteran problem: "In any war where great masses of men are involved, the demobilized soldier, trying to find his way back to civil life, is the pivot on which turns this group conversion from war to peace."[7] Waller's and Wecter's books circulated amid myriad academic and popular articles about the veteran problem, all of which "assumed that all men would have difficulty adjusting to civilian life, whether or not they had seen action or were visibly wounded or psychologically distressed."[8] In concert with this frenzy of public concern, in June 1944, producer Walter Wanger, then serving as president of the Academy of Motion Picture Arts and Sciences, announced that "postwar is now." In an address to newspaper publishers, Wanger declared that "the most urgent home front problems to be dealt with by screen and press are veterans' rehabilitation, post-war employment, housing, inter-racial friction and education. The Number One problem for the people of the United States is the reincorporation into our national life of the men and women of the armed forces."[9]

While we often associate the soldiers of the "greatest generation" with stability and conservative values, these concerns over the veteran problem remind us that postwar success and stabilization were by no means taken for granted. If, as I suggested in the previous chapter, the coming of World War II marked, by and large, the end of the tramp as a large-scale phenomenon and cause of moral panic, this was not because the war itself instantiated a period of stabilizing normativity. Rather, the postwar period eventually led to such stabilizing influences as the expansion of employment, widespread college education, and home ownership, as well as the stereotypical midcentury cult of domesticity, only because the war *first* unhomed millions of men and women and, as a result, produced a wholesale crisis in domesticity.

World War II engendered the mass movement of men and women both within the United States and abroad. The Selective Service and Training Act of 1940—the nation's first peacetime draft—required all men between the ages of twenty-one and forty-five to register for the draft. Those selected by lottery were required to serve at least a year, but once the United States entered the war, service was extended for the duration and the draft age expanded to include those eighteen to sixty-four.[10] By the end of the war, fifty million men had registered for the draft and more than eleven million draftees and more than six million volunteers served in the Army, Navy, Marines, Air Force, and Coast Guard, with 73 percent serving overseas.[11] In addition, approximately 350,000 women served in the Women's Army Corps (WAC), Navy Women's Accepted for Voluntary Emergency Service (WAVES), Women's Airforce Service Pilots (WASP), Coast Guard and Marines Reserves, and Army and Navy Nurse Corps, with another six thousand women employed by the Red Cross and United Service Organization (USO) to provide recreation and entertainment services for servicemen abroad.[12] Beyond those serving directly, in the three and a half years after Pearl Harbor, more than fifteen million male and female civilians moved to find jobs in wartime industrial production or to be near military bases in small and large cities all over the country, including female "camp followers," who trailed their husbands from base to base.[13] According to historians Ken Coates and W. R. Morrison, the United States' World War II mobilization produced to that time "the fastest and most widespread dispersal of a country's citizens in the history of the human race."[14]

While viewed as patriotic and temporary, this mass mobilization nonetheless stirred anxieties about mobility and placelessness. These anxieties included a concern about the behavior of men and women distanced from the civilizing influence of home through migration, a process that was seen to provoke multiple broad-based disruptions to traditional family and gender roles. The litany of uncivilized behaviors that caused such anxiety included sexual promiscuity among both sexes, including teen sex, and sex with prostitutes, and thus venereal disease; quickie marriages and a concomitant rise in divorce; an increase of single and unmarried mothers; women's mobility and liberation through wartime work; housing shortages that compromised conventional opportunities and boundaries for privacy; and more. In addition, migration unsettled many taken-for-granted ideals related to class and race, as well as gender, as servicemen were unmoored from familiar hierarchies and privileges. While these behaviors and issues occurred both at the home front and among soldiers abroad, they were not simply resolved by demobilization. Rather, as the moral panic about the veteran problem indicates, the return of sixteen million veterans—constituting more than 10 percent of the population in 1940—underscored and exacerbated the effects of such disruptions and revealed conventional ideas of home and family to be deeply contingent and precarious.

This sense of being outside home, even and especially on returning home, marks the soldier's experience as a form of unhomeliness akin to Homi Bhabha's formulation of the unhomely. Rather than unhoused, *per se,* they experience the "uncanny ... effects of enforced social accommodation, or historical migrations and cultural relocations."[15] While this condition of unhomeliness is most clearly related to the experience of migrants and postcolonials—and the experience of migration during World War II is, of course, different from the displacement of present-day postcolonials—the experience of World War II soldiers and migrants enacted, in accelerated and temporary form, a very similar kind of dislocation. World War II migration entailed many kinds of displacement. Servicemen might have lived in institutional settings such as bases and hospitals that fit Edward Relph's definition of placeless homogenized "spaces that seem detached from the local environment and tell us nothing about the particular locality in which they are located." But soldiers also lived or furloughed in unfamiliar and sometimes exotic countries or regions, where they existed as something between temporary residents and tourists.[16] Massive housing shortages during and after the war left many people unhoused and forced people to double-up with family, take on boarders, live in trailers and Quonset huts, and crowd into hotels and shared rooms; and housing shortages produced alternatives to the conventional heterosexual family household, including all-female households, multigenerational households, households comprising mixed-sex friends, communal households, and more.

Crucially, when servicemen returned home, they were widely seen as alienated, uncomfortable, and restless; and their home seemed to register the uncanny effects of the familiar made strange. As the prominent philosopher and sociologist Alfred Schuetz argued in 1945 in his analysis of returning veterans: "To the homecomer home shows—at least in the beginning—an unaccustomed face. He believes himself to be in a strange country, a stranger among strangers." Even if nothing substantial had changed in the veteran's home, Schuetz argued, "even then, the home to which he returns is by no means the home he left or the home which he recalled and longed for during his absence. And, for the same reason, the homecomer is not the same man who left."[17] In this sense, the serviceman was doubly unhomed, separated from his familiar home, then returned to a home that felt strange and alienating.

In comparison to other unhomely experiences, such as that of refugees, the experience of American World War II servicemen represents a somewhat unusual and privileged case. Not only did sociologists and popular discourse address the problem early, but the government put in place expansive policies to ensure that rehabilitation succeeded. The Serviceman's Readjustment Act, commonly referred to as the GI Bill of Rights, was signed into law by President Franklin Delano Roosevelt (FDR) on June 22, 1944, a year before the war's end. Describing GIs as "caught between two worlds, neither soldier nor citizen," the "Bill of Rights for G. I. Joe and Jane" was famously drafted on a hotel notepad by Harry Colmery of the American Legion.[18] The GI Bill largely took proposals that had been developed by the Conference on Postwar Adjustment of Civilian and Military Personnel (a.k.a. the Postwar Manpower Conference) of June 1943 and disseminated to the public by FDR in a Fireside Chat on July 28, 1943.[19] The American Legion took the ninety-six distinct proposals of the Postwar Manpower Conference and FDR's comments to create an omnibus plan to address housing, education, training, job placement, unemployment compensation, and—an addition by Colmery—loans for home ownership and small businesses. Congress debated how restrictive or unrestrictive the bill should be, but they passed it with few significant modifications.

The G. I. Bill was developed and passed with the idea that Congress should not repeat past mistakes with veterans of previous wars (a lesson seemingly unlearned again with later wars in Vietnam, Iraq, and Afghanistan). Revolutionary War soldiers had been denied overdue back pay and pensions by a "fledgling cash-strapped government."[20] Congress did not award pensions to those veterans in financial need until 1818, and pensions were not extended to all Revolutionary War veterans without regard to rank, financial distress, or physical disability until 1832.[21] After the Civil War, the federal pension program was denied altogether to Confederate soldiers; and what was due Union soldiers was "mired in fraud, graft, and patronage."[22] Individual Southern states granted pensions to Confederate veterans and widows but in many cases not until 1911 or later.[23] As mentioned in the preceding chapter, many Civil War veterans, not only those with disabilities, faced significant challenges in reintegrating into society, finding and keeping work, and maintaining personal relationships; thus, many became tramps.

Most proximate for those developing plans for World War II veterans were the failures of World War I. World War I veterans were disadvantaged by their service as they received no consideration for lost income and jobs.

Unemployment was a third higher among veterans than the general population, leading to the World War I veteran having the status of the "forgotten man," FDR's famous 1932 characterization of those at the bottom of the economic ladder.[24] Instead of a pension, World War I veterans were given a bonus in the form of a government bond. They could borrow up to a quarter of the face value of the bond, but it would not mature until 1945. In Spring 1932, suffering the effects of the Great Depression, more than forty thousand veterans, including many who were tramps, joined the Bonus March on Washington, DC. President Hoover viewed the protesters as communists and criminals, and he used the military to forcibly oust them after three months of mostly peaceful protest.[25]

Because so many Americans were directly impacted by the war, and because they remembered the history of World War I and the Great Depression, the GI Bill had overwhelming public support. It helped build the white middle class in postwar America. Eight million veterans took advantage of the bill's education benefit to attend college and nearly five million vets bought homes with the GI loan program, their purchases representing nearly half the new homes constructed nationwide in the decade after World War II.[26] In adopting the GI Bill as policy, government worked to reintegrate soldiers back into civilian life, solved a housing crisis, and averted a massive economic crisis. The GI Bill was not perfect—it was still limited by institutional racism that denied Black servicemen the full benefits accorded white soldiers—but it showed a more forgiving, forethinking, and intelligent response to problems of precarity, housing, and inequity than at any other time in US history.[27] Still, the massive scale of the GI Bill suggests how imperative and dangerous the veteran problem was perceived to be and how much effort and work was required to successfully reintegrate veterans into American society.

Without denying the success of rehabilitation for millions of Americans after World War II, this chapter focuses on the destabilization that made the GI Bill necessary and will consider the narratives of dislocation and displacement that get repressed in nostalgic visions of the postwar period, especially as they relate to domesticity. Popular films about the veteran problem—including problems on the home front, housing shortages, adjustment, and rehabilitation—proliferated in the 1940s in narratives that made manifest anxieties about the mobility of soldiers and citizens and revealed ruptures in the stability of home and family. All the films discussed in this chapter are, broadly speaking, social problem films that dramatize concerns that are seen as broadly representative of contemporary issues and that are typically set in the present day.[28] While films about World War II have appeared intermittently over the seven decades since the war, I mainly limit my analysis to the cycle of films that appeared during and shortly after the war, allowing for a few exceptions in the late 1950s that take up civil rights in tandem with the veteran problem. Some films address the veteran problem comedically via established genres of the romantic comedy or musical, while others more clearly state their purpose as social problem films by employing a serious tone, realistic mode of representation, and a somewhat didactic approach to the subject matter.[29] The veteran problem entailed the necessity for personal, medical, educational, economic, and housing readjustments, but in Hollywood all of these were subsumed into the personal and individual. Whether comedic or serious, as Hollywood social problem films, they tend to point to large-scale social problems but offer individual solutions, "inviting audiences to identify with the suffering of individual characters and to applaud the relief of that suffering at the resolution of the narrative."[30]

In these personal and individual narratives, fantasies of domesticity go hand in hand with the filmic narratives of dislocation and displacement; thus, they feed into views of the period as conservative and homebound. In particular, these narratives often resolve the crises at the heart of the films through romantic happy endings that either form a new couple or restore a broken one, offering a promise of future marriage and domesticity. In part, this is in line with the formation of the couple that Raymond Bellour identified as "absolutely central" to Classical Hollywood cinema as a whole.[31] But in the context of mass mobilization and migration, the fantasy of domesticity in these films can be seen as akin to forms of "shelter writing" that Susan Fraiman describes in her book *Extreme Domesticity: A View from the Margins*. The characters she describes are unable or unwilling to take "home" as a given; thus, "for them, contriving a livable space is all the more urgent, fraught, and potentially gratifying." Among those "driven to domesticity ... by desperate circumstances," Fraiman counts "anyone whose smallest domestic endeavors have become urgent and precious in the wake of dislocation."[32] A similarly desperate drive to domesticity motivates the urgent romances and *deux ex machina* marriages of romantic comedies and musicals; films about the housing shortage, comedic and sentimental alike, that detail the mise-en-scène and logistics of shared domestic space; and melodramas about the returning veteran that show home as alienating and uncomfortable.

Thus, rather than dismiss the nostalgic view of the postwar middle-class family as merely an after-the-fact falsification of the period, we can see that these films are, in effect, nostalgic for the future. The drive to domesticity in these films highlights the fact that even as they underscore a national crisis around the *unhoming* of soldiers and civilians, they also participate in a national project aimed at *rehoming* them. This differs markedly from the cycle of films about tramps in the last chapter, which never assume that the tramp can or should be rehomed, and from the hitchhiking films in the next chapter, which emphasize the voluntary unhoming of drifters and runaways. Here, mobility and placelessness are always imagined to be temporary and domesticity desirable.

Borrowing Elisabeth Bronfen's phrasing, however, even as World War II films project a fantasy of home in "scenarios that fill an originary sense of plenitude, the traumatic core of dislocation can never be fully erased."[33] In other words, even as films seemingly repress or resolve the anxiety and fear engendered by the war's disruption to social norms by bringing soldiers and other mobile wartime figures into line with the social norms of society—through the civilizing influence of marriage especially—the happy endings never fully expunge or obliterate the expressions of sexual desire, rage, despair, violence, self-loathing, restlessness, or other feelings generated by the narrative middles.[34] The unresolved nature of these narratives are attested to by the fact that films—and audiences—turn to the same topics over and over in a kind of repetition compulsion that relives the veteran problem over and over again across cycles of films that variously take up the soldier's unhoming, the housing crises, and the veteran's return.

My analysis touches on almost thirty films, a relatively small corpus if we consider all films about shore leave and furlough, soldiers abroad, housing shortages, and postwar adjustment, not even counting newsreels and shorts.[35] Some of the films I discuss, such as *The Best Years of Our Lives* (Wyler 1946) and *On the Town* (Donen and Kelly 1949), are well-known, but they are not generally considered together. Here, as in the last chapter, my goal is to place such canonical films amid the plethora of social problem films that were in circulation then but have been largely forgotten. Rather than think of these films as extraordinary approaches to the topic of the soldier's return, as with *The Best Years of Our Lives,* or as outstanding and somewhat timeless variants of a genre, as with *On the Town,* I view them in their historical context to emphasize their commonality with lesser-known films, not to diminish them but to show shared cultural investments and narrative patterns across a larger cycle.

The serviceman offers a very different model of mobility and placelessness from that of the tramp. Whereas the tramp was socially marginal and had "no place in contemporary society," the World War II serviceman and veteran are seen as dominant and representative figures—for, indeed, a whole "great" generation.[36] While the tramp was ubiquitous—traversing urban and rural areas and appearing at the doorstep of every family—the serviceman's movements are dictated by the government and are more restricted. Most important, where the tramp largely existed outside the bounds of domesticity and feminine influence, the serviceman's movements are understood as only temporarily uprooting, with the promise of a return to home and family.

One way to consider the difference between these two models of mobile masculinity is to look at their relationship to the train. As discussed in the previous chapter, the train is crucial to the existence of the tramp, as it extends his reach past that of previous vagabonds; and the train is a defining aspect of the mise-en-scène in tramp films, with tramps frequently hopping freights, riding the rails, contending with railroad "dicks," and so forth. The train is also vital to World War II migrations. During the war, each railroad had to allocate a quarter of their cars to military personnel, and about half of all Pullman sleepers were commandeered. Railroads carried more than 97 percent of all troops, some 43.7 million military passengers between 1941 and 1945.[37] A short 1943 propaganda film by the Office of War Information, *Troop Train*, highlights the importance of troop trains to carry personnel and equipment. "This is a war of movement," an intertitle announces. "Our new Army is mobile not only on the highways, but on the rails." The film shows the government's control of the trains through a centralized system, as well as masses of men inside the trains and in sleeper cars. As opposed to the illicit movements of tramps, the train in World War II operates as an institutionalized space run by the government to transport men between bases, ports of call, and home.

In the World War II cycle of films about servicemen and returning vets, train stations provide a stage for the soldier's leaving. In *Tender Comrade* (Dmytryk 1943), for example, a flashback shows Jo Jones (Ginger Rogers) saying goodbye to her husband, Chris (Robert Ryan), on the train platform. As they part, they imagine and describe his return: she will meet him at the station, and they will return to their hometown of Shale City, where his job will be held for him; they will have a child and a garden and will barbecue for friends. In *Pride of the Marines* (Daves 1945), Al (John Garfield) initially

FIGURE 2.1. Lovers Bill (Robert Walker) and Jane (Jennifer Jones) say goodbye at the train station in *Since You Went Away*.

resists a teary goodbye from girlfriend Ruth (Eleanor Parker), but when she appears on the platform, he asks her to wait and offers a ring inscribed "Till I come home, Al," as she declares that she is "the sticking kind." In *Since You Went Away* (Cromwell 1949), when Bill (Robert Walker) leaves, he asks girlfriend Jane (Jennifer Jones) to promise to marry him when he returns (fig. 2.1). He also apologizes for not marrying her before leaving but explains that he didn't want her stuck "if something happened," such as death or debilitating injury. Of course, in each of these films, "something" does happen: Chris and Bill are both killed in action, and Al is blinded. In a more comedic vein, *Skirts Ahoy* (Lanfield 1952) reverses the trope to show three men saying goodbye to three WAVEs (Esther Williams, Vivian Blaine, Joan Evans) before they head overseas, and *Since You Went Away* shows one man saying goodbye to numerous different girls in the same area where Bill and Jane say goodbye.

In other films, the train becomes a vehicle for a pickup or sexual encounter. In *I'll Be Seeing You* (Dieterle 1944), a soldier on medical furlough, suffering from psychoneurosis meets a female prisoner, Mary (Ginger Rogers), who has been given a good-behavior leave. The smitten soldier, Zachary

(Joseph Cotten), pretends to have family in town in order to exit the train at the same station as Mary, and they begin a romance. *The Clock* (Minnelli 1945) operates on the narrative principle of the deadline as a soldier, Joe (Robert Walker), on a two-day leave meets and marries a girl, Alice (Judy Garland): their romance begins and ends at Grand Central train station. In *My Foolish Heart* (Robson 1949), Eloise (Susan Hayward) joins boyfriend Walt (Dana Andrews) at Grand Central. Rather than say goodbye on the platform, she boards the train and ends up spending the night with him, loses her virginity, and becomes pregnant. He then dies on base in an accident, having just written her a proposal letter.

Rather than position any narrative as wholly unique, the train consistently situates characters among large groups of men and women experiencing similar dislocations, to suggest a commonality of experience, underscoring what Kaja Silverman has characterized as "historical trauma," a historically precipitated disruption with ramifications that exceed the individual psyche.[38] In each film, when the couple are saying goodbye, they are one of many couples on the platform, all saying goodbye or welcoming a soldier home. In *Since You Went Away,* Anne Hilton (Claudette Colbert) and her daughters Jane and Brig (Shirley Temple) travel by train unsuccessfully to meet Anne's husband and say goodbye before he goes overseas. They share the train with refugees, injured soldiers, other women going to meet their men, and others impacted by the war, as well as unpatriotic travelers who express selfish and unsympathetic views of the war. While showing crowded and uncomfortable conditions, the films emphasize camaraderie over discomfort. For example, in *Since You Went Away,* as Anne makes her way through a crowded train car, soldiers sing the Andrews Sisters' hit "Shoo Shoo Baby" with the pertinent lyric "Your papa's off to the Seven Seas." Similarly, in *In the Meantime, Darling* (Preminger 1949), when Maggie Preston (Jeanne Crain) and her parents travel by train to join her fiancé—for a quickie marriage intended to take advantage of a vacancy in married housing near the base—soldiers on board sing "Oh, My Darling Clementine."

Another way that World War II films assert the commonality of experience is through the use of mass media. In numerous films, radio brings news of the war in ways that not only mark a turn in the narrative for characters but also serve as evocative *aides-mémoires* for the audience that may have heard the news the same way. For example, in *Pride of the Marines,* as Al's landlords—Jim Merchant (John Ridgely) and his wife, Ella Mae (Ann

Doran)—call Al and Ruth to the dinner table, the radio announces the attack on Pearl Harbor. As the four friends ponder "Where's Pearl Harbor?" a second announcement declares that the US is at war with Japan, precipitating Al's entry into the military. In *Tender Comrade,* similarly, we hear news of the war in Europe as Jo and Chris argue one night, foreshadowing his eventual enlistment. Later in that film, a radio broadcast describes the Battle of Midway and, personalizing it for the narrative, erroneously names the husband of one of Jo's female housemates as having been killed. In *The Homecoming* (LeRoy 1948), an all-caps newspaper headline reading LONDON BLITZED AGAIN foreshadows the US entry into the war and underscores the naivete of Dr. Johnson (Clark Gable), who mansplains to his worried wife that the war in Europe is far away and not likely to impact them—before he appears in the very next scene in uniform and about to head to base camp.

These radio broadcasts and newspaper headlines, like the scenes of train travel, highlight the veteran problem as a shared experience but also stitch that experience to the emotions and actions of particular couples. To be clear, this commonality is limited to mainly white men and women—Black soldiers and women appear very rarely and only in the background of train scenes—and both race and class are submerged in the imagination of commonality.

ON THE TOWN

While the emphasis on commonality of experience and the formation of the couple extend across most of the World War II films presented here, there are subcycles of films corresponding to different aspects of the soldier and veteran's unhoming. One subcycle of films, largely consisting of musicals and romantic comedies, especially addresses the concern about sexual promiscuity while servicemen are away from home—at embarkation sites, located on base in the US or abroad, or on furlough or shore leave.

As scholars such as Amanda Littauer, Mary Hegarty, and Frank Krutnik have argued, the war "troubled (the) heterosexual order" on the home front and abroad and generated moral panics about venereal disease, promiscuity, prostitution, teen "victory girls" who offered sex to servicemen, unwed mothers, quickie marriages, and divorce.[39] Removed from what Dixon Wecter referred to as the "petticoat government—of mothers, sweethearts, wives," servicemen adopted a tendency toward "low brow virile vices."[40] At the same time, women—single, married, and teen—were also seen as becoming more promiscuous. When the army tried to lower incidents of venereal disease by banning prostitution near military bases with the May Act in July 1941, it found that "the campaign against prostitution has been partly offset by an increase in infections due to pick-ups, waitresses, tavern and dance hall girls, and the like, who at most are only part-time prostitutes and many of whom are teen age girls."[41] While worries about male and female promiscuity were partly a moral panic, statistics suggest that adolescent girls *were* having more sex than prior to the war, that soldiers *were* getting sexually transmitted diseases while on furlough, that single motherhood increased by 40 percent, and that there was an uptick in admissions to homes for unwed mothers.[42] As Waller admitted, "Soldiers and civilians alike participate in the relaxation of sexual morality in time of war. Wherever men and women meet, they may join in illicit unions."[43]

From Here to Eternity (Zinnemann 1953), set at a Hawaiian base just before and during the attack on Pearl Harbor, implicitly references prostitution, though the character of Loren (Donna Reed) is changed from a prostitute in the original novel to a "hostess" at a "social club" in the film. Most films focus, instead, on "pick-ups, waitresses, tavern and dance hall girls, and the like" but divert attention away from casual sex and toward romantic coupling, usually with a promise of marriage. Two musicals starring Gene Kelly and Frank Sinatra, *Anchors Aweigh* (Sidney 1945) and *On the Town*—a postwar film adapted from a wartime Broadway musical—are both about sailors on shore leave, and both shift narrative emphasis from the pursuit of sex toward romantic longing and the promise of marriage. In *Anchors Aweigh*, Kelly's character, Joe Brady, is characterized as a "wolf" or would-be seducer. Granted shore leave as reward for a heroic act, he sets out to meet the never-seen Lola, a woman he describes to his shipmates using hand gestures to indicate curves, saying, "Whatever the others have, Lola has more." In *On the Town*, Kelly's Gabey and Jules Munshin's Ozzie are both marked as wolves. When they land in New York for a twenty-four-hour leave, Gabey and Ozzie, along with Frank Sinatra's Chip, imagine a perfect day as they sing "New York, New York" during a montage that shows them traversing the city in various vehicles and on foot. Where Chip mostly sings of "the famous places to visit" listed in guidebooks, Gabey and Ozzie mainly sing of picking up women:

> Manhattan women are dressed in silk and satin,
> Or so the fellas say.
> There's just one thing that's important in Manhattan,
> When you have just one day;
> Gotta pick up a date,
> Maybe seven
> Or eight
> On your way.
> In just one day!

Gabey and Ozzie then enact a pretend date, with Ozzie pretending to be Gabey's pickup as they move through a hurried timetable of prenoon seduction in giggling falsettos: "10:30? Hello! 10:45? Hold hands," as they hold hands. "11? Shall we dance?" They take a quick spin. "11:15. Our first kiss." Gabey plants one on Ozzie's cheek. With "11:30?" they do not announce what will happen, but shift their voices into a more masculine register and whoop "Wowowow" with wolfish excitement.

Emphasizing the importance of the serviceman's sexual pursuits, Sinatra's sexual innocence in both films is seen as out of line with his status as a serviceman and as a problem to be solved. In *Anchors Aweigh*, his character, Clarence, stalks Joe and begs him to teach him how to pick up women. But the police ask Clarence and Joe to help with a runaway boy who wants to join the navy. Taking him home, they meet his Aunt Susie (Kathryn Grayson), and the narrative quickly shifts from sexual pursuits to romance: while Joe half-heartedly claims to want to go visit Lola, he lingers with Susie, first to help Clarence, who is smitten, then because he has fallen in love himself. In *Anchors Aweigh*, Joe nicknames Clarence "Brooklyn" for his hometown; he is seen as an innocent in Los Angeles, destined to couple not with the exotic high-class beauty Susie but with the unnamed working-class waitress (Pamela Britton), who is also from Brooklyn, thus affiliating Sinatra with the urban working class, as is typical of his populist 1940s persona. Whereas virtually every other film emphasizes Sinatra's presumed New York origins, *On the Town* maintains his ordinary working-class image but abandons his star attachment to New York to cast him as another out-of-place rube who has never visited New York and seeks outmoded tourist pleasures rather than the more sophisticated sexual pursuits of his comrades.

As much as they highlight male desire, these films also highlight *female* sexual desire. In *Anchors Aweigh*, Kelly and Sinatra sing three duets—"We Hate to Leave," "If You Knew Susie," and "I Begged Her"—all falsehoods in song and all initiated by Joe.⁴⁴ Whereas "We Hate to Leave" has Joe and Clarence tease their shipmates by pretending they do not want to go on shore leave, the other two duets conjure an image of unrestrained female desire as a fantasy ideal. Most of the songs in *Anchors Aweigh* were written for the film by Jules Styne and Sammy Cahn, but "If You Knew Susie" was written by Buddy DeSylva and Joseph Meyer in 1925 for Al Jolson and became a standard for Eddie Cantor. The original song intimates that a woman named Susie is less restrained than her public image, but the film's revision pushes the implications further. Clarence and Joe are trying to thwart a date who has arrived to take Susie out. To tarnish the date's view of Susie, Joe pretends that Susie is the sweetheart of the navy and that she is so well-known among sailors that they have a song about her. Amplifying the original "If you knew Susie like I know Susie, / Oh! Oh! Oh! What a girl!," Joe and Clarence improvise:

> If you knew Susie, like *we* know Susie
> Oh! Oh! Oh! What a gal!
> She's not so choosy, no, not our Susie.

In "I Begged Her," when Joe and Clarence arrive at a hotel that has been turned into temporary accommodation for sailors, to hide the fact that they spent most of the night babysitting, they brag of imaginary sexual conquests. Joe's verse positions him as begging a girl for a kiss in terms that, today, sound like coercion:

> I argued, I threatened
> I said, "You can't send me home, not like this."
> Then I finally got my kiss.

When Clarence sings, the subject position reverses to cast him as object of female pursuit, in a manner typical of his 1940s feminized crooner image; rather than "I," in his verse, "she" argues, threatens, and finally gets *her* kiss.⁴⁵

Similarly, in *On the Town,* Hildy (Betty Garrett), masculinized by her job as a taxi driver, pursues Chip tenaciously (fig. 2.2).⁴⁶ She refuses to drive the sailors unless Chip sits up front with her; then, when they are alone, she deflects all his plans for sightseeing to demand that he join her at her apartment in the duet "My Place." The socialite Claire (Ann Miller) in *On the Town* is also shown as sexually voracious. When she meets Ozzie and the others at the Museum of Natural History, she explains that she is studying anthropology to distract herself from men. But seeing Ozzie, a dead ringer

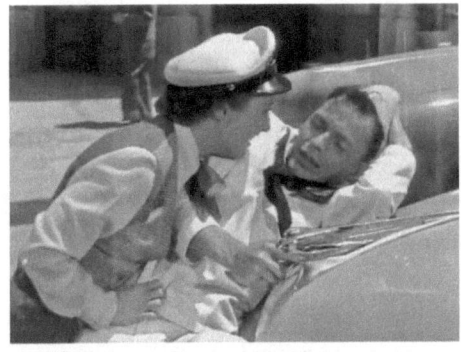

FIGURE 2.2. Hildy (Betty Garrett) shows unrestrained desire as she urges Chip (Frank Sinatra) to come to "My Place" in *On the Town*.

for a statue of prehistoric man, stirs her imagination, and she declares in song her preference for the "bare skin" and "free expression" of "Prehistoric Man." Indeed, the film indicates rather unmistakably that the couples Chip and Hildy and Ozzie and Claire each spend the afternoon in bed.[47]

To a large degree, without fully expunging or obliterating the expressions of sexual desire generated by the narratives, *Anchors Aweigh* and *On the Town* repress or resolve the anxiety and fear engendered by the war's disruption to social norms by bringing their mobile sailors and women into line with the social norms of society through the promise of the civilizing influence of marriage. In *Anchors Aweigh*, Joe and Susie fall in love. In *On the Town*, Gabey falls for Miss Turnstiles, Ivy (Vera-Allen) whom he imagines to be a glamorous New Yorker but who turns out to be a working-class girl from his small midwestern hometown. Chip and Hildy proclaim their love in the duet "You're Awful" ("I'm the one who needs you, / And I think you're awful, awful nice to say you're mine."). And Ozzie and Claire also fall in love. In the film's final scene, Gabey, Chip, Ozzie, Claire, and Hildy are chased by police as they rush to locate Ivy—who, in another sign of the loosening of wartime morals, is working as a cooch dancer at Coney Island—so Gabey can say goodbye. After the men are arrested, Claire and Hildy implore the police to overlook their crimes as a patriotic gesture of "civic pride." Explaining why she did not turn in her taxi at the end of her shift and why she was speeding, Hildy declares, "I know my duty to the servicemen," and, suggestively: "He wanted to see the beautiful sights of our beautiful city of New York, and I showed him plenty." This patriotic blarney wins over the police, who not only escort the women to the ship to say goodbye but also collect money to pay the exorbitant cab fare.

As films about sailors on leave, *Anchors Aweigh* and *On the Town* deflect but do not totally repress the grim realities of war. As Beth Genné suggests, in these films, the final clinch in which lovers unite to say goodbye conjures the "poignancy" of shore leave, "that hiatus between tours of duty that gave a special urgency to the romance." There is a tension between the Hollywood convention of the clinch, which indicates the promise of marriage and futurity, and the reality of war, where "a tour of duty might mean a final, rather than temporary separation"; thus, "the theme of a final leave before going overseas took on a real emotional intensity."[48]

These films also deflect but rely on a central contradiction of wartime discourse about women. As Hegarty discusses, on the one hand, the media "covertly and overtly urged wartime women to provide sexualized support for the military in various types of private and public entertainment" (General Patton famously said, "If they don't fuck, they don't fight!"); but, on the other, they cast women who engaged in sexual relations with soldiers as deviant, promiscuous, or as prostitutes.[49] The brilliant satire *The Miracle of Morgan's Creek* (Sturges 1944) addresses this contradiction head-on.[50] Trudy Kockenlocker (Betty Hutton) is a small-town hoyden who lives near a military base and likes to kiss "the boys" goodbye. Trudy becomes pregnant after attending a series of parties for soldiers about to head overseas. Evading the Production Code, we see her get "knocked up" in a delightful visual pun as she hits her head on a disco ball after she has unknowingly drunk spiked punch. Realizing at first only by a curtain-ring on her finger that she was married in a quickie ceremony, she cannot recall the soldier's name except that it was something like Ratzkiwatzki: her "husband" could be any number of men with whom she danced. Here, rather than marry Trudy to the missing soldier, Sturges has her discover true love with the boy she previously dismissed—her childhood friend Norval Jones (Eddie Bracken), who has been unable to enlist owing to a nervous condition that makes him see "the spots" and be registered 4F every time he is examined. To get a legitimate marriage certificate and thus legitimize the baby, Trudy and Norval attempt to redo the wedding, with Norval posing as Ratzkiwatzki (fig. 2.3).

But they slip up: Trudy's pregnancy becomes public, and Norval is accused of impersonating a soldier. When Trudy delivers male sextuplets, however, the births are heralded as proof of American military power, and we see a montage of newspaper headlines—"Canada Protests!" "Nature Answers Total War"—including headlines about the births in Russia, China, and Italy, the latter followed by shots of Mussolini reacting with shock and anger, then a headline: "Mussolini Resigns"; and finally a mocking shot of a very diminutive Hitler (over)reacting and the headline "Hitler Demands

FIGURE 2.3. Trudy (Betty Hutton) and Norval (Eddie Bracken) attempt to make Trudy's quickie marriage to Ratzkiwatzki official in *The Miracle of Morgan's Creek*.

Recount." Cynically stitching Trudy's sexual liaison to patriotism, the governor (Brian Donlevy, brilliantly reprising his role from Sturges's 1940 film *The Great McGinty*) intervenes to annul Trudy's marriage to Ratzkiwatzki, formalize her marriage to Norval, and give Norval a retroactive commission in the State Guard, allowing him to legally wear a uniform—thus ensuring that the babies are a product of the American military.

MARRIAGES MADE IN A MOMENT

As Trudy's marriage to Ratzkiwatzki in *The Miracle of Morgan's Creek* suggests, just as films channeled sexual impulses into marriage narratives, so, too, did real servicemen and civilians. The film plays on the moral panic about such marriages, showing Trudy's father, Constable Kockenlocker (William Demarest), read a newspaper headline: "Are Military Marriages a Menace?" "This is war," the newspaper story reads. "Our homes, full of lonely young women, are surrounded by camps full of lonely young men. This is war. Death may be just around the corner and life moves at a desperate pace. Forgotten are caution and circumspection. Haste is the by-word.... Marriages made in a moment..." While the panic about such marriages is mocked here, the buildup to the war did trigger a marriage boom with "conscription" marriages aimed at dodging the draft in 1940; then, as war began, courtship and marriages were accelerated among servicemen before deploying. In the first five months of 1942, there were about one-third more marriages than in the previous year—one in four creating war brides—with approximately one thousand servicemen married every day from 1940 to 1942 and a concomitant divorce boom at the end of the war, with sixty thousand divorces in 1946.⁵¹ At one church in Manhattan, the pastor, Randolph Rey, indicated that six wedding ceremonies a day represented a "quiet midweek schedule" for him. Even as he performed more than two thousand marriage ceremonies in 1942 and 1943, however, Rey worried that young couples were marrying for the wrong reason. In a pamphlet he published, titled "Marriage Is a Serious Business," he derided "the hasty marriage, caused by glamour and excitement rather than genuine affection," and he called quickie marriages "one of the evil products of war."⁵²

The film *Allotment Wives* (Nigh 1945) plays on the fear that "unscrupulous women" will prey on servicemen. This B movie begins with documentary-like footage and a voiceover explaining the function of the Office of Dependency Benefits (ODB), which handles family allowances and allotments to protect "wives and children and helpless relatives" from want and scarcity; it then shifts into a fictional narrative about an ODB undercover investigation intended to root out the criminal element that abuses the system. Sheila Seymour (Kay Francis) runs a nationwide racket in which women marry unsuspecting servicemen—often bigamously—to get allotments, steal insurance, and even liquidate wedding gifts. Most films, however, and most of the discourse about quickie weddings focus on sexual and romantic motivations rather than criminal intent.

Quickie marriages in film highlight the sexual urgency that motivates the wedding even as they nominally legitimize the sex. Some films romanticize quickie weddings, while others underscore their flimsiness. *The Clock* does both. In this film, Joe, a soldier on a two-day furlough before being shipped overseas, arrives at Grand Central Station in New York. He is a rube who has never ridden an escalator. He meets Alice, a working girl who has been in the city for three years and loves it. He convinces her to spend the afternoon with him; then she cancels her evening date to meet him again. Missing the last bus home that night, they end up hitching a ride in a milk truck, helping the driver make his deliveries and then finishing his route for him when he is hurt in a fight with a drunk. Joining the driver, Al (James Gleason), and his wife for breakfast, they talk about service marriages. Joe says that he isn't sure marriage is fair to the girl as the soldier may not make it back, but Al argues that "if you think about everything that will happen, you'll never do anything." Later that day, Joe and Alice are separated on a busy subway platform and realize that they do not know each other's last names or how to get in touch. When they meet by luck again in Grand Central, Joe proposes, their lack of knowledge about each other paradoxically spurring them to secure a connection.

FIGURE 2.4. The "ugly" quickie wedding between Joe (Robert Walker) and Alice (Judy Garland) in *The Clock*.

The scenes that follow in *The Clock* accentuate how common, and even banal, war weddings are: we see a marriage license clerk's office packed with servicemen and a waiting room for blood tests, where Alice wears the exact same dress as another would-be war bride. Managing to secure a waiver so they can get married without a three-day waiting period—courtesy of Al's cousin—they have a rushed ceremony just before the clerk's office closes with no ring or flowers and with trains running by the window outside so that they cannot hear their own vows (fig. 2.4). "I don't feel very married," Alice says. "It was so ugly." The quickie wedding in *The Clock* is redeemed, however. In a scene reminiscent of the scene of marital redemption in Murnau's *Sunrise* (1927), Joe and Alice enter a church after seeing a crowd gathered outside following a wedding. Inside, Alice reads aloud the marriage ceremony in the liturgical book, and they redo their ceremony privately. After this, we cut to a scene in a hotel where Alice relaxes in a negligee and smiles as she looks out the window, the marriage consummated. The film ends at the train station where we see numerous couples saying goodbye alongside Alice and Joe; then we see Alice exiting the station alone, triumphant and proud, but with an uncertain future.

The Clock ends on a romantic note, but many other films show the negative aftermath of quickie weddings. In *Till the End of Time* (Dmytryk 1946), Dorothy McGuire's character, Pat, is a grief-stricken war widow. She explains her decision to marry in terms similar to Fraiman's notion of shelter writing, contriving a home in the context of urgent and fraught dislocation: "We had a choice to make and we made it. My John married me because when he went to war he wanted to be able to dream of home. That's why I married him. I wanted him to be able to have that dream. The thing I didn't count on is, at the end of the war, John's coming home would be my dream." Pat marries to create an imaginary home but loses her husband before ever being able to do so. This echoes Waller's concern about war weddings. The young wife, he warns, "although she may have been married for some years, . . . has not yet established a home."[53]

Other films emphasize sexual desire as motivation for marriage and show the rift between couples as a gap between their imagined future and their present postwar reality. In *Living in a Big Way* (LaCava 1947), Leo (Gene Kelly) and Margo (Marie McDonald) know each other for only nine days before they marry; then he is arrested for being AWOL, and they never consummate the marriage. Unsurprisingly, she comes to regret the hasty marriage and seeks an annulment. Equally unsurprisingly, Leo will win her back. *The Impatient Years* (Cummings 1944) similarly shows the aftermath of a quickie marriage. When Andy Anderson (Lee Bowman) returns home to wife Janie (Jean Arthur), they discover that they do not know each other very well, and they come to hate each other. In this case, before allowing them to get a divorce, a judge sentences them to recreate their initial whirlwind romance, which, unsurprisingly, reignites their love. Arguing against the divorce and claiming war marriages as a social problem and not just an individual one, Janie's father (Charles Coburn) tells the judge, "This isn't just one divorce case. It is about a million. . . . There's going to be a million more like it."

THE MORE THE MERRIER

While the films above reckon with the servicemen's leaving home, another subcycle of films relates to the housing shortage on the home front. The housing shortage extended from 1942 until at least 1949 and correlated to both internal migration and the postwar return of servicemen. During the war, there was a dramatic housing shortage as fifteen million people moved to labor in industrial production and governmental war jobs. Large and small cities witnessed huge booms in residents who came to work in shipyards, aircraft plants, munitions factories, and military installations.[54] The housing shortage was compounded because, from 1942 forward, housing materials were channeled into the war effort, so housing starts plummeted.[55] Between 1940 and 1943, workers piled into single-family homes and made them multifamily; moved into motels and hotels; converted small retail spaces to living quarters; slept in shifts in the same bed; and used trailers, tents, shacks, barns, garages, and cars as living spaces.[56] The Lanham Act of 1940 provided funds for defense housing, which was meant to be temporary and easily assembled and disassembled, and the federal government purchased nearly thirty-six thousand trailers as stopgap housing.[57]

Demobilization furthered the housing crisis. The number in the military dropped from twelve million servicemen in the last months of WWII to three million a year later, so there were nine million men and women returning home in 1945 and 1946. In December 1945, President Truman authorized the Federal Public Housing Authority to allocate unused military and wartime housing—barracks, Quonset huts, demountable units, trailers—as housing for vets and then appointed a "housing czar," Wilson Wyatt, to channel building supplies into production and keep prices low.[58] Wyatt proposed creating the Veterans' Emergency Housing Program (VEHP) aimed at building 2.7 million homes in two years, keeping the costs of home ownership down, and maintaining wartime rent controls. On May 22, 1946, Congress declared a national housing emergency and granted the Executive Branch special powers to deal with it. The special powers were to continue until December 31, 1947, under the assumption that the acute housing shortage would not be resolved before that date. Under the emergency program, more housing was built during 1946 than in any peacetime year since 1928; but the new construction still did not meet the pent-up demand, and Truman, bowing to the construction industry and no longer courting voters, scuttled the VEHP.[59] The GI Bill provided vets with a loan guarantee of up to $2,000 with a maximum interest rate of 4 percent, but many vets did not have ready cash to buy homes, and those who had money could not find homes for sale. Redlining and restrictive covenants further limited opportunities for Black and other minority servicemen, even when housing was available. The Housing Act of 1949 declared that "the housing shortage is still acute" and that "the general welfare and security of the Nation requires the establishment of a national housing policy to realize, as soon as feasible, the goal of a decent home and a suitable living environment for every American family." But it shifted funds away from war and defense housing projects toward broad programs of loans, grants, slum clearance, and urban renewal. Eventually, it was not government policy, but private loan programs, increased employment, and suburban development—spurred by techniques of prefabrication developed by the defense industry—that eased the housing crisis.

The subset of housing-shortage films begins during the war, with many set in Washington, DC, and other home-front defense areas. Showing both the commonality of experience and the desperation around housing, these films often begin with a montage sequence of "No Vacancy" signs and newspaper ads for rentals, with lines forming at vacant apartments, and battles between would-be tenants over open spots. For example, in *Rosie the Riveter* (Sentley 1944), after the credits roll over images of a California defense plant, we see a montage of "No Vacancy" signs, people moving into a gas station, and a man and a woman each separately reading an ad in a newspaper outside a boarding house. They race each other to the door and fight to get in, as another man and woman arrive in two separate taxis and also race to the door, all four claiming the right to the room. In *Johnny Doesn't Live Here Anymore* (May 1943), after defense worker Kathie (Simone Simon) arrives in an unnamed city, she loses a room with a friend because the friend has suddenly gotten married. We see Kathie walking the streets in a montage that shows multiple "No Vacancy" signs, until she stops a soldier, Johnny (William Terry), leaving a building with his rucksack and convinces him to let her rent his apartment while he is away with the marines.

In *The More the Merrier* (Stevens 1943), a newsreel-like opening voiceover intones, "Our vagabond camera takes us to beautiful Washington, DC." What follows is a sardonic dissonance between the voiceover and the images we see. As the voice describes the living as "pleasant and leisurely," we see people run from an office building across a crowded street; as numerous people cram into a taxi, the voiceover mentions "manners"; "epicurean culture" is matched with an outdoor hot dog stand. When the montage describes "Washington's beautiful homes," we see an apartment with three people sleeping in one bed and another four people sleeping on the floor. As we approach the "quiet residential section" and "friendly Washington welcoming us to her doorstep and throwing open her doors," we see a multitude of "No Vacancy" signs. Beyond this opening, as we enter the diegesis, when government official Benjamin Dingle (Charles Coburn) finds that his hotel reservation is no good because he has arrived two days early, we see him reading the paper and finding many ads for "Rooms Wanted" and only one "Room for Rent." When he arrives at the room for rent and sees a long line outside the apartment building, he walks past the line and into the building; he then replaces the "For Rent" sign with a "No Vacancy" sign to secure the room for himself.

In the Meantime, Darling gives a sense of the urgency of both housing needs and wartime weddings. During maneuvers, Lieutenant Daniel Ferguson (Frank Latimore) abruptly asks for leave, telling his commanding officer that there is "a room being vacated at the Craig Hotel." "Well, what are you waiting for?" the officer replies, encouraging him to abandon maneuvers. Ferguson not only has to race to the Craig, a hotel for wives of married soldiers, but also has to bring his fiancée to town and get married within a day. When her train arrives late, another married service couple oblige the justice of the peace to keep his convenience store open until she arrives; then, as the wedding takes place, soldiers come and go buying cigarettes, the justice's wife puts out a bowl to catch rain dripping in the ceiling, and the justice's daughter wanders through, brushing her teeth.

As with migration, the housing shortage seemed to challenge the dominant heterosexual order, particularly with regard to family. In the 1945 article "What's the Matter with the Family?," anthropologist Margaret Mead detailed the concerns that the housing shortage created about the family: worries that camp followers were living in miserable small spaces while following their husbands from camp to camp; that mothers were too young, married too early, and unable to care for children; that families moved too much; that there would be large numbers of divorces; and, overall, that the family was in danger because it was unstably housed. Mead maintains a fairly traditional definition of family: "just a name for the institution under which men marry women and have children."[60] But she suggests that family is not a static institution but a pliant one that changes according to historical circumstance: "Today we know that the family, no matter how sacred or secular we may personally feel it to be, changes its form, as house forms, methods of employment, [and] methods of making war change through the centuries." Countering claims that the family was in danger, Mead argued that it was not dead but "undergoing some changes in form, perhaps adjusting its code to wartime and migration and cramped quarters, but still a very flourishing institution, more valued, more yearned for, more patronized than usual."[61]

While pointing to a housing crisis, the cycle of films about the housing shortage evidence a wide array of experimentation with the "form" and "code" of family living. Many housing-shortage films, as Krutnik argues, "tackle the disarray in which mobilization has thrown established codes of sexual intimacy" by placing men and women in close quarters that break down boundaries between them.[62] At the same time, these films engage in a form of shelter writing by attending to the logistics and mise-en-scène of shared domestic space. In *Rosie the Riveter*, for example, the two men and two women agree to share the room, with the men working the night shift at the plant and sleeping daytime and the girls working days and sleeping nights. They organize the room, labeling the wardrobes and bureaus for men or women and setting up a dressing screen for privacy. In *Johnny Doesn't Live Here Anymore,* Kathie discovers that Johnny has lent keys to numerous male friends who stop by to use the apartment to sleep, meet girls, or grab a beer; one even stops by to use the bathtub. So Kathie organizes shifts for their visits: she lets them sleep there while she works, or she takes her bath while they drink beer in the living room. In *The More the Merrier,* when Dingle rents a room in Connie's apartment, Connie (Jean Arthur) attempts to impose order to ensure privacy, a minute-by-minute schedule that allocates precises times for the bathroom, breakfast, dressing, and leaving the house. Dingle not only bungles this—by, for example, entering the bathroom at the wrong time—but he invites a young man to rent space in the apartment, too, thinking Connie needs a beau. This matchmaking venture on Dingle's part works, as the new tenant, Carter (Joel McCrea), and Connie fall in love. When Connie's unusual living situation—a woman with two men—is exposed, she and Carter marry to avoid scandal and then, as they discover the wall between their bedrooms has been removed by Dingle, they consummate the marriage.

"The restrictive opportunities for privacy and intimacy" engendered by shared living quarters trouble the terms of the quickie marriage in *The Impatient Years.*[63] Andy arrives at his wife Janie's apartment on a convalescent furlough, having married after knowing each other only three days and then being apart for a year and a half. He finds Janie sharing space with their baby and her father, neither of whom Andy has met before. Janie also has a tenant, Henry (Phil Brown), who has been living with Janie for a year, helping to take care of the baby and perform household chores. When Andy fails to adhere to Janie's rigid schedule—similar to that of Connie in *The More the Merrier*—Henry speaks the dreadful truth that, owing to his residency in her home while Andy has been away, "You've never been as much married to Janie as I have."

The housing shortage unsettles conventional ways of living not only in relation to sexual propriety but also in reimagining domestic space in ways that queer the family away from the conventional husband-wife-child model. For example, a subset of films feature women setting up all-female households that reimagine domestic space as a collective. *In the Meantime, Darling* shows a boarding house for wives of soldiers. While the men are at the barracks, the women work together as a cooperative—cooking, gardening, knitting, and taking care of babies in a manner similar to what first-wave feminist

Charlotte Perkins Gilman imagined in *Women and Economics* (1989), where she proposed a model of centralized domestic and childcare chores as a shared collective practice that would free women from individual domestic ties. *Tender Comrade*—read at the time as "written with a deep and flaming sympathy for the women who are left behind to carry on with their war work" and "a preachment for all democracy stands for" but later seen as communist owing to the involvement of Hollywood Ten director Edward Dmytryk and blacklisted writer Dalton Trumbo—also imagines its all-female household as a collective.[64] Four female defense workers, all with husbands, and one older woman with a son in the military, decide to pool their resources to save money and get a better living situation. Jo Jones asserts, "We could run the joint like a democracy. If anything comes up, we can vote. Share and share alike." As in *In the Meantime, Darling*, they initially share household duties, but, realizing how inefficient it is because they all have jobs, they decide to hire a housekeeper. They hire a German woman, Manya (Mady Christians), whose husband is also fighting Nazis and who agrees to work for free, proffering that this will be her contribution to the war effort since, as a German national, she is not allowed to work in the defense plant. When Jo gives birth, the women share caretaking duties that enable Jo to continue working at the defense plant. At film's end, when Jo learns that her husband has been killed, we are left to assume that she will continue to live in the collective until war's end.

Other films imagine multigenerational alternatives to conventional families. In *Since You Went Away*, with her husband off to war, Anne Hilton and her daughters decide to take in a boarder, retired Colonel Smollet (Monty Woolley), and they also occasionally host Anne's friend Lieutenant Tony Willet (Joseph Cotten). In *It Happened in Brooklyn* (Whorf 1947), after again establishing Brooklyn as the Sinatra character Danny's hometown and having him sing a ballad to the Brooklyn Bridge on his return from service in England, the film mysteriously indicates that he has no friends or family there and, because of the housing shortage, has to live with his lonely grammar-school janitor, Nick Lombardi (Jimmy Durante), in the school basement. They then welcome posh British veteran Jamie (Peter Lawford) as a roommate who visits from England hoping to learn how to live authentically from working-class Danny. In *Apartment for Peggy* (Seaton 1948), Peggy (Jeanne Crain) convinces elderly college professor Henry Barnes (Edmund Gwynn) to rent her his attic so that she and her husband, Jason (William Holden), can move out of GI student trailer housing on campus. Once there,

FIGURE 2.5. Everybody pitches in to build housing for veterans in *Living in a Big Way*.

their presence revivifies the previously suicidal professor and gives him a new sense of family.

Many films show collectives of young veteran families working together to build housing. These films highlight alternative modes of living that challenge traditional single-family ideals, highlight the appeal of the collective, and also privilege building as an ideal postwar job for veterans. Recall *It Happened on Fifth Avenue* (Del Ruth 1947), discussed in the previous chapter, where army vet Jim (Don DeFore) convinces war profiteer Michael O'Connor (Charles Ruggles) to let him and other vets start a business building houses for returning vets in the deserted barracks O'Connor was going to use to expand his business. In *Something for the Boys* (Seiter 1944), when the Hart cousins—singer Blossom (Vivian Blaine), con man Harry (Phil Silvers), and munitions worker Chiquita (Carmen Miranda)—inherit the Magnolia Mansion, it turns out to be a tax liability and termite trap. But Sergeant Rocky Fulton (Michael O'Shea) from a nearby army camp arrives with plans to convert the mansion into a home for army wives. Soon, the place is swarming with soldiers and their wives, all pitching in to fix the place up. In *Living in a Big Way*, when Margo rejects her war husband, Leo, and demands a divorce, her grandmother (Jean Adair) offers to give Leo the $4,000 in allotments he sent Margo, plus a dilapidated family mansion "going to waste in times like these." She encourages him to use the mansion to provide housing to returning vets. As in *Something for the Boys*, we see men and women working side by side, repairing the home, setting up apartments, doing laundry and cooking together, and making do with no bathtubs or proper kitchens (fig. 2.5). As the multiple units in the mansion are completed, Grandma and Leo announce plans to build three hundred more houses.

Margo discovers her love for Leo and proves her mettle when she sets up an apartment, complete with a nursery, in the renovated veteran compound.

In each case, homebuilding is a collective effort, with women doing as much physical labor as men; but, in each case, a man's vision shapes the activity. The work of building gives the veteran a new lease on life and a worthwhile occupation that helps him adjust while he enables the rehabilitation and adjustment of his fellow veterans. The idealization of builders helps define Joe's character in *The Clock,* too, as he woos Alice by telling her that he wants to build houses—not prefabricated ones—in his hometown of Mapleton, Wisconsin. In imagining the veteran as builder, these films proffer solutions to two problems at once: the veteran problem and the housing shortage. They also accurately suggest that it will be private enterprise, not government policy, that will shape the future of housing.

WOMEN'S WORK

As suggested at the start of this chapter, the veteran's return was of paramount concern for government and Hollywood alike, and this concern generated a subset of earnest and often didactic films about the veteran's reintegration and adjustment. These include films about the veteran's physical and mental rehabilitation and about his alienation on returning home.

The imagined spectators of reintegration dramas were not the veterans themselves but the home-front audience, especially women. Not only were women Hollywood's most important audience, but, more important, rehabilitation and reintegration were seen as their responsibility.[65] In an article in *Ladies Home Journal,* "What You Can Do to Help the Returning Veteran," Waller notes that the "soldier had an experience which somehow changed him, an experience beyond the ken of his mother and all others who stayed home." He argues that while she may not understand the soldier's experience, the "woman's task is to help her own man when he needs it. . . . The personal side of reconstruction is women's work."[66] The film *The Homecoming* makes explicit the didactic purpose of the reintegration drama and its intended audience. As Colonel Johnson sits on a ship home, he is approached by a newspaper reporter who wants to hear his story. When Johnson balks, the reporter reminds him that "people at home have to live with the men returning home. They need to know how they've lived and changed." And in rehabilitation dramas, "women appeared to shoulder the burden—practical, emotional, sexual—of reintegration."[67] As Martin Norden suggests, the films show vets being "heroized, remasculinized, and reassimilated into society at all costs," with women as "the primary agents for the task."[68]

In part, the woman's role in aiding readjustment required her to give up her own newfound freedoms. As Mark Van Ells notes, the message of postwar pop culture was clear: "The reestablishment of traditional gender roles would provide further reassurance in the uneasy postwar world."[69] According to Sonya Michel, expert advice to women about how to help with readjustment "assumed that all men would have difficulty adjusting to civilian life, whether or not they had seen action or were visibly wounded or psychologically distressed. At the same time, the advice betrayed a nagging fear that women would not—or perhaps could not—readily yield their newfound freedom and sense of identity."[70] An article in *Ladies Home Journal* asks, "Has Your Husband Come Home to the Right Woman?" and articulates the woman's point of view: "Everybody's talking about how to treat your soldier and help him reconvert to civilian life! Well, what about wives? They've got a job of converting, too. They've got to stop being independent and getting used to having a full-time boss around the house. They've got to adapt themselves to the male ego after being comfortably female for several years. It isn't so easy!"[71]

A frequent trope in reintegration dramas underscores the tension between the woman's role in shepherding the veteran through his readjustment and giving up her newfound freedom. In numerous films, a woman drives a car with a male veteran as passenger. In *The Impatient Years*, for example, Janie picks Andy up at the train station and drives him and her father back to their apartment (fig. 2.6a). In *It Happened in Brooklyn*, when Danny gets back to Brooklyn, a policeman commandeers a passing car driven by Anne (Kathryn Grayson) and orders her to give Danny a lift. In *The Best Years of Our Lives*, Peggy (Teresa Wright) drives her father, Al (Fredric March), and fellow veteran Fred (Dana Andrews) along with her mother, Milly (Myrna Loy), after Al has dragged them from bar to bar getting drunk on his first night home and has run into Fred, who is also drunk. The next morning, Peggy drives Fred home (fig. 2.6b). In *Till the End of Time*, recently widowed Pat drives newly returned veteran Cliff (Guy Madison) from the bar where they met back to her house and, later, on a date to the beach; the girl next door, Helen (Jean Porter), drives Cliff and his army buddy Bill (Robert Mitchum) to visit another buddy, amputee Perry (Bill Williams) at his house; and Pat drives Cliff to see Perry a second time. In *Bright Victory* (Robson 1951), Judy (Peggy Dow) drives blind veteran Larry (Arthur Kennedy) to her sister and brother-

FIGURE 2.6A AND 2.6B. Women drive returning veterans in *The Impatient Years* and *The Best Years of Our Lives.*

in-law's cottage. In *Pride of the Marines,* Al refuses to see Ruth after the war because he is blind, but she tricks him by pretending to be a navy nurse and drives him home from the train station. In *The Men* (Zinnemann 1950), Ellen (Teresa Wright) drives her boyfriend, paraplegic veteran Bud (Marlon Brando), until he learns to drive using a device that allows him to control the pedals using his hands.

These scenes of women driving men are striking as they provide a visual metaphor for the idea of women as the driving force behind men's rehabilitation. They are also conspicuous because they suggest the woman's in-between status in relation to wartime and postwar expectations of femininity. As Jessica Brockmole explains, prior to the war, car manufacturers appealed to women consumers by linking driving to "independence, adventure, or sheer enjoyment."[72] During the war, women were the primary drivers on the home front, and car manufacturers, unable to sell new cars owing to restrictions, encouraged women to contribute to the war effort by maintaining cars; and they provided women with advice and information about "better gas mileage, longer tire life, and lower upkeep to keep cars going until the end of [the] war."[73] In the postwar period, rather than frame driving as enjoyable, or appeal to women as educated consumers interested in car maintenance, marketing for cars aimed at women primarily targeted as suburban homemakers and showed women driving solely for domestic chores, alone or with children. Driving for pleasure or adventure was portrayed with the man at the wheel and the woman as passenger.[74] Thus, we can see these frequent scenes of women driving as representing, on the one hand, a kind of lingering autonomy from the war years and, on the other hand, as transitional women's work focused on veteran rehabilitation prior to shifting into childcare and grocery shopping.

In these scenes of women driving, we can also see the veteran marked as lacking—castrated, feminized, or infantilized—by being placed in the passenger seat, with the woman assuming his place in the driver's seat. In reintegration dramas, as Silverman describes, "the 'hero' returns from World War II with a physical or psychic wound which marks him as somehow deficient, and which renders him incapable of functioning smoothly in civilian life."[75] As social problem films, reintegration dramas must explore the veteran's feelings of deficiency and attendant feelings of alienation, rage, and helplessness, to then restore the male—or, in the lingo of the time, "adjust" him—to wholeness. Beth Linker and Whitney Laemmli note that these films embody "lofty hopes that veterans might be seamlessly reincorporated into civil society, while also conceding that these men's feelings of anger, alienation, and frustration could easily undermine postwar harmony."[76] Still, just because the films reassert somewhat the man's mastery and control, they do not erase the memory of the man's frustrations. Rather than disavow these feelings entirely, reintegration dramas give space to them and provide didactic models for how to manage them.

THE SECOND BATTLE

The main challenges to veteran rehabilitation were psychological in nature. By war's end, many more veterans were suffering from mental illness than physical. Of the 671,000 who had been wounded, 300,000 required long-term hospitalization and rehabilitation; 500,000 were hospitalized for neuropsychiatric treatment in 1945 alone.[77] Prior to the war, to avoid the problems of "shell shock" from World War I, the Selective Service adopted a more stringent psychiatric evaluation than ever before, screening out the "maladjusted" to prevent psychiatric problems on the battlefield; up to 25 percent of potential recruits were found unfit to serve. Even so, mental breakdowns on the battlefield, including anxiety, nightmares, tremors, stuttering, mutism, and amnesia were significant, and somewhere between 20 and 34 percent of all casualties in the Pacific were neuropsychiatric, not physical.[78]

In films, however, clinical psychological deficiencies are represented relatively rarely: *I'll Be Seeing You* is one of the rare films that focus on a neuropsychiatric disorder. In this film, a soldier, Zachary Morgan, is on a ten-day medical furlough, suffering from what he refers to in a subjective voiceover as a "mental wound." In a scene clearly intended to educate the audience, we see Zachary reading a magazine article titled "The Problem of Neuropsychiatric Soldiers," and we learn that such soldiers will "respond to mental, physical upbuilding." Trying to avoid the "insane asylum," Zachary adopts a program of self-help, repeating to himself, "You'll get well." When he takes his date, Mary, to a combat movie, he explains to her the difference between his experience and "the way they see the war." The film shows war as a large-scale dramatic phenomenon, but for Zachary, it is smaller, "about ten feet wide and kind of empty," and varies depending on context: "Sometimes it's all full of noise and sometimes it's quiet. . . . It depends on how scared you are and how cold you are and how wet you are. I guess if you ask a hundred guys what the war is like, they'd all give you a different answer." Here, individual experience counters narratives of commonality and patriotism to allow for fear and discomfort. But, in the logic of the film, Zachary's individual experience is meant to represent broader trends.

Zachary's successful rehabilitation depends on Mary. After they have a date one night, Zachary goes back to his room at the YMCA and has a panic attack. He spins and stumbles, and tells himself in an internal monologue to "hold on . . . sit down . . . You know what you're about to go through." As his heart beats audibly, he says, "You're in for it now." But he hears the sound of Mary's voice in his head, telling him that he has to believe in his recovery, and he is soothed. Mary's ability to empathize with Zachary depends, in part, on her own dislocation. Jailed after killing a man who attempted to rape her, Mary is unhomed as much as Zachary. He describes himself to her as homeless: "I haven't got any regular home or family"; and Mary, likewise, describes herself as not fitting in or belonging anymore and considers her dream of a home—"a home like this with a kitchen and a stove and an icebox and a husband and a child"—as impossible. In the end, she returns to finish her jail sentence, and he promises to get well, their future together far from certain.

Rather than psychological trauma, rehabilitation films tend to focus on physical wounds, "a visually startling means for exploring the psychological and social consequences of war."[79] Dana Polan has referred to narratives of physical wounds as conversion narratives in which the individual veteran is converted to "appropriate beliefs and commitments."[80] In particular, wounded vets must be converted from feelings of aberrant individuality to communality, from bitterness and self-pity to acceptance, from pride to humility. These conversions involve the veteran accepting the persistent love of a woman such that "the two ideologies coincide: It is for the nuclear family and not for the rampant male adventure that we are fighting the war."[81] While conversion narratives hinge on a woman's love, they are cast in militaristic terms as narratives of grit and "battle." For example, *The Men* opens with an intertitle reinforced by a male voiceover that describes rehabilitation as a second war: "In all wars, since the beginning of history, there have been men who fought twice." The second battle is fought "with abiding faith and raw courage."

Conversion narratives take place primarily in hospitals that emphasize the programmatic help available to veterans and create a form of shelter writing as the veteran establishes patterns of living in the hospital as an alternative home. In *Pride of the Marines* and *Bright Victory*, the blind veterans are placed on a ward with other blind veterans, where they form a community away from their former homes and families. Similarly, in *The Men*, Bud is moved onto a ward filled with other paraplegics—and the film features forty-five patients from the Birmingham Veterans Administration Hospital as extras for added authenticity. Most of the men do not have family. Bud is an orphan. Fellow paraplegic Doolin (Richard Erdman) is visited by his father, who apologizes because Doolin's mother is again unable to visit, then leaves immediately after Doolin gives him some cash to cover his gambling debt. Only the Mexican American character Angel (Arthur Jurado) has a loving family—a mother and sister who visit—and he is saving money to buy a home. Despite being the model patient, however, Angel dies of his injuries before he can purchase that home. That Angel is played by Arthur Jurado, a World War II veteran who lost his legs in a plane crash coming home from the war, adds both authenticity and pathos to his death.

In conversion narratives, the veteran's acceptance of his condition initially occurs within the context of other men suffering the same illness. In this way, the narrative is shown to be one of many possible narratives, and the main character's experience is not fully unique. At the same time, the multiplicity of patients can give voice to a spectrum of feelings, including frustrations with rehabilitation. Thus, in *The Men*, one of Bud's wardmates, Butler (Jack Webb), expresses frustration with the ethos of rehabilitation: "I don't want to be rehabilitated, readjusted, reconditioned or re-anything. And if you don't mind, I don't want to take my proper place in society either." In *Pride of the Marines*, patients debate whether things are really better for veterans now than after the First World War. "Things are different now," one argues, citing the GI Bill of Rights. But others question whether they can get their jobs back, given their injuries, and others recall the Bonus March.

For the most part, however, the other patients provide role models for rehabilitation and perseverance. In *Pride of the Marines* and *Bright Victory,* the blind veterans Al and Larry, respectively, are surrounded by other blind men, all of whom have adjusted to their condition. Initially resistant, and in Larry's case suicidal, Al and Larry learn how to eat, walk, use a cane, and navigate unfamiliar spaces. In *The Men,* similarly, Bud is initially bitter and fatalistic, but after Ellen presses him to accept her love, he works to improve. In montage sequences, we see him working out with Angel. In both *Bright Victory* and *The Men,* we see the injured veteran participating in various sports, such as swimming, bowling, and wheelchair basketball, that remasculinize him in a homosocial world.

The injured veteran's difficulty arises when he tries to rejoin the world outside the hospital, especially when he enters domestic space. In *The Men,* for example, Bud and Ellen get married. Determined to stand for the ceremony, which takes place in the hospital chapel with only fellow patients for guests, Bud stumbles when the preacher asks him to take Ellen's hands. Afterward, when he enters the new house she has decorated, as Ellen natters on about the curtains, ashtrays, and lamps she has chosen, we hear the wheels of Bud's chair squeak on the carpet. When they try to celebrate their marriage with champagne, Bud pops the cork but spills the champagne on the carpet—a not too subtle metaphor for sexual inadequacy. After Ellen reacts with horror to Bud's leg tremors, their marriage fails on their wedding night—the wedding a false conversion in which neither one of them is truly ready to accept his condition—and Bud leaves their new house and returns to the hospital, declaring, "I'm home. This is my home. This is where I belong." Similarly, in *Bright Victory,* when Larry goes home on furlough, he attends a party in his honor. Despite having excellent skills at the hospital, at the party he accidentally spills drinks and misses his plate because other guests have thoughtlessly moved items. After his fiancée, Chris (Julie Adams), confesses that she is "just not strong enough" to marry him, we see him stumble and bump into things inside his parents' house.

In each film, in order to acclimate to the outside world, the man must accept the woman's help. In *The Men,* after Bud gets into a drunk-driving accident, following an altercation in a bar, he is kicked out of the hospital by the Paraplegic Veterans Association. Initially resistant to leaving—"What am I going to do? Where am I going to go?"—Bud then drives in his modified car to Ellen's parents' house, wheels himself up the hilly walkway, and stops at the stairs. The film ends as Ellen asks if he wants her to help him up the stairs and he says, "Please." In *Bright Victory,* after Chris rejects Larry, he returns to Judy (Peggy Dow), who befriended him at the hospital and whom he credits with his cure. In *Pride of the Marines,* Al accepts Ruth's love after she scolds him, "You haven't got enough pride to face the truth, to accept being blind like a man," and assures him that needing someone is not bad: "Everyone has problems."

These conversion narratives resolve the veteran problem through the formation of the couple. But none of these films fully restore the man to wholeness. In *The Men,* Bud sits outside the family home, willing to accept Ellen's help, but it is unclear what work he will do or whether he and Ellen can have children. In *Bright Victory,* Larry is returning to the hospital and planning to train as a lawyer, but he faces a long and difficult path to success. *The Pride of the Marines* ends with a glimmer of light as Al sees color on a taxicab and orders the taxi driver to take him and Ruth "home." But where is home? Prior to serving, Al was a boarder with the Merchants, and it is to their house that Ruth drives him when he gets off the train. He and Ruth have not created a home, so home here is a fantasy, an idea more than a place.

NERVOUS OUT OF THE SERVICE

Along with psychological and physical wounds, veteran rehabilitation focused on more general feelings of unease. As Van Ells states, "In leaving the familiar, structured environment of the military for the unfamiliar civilian world, veterans sometimes felt adrift in postwar America."[82] According to Franklin Reck, the soldier may be homesick at home because in the service he "dreamed of home so longingly that he has conjured a paradise.... Home has become a fantasy. No home could possibly be as good as the one Bill dreamed up in his Quonset hut.... Home will be a disappointment."[83] Waller concurs: "When the soldier returns to the home of which he has dreamed through the years of war, he finds it smaller, dingier, more sordid than he ever imagined it to be, and his life within it is flavorless."[84]

This general feeling of alienation, unease, and restlessness permeates postwar dramas. *Till the End of Time* and *The Best Years of Our Lives*—probably the best known reintegration drama—each detail the difficulties faced by three different returning veterans, one of whom is an amputee.[85] These films differ from the conversion narratives I discussed above because the veteran's reintegration occurs in his family home, not in the institutionalized space of the hospital, and because the amputees' problems are shown in tandem with those of uninjured veterans who face similar difficulties adjusting to civilian life. As with narratives about wounded soldiers, the veterans' adjustments depend on women.

Till the End of Time begins with scenes of marines at a San Diego base being discharged, then taken to a Separation Center, where they learn about rehabilitation, pensions, and educational opportunities. When Cliff arrives home, taking a taxi from the train station, he finds the house empty and lets himself in using a key hidden in a planter outside. He explores the house, tastes food in the oven, takes down the service star in the window, and goes to his room, There, he and we examine signs of his youthful prewar self: a high school pendant, a STOP sign, lots of pictures of airplanes, jokes, pictures of his mom and dad, a signed football, an out-of-style necktie. In a familiar image of rehoming in which the veteran discovers that his old clothes no longer fit—a clear marker of how much he has changed and of his ill-fit in home environs—Cliff takes off his uniform and puts on an old jacket, but it is much too small, so he puts his uniform back on.[86] Restless, he goes to the local bar.

In *Till the End of Time,* Cliff's fellow veterans suffer from mental and psychological damage. Bill has a silver plate in head. When he first visits Cliff, he is a swaggering image of postwar machismo. He wears a new flashy suit and discusses his postwar adventures with women and gambling. Cliff becomes a different, rougher, man with him, and his mother uncomfortably witnesses the serviceman in her son. Later, Bill returns, broke and nervous. He says his head is "busting open," but he will not go to the VA hospital and has not told his family about his injury. Their friend Perry is a paraplegic who lost both legs. He is bitter and resists the help of the veterans' rehabilitation officer who visits him. "Twenty-one and I'm dead," he complains. Only when Cliff asks him to help get Bill to a hospital does Perry rally; he puts on his prosthetic legs and uniform and joins them at a bar.

The Best Years of Our Lives starts with soldiers struggling to get home: three veterans—Al, Fred, and Homer (Harold Russell)—share a bare-bones flight back to their hometown, Boone City, then a taxicab to their respective homes. On the plane, Al and Fred learn about Homer's accident, which left him without hands, and they witness how confident and comfortable he is using his hooks—these scenes and all involving Homer made more authentic and poignant because the actor, Harold Russell, like Angel in *The Men,* is a real veteran who lost both hands in an accident. Fred confesses that he is "nervous out of the service," and Al says that what worries him most about going home is "that everybody's going to try and rehabilitate me."

Each of the vets in *The Best Years of Our Lives* has an uncomfortable homecoming. When they drop off Homer, Fred and Al see Homer's mom break down crying when she sees his hooks and Homer's stiff response when his fiancée, Wilma (Cathy O'Donnell), hugs him. "You gotta hand it to the navy," Fred says as they drive off, with Homer saluting them, "They sure taught that kid how to use those hooks." "Yeah," Al says, "but they couldn't teach him to put his arms around his girl or stroke her hair." As the taxi arrives at Al's home, we discover that while he was only a sergeant in the army, he is a wealthy banker and lives in a posh high-rise. Still, he says that going home makes him "feel as if I'm going to hit a beach." At home, he is restless and uncomfortable. In contrast, Fred, a captain in the air force, is revealed to be poor, a former soda jerk. When Fred arrives home, his wife, Marie (Virginia Mayo), from a quickie war wedding, isn't even home. Fred goes to the ramshackle shack where his father lives with his girlfriend and learns that his wife has moved and is working in a nightclub. Unable to get into her new apartment, he is temporarily homeless. Meanwhile, Homer bolts from a family dinner, later telling his friends that at home, "they got me nervous ... staring at these hooks or else they keep staring away from them." Within a few hours, all three veterans end up together at a bar owned by Homer's Uncle Butch (Hoagy Carmichael), all more comfortable with each other than with their loved ones.

As in *Till The End of Time*, in *The Best Years of Our Lives*, the veteran's unsuccessful return to civilian clothing is a crucial motif. Al discovers that his pants are too big for him, their ill-fit mirroring his ill-fit for his "nice fat job in a nice fat bank." When Fred eagerly abandons his uniform, Marie complains and forces him to put it back on so she can show him off to her friends. "Now you look wonderful," Marie exclaims. "You look like yourself." Then, when Fred is unable to find a job commensurate with his air force experience, he ends up back in a soda jerk uniform, a marker of his lowly status out of the service.

Both films mark out appropriate and inappropriate ways for women to behave. In *Till the End of Time*, despite telling her son that "we have so much to talk about," when Cliff begins talking about the war, his mother repeatedly shuts him down, saying, "I know you don't want to talk about it." In contrast, the war widow Pat listens to Cliff. When he gets mad at his work in a factory, Pat follows him to a diner and lets him talk about how he lost three years of his life and feels edgy. In *The Best Years of Our Lives*, Fred's wife, Marie, seeks only fun, resents his poverty, is unfaithful, proudly discusses using the black market for purchases, and, above all, wants their life to be "as if nothing happened." When Fred has nightmares, Marie asks if he is all right, "I mean, in your mind," and tells him he "won't get anyplace" until he gets over the war. In contrast, when Fred sleeps at Al's family's apartment, and has a nightmare, Peggy soothes him, wipes his tears away, and tucks him into bed. In the morning, she does not mention what she saw. Wilma is stalwart in her love for Homer, even as he pushes her away. When she confronts Homer about his feelings for her, he takes her up to his bedroom to show her the reality of his condition. Taking off his harness and prosthetic arms, he tells her he is "helpless as a baby now." Rather than be repulsed, she declares her love, tenderly puts his prosthetics away and tucks him into bed. As Silverman and other scholars have noted, Milly also tucks Al in when he comes home drunk. In each case, the woman's nursing gestures reveal a deep tenderness; at the same time, as Silverman suggests, the woman's "privileged access to the spectacle of male lack" also engenders female desire and does not restore the man to wholeness but provides acceptance for his lack.[87]

In both films, marriage offers a promise of domesticity. In *Till the End of Time,* Cliff's mother brings Pat to the hospital to join Cliff, stitching together Cliff's reintegration into his family and his maturation into marriage. But as Pat and Cliff kiss outside the hospital, their future is uncertain, Cliff's adjustment incomplete. As Cliff's dad says, "You didn't make yourself a soldier overnight. You can't make yourself a civilian overnight." In *The Best Years of Our Lives,* the film ends with a wedding and an engagement. Homer marries Wilma, placing a ring on her finger using his hooks—which Silverman views as a moment of crisis, "eliciting fear, anxiety and pain," but which can also be read as restorative, allowing Homer to prosthetically fulfill his masculine role.[88] During the wedding ceremony, crosscutting connects Fred and Peggy, who then become engaged. But Fred's proposal makes clear that their union will not engender stability. "We'll have no money, no decent place to live," he warns.

Similar to films about the housing shortage, the promise of futurity for Fred relates to the ideal of home building. Fired from his job as a soda jerk and unable to find work that values his experience as a pilot, Fred despondently wanders into an airfield of discarded planes and, learning that they will be recycled for use in prefabricated houses, secures a job. In a fairly clear parallel to his own condition, Fred, a former pilot, will remake himself by recycling the unwanted artifacts of war, the cast-off planes that he flew.

While these films focus on the recuperative effort to rehabilitate veterans, they also showcase hostile and divisive attitudes toward veterans in ways that underscore threats that jeopardize successful rehabilitation. In *The Best Years of Our Lives,* Al encounters unfeeling attitudes toward veterans in his work at the bank. When he returns to work, he is offered a job as vice president in charge of small loans related to the GI Bill: "We need a man who understands the soldier's problems." But when Al gives a loan to a GI who wants to buy a farm, and who views the loan "not as a handout but a right," the bank manager questions Al about the loan because the veteran has no collateral. "His collateral is in his heart and his right as a citizen," Al argues, and at a bank banquet in his honor, he drunkenly asserts that he will continue to "gamble on the future of this country." Fred and Homer encounter a different kind of hostility in the lingering isolationist views of a civilian. When Homer visits Fred at the diner, he meets a man who looks at his hooks and tells him he has "plenty of guts" but says that it is "terrible seeing a guy like you sacrifice so much, and for what?" Homer asks angrily, "So we're all a bunch of suckers, eh?" He and Fred end up brawling with the man, getting Fred fired.[89]

In *Till the End of Time,* the threat to stability comes from a shady veteran's organization. This organization is clearly distinguished from the friendly, helpful veteran rehabilitation services offered to Perry by Sgt. Gunny Watrous (William Gargan) throughout the film. When Perry meets Cliff and Bill at the bar, they are approached by four veterans who ask them to join their organization, American War Patriots. They tell Cliff and the others that they offer monthly bonuses, but they criticize labor unions, stating that the unions do not represent the freedom they fought for; they also make clear that they have restrictions on membership: "No Catholics, Jews, or Negroes." As they talk, we see offended reaction shots of Perry, Cliff, and Bill, each in close-up. Prior to this, we have seen a Black serviceman (Caleb Peterson) playing pinball in the background in the bar, framed between Bill and Cliff (fig. 2.7). When Bill had stepped away from the game, he had asked the Black soldier to "run up my score" and then congratulated him on his score when he returned. As the American War Patriots talk, the Black soldier is again framed in the background, but, when they list restrictions, the film cuts to a solo shot of him in a medium-close reaction shot before he walks away. Bill describes a Jewish friend in the service who died and spits in one of the Patriots' eyes. Then Cliff, Perry, and Bill brawl with the men, eventually landing Bill in the hospital with a new head injury, forcing him to have his much-needed surgery.

Until this moment in *Till the End of Time,* the differences among the three veterans was foregrounded, as Cliff, Bill, and Perry—like Al, Fred, and

FIGURE 2.7. The Black soldier (Caleb Peterson) in the background in *Till the End of Time*.

Homer in *The Best Years of Our Lives*—each experience a different variation of the veteran problem (unease, psychiatric problems, physical wounds) and different class and age positions (Cliff is solidly middle class and college-age, Bill is older and seemingly on his own, Perry is seemingly lower middle class). At this moment, as the three characters push back against white supremacist views, they, ironically, come into focus as white. As Richard Dyer famously argues, whiteness "secures its dominance by seeming not to be anything in particular," and white characters are differentiated according to characteristics other than race, such as Italian American identity, lower-class status, a Brooklyn accent, and so forth.[90] But when the Black serviceman enters the frame, visually wedged between and behind the white characters, "whiteness *qua* whiteness" comes into focus.[91] As Christine Goding suggests, in this moment, race *happens*. Goding argues that "race itself is an *event*. It is not just a relation," between, say, the white and Black servicemen "but an event of *relating* . . . generated by the interaction of at least two bodies . . . the character and outcome of their interaction."[92] Beyond this film, in particular, I suggest that the insertion of this unnamed Black character (and not coincidentally uncredited Black actor) into the background of this reintegration drama serves to bring to the foreground the whiteness *qua* whiteness of these World War II films as a whole.

WHITE PEOPLE PROBLEMS

In Walter Wanger's call for films to address "urgent home front problems," he listed "interracial friction" as a crucial topic alongside housing and rehabilitation. As Kevin Kruse, Stephen Tuck, Ken Coates, and W. R. Morrison discuss, the institutionalized racism of segregated troops and the explicit racism of servicemen shocked foreign observers. Hitler gave racism a bad name, American policymakers discovered that domestic racial discrimination could harm their diplomatic overtures to nonwhite nations, and African Americans demanded equal rights in return for their contributions to the defense economy and war effort.[93] In 1942, representatives from the National Association for the Advancement of Colored People (NAACP) met with executives from several major Hollywood studios and brokered an agreement to improve the portrayals of African Americans in film by decreasing the reliance on traditional stereotypes and to increase opportunities for African Americans working behind the scenes, thus improving the representation of African Americans throughout the film industry. Hollywood mainly responded to demands from the NAACP for better representation with all-Black-cast musicals such as *Cabin in the Sky* (Minnelli 1944), as opposed to large-scale transformations in representation. In 1944, the Office of War Information produced the short film *The Negro Soldier*, directed by Frank Capra, to show Black contributions to the war effort and to stir Black patriotism. For the most part, however, the cinematic image of America's military remained largely white. The cycle of social problem films around the veteran's unhoming, housing crisis, and return that I discuss here focuses almost exclusively on the problems of white soldiers and veterans. A small slate of films address the intersection of the veteran problem with race, but it is seen mainly through the eyes of the white serviceman confronting his own racism. In the context of the civil rights movement, the films' didactic approach to race is aimed primarily at white spectators in narratives that show a serviceman's conversion from racist attitudes toward acceptance.

Bright Victory, for example, includes a change in racist attitudes as part of Larry's conversion narrative. When Larry is first blinded, we see him, still in bandages, on a transport plane heading to the hospital. He meets a fellow southerner, a Black soldier in a neck brace (Bernie Hamilton), and they learn that they grew up near each other (sort of—Seminole, Florida, and Atlanta, Georgia, respectively). Larry asks if the soldier knows of a certain country club. When the Black man answers that he waited tables there, Larry, realizing the man is Black—apparently not being able to *hear* race and thus not *see* it, but understanding the codes of servitude—bristles and stops talking. He asks the Black man to go get the nurse and then has her sit by him, displacing the Black soldier. Later, in the hospital, Larry bumps into a blind Black patient, Joe Morgan (James Edwards), from New Orleans. They share stories of their war wounds, and Larry, again unable to *hear* racial difference, offers to buy Joe a drink. Then, in a montage sequence, we see Larry and Joe swimming together, bowling, and hugging each other playfully. But one night, someone mentions that the ward is getting new men soon. "So I hear," Larry says. "Three of 'em n——rs. I never knew they let n——rs on this ward." Joe and the other men stop. "Did you, Joe?" Larry asks. "Yeah. I've been here seven months now," he says and walks away.

Later, when Larry is home on furlough, he sees his own racism reflected in his mother's attitude toward her Black servants. "The Civil War is over, ma; haven't you heard?" Alone with his father, he tells him of his broken friendship with Joe and says that he realizes his mother taught him to be racist. "She taught you those things because she was taught them, son, and I was, too. But the whole world is changing and you more than we because you helped to change it." At the end of the film, after reuniting with Judy on the train platform, Larry meets Joe on the troop train taking them to the next hospital. Barely asking how Joe's furlough went, Larry asks, "We're still friends, right?" "Sure," Joe answers, "if you want to be, Larry." "I want to be." Without any deep reckoning with the deep bias that shaped him, Larry resolves his racism through personal friendship, a friendship dictated by his desire, not Joe's. Joe exists in the narrative only as a prop for Larry's conversion: he has no story apart from Larry.

Bright Victory suggests that Larry was taught to be racist in the American South and that being freed from familiar conventions and hierarchies—both in hospital and as a blind man—he can unlearn his racist tendencies. Similarly, and famously, in *South Pacific* (Logan 1958), the Rodgers and Hammerstein song "(You've Got to Be) Carefully Taught" argues that racism is not born in one but is a learned social bias. In the film, based on the 1949 Broadway musical, nurse Nellie (Mitzi Gaynor) falls in love with a French plantation owner, Emile (Rossano Brazzi), when she is stationed on a South Pacific Island. She learns that Emile left France because he killed a man, and she readily accepts that. But Nellie cannot accept that he was married to a now-dead Polynesian woman and fathered two children with her. Meanwhile, one of the Americans on base, Lt. Joe Cable (John Kerr), falls in love with a local island girl, Liat (France Nuyen). Joe and Nellie both admit that they love but cannot marry their respective paramour because of race. Nellie comforts Joe by telling him, "You're just far away from home, Joe, we're both far away," indicating that their unhoming has made them both abandon conventions regarding race; and she counsels, "We just have to go back where we belong." While Nellie claims that her feelings of disgust toward Emile are "just something that's born in me," Joe counters in song: "You've got be taught to hate and fear." Eventually, after he is nearly killed, Nellie decides to marry Emile, who, after all, is a white man. The limits of the film's antiracist politics are clear when Joe is killed before he can marry Liat and insofar as Nellie never does go back where she "belongs" but stays in the South Pacific, where we see her join Emile and his children at an outdoor table but never inside a home.

Like *South Pacific*, *Kings Go Forth* (Daves 1958) grapples with homegrown racism by displacing it onto foreign soil and making it strange to the American abroad. In this film, Sinatra plays Lt. Sam Loggins, a soldier stationed in Southern France, who meets and falls in love with a young French woman, Monique (Natalie Wood). After he has spent time with Monique and her mother (Leora Dana), her mother tells Sam that Monique is mixed-race. Monique's white mother and Black father came to France to escape the racism of America, thus marking America as inherently racist and imagining France as free of such views. When Sam first hears of Monique's racial heritage, he is shocked and walks out. But, back on base, he mulls this information over in an internal subjective voiceover as the camera slowly zooms into his face in a black-and-white close-up. As with the struggle to deal with physical wounds of war in *The Men*, Sam's struggle with his own racism is described as a war: "I fought two wars that week, my own and the army's." "Mostly I thought about that word," he says, and admits, "I learned it early and used it often. It showed just how tough I was." He acknowledges the color line that existed where he grew up in Harlem, "They were on one side and we on the other. Why? I don't know why except a lot of people want someone to look down on, or they think they do." Sam comes to accept Monique—the choice, as in *Bright Victory*, belongs to the white man. But she refuses his romantic attention and opts instead to give herself to Corporal Britt Harris (Tony Curtis), a rich white playboy type who flaunts his affinity for Black culture by playing jazz trumpet in a nightclub. Pretending to love Monique, he deflowers her and then refuses to marry her. He explains to Sam that sex with Monique "was like a new kick for me," as Monique is the first nonwhite woman he had slept with. Britt dies in battle alongside Sam, who loses an arm. After recuperating in hospital, Sam returns to Monique's home, which she has turned into a school for children. At film's end, Sam, debilitated, joins Monique for an uncertain and likely unromantic future. As in *Bright Victory* and *South Pacific*, the white racist remains away from home, unmoored from the familial and familiar context that engendered his or her racism, and seemingly unable to return.

In contrast, *Home of the Brave* (Robson 1949) seemingly centers on the Black soldier's experience. It shows a Black soldier, Peter Moss (James Edwards), who has a psychosomatic illness that makes him paralyzed and amnesiac. His white doctor (Jeff Corey) surmises that his illness is caused by the racism of white soldiers. Indeed, Moss faces racism as the only Black soldier on a reconnaissance mission with three white men: T. J. (Steve Brodie), who believes Black soldiers should not be in combat roles and makes frequent racist cracks; Sgt. Mingo (Frank Lovejoy), who adopts a universal humanistic view that there are good and bad white men and good and bad Black men; and Finch (Lloyd Bridges), who is an old friend from childhood and who had developed a playful lingo with Moss in which they called each other "charming" and "delightful." The doctor drugs Moss to lead him through a talking cure that produces a flashback narrative. While T. J.'s racism is problematic, the real problem on the mission is that Finch, who had been Moss's good friend until college and is seemingly not racist, slips at one point and uses a racist slur against Moss. Finch then dies in an ambush, and Moss is unable to save him. Though Moss assumes his illness relates to guilt over not saving Finch, he discovers through psychotherapy that he felt glad when Finch died. This seems to be a moment that Moss might admit his righteous anger at a racist, but, instead, the doctor advises Moss that all soldiers are glad when someone dies and it is not them: "I'm just like anyone else," he happily intones; "we're all different, but we're all guys." Mingo, now crippled with one arm missing, compares his disability to Moss's race and suggests that they partner together and open a bar back home, where negative attitudes toward a Black bar owner would, he thinks, be lessened by partnering with a disabled white man. The film ends on an optimistic but ambiguous note as Mingo adopts the mannered language that Moss shared with Finch, using the words *charming* and *delightful* as they head to transport home.

In *Bright Victory*, *South Pacific*, *Kings Go Forth*, and *Home of the Brave*, the white veterans who overcome their racism do so in relation to one specific person of color. They level the playing field but only on a one-to-one basis. They do not change or investigate systemic racism. They also resist the tendency of reintegration dramas to resolve the narrative through the formation of a couple. The one white soldier in *South Pacific* who might marry a woman of color dies before he can do so, and Nellie only encounters a person of color by proxy—the dead woman previously married to Emile—and she still marries a white European. Larry in *Bright Victory* pairs with a white woman, but the film ends not with their clinch but with his reconciliation with Joe in parallel but not intersecting resolutions. The white veterans in *Bright Victory, Kings Go Forth,* and *Home of the Brave* are all diminished in some way—blind or amputees—rather than figures of power and privilege.

These films illuminate the degree to which the veteran problem is perceived to be a white problem, and they make people of color subservient to the white serviceman's narrative. In introducing people of color into these narratives of white dislocation, however, these films open space to imagine different neglected and repressed narratives that might have been told—such as the story of Black soldiers' unhoming in World War II, or the movement of Mexican American and Puerto Rican serviceman, or the forced rehoming of Japanese Americans into internment camps—stories that did not get told until much later.

COMING HOME AGAIN?

World War II migrations encompass many different modes of mobility: home leavings and homecomings; forced mobility via the draft, voluntary mobility for those soldiers who enlist, and civilians who move for work or family; social mobility and immobility; and including the transience and instability of the unhoused. World War II mobility sometimes reads as freedom, in stories of shore leaves and touristic narratives or women's mobility, but is most often portrayed as instrumental, in service to the nation, in one way or another.

Overall, films related to World War II migration underscore the degree to which *responses* to mobility shape the experience. Where the tramp's mobility was viewed with suspicion and distrust, and the tramp was thus a marginalized figure, the mobility of the servicemen and civilians engaged in the cause of war is framed as central to the culture, pervasive rather than invasive. As "the major social problem" of the day, the veteran problem—and the widespread massive unhoming that phrase encompasses—became a shared ideological project that not only motivated expansive proactive policy solutions but also produced myriad films that provide capacious and multifaceted attention to the problem.[94] These films allowed a broad-based societal acknowledgment of not only the pleasures but also the difficulties inherent to the condition of the unhomely, including neuroses and alienation, which were treated not as aberrant or pathological but as normal and manageable. These films also provided glimpses of new codes and forms for imagining family and domestic life and showed home not only as desirable but also as contingent and pliant.

It is perhaps because the veteran problem was a shared ideological project that it seems, in retrospect, so frictionless, especially when compared to the problem of the Vietnam veteran. At the end of the United States' years-long intervention in Vietnam, from 1964 to 1973, Vietnam veterans returning home were met "with none of the fanfare and received none of the benefits bestowed upon World War II's 'greatest generation.'"[95] This is due, in part, to the very different logistics of the war, where rather than a mass demobilization all at once, servicemen, who typically served a year, came back intermittently and one by one. More important, the different response to Vietnam vets relates to the negative feelings about the war, "a negative consensus about that bloody and divisive struggle... a consensus born of anger, despair, disillusion, and a weariness in the face of all the costs of the war," and a "national implication of guilt and shame placed on Vietnam veterans as participants in and avatars of a brutal and unsuccessful war."[96]

Not surprisingly, perhaps, compared to the dozens of films made about the serviceman's unhoming, the housing shortage, and the veteran's return in World War II, the vast majority of which I have not discussed here, it took four years after the end of US involvement in Vietnam for the first significant films about the Vietnam veteran to appear. *Heroes* (Kagan 1977), *Coming Home* (Ashby 1978), and *The Deer Hunter* (Cimino 1978) each examined the lingering effects of Vietnam service, encompassing amputation, dis-ease at home, and post-traumatic stress disorder (PTSD) (a diagnosis only recognized by the American Psychiatric Association in 1980 specifically due to the lingering trauma of Vietnam veterans). Unlike their World War II predecessors, these films mostly did not offer the promise of successful reintegration. The latter two films, especially, end in a veteran's suicide. The release of Oliver Stone's angry film *Born on the Fourth of July* in 1989 indicates the degree to which the Vietnam veteran's rehoming was still unfinished business.

These dark films and the distinction often made between the denigrated Vietnam vet and the "greatest generation" retroactively render the World War II veteran as a relatively unproblematic figure. As I hope to have demonstrated, however, the World War II veteran problem was the major social problem of its day. What made the World War II veteran problem different from that of Vietnam or later wars is that the effort to address the veteran problem, to turn the soldier back into a citizen, was a civilized effort, engaged in by both government and Hollywood, that aimed to help the soldier find his place in society with education and empathy.

THREE

Adrift

THE AMBIVALENT FREEDOM OF
THE FEMALE HITCHHIKER

It allowed her to feel what she had not felt till now: *a feeling of happy-go-lucky irresponsibility.* The alien life in which she had become involved was a life without shame, without biographical specifications, without past or future, without obligations. It was a life that was extraordinarily free. The girl, as a hitchhiker, could do anything, *everything was permitted her.* She could say, do and feel what she liked.

MILAN KUNDERA, *"The Hitchhiking Game"*

She could not think of freedom as a destination but as a practice, full of intervals and regressions.

PARUL SEHGAL,
reviewing a biography of Lorraine Hansberry

IN QUENTIN TARANTINO'S *Once Upon a Time . . . in Hollywood* (2019), set in 1969, the stuntman Cliff Booth (Brad Pitt) has an encounter with a young female hitchhiker. Cliff first spots the young hippie Pussycat (Margaret Qualley) when he is driving his boss, the actor Rick Dalton (Leonardo DiCaprio), in Rick's Cadillac Coupe de Ville. Pussycat and a group of young female hippies have been dumpster-diving for food. When Cliff passes by in his car, she gives him the peace sign. Whereas Rick dismisses the group as "fucking hippie motherfuckers," Cliff exchanges flirtatious glances with Pussycat. The next day, Cliff sees Pussycat hitchhiking in front of Pandora's Box on the Sunset Strip—an anachronistic inclusion as the youth-oriented coffeehouse had been razed in 1967, following riots over an imposed curfew—but he is traveling in the wrong direction, so she makes a mock crying face as he drives off. Finally, he spots her hitchhiking again on Burbank. She says she is going to Chatsworth and acknowledges her own trendy status when she says she can usually get rides because tourists will dine off the story of picking up a "hippie girl" and taking her to "a movie ranch." Cliff knows the "movie ranch" she mentions as Spahn Ranch, having worked there shooting westerns in the past, and agrees to take her there. In the car, Pussycat offers Cliff a blow job. He asks her how old she is. When she claims to be eighteen, he asks for ID. Correctly gauging that she has no ID because she is not yet eighteen, Cliff refuses her offer and says he is "too old to go to jail for poontang." On their arrival at the ranch, Cliff seeks George Spahn (Bruce Dern), the owner, to make sure he is okay, as the ranch has been taken over by a hippie commune, whom we, the audience, recognize as the Manson family. Cliff disappoints and embarrasses Pussycat with his insistence on seeing George, and she and all the hippies view him suspiciously. When one hippie slashes the Cadillac's tire, Cliff brutally beats him and forces him to fix it—prefiguring the film's violent end when Cliff and Rick dispatch the Manson family members who visit Rick's house instead of next-door neighbor Sharon Tate's in Tarantino's wish-fulfilling alternate history of the Manson murders.

The fictional Pussycat's hitchhiking has some basis in historical fact, as the Manson girls frequently hitchhiked and used hitchhiking as a recruiting tool.[1] But in addition to being a fictional stand-in for the world-historical Manson girls, Pussycat also functions partly like other aspects of the late 1960s and early 1970s that populate the film's soundtrack and mise-en-scène—such as music by Paul Revere and the Raiders and Deep Purple, wood-paneled walls, shag carpets, rooftop TV antennas, reel-to-reels, miniskirts, *Mad Magazine,* the Playboy Mansion, and a range of Volkswagens, including a van, a Beetle, and a Karmann Ghia—as a nostalgic icon of a bygone period when hitchhiking, and especially young female hitchhikers, were briefly at the cultural forefront. As the nostalgic website *Flashbak* describes it in "The Hitchhiking Craze: When Women Thumbed a Ride," hitchhiking was a "highly popular means of transport for girls in the hippy era," yet the image of the female hitchhiker indexes a seemingly more innocent and trusting time: "The idea of a female hopping into a random stranger's car is so foreign to today, that it almost seems impossible that a world existed where this was actually a thing."[2]

The female hitchhiker in Tarantino's film not only denotes the real practice of hitchhiking among young women, especially underage runaways, but also conjures a crucial cinematic trope. Pussycat resembles the multitude of hitchhiking hippie girls who populated movie screens in the late 1960s and early 1970s in films inspired by "the hitchhiking craze" among women. Fans and critics have documented many of the film references built into *Once Upon a Time... in Hollywood,* including, among many others, the films *The Wrecking Crew* (Karlson 1968) and *Valley of the Dolls* (Robson 1967), featuring the real-life actress Sharon Tate played by Margot Robbie in the film;[3] films representing the acting career of the fictional character Rick Dalton, including spaghetti westerns such as *Savage Gringo,* a.k.a. *Nebraska Jim* (Román 1966), TV westerns such as *Lancer* (1968–70), and the Steve McQueen vehicle *The Great Escape* (Sturges 1963), reimagined with Dalton in the lead; the countercultural biker film *Easy Rider* (Hopper 1969) as signaling the New American cinema; and the grindhouse biker film *C.C. & Company* (Robbie 1970), along with Tarantino's own tribute to grindhouse, *Death Proof* (2007), both marking the broader context of low-budget independent cinema of the time. Along with these explicit references, of course, *Once Upon a Time... in Hollywood* additionally seeks to evoke the cinema of the late 1960s and early 1970s via the careful selection of camera, lenses, and film stock to evoke a 1970s retro feel for the narrative, as well as recreating a 1950s black-and-white TV aesthetic for Dalton's past TV series, and other fictionalized TV shows and films.[4] Additionally, the film contains "colorful nods to grindhouse culture" such as the "staggering and brutal," "outlandish, cartoonish, and juvenile" culminating violence of the film, taken as evincing Tarantino's penchant for the over-the-top aesthetics of exploitation cinema—and rightfully castigated for its misogyny and "obscenely regressive" celebration of white male power.[5]

With Tarantino's particular auteurist imprimatur as an especially knowledgeable fan of B movies and grindhouse cinema, it is notable that neither he nor his fans acknowledge the cycle of hitchhiking films that may have influenced his depiction of Pussycat in *Once Upon a Time... in Hollywood,* focusing instead on more masculinist westerns and biker films.[6] Yet the plotline centered on Pussycat certainly summons such exploitation pictures as *The Hitchhikers* (Sebastians 1972)—a narrative clearly modeled on the Manson story, in which a runaway white female hitchhiker joins a commune led by a charismatic white man who uses sexy female hitchhikers to lure and rob men—as well as numerous other low-budget exploitation pics about dangerous, sexually aggressive young white female runaways, such as *Little Miss Innocence* (Warfield 1973) and *Teenage Hitchhikers* (Sedley 1974). In her flirtation with Cliff Booth, Pussycat also invokes more mainstream studio films such as *Breezy* (Eastwood 1973) or *Ginger in the Morning* (Wiles 1974), in which a hitchhiking hippie girl meets and loosens up a staid middle-aged man.

True, the 1969 setting of *Once Upon a Time... in Hollywood* slightly predates the bulk of the female hitchhiking cycle that is most densely populated between 1970 and 1974, but Tarantino and his cinematographer Robert Richardson have cited cinematic influences that extend beyond the immediate temporal setting of the film, including those that predate that setting by a wide margin, such as *Gunman's Walk* (Karlson 1958) and *Battle of the Coral Sea* (Wendkos 1959), and those that postdate it somewhat, including *Getting Straight* (Rush 1970), *Evel Knievel* (Chomsky 1970), and *The Exorcist* (Friedkin 1973).[7] Given that the female hitchhiker was the subject of earlier titillating exploitation films such as *Highway Hell*, a.k.a. *Hitchhike to Hell* (Carlyle 1937), and *Live Fast Die Young* (Henreid 1958), as well as numerous early 1970s films—including TV movies, drive-in films, studio pictures, and low-budget independents—the omission from the pantheon of references is striking.

Tarantino and his fans and critics are not alone in their neglect of female hitchhiking films. When most people think of mobility and placelessness in the late 1960s and early 1970s, they think of films like *Easy Rider*, *Vanishing Point* (Sarafian 1971), and *Two-Lane Blacktop* (Hellman 1971). All of these include at least some attention to hitchhiking, but the focus of the films and the discourse around them tend to emphasize masculinist fantasies of freedom and existential crisis. In *Easy Rider*, the male hitchhiker (Luke Askew) leads Wyatt (Peter Fonda) and Billy (Dennis Hopper) to the commune and fantasies of free love. In *Vanishing Point*, the gay male hitchhikers (Anthony James and Arthur Mallet) are little more than a homophobic footnote in the narrative. The female hitchhiker has a more substantive role in *Two-Lane Blacktop*, but where the male characters in the film are all tagged by their relation to cars—Driver (James Taylor), Mechanic (Dennis Wilson), and GTO (Warren Oates)—the hitchhiker is defined only by gender, as the Girl (Laurie Bird). She is passenger, not driver, within the narrative's competition among men. More, the hitchhikers disappear from these narratives before the male drivers face their bleak (presumed) deaths in the films' endings. To be sure, these films are crucial touchstones for a consideration of countercultural mobility. But in focusing on these masculine-centered films, while ignoring the female hitchhiking films, we not only fail to understand broader conceptions of the road and countercultural travel in the late 1960s and early 1970s, but we also obscure—once again—both the reality and representations of female mobility. Similarly, when critics discuss youth cinema of the period, these films about young runaways and female hitchhikers are never mentioned, even in instances when critics seek to expand the conception of what "counts" as youth cinema.[8] Largely viewed as a period lacking almost any youth film—save the nostalgic *American Graffiti* (Lucas 1973), set in the early 1960s—let alone films focused on girls, this critical lacuna about the early 1970s negates the place (or rather placelessness) of young countercultural women who were quite prominently represented, but who do not fit most conceptions of youth or youth film.

In the opposite direction, when scholars acknowledge hitchhiking in films, they mention 1930s comedic treatments such as *It Happened One Night* (Capra 1934), the smaller midcentury film noir cycle of films about male hitchhikers such as *Detour* (Ulmer 1945) and *The Hitch-Hiker* (Lupino 1953), or the late posthitchhiking film *The Hitcher* (Harmon 1986), without mentioning the early 1970s cycle at all. This is partly a question of the self-perpetuating film studies canon, which favors film noir over both female-centered and youth-driven films, and partly the result of a process of historical forgetting and marginalization that perpetually elides the presence of women so that we consider their presence unlikely or counterfactual.

The lack of attention to hitchhiking in film is not just a failure of the canon but a reflection of a broader dismissal of hitchhiking as a largely forgotten fad. Hitchhiking, however, has a much more complex history that, in itself, shows changing attitudes toward mobility related to changing ideals of car culture, shared sacrifice, patriotism, gender, race, and more. Moreover, in both its practice and its filmic representation, hitchhiking represents a once-important cultural dominant that offers an alternative model of mobility and placelessness. Rather than only a means of getting from point A to point B, hitchhiking was, for a time, a crucial mode of travel and lifestyle for a generationally defined counterculture who were mobile and deliberately unhomed. This practice hearkens back to but differs from tramping, and it prefigures in many ways the countercultural aspects of #vanlife I discussed in my introduction and the generational unsettling that I will discuss in the epilogue.

This chapter will consider the hitchhiker, especially the young female hitchhiker, as a crucial emblem of mobility and placelessness. I will trace the history of hitchhiking in America and changing attitudes toward the risk and pleasures of hitchhiking as it shifts from a mode of commuting and adventure tourism to countercultural lifestyle, especially as the number of women hitchhikers dramatically increases from the late 1960s forward. I will consider earlier representations of hitchhiking in film as they negotiate contemporary attitudes toward hitchhiking, including minor instances of hitchhiking in 1930s films that mainly gender hitchhiking female and comedically link hitchhiking to sexuality. I will attend especially to the film noir cycle of films that tap into a moral panic about masculinity, conjoining fears of the new interstate highway system, increased car ownership, and neoliberal individualism through the figure of the drifter and the sociopath. The gendering of the risks and threat of hitchhiking in these films will be contrasted with that of the 1970s female hitchhiking films, which yoke female hitchhiking not only to transgressive sexuality and criminality but also to freedom, stitching together anxieties related to the counterculture, voluntary precarity, runaway youth, and women's liberation. In addition, I will claim these films as youth films, suggesting that their absence indicates a broader inability to reconcile countercultural girls with the conception of young women in discussions of youth film.

In part, acknowledging this 1970s cycle of films fills in numerous gaps in film history to broaden the conception of countercultural representation, female-centered narratives, and youth film. Crucially, recognizing these films also enlarges our understanding of women's liberation to more fully include narratives of young women and teens who push back against conventional gender roles, sexual roles, and domesticity. While not always explicitly framed within feminist discourse, and often offering contradictory and troubling views of rape and sexual exchange, these films stake a claim for female mobility against security and stability, as a possible form of resistance. As my epigraph from Milan Kundera's short story "The Hitchhiking Game" suggests, the female hitchhiker in this brief but intense cycle of films intimated the possibility, however tenuous and temporary, of extraordinary freedom—freedom not as a destination but "as a practice, full of intervals and regressions," as Parul Sehgal puts it in a different context—and, at the same time, she disclosed a moral panic engendered by the seeming threat of young women running away from home, asserting their sexual freedom, and claiming their right to the road.[9]

FROM FRIVOLITY TO CIVIC DUTY

As with other modes of mobility, views on hitchhiking in the United States vary at different points in time and for different populations of travelers.[10] At certain points, hitchhiking is accepted as an economic necessity or thrifty mode of travel, a harmless form of adventure for youth, a safe mode of commuting—even for children—in cities with few transit options, a patriotic good deed to servicemen and defense workers under conditions of rationing, or "even an underground railway for runaways trying to escape unlivable conditions."[11] At other times, more sinister views predominate, and hitchhiking is deemed unnecessarily risky to hitchers and drivers, "the road to rape and murder," as one 1970s guidebook frames it.[12] While it is initially considered a mode of touristic travel, or convenient for short hops across town, hitchhiking eventually becomes associated with a countercultural, if not deviant, lifestyle, less about the getting from here to there than about the practice.

Hitchhiking needs to be understood in tandem with automobility and the changing dynamics of car culture in America. As hitchhiking occasions "a voluntary agreement between pedestrian and driver," it depends on feelings of trust, willingness to share, and an openness to contact, all of which are impacted by the expanding demographics of car ownership and changing conceptions of individualism and privacy.[13] Of course, changing opinions about hitchhiking are animated by "conceptions of gender, race, and class" that inform "categories regarding who belonged in public space and who had access to various forms of mobility" and are "a culturally constructed means of separating the desirable from the undesirable, whether people, activities or cultural objects."[14] As Jeremy Packer observes, there is "no necessary correspondence between the statistically determined relative risk of hitchhiking... and the extent of media coverage, the level of social concern, and the degree of governmental response" this practice received.[15] Instead, the cultural, economic, and political context determined the degree of concern at any given point.

According to the *Oxford English Dictionary*, the first use of the word *hitchhike* defined as "to travel by means of lifts in vehicles" is from 1923 in *The Nation*.[16] Hitchhiking only begins in the 1920s, once Henry Ford's assembly-line mass production made cars more accessible and affordable. First produced in 1908, there were fifteen million Ford Model T cars on the road before Ford stopped production in 1927; and, by the end of the decade, there were twenty-three million registered drivers. As Jack Reid notes in his history of hitchhiking, white male college students made up the largest population of hitchhikers in the 1920s.[17] Students hitchhiked for vacation travel, and they associated hitchhiking with "thrift, exploration, and the opportunity to meet other people."[18] Viewed in large part as a fad and a "frivolous hobby for affluent youth," hitchhiking was also popular with children going to beaches and playgrounds.[19] Women hitchhiked, too, ignoring social norms and appreciating hitchhiking for the adventure, autonomy, and spontaneity.[20]

Linked to the freedom of flapper culture, hitchhiking provided women with "an escape from the domestic expectations of 1920s womanhood."[21]

If hitchhiking was viewed largely as a recreational fad in the 1920s, the Great Depression made hitchhiking more an economic necessity and, therefore, more widely available and more broadly socially acceptable as a practice. In Packer's schematic of perceptions of hitchhiking, the Depression engenders the "civic Samaritan" phase of hitchhiking, a time when hitchhiking was primarily performed out of economic need and "picking up an out-of-work traveler or family was seen as providing a needed hand to the many who were suffering a worse fate than one's own."[22]

Of course, this sympathetic acceptance of hitchhiking was unevenly distributed. Hitchhikers were not the only itinerant poor on the road in the 1930s. As I discussed earlier, tramps constituted a large mobile population traveling mainly by rail, while migrant families motivated by Dustbowl economics were traveling primarily by automobile. So-called thumb waggers were sometimes migrants, but they sought to differentiate themselves from tramps and "shiftless wanderers," as they sought new opportunities for work or to improve their family's welfare.[23] Positive accounts of hitchhiking linked it to self-reliance, goal-oriented travel, and personal uplift; and hitchhikers were differentiated from tramps in media reports that emphasized that hitchhikers were clean, did not beg, and had not abjured the responsibilities of family and career.[24]

Despite a populist understanding of broad-based economic need, hitchhiking in the 1930s was still viewed through a gendered lens. Conservative estimates suggest that a quarter of a million women were transient in the mid-1930s, and many of these women opted to hitchhike because they could not afford to own cars or ride buses or trains.[25] But the "civic Samaritan" did not necessarily view women as part of the deserving poor. As in the 1920s, female hitchhikers were seen as acting outside acceptable gender roles and were cast as aberrant. Rather than being viewed as able-bodied workers who could seek work to be self-supporting, women were told that they should relocate to live with, and off, male relatives—advice that betrays little understanding that living with relatives was not always a financially tenable, or safe, position.[26]

Views on hitchhiking were also framed by racial prejudice, in part because automobility itself was contoured by racism. African American car ownership increased between the two World Wars—as both an emblem of Black economic success and a practical tool for Black farmers—giving Black people access to greater mobility; but, as Mia Bay details, "racial power struggles played out on the road."[27] Black driving provoked resentment among whites, and Black drivers were expected to give deference to white drivers in a coded "racial right-of-way."[28] In the South, at least, parking was segregated, insurance for Black drivers was hard to come by, gas stations discriminated against Black drivers, and roadside sleeping accommodations were largely off-limits to Black travelers—hence the need for *The Negro Motorist Green Book* and other guides for Black travelers that helped African American tourists find accommodations and other amenities and services on the road.[29]

As Black drivers were constrained in myriad ways, Black and other minority hitchhikers could not rely on finding rides from nonwhite drivers. White drivers were still the majority of car owners and dominated the roads. Black hitchhikers were much less likely to secure a ride from a white driver and, when they did, were still subject to the racial hierarchy of the South—possibly offered rides in the back of a truck but not in the car of a white driver.[30] Black riders were also vulnerable on the road to attacks by the Ku Klux Klan and harassment by police.[31] Furthermore, the media portrayed Black hitchhikers less sympathetically than whites and paid heightened attention to criminality among nonwhite hitchhikers, promulgating a "concerted effort to keep drivers, assumed to be white, from offering lifts to racial minorities."[32]

GOING MY WAY, MISTER?

Hitchhiking is much less well-represented in film during the 1930s than either migrancy or tramps. Rather than a dominant narrative thread, hitchhiking appears as an incidental activity in just a few films. *Girls of the Road* (Grinde 1940), for example, discussed in chapter 1, shows women hitchhiking as one mode of transport, but that film's focus is less on hitchhiking per se than female tramps who also travel by bus, train, and walking. To different ends, John Steinbeck's 1939 novel *The Grapes of Wrath* and its 1940 film adaptation, directed by John Ford, start with Tom Joad (Henry Fonda) hitchhiking home to Oklahoma, having been paroled after serving four years of a seven-year sentence for homicidal self-defense.

Other representations are gendered female, and, while they tend toward the comedic, they nonetheless play off associations between female hitchhikers and sexuality. Famously, in *It Happened One Night*, Claudette Colbert's

FIGURE 3.1. "Going my way mister?" Hitchhiking as prostitution in *Highway Hell*, a.k.a. *Hitchhike to Hell*.

runaway bride Ellie Andrews proves her mettle when she bests Clark Gable's hard-boiled reporter Peter Warne's efforts at hitchhiking in a scene that links female hitchhiking to sexuality. Warne brags to Ellie about his thumb skills, saying he ought to write a book about it, and demonstrating various techniques and postures for signaling drivers; but when he tries them out, he fails to catch a ride, even as numerous cars whiz by. "You mind if I try?" Ellie asks. Saying she can stop a car without using her thumb, she lifts her skirt to show some leg, and we see a car screeching to a halt as she secures a ride. While this scene authenticates the heiress Ellie—as she has left the rarified world of yachts and is able to master a mode of travel associated with economy and thrift—it also makes female hitchhiking seem like a sexual exchange. Thus, it plays into both the civic Samaritan model and concerns about women's mobility.

While *It Happened One Night* offers a comedic view that largely fits the civic Samaritan model in treating hitchhiking as safe and thrifty, the exploitation film *Highway Hell* links female hitchhiking more squarely with prostitution. The film's opening credits show a sequence of five white women in direct address, each flourishing her thumb as she asks, "Going my way, Mister?" (fig. 3.1). Following this, a police bulletin announces that "crime and vice may often take the guise of an innocent hitchhiker" and labels "Going my way, Mister?" a "dangerous call." The narrative shows the women working for a pimp who drops them off at intervals every three hundred feet along the highway, where they are meant to solicit rides and then bring the drivers to rented cabins for paid sex. This narrative suggests both that girls who hitchhike are susceptible to being trafficked by pimps and that girls who hitchhike may be dangerous seductresses who will steal men's money. This narrative works against the more positive representations of hitchhiking as civic duty to emphasize the risk and dangers of it and, especially, to cast aspersions on women hitchhikers as morally suspect and, in a manner typical of exploitation cinema, to moralize while it titillates.

FROM PATRIOTISM TO PATHOLOGY

During World War II, the ethos of the civic Samaritan is sutured to patriotism.[33] In August 1941, President Roosevelt's Executive Order 8875 created the Office of Price Administration (OPA). After the attack on Pearl Harbor, the OPA's main responsibility was to place a ceiling on prices of most goods and to limit consumption by rationing, setting limits on the purchase of certain high-demand items, such as sugar. Along with this, the War Production Board (WPB) worked to prohibit nonessential production, convert industries from peacetime work to war needs, and allocate scarce materials. As Japanese control of the Dutch East Indies (now Indonesia) led to a shortage of rubber in the United States, tires were rationed starting in January 1942, so everyday consumers could not purchase new tires and, thus, drove less to preserve them. In January 1942, the WPB ordered the end of all civilian automobile sales, and in February 1942, car manufacturers converted their factories to the manufacture of jeeps, tanks, and ambulances. Gasoline began to be rationed in May 1942, so even those with cars needed to limit travel. As a result of these policies, Americans drove less, carpooled more, took public transportation, and walked. In this context, hitchhiking—and picking up hitchhikers—was deemed not only acceptable but part of the larger homefront war effort.

During World War II, the most dominant image and privileged case of the hitchhiker became the American serviceman, who would hitch back and forth between base and home when given leave. So common was hitchhiking among servicemen that the War and Navy Departments created a workaround for servicemen in relation to various states' antihitchhiking laws, specifically permitting men in the armed forces to accept rides, although they were banned from using their thumbs to attract those rides. To avoid thumbing a ride, servicemen would walk facing traffic or stand by the side of the road and hope someone would stop to offer a ride. To accommodate military hitchhikers, some towns built special shelters where servicemen could gather to hitch rides without using their thumbs.[34] While most hitchhikers were still white, the privileging of servicemen produced a somewhat "more racially inclusive hitchhiking identity than previous decades."[35]

Women's wartime hitchhiking was also regarded through the lens of patriotism. As the *New York Times* noted in December 1942, "Emily Post Gives the Nod to Hitch-Hiking and Frames the Rules for 'Defense Debutantes'": "Hitch-hiking now has Emily Post's approval if (and of course there is an if) it's a woman war worker thumbing a ride from a gentleman motorist—if the gentleman motorist has any gasoline!"[36] In a letter to the Regional News Bureau of the Office of War Information, Post commended women defense workers for their patriotism in working and securing rides to work. She offered revised etiquette rules for "defense debutantes," such as using their defense identification tags rather than a thumb to signal rides; to only travel with other defense workers driving cars with approved rationing stickers; to try and travel with two or more girls; and to avoid any personal or work-related conversation, to protect one's own privacy and classified information alike.

Despite this early 1940s approval for hitchhiking, following World War II, hitchhiking became newly disreputable, more than at any other time before. A number of factors contributed to hitchhiking's newly negative image.[37] First, rationing and controls on production eased and the OPA and WPB were abolished. With rations lifted and manufacturing reoriented to civilian consumers, car ownership multiplied. Increased affluence and minimal unemployment made people less likely to feel a sense of shared purpose or sympathy for those without cars. More privatized transportation options made people more isolated, less likely, and then less willing, to open the private space of their car to strangers. Cold War tensions further pushed people to see cooperative behaviors such as ride-sharing as communistic. As Ginger Strand argues, fears of hitchhiking are partly linked to the development of the interstate highway as a new unknown arena of mobility.[38] The development of major highways such as the New Jersey Turnpike and passage of the 1956 Federal-Aid Highway Act (a.k.a. the National Interstate and Defense Highways Act) created controlled-access, high-speed expressways that made hitchhiking much more difficult. The new highways did not carry passengers through towns and cities; there were no intersections or lights; stopping a car at high speeds became harder and potentially dangerous. Police began cracking down on hitchhiking as a safety measure, and they limited hitchhikers to the safety of on-ramps.

While the late 1940s and early 1950s witnessed a significant reduction in hitchhiking, there were still those who chose to hitchhike.[39] College students hitchhiked home for the weekend; teens hitchhiked to school and for recreation; servicemen still hitchhiked home from their bases; and ethnic minorities, largely left out of the postwar economic boom, still hitchhiked out of economic necessity. In a different vein, during the Montgomery bus boycott of 1955–56, when African Americans protested to desegregate public transportation, hitchhiking, along with car pools and community taxi services, helped transport former bus riders across town.

On the whole, however, in this largely fallow period for hitchhiking, it came to be seen as inherently dangerous and risky in what Packer labels "The Homicidal Hitchhiker" phase.[40] While there had been crimes such as robbery, rape, and burglary associated with hitchhiking in the 1930s and early 1940s—with hitchhikers and drivers equally likely to be perceived as potential criminals—those crimes had been treated as isolated events. Now, however, rather than treat hitchhiking crimes as unfortunate events that were no more or less common than in other spheres of life—viewing hitchhiking as an activity requiring caution but not panic—hitchhiking came to be seen as something to be avoided altogether.

In the late 1950s, the Automobile Association of America launched an antihitchhiking campaign, "Thumbs Down on Thumbers," suggesting that ride solicitors might be felons or con men. FBI director J. Edgar Hoover wrote several articles decrying the practice of hitchhiking, and, under his aegis, the FBI launched the poster campaign "Death in Disguise," which featured a clean-cut young man standing by the side of the road as a car with a family slowed to pick him up, a skull superimposed over the image. "Don't pick up trouble," the ad warned. Suggesting that picking up hitchhikers was a "gamble" and "risk," the ad played on uncertainty about appearances: "Is he a happy vacationer or an escaping criminal—a pleasant companion or a sex maniac—a friendly traveler or a vicious murderer?"[41] In this period, the hitchhiker, more than the driver, was perceived as a danger, and drivers were deterred from picking them up.

"FATE STICKS OUT A FOOT TO TRIP YOU"

Despite the broad-based acceptance of hitchhiking during World War II, hitchhiking appears only rarely in films of the early 1940s, even in films about servicemen. As I mentioned in the last chapter, trains are the dominant mode of travel represented in films about servicemen, and servicemen are shown in cars driven by women they know, not hitchhiking. In tandem with the postwar suspicion of hitchhiking, however, a small number of films in the postwar era took up the figure of the hitchhiker. As a seemingly outmoded system of transportation by the end of the war, in film noir, hitchhiking figures not as an incidental activity—as in Depression-era films—but as emblematic of character. To a large degree, representations of hitchhiking in this period link the contingency and chance involved in hitchhiking to narratives of doomed fate or, in the parlance of the FBI, picking up trouble. As Mark Osteen suggests, the figure of the hitchhiker in films of this period not only challenges the symbolic power of the car as a commodity that marks its owner's status but also embodies "risk, the intrusion of chaos, and the fragility of postwar prosperity and security that automobiles represent."[42] In other words, by encroaching into the private space of the family car, the hitchhiker represents a challenge to ideals of autonomy, safety, and upward mobility.

A few girl hitchhikers play into the stereotype of the noir femme fatale, such as the doomed hitchhiker Christina (Cloris Leachman) in *Kiss Me Deadly* (Aldrich 1955) and the criminal Laurie (Peggy Cummins) in *Gun Crazy* (Lewis 1950). For the most part, however, the film noir cycle features criminal male hitchhikers. By most accounts, film noir's complex male figures disclose a crisis of masculinity engendered by the physical and psychological damage of World War II and the difficulty of reintegrating into civilian life, particularly the lingering, unresolved, marginalized effects plaguing veterans. In noir, male hitchhikers are placed in opposition to postwar ideals of hegemonic masculinity associated with marriage, domesticity, suburban life, breadwinning, and middle-class white-collar professional work.[43] Hitchhikers exemplify subordinate masculine types who are repressed in the cultural imaginary, such as working-class and transient men, or they are linked to psychopathology and crime that not only runs counter to but also threatens hegemonic masculinity.[44] They are perceived as, at best, drifters and, at worst, sociopaths.

In *The Postman Always Rings Twice* (Garnett 1946), Frank Chambers (John Garfield) is introduced as a societal anomaly, a drifter who bucks the standards of hegemonic masculinity. The film opens with a close-up of a sign reading "Man Wanted," then cuts to an establishing shot that shows the sign is posted at a combination gas station and roadside lunch stand as we hear Frank in voiceover: "It was on a side road outside of Los Angeles. I was hitchhiking from San Francisco to San Diego, I guess. A half hour earlier I'd thumbed a ride." As a car pulls up to the gas station, Frank exits the car's passenger seat and thanks the male driver. Indicating a difference in status between the two men, Frank wears an open collar, no tie, and no hat, whereas the driver, who we discover is the district attorney Kyle Sackett (Leon Ames), wears a more formal striped suit, hat, and tie. As Frank thanks him, Sackett complains, "But you broke off right in the middle of a sentence. Why do you keep looking for new places, new people, new ideas?" Rather than shirking work, Frank's mobility and indefiniteness—the "I guess" of his hitchhiking plans—suggest that he is seeking something: "Well, I never liked any job I had. Maybe the next one is the one I've always been looking for." Sackett values security. "Not worried about your future?" he asks. "I got plenty of time for that," Frank says, and, gesturing at the "Man Wanted" sign, says, "Besides, maybe my fortune starts right now." This exchange underscores the fate-driven narrative in which Frank's "fortune starts right now," as his stop at this lunch stand will lead him to commit adultery and murder, eventually leading to his execution, and also works to place Frank in opposition to the more conventional patriarchal masculinity embodied by Sackett, as one driven more by contingency than concerns over the future.

While Frank Chambers begins the film as a happy hitchhiker unconcerned about his future—a figure who, in a different genre or time period, might be linked to the romance of the road—his relationship with the married Cora Smith (Lana Turner) casts aspersions on hitchhiking as a lowly activity. When Frank and Cora fall in love, they first decide to run away together. Frank refuses to steal Cora's husband's car, applying both a moral and legal logic that indicates the heightened importance of car ownership: "Stealing a man's wife, that's nothing. Stealing his car, that's larceny." As Frank and Cora walk down the dusty road hitchhiking, Cora—impractically but glamorously dressed in white suit, white beret, and white high heels—dejectedly asks where they are going. Frank answers according to his openness to indeterminacy, "Anywhere." But, for Cora, "anywhere" means "back to the hash house" and a life without ambition. "I'm ashamed of standing out here begging for a ride that will take me right back where I started," she says, and declares that she doesn't want to start her life with Frank "like a couple of tramps." Here, Cora's ambition renders her a femme fatale who leads Frank to agree to murder her husband, homicide being viewed as a better option than hitchhiking insofar as it offers promise of social mobility.

Unlike *The Postman Always Rings Twice,* where hitchhiking indicates character through just two key moments, in *Detour,* hitching is more central to the narrative and its worldview, as well as to our understanding of the main character, Al Roberts (Tom Neal). The film's opening credits run over a rear-view image of the road as seen from a traveling car—a rearward look suggestive of the film's flashback structure, also providing a sense of running from something and, as Vivian Sobchack argues, an image filmed using obvious back projection that shows the receding road to be "a fabulation, a lie, a metaphoric stand-in for—and forestallment of—... real and present forward movement in space and time."[45] As the credits end, we see Al walking along the road, then in a car with a driver, arriving in Reno. Inside a diner in Reno, he meets a truck driver who, seeking companionship and conversation, offers him a ride. As portrayed by Tom Neal, whom Noah Isenberg describes as having a "preternatural capacity for sulking," Al peevishly rebuffs the driver and then becomes angry when he plays the song "I Can't Believe That You're in Love with Me" on the jukebox.[46] This initiates Al's subjective voiceover in which he describes losing his girlfriend, Sue (Claudia Drake), to her dreams of Hollywood—"I Can't Believe That You're in Love with Me" being their song—and then his venturing away from New York to join her. We see an image of a map with a star near New York City. This image zooms out and dissolves to a blur, indicating no clear destination or path, a map of indeterminacy rather than planning. Al catches a ride on a flatbed truck, and then we return to the image of the map, now with a shot of Al's legs walking superimposed over it, somewhere in Ohio. Al's voiceover makes clear that he hitchhikes only because he can't afford any other mode of travel, and he describes money as "the stuff you never have enough of, little green things with George Washington's picture that men slave for, commit crimes for ... the stuff that has caused more trouble in the world than anything else we ever invented, simply because there's too little of it." As we listen to Al discuss money, and his lack of it, we see a montage that alternates between images of Al as passenger in different vehicles and repeated images of him walking superimposed on the map, showing his progress across the country until he arrives somewhere West of Oklahoma. Here, as Al hitchhikes, an inverted negative shows him hitchhiking in the wrong direction, with traffic moving on the left side of the road (fig. 3.2). Probably a continuity error, the shot nonetheless underscores Al's unreliability and seeming aimlessness even as he presumably heads to Los Angeles.[47]

In contrast to *The Postman Always Rings Twice,* which initially allows for some sense of the romance of hitchhiking and the possibility that it might indicate a refusal to conform, rather than failure, *Detour* quickly locates hitchhiking as a last resort. Al's voiceover narration undercuts any romance associated with hitchhiking: "Ever done any hitchhiking? It's not much fun, believe me. Oh yeah, I know all about how it's an education and you get to

FIGURE 3.2. Al Roberts (Tom Neal), an unreliable and wayward hitchhiker in *Detour*.

meet a lot of people and all that. But me, from now on, I'll take my education in college or P.S. 62 or I'll send a dollar ninety-eight in stamps for ten easy lessons." Beyond discounting the merits of hitchhiking as an education, Al also warns against the dangers of the road: "Thumbing rides may save you bus fare, but it's dangerous. You never know what's in store for you when you hear the squeal of brakes." Then, ironically ascribing the danger to the driver's agency rather than his own, Al laments, "If only I'd known what I was getting into that day in Arizona." While Al seems to indicate that he suffered at the hands of the driver, this comment also must be read as part of his notoriously unreliable narration and what Robert Polito refers to as "the film's mastery of the nuances of subjective narration," for what happens that day is not Al himself being endangered but, instead, the death of the driver, Charles Haskell Jr (Edmund MacDonald), who dies mysteriously in his sleep while Al drives the car.[48] Al claims the death was accidental—perhaps related to pills Haskell was taking—but he furtively covers it up, hiding Haskell's body in some brush, and stealing his clothes, wallet, car, and identity as he does.

Isenberg reads *Detour* as a thematic exploration of "the lone wanderer" who "ambles about without a clear destination on a journey that places him completely at the mercy of others, subject to change and the contingencies of modern life," but Al considers his to be a story of cruel fate.[49] "That's life," he says. "Whichever way you turn, fate sticks out a foot to trip you." His emphasis on fate over either accident or agency underpins Al's unreliable narration, in which he admits no culpability but instead proffers a paranoid belief that nobody would believe the truth. In the film, contingency or fate puts Al in the sightlines of a femme fatale. As Al continues on his journey, now pretending to be Haskell, he meets a woman hitchhiker who knows Haskell. Earlier, Haskell had told Al that he got scratches on his hand from "the most dangerous animal on Earth, a woman." Evincing the misogynist view of female hitchhikers, Haskell explains, "You give a lift to a tomato, you expect her to be nice, don't you? After all, what kind of dame thumbs rides? Sunday school teacher?" When Al sees Vera (Ann Savage)—whom *Variety* described as "a tough girl of the roads"—hitchhiking, he picks her up and agrees to take her to LA.[50] After a while, she confronts him with the knowledge that she knows he is not Haskell and tries to force Al to continue posing as Haskell to get his inheritance. Ultimately, Al commits another "accidental" murder in a wildly unlikely scenario in which he strangles Vera with a phone cord from behind a locked door, as he yanks the phone cord away to prevent her from calling the police and she drunkenly wraps the cord around her own neck. With this murder, Al has to remain on the move permanently, unable to meet his girlfriend, Sue, in LA and unable to return to New York, moving without terminus until "someday a car will pick me up that I never thumbed," and the cops arrest him.

In *Detour*, hitchhiking not only initiates a series of encounters—unlucky or criminal, depending on how one views them—but also underscores what Isenberg calls "a pervasive sense of homelessness" that he links to the experience of exile, on the one hand, and a more general sense of dislocation engendered by the war, on the other. As Isenberg notes, *Detour* shows characters unmoored from any sense of home or rootedness, and he draws on German scholar Stefan Grissemann's "apt summation": "Ulmer hands over his characters to a labyrinth of bars, motel rooms and highway rest stops—to anonymous spaces that could be anywhere—or to a nowhere, a world for nothing and nobody . . . way stations, places of passage . . . without any proper home, without living or private quarters."[51] As this suggests, *Detour* occurs across a series of nonplaces that Dana Polan describes as the "new space of modernity" and "the new alienation of endless roads all looking the same."[52] In this sense, hitchhiking operates in the film not only to move Al from one part of the country to another but to indicate a deeper sense of rootlessness and drift.

While both *The Postman Always Rings Twice* and *Detour* stitch hitchhiking to narratives of transience and criminality, other films in the film noir cycle more clearly play on contemporary fears of highway menace and the potential danger of the stranger and use hitchhiking as the inciting incident. *The Devil Thumbs a Ride* (Feist 1947), *The Night Holds Terror* (Stone 1955), and *The Hitch-Hiker* hew closely to the FBI "Death in Disguise" scenario as a sadistic male hitchhiker gets picked up by an unwitting family man or, in the case of *The Hitch-Hiker*, pair of men.[53] These films not only place the hitchhiker in opposition to the family man but use the figure of the hitchhiker to place pressure on the sanctity of the family and the security of the patriarchy.

The Devil Thumbs a Ride shows an innocent man victimized by a brutal hitchhiker who kills two people and tries to frame the driver for the murders, whereas *The Night Holds Terror* more clearly proffers a "message" about the dangers of picking up hitchhikers. As Amanda Klein suggests, film cycles often exploit moral panics that are triggered by actual events. These moral panics allow film studios to "exploit contemporary concerns while also making claims to the educational value of their films."[54] *The Night Holds Terror* is a "ripped from the headlines" narrative based on the real-life kidnapping of an Edwards Air Force Base technician and the subsequent overnight encampment of three criminals in his home before they could get money from him in the morning. Typical of pseudo-educational exploitation films, *The Night Holds Terror* employs a "square-up" or prefatory statement that describes the topic as real.[55] A deep male voiceover intones, "In practically all important respects, this is a true story. Wherever possible, we have used the original locations and even the actual words spoken. It is the account of a family [images of the film family come into focus here], the Courtier family. There they are—Gene, Doris, and their two kids—who because of one of those split-second decisions learned that [as the title appears onscreen] *The Night Holds Terror*." After showing and naming the characters and actors, the voiceover warns, "What happened to the Courtiers could happen to you!" After the initial credits, a different voiceover, spoken by Jack Kelly as Gene Courtier, opens the narration. As we see Gene driving his car, his voiceover says that he was driving home from LA to Edwards Air Force Base. "I had a wonderful family and a good job. What more could a man ask for?" Then, underlining again the "split-second decision," he describes how a "quick impulsive decision" led him to pick up a lone male hitchhiker. After the hitchhiker forces him to stop, and two men in a second car join to rob him, Gene's voiceover reminds us of the risks of hitchhiking: "Why, why had I stopped to give that guy a lift? It was taking a chance. I knew that. Yet nearly everyone's picked up a hitchhiker at one time or another. Haven't you?"

Similar to *The Night Holds Terror*, *The Hitch-Hiker* opens with a square-up title asserting the film's educational value and real-world resonance. Over a still image of a man's legs standing on the side of a road, the sound of traffic roaring in the background, a title reads, "This is a true story of a man and a gun and a car. The gun belonged to the man. The car might have been yours—or that young couple across the aisle. What you will see in the next seventy minutes could have happened to you. For the facts are actual." Indeed, the film is based on William Cook, who engaged in a hitchhiking murder spree two years prior, killing six people in twenty-two days between Missouri and California, triggering a massive manhunt, before kidnapping two men on a hunting trip and forcing them to take him to Santa Rosalia, Mexico, where he was arrested.

A quick series of opening shots in *The Hitch-Hiker* establishes the pattern for a series of hitchhiking murders and sets up a chase for the murderous hitchhiker. Under the credits, we see a man walking on the side of the road, his head out of frame, his thumb lifting. We see a close-up of an Illinois license plate on a convertible that stops and, in a long shot, that car driving away with two men and a woman in it. As the credits pause, a close-up shows the front tire roll up on a dirt road; we pan left to see a man's feet step out of the car as the passenger door opens, and then we hear a woman's offscreen scream. We hear a gunshot and see the woman's purse, cigarettes, and a small gun fall out of the car. The man bends to pick up only the gun. The credits continue over the shot of the dirt road; then, after a title names Ida Lupino as the director, we see a flashlight search the area, showing the license plate, and then a policeman finding the two bodies in the car. Three spinning newspaper front pages evince responses to the crime: the first declares robbery a probable motive for the murder; the second announces a nationwide hunt for the man now referred to as the "Hitch-Hike Slayer" and identifies the suspect as an ex-convict named Emmett Myers (William Talman); and the third newspaper labels the crime as "Hitch-Hike Atrocities" and shows a picture of Myers under a heading "Be on the Lookout for This Man!" Then, we see the hitchhiker's shadow on the road; a car stops, and a male passenger opens the door to let in the hitchhiker (his face still out of frame). We cut to a low-level shot of the hitchhiker taking a wallet from one of two dead men on the ground and then getting into their car and driving off. Then, we cut to the two main protagonists of the film, Roy Collins (Edmund O'Brien) and Gilbert Bowen (Frank Lovejoy), as they drive along discussing their itinerary.

The male drivers in *The Devil Thumbs a Ride* and *The Night Holds Terror* are relatively blameless family men: they are away from their wives when they pick up the hitchhiker, but both are returning home—from a homosocial gathering in one case, from work in the other. In contrast, the men in *The Hitch-Hiker* are more blameworthy because they are wayward. On their way to the Chocolate Mountains in California to go hunting, Gilbert suggests

FIGURE 3.3. The sociopathic hitchhiker (William Talman) holds married men Roy (Edmund O'Brien) and Gil (Frank Lovejoy) hostage in *The Hitchhiker*.

that they turn South to go to San Felipe in Mexico instead. Roy then reminiscences about Florabelle, a showgirl both men knew at the Alhambra Club, and suggests that they stop at the iniquitous border town of Mexicali. Gil agrees, and he mentions that, aside from the war, this trip is the first time he has ever been away from his wife and children. With Gil asleep in the passenger seat, we see Roy cruise the Mexicali streets, which are densely populated with nightclubs, bars, and tourists. Hustlers approach the car and invite Roy to see a fan dance, and he tries unsuccessfully to wake Gil. Roy gives up and drives away, saying "San Felipe, here we come." Although the men have evaded a situation in which they might stray from their marriages, they have nonetheless drifted from their itinerary and now are neither at home nor where they are supposed to be. Of course, the next shot shows Myers's feet as he flags down Roy and Gil's car for a ride, then pulls a gun (fig. 3.3).

The Devil Thumbs a Ride, *The Night Holds Terror*, and *The Hitch-Hiker* are all in large part police procedurals that crosscut between scenes of the criminals and the police, showing the police investigating and closing in on the criminals. Unlike other noir films that show the police as ineffectual or corrupt, these films emphasize the role of smart and capable police using sophisticated technology to find criminals. In both *The Night Holds Terror* and *The Hitch-Hiker*, the police even manipulate the media to put out false reports on the radio so the criminals do not know their plans. This aligns the films with the FBI's antihitchhiking campaign as they scold drivers who take risks by picking up hitchhikers, render hitchhikers sociopaths, and show the police competently restoring order.

In distinction from more prestigious studio films of the 1930s, such as *It Happened One Night* and *The Grapes of Wrath*, this midcentury cycle of film noirs needs to be understood as consisting largely of B movies and low-budget independents that teeter on the edge of exploitation. As a relatively prestigious picture from MGM, *The Postman Always Rings Twice* is the outlier. Adapted from the well-regarded 1934 novel of the same name by James M. Cain, and following on the heels of Paramount's adaptation of Cain's *Double Indemnity* (Wilder 1944), it was a full feature-length major studio production budgeted for major stars and location shooting with a respectable studio director. Nonetheless, reviews described it as a B picture and as "a film that lends itself in every respect to dynamic exploitation."[56] More clearly a B picture, the sixty-eight-minute *Detour* was made at the short-lived Poverty Row studio Producer's Releasing Corp (PRC), which existed only from 1943 to 1946 and was nicknamed "Pretty Rotten Crap."[57] It was directed by Edgar Ulmer, a Viennese émigré who had bounced around Hollywood making "a string of pictures outside the studio system and far from Hollywood in nearly every respect" before landing at PRC, where he made numerous low-budget films across a wide range of genres.[58] *The Night Holds Terror* was distributed by Columbia but made by the independent Andrew L. Stone Productions. Reviews described it as "a good entry for the exploitation market" and an "expertly made low budget suspense movie."[59]

The Devil Thumbs a Ride and *The Hitch-Hiker* were both made at RKO when it was long past its heyday as one of the Big Five. RKO had shifted to mostly B movies, and especially film noir, in the 1940s, when it produced *The Devil Thumbs a Ride;* and it was operating under the turmoil of Howard Hughes's leadership in the 1950s when Hughes partnered with Lupino's independent production company The Filmmakers to make *The Hitch-Hiker* and four other films. Both *The Devil Thumbs a Ride* and *The Hitch-Hiker*, in their use of prefatory statements that assert the "factual" quality of their narratives, employ the tactics of exploitation cinema. Described in *Variety* as "a melodrama with exploitation values," the sixty-two-minute *The Devil Thumbs a Ride* was dismissed by critic John T. McManus as "really pretty cheap low-level stuff"; but, oddly, as "the lower half of a double-bill, it played alongside such innocuous fare" as Loretta Young in *The Farmer's Daughter* (Potter 1947) and *Love Laughs at Andy Hardy* (Goldbeck 1946).[60] Clocking in at seventy-one minutes, *The Hitch-Hiker* was second-billed with the gritty noir *Pickup on South Street* (Fuller 1953) and the short titillating film *The World's Most Beautiful Girls* (Hibbs 1953), featuring Miss Universe winners in provocative poses.

In referring to these films as exploitation, critics indicate a reliance on melodrama, sensation, action, and thrills more than they do a distinct cinematic practice. As Guy Barefoot reminds us, exploitation has been central to cinema all along, existing both "as a core element of Hollywood and an area of cinema that existed beyond Hollywood and even beyond Poverty Row."[61] Likewise, the B movie in the 1950s could be a studio film with a modest budget, a more ambitious film bidding for commercial or artistic success, or a "bad" cheapie aimed at the teen market.[62] These films are mostly Hollywood-adjacent, lower-budget films that play off contemporary fears about hitchhiking as part of a broader melodrama or thriller. The relatively low status of all these films—despite the critical and popular regard that *The Postman Always Rings Twice*, *Detour*, and *The Hitch-Hiker* now enjoy—harmonizes with the perceived lowliness of hitchhiking at this time, its relegation to the realm of criminals, and its distance from mainstream ideologies of family, privacy, and consumerism.

FROM BEATS TO FREAKS

Despite the attacks on hitchhiking from the FBI and the lurid film noir cycle about sociopathic hitchhikers, the postwar turn against hitchhiking did not last long.[63] In the early 1960s, hitchhiking was viewed more sympathetically again and especially closely affiliated with college-aged youth. Between 1960 and 1972, the college population tripled, from three million to ten million. Early 1960s college-aged students engaged in "sport hitchhiking" similar to the adventure-seeking youth of the 1920s, but the new breed of hitchhikers were inspired by the Beats, especially by Jack Kerouac's accounts of his own hitchhiking, as well as riding the rails and driving, in *On the Road* (1957) and *Dharma Bums* (1958).[64] As Gwyneth Cravens stated in 1972, "Jack Kerouac set off a time bomb in the Fifties: *On the Road* with Dean Moriarty and Sal Paradise zigzagging across the country in search of the great beatific scene, its people going off like Roman candles; *The Dharma Bums* with Japhy Ryder spinning out visions of the great Bhikkhu movement, the rucksack revolution."[65] Karen Staller describes the Beats as providing "an anthem to perpetual motion" that "modeled the image of American youth on the move."[66] Inspired by the Beats, hitchhikers were searching for authentic experience tied to ideals of spontaneity and freedom "in a culture increasingly regimented and risk averse" and participated in hitchhiking as a "rejection of mainstream norms."[67] This phase of hitchhiking, which Packer calls the "Romance of the Road," was characterized by "themes of freedom, adventure, escape, discovery, and community."[68]

As Abraham Miller notes, the early 1960s hitchhiker may be seeking authenticity, but his—and at this point the dominant hitchhiker is still a college-aged white male—hitchhiking functions largely as a time-out or detour from conformity rather than a wholesale rejection. In part, Miller argues, the early 1960s student hitchhiker partakes of a "romance with poverty" in which he "tends to view his adventure as a demonstration of his independence and his ability to survive at a minimum economic level by his wits and restraint," as well as a "quest for escape from the responsibilities and constraints of adulthood," despite the fact that he is technically preparing for adulthood by going to school.[69]

In the late 1960s, however, as youth culture becomes the counterculture, hitchhikers are less likely to be students seeking a temporary reprieve from the mainstream and more likely to be what Miller describes as "road people," hippies, or, in the lingo of the time, "freaks" with transplantable roots who have chosen an itinerant life, denying themselves security in favor of freedom.[70] The counterculture embraced hitchhiking as part of a subversive and communal lifestyle, with the sense of going as more important than the destination. Miller linked it to "a compelling need to live life intensely, to seek the heights of physical and mental experience, and to do it as if life itself were a fleeting opportunity."[71]

Broadly speaking, the counterculture that emerged in the late 1960s had as its "central essence and purpose" the "profound" desire to "create a new, freer, superior society based on an alternative culture, ideas, values, and institutions."[72] Predating hippies, the Beats foreshadowed the counterculture and offered a model for cultural dissent from the social order that embraced art over commerce, mobility over domesticity, and spontaneous authentic experience over "plastic" suburban lifestyles. But the Beats were generationally distinct from the late 1960s counterculture. The late 1960s hippies were defined by values of love, harmony, beauty, togetherness and community, environmental concerns, sexual liberation, Eastern religions and mysticism, and drug experimentation. While Kerouac experiments (especially in *Dharma Bums*) with Eastern religion and mysticism, the Beats were defined by the consumption of alcohol as opposed to dope, jazz as opposed to rock and roll, and a logic of marriage and adultery as opposed to free love. While the Beats offered a counter to the dominant, hippies marked a divide not only from "straight" America but also specifically from the older generation, which, by the late 1960s, included Beats such as Kerouac, who was forty-six in 1968 and died at age forty-seven from an abdominal hemorrhage associated with heavy drinking. As Cravens claims, more than a Beat or Whitmanesque mystique of the road, hitchhikers in the late 1960s and early 1970s were reacting to a generational divide and what they saw as the false promises of their parents: where the older generation told youth to work conscientiously and follow the straight path to be able to gain what their elders have (home, marriage, job), the hippies proclaimed that "what many of these elders had was emptiness."[73]

Benjamin Brazil situates hitchhiking amid a larger movement of youth travel "as a massive cultural fact and as a style of travel with distinctive practices, institutions, and moral logics" tied to "popular existentialism," which opposed the "free and authentic individual to modern social structures."[74] As Brazil notes, the larger culture of youth travel included van-dwelling and the development of youth-oriented travel guides such as Arthur Frommer's *Europe on $5 a Day*, which started in 1957, and the *Let's Go* series of travel guides, which were researched, written, and edited by students at Harvard starting in 1960. The new mode of youth travel emphasized traveling cheaply rather than as part of the mass tourist industry, choosing poverty as a form of authenticity, and embracing the language of liberation and self-transformation underpinning travel. The backpack was a crucial symbol of this new conception of youthful existentialist travel. As Damon Bach writes, "in contrast to the suitcase, which usually marked a temporary traveler with a permanent home, the backpack represented 'transience and unfettered spirit'" and implied that you were an "adventurous traveler."[75]

The countercultural travel writer Ed Buryn, author of a series of "Vagabonding" books (half a dozen titles with multiple revisions) that were premised on the idea that "meaningful travel required genuine encounters with other human beings," articulates the difference between this "popular existentialist" travel and conventional tourism:[76]

> Travel is not just moving over the earth from one place to another in some kind of conveyance. It's not about where you're going or how you're getting there. It's not about getting away from it all, at all. In fact, more the opposite . . . [it is] a way of getting to it all. Travel is a metaphor for life. By that I mean travel is a dramatization of life, a way of experiencing it more intensely and self-consciously. Traveling is not so much an action as an enlightened state of consciousness, opening you to fresh experience, to [a] fresh look at the world and yourself in it.[77]

Conventional tourism was viewed as being an "adjunct of mass society."[78] Buryn, for example, says that the tourist industry "corresponds in its own modest way to the military-industrial complex" as a system of chain hotels, motels, restaurants, airlines, and travel agencies, with interlocking synergistic businesses "offering profit-prompted tours and packages, setting phony standards of taste and popularity, employing advertising budget outlays that equal the gross national product of dozens of foreign countries." By contrast, the "vagabond" or hippie is "someone not entangled in travel arrangements," someone who travels light "because 'things' rob you of firsthand experience," someone who books details of his trip with "an agent called Chance" and pays for travel with "pocket money instead of bank loans."[79] Chance here is not the fatalistic accident of film noir, where chance encounters led to danger and even murder. Rather, chance is celebrated as contingency, authenticity, and the opportunity for encounter.

Hitchhiking was central to this conception of travel. Hitchhiking engendered its own boom in travel publications with at least ten guides to hitchhiking published in the US between 1969 and 1973, including Buryn's Vagabonding books, Paul DiMaggio's *The Hitchhiker's Field Manual,* Tom Grimm's *Hitchhiker's Handbook,* Ben Lobo and Sara Links's *Side of the Road: A Hitchhiker's Guide to the United States,* and Phil Wernig's *The Hitchhikers,* as well as Patricia Valian's sensationalist *Hitchhiking: The Road to Rape and Murder.* Giving a sense of how ubiquitous the figure of the hitchhiker was, in 1972 Wernig claimed, "You never have to drive very far to find a hitchhiker. If you are in a city, chances are there is someone within a few blocks, standing on a corner, thumb out over the curb. If you are in the country, you need only find the nearest interstate highway to notice someone sitting on his pack on the shoulder of the road, waiting for the nod that means the next ride to the coast."[80]

Hitchhiking in the late 1960s and early 1970s was viewed in starkly generational terms. As Miller wrote, distinguishing hippie hitchhiking from that of earlier modes of youthful hitchhiking, "no generation has taken to the road in such large numbers or with such deliberate purpose as the current generation of young people."[81] Ben Lobo and Sara Links noted that while the road was always "the recurrent destiny of the dispossessed, the avenue of social dislocation, turf of the jobless, homeless, propertyless, destitute" and "did provide an alternative to the legitimized social order" for those people, "we are the first generation to voluntarily place ourselves adrift, *en masse,* on the roads of America."[82] Tom Grimm agreed: "What the present generation is doing with this mode of travel is what they seem to have done with much else in the subculture.—done it *en masse* and done it more openly than ever before."[83]

Hitchhiking was viewed as a means of distinguishing the ideals of the hippies from those of their parents. As Reid says, hippies "found the practice appealing because it fostered a life of unrestrained mobility" that proved the opposite of their parents' more rooted and "square" lifestyles: "Freaks viewed this freedom as a key component of breaking away from the square responsibilities of work schedules and family life that moored many adults to what young people understood to be unhappy, repressive existences."[84] In 1974, the sociologist Walter F. Weiss approached hitchhiking from a conservative religious viewpoint; and he, too, saw hitchhikers as rejecting their parents' values, though he viewed the rejection as fear-driven rather than as critical. He described hitchhikers as "running away from that which they consider unpleasant.... They are afraid to establish roots, to be successful, to join the establishment."[85] Where Weiss hoped that hitchhiking would eventually lead youth to discover "the meaning of home," most hitchhiking guides considered hitchhiking to be emancipatory from all domestic ties.[86] Lobo and Links, for example, identified themselves as the "mobile army of outlaw culture" who had left bonds to home behind: "We who live on the road are conscious of the gulf that separates us from those who stay behind. We think of ourselves as being apart from a mainstream, as, in a sense, we are. We have broken the bonds, sometimes the binds, which once held us, and now we find ourselves far out onto an infinite range of possibilities. It is the newfound freedom we have always celebrated as myth. Road freedom."[87] Hitchhiking, by this account, is less about a convenient and inexpensive ride than it is about rejecting mainstream lifestyles and embracing freedom.

While countercultural hitchhiking was partly tied to ecological concerns, and the cost of maintaining a car, more than anything it was tied to ideals of mobility: "Hitchhiking—with its promise of free, untethered, and spontaneous mobility—offered youths of the time the ability to maintain a largely nomadic existence while living out the values of the hippie (or freak, as many self-identified) lifestyle."[88] The freak lifestyle emphasized having contact with people, as well as spontaneity and contingency, understood as freedom. As Paul DiMaggio wrote, "Hitchhiking throws people together in an unstructured setting with the knowledge that, after the episode's completion, they will never see one another again. This provides a kind of intensity and freedom rare in our modern society."[89]

Hitchhiking's affiliation with the counterculture led to increased policing. While there were no federal laws against hitchhiking, states and counties set their own laws and could ignite temporary crackdowns for any number of reasons. Many of these laws and crackdowns seemed geared toward giving police an excuse to question travelers or regulate perceived vagrancy. Because police had a great deal of latitude in deciding when to enforce antihitchhiking laws, hippies ascertained that "what's illegal may not be what you've done but who you are and what you represent"—namely, freaks.[90] As Lobo and Links state, "In its freest form, youth culture is illegal and even if you've broken no law, they'll invent a way to put you away."[91] Law enforcement agencies and municipalities began to use the excuse of highway safety to "reign in the countercultural movement by strictly regulating one of its primary forms of mobility—hitchhiking."[92] Nearly all hitchhiking guides provide full chapters on how to deal with differing hitchhiking laws and how to avoid contact with the police, including not carrying dope, staying on the shoulder of the road, carrying identification, and being polite.

In many ways, including the efforts to police a mobile population, the discourse on hitchhiking in the late 1960s and early 1970s echoes that of early twentieth-century tramp culture, and hitchhikers were sometimes linked to hoboes as figures feared for their placelessness.[93] But the discourse on and by hitchhikers sought to differentiate hitchhikers from vagrants and tramps. Crucially, hitchhikers are not generally linked to charity or begging. As Schlebecker writes, "Unlike knights of the road, the hiker wanted only transportation."[94] Brazil points out that despite the romance with poverty among hippie hitchhikers, hitchhiking travel guides tended to assume that their readers were middle-class, educated, and hitchhikers by choice, not necessity.[95] Making clear the perceived generational distinction between youthful hitchhikers and tramps, Grimm warns hitchhikers not to hitch with vagrants whom he describes as older looking dirty men.[96] In the other direction, DiMaggio suggests that the small but persistent class of contemporary hoboes were hostile toward hitchhikers and considered hitchhiking to be faddish, believing that hitchhikers could not survive an itinerant lifestyle for the long haul, as tramps did.[97]

FEMALE RUNAWAYS

Perhaps the biggest difference between countercultural hitchhikers and hoboes was that whereas tramps were largely single adult men, hitchhikers included a large population of young women and girls. According to Reid, one-quarter of all hitchhikers in the late 1960s and early 1970s were women.[98] Among female hitchhikers, many were runaways. Hitchhiking guides routinely set aside space dedicated to women's hitchhiking and runaways, and, as I will discuss, literature and film places strong emphasis on the image of the runaway female hitchhiker.

In the late 1960s and early 1970s, running away was framed as a large-scale social problem. In 1974, Congress enacted the "Runaway Youth Act," recognizing a stand-alone population of runaway children deserving of policy intervention. According to Staller, although there had been wayward youth for decades, the problem seemed especially acute in the early 1970s.[99] In part, Staller argues, the sense of crisis around runaways was because the baby boomers constituted an enormous dominant demographic of teenagers and young adults, ranging in age from ten to twenty-eight in 1974, that drew attention to youthful home-leaving.

Seemingly overnight, the nature and understanding of running away underwent a significant shift in the late 1960s. Earlier in that decade, running away was seen as a safe, harmless, even relatively predictable activity, lasting for a few days at most, and mainly undertaken by boys seeking innocent adventure at an attraction such as a rodeo or World's Fair.[100] But in the late 1960s and 1970s, there was more emphasis on girls leaving and staying away from home, "running *away* from home, rather than being lured toward an attraction."[101] In 1969, some five hundred thousand children and teens under the age of seventeen and another five hundred thousand between the ages of seventeen and twenty-one left home, and by 1971 half of these runaways were girls, with numbers rising.[102] Instead of short-term local male runaways, long-distance and long-term female runaways became the dominant image.

Most of these runaways ended up as part of the counterculture. By one estimate, during its height, from 1970 to 1972, the counterculture included an estimated half million runaway teens.[103] Sites such as Haight-Ashbury in San Francisco became a haven for runaways starting back in 1967, when advertisements for the Summer of Love hyped the idea of traveling to San Francisco.[104] In the context of the Summer of Love, there was a perceived mass migration of teens to San Francisco and a new population of would-be or part-time hippies; however, the part-time or seasonal hippies did not leave but assimilated, as they found crash pads and free food to sustain them long term. As runaways joined the counterculture, it became harder to differentiate runaways from hippies: "Children who were once deemed easily recognizable by appearance now blended in with the disheveled, hairy hippie crowd."[105] This made it harder to differentiate runaways from other kinds of countercultural "dropouts" who "attempted to live on the fringes of mainstream society as much as possible; [and] included drifters, some communards in rural areas, runaways, and itinerant street people."[106]

Runaways were attracted to the counterculture as an alternative to both familial abuse and what they perceived as false values at home. Lillian Ambrosino notes that among common reasons for running away were parental divorce, alcoholism of parents, harsh rules or expectations, and parents who "don't understand."[107] As with the hippie, the runaway often claimed to be leaving the "hypocrisy of his household or society" to search for "the warmth, integrity, and meaning he has been led to believe thrives within communities or among groups of flower folks who have also turned to the city for renewal."[108] Runaways were drawn to hippies by the "utopian suggestion that an ideal kind of family could be acquired by conscious choice rather than by biological chance."[109] For Lobo and Links, running away attested to the generation gap and showed youth's alienation from conformist ideals: "Splitting home is one way kids turn off to a system that offers school, Army, or jail as the range of potential alternatives. America's young aren't relating to Mickey Mantle or some spaceman anymore. The Huck Finn type of mischief pales beside the adventurism and romanticism of a Mick Jagger, the strength and power of a Bernadine Dohrn."[110]

FEMALE HITCHHIKING AND/AS WOMEN'S LIBERATION

The figure of the female runaway and the figure of the female hippie are largely collapsed in both reality and the cultural imaginary. But where the runaway is usually viewed as running away from home to escape something bad, the female hitchhiker is widely seen as seeking freedom. These are not contradictory impulses, however, just questions of emphasis on why she leaves and what she seeks instead.

Most recent analyses view young women's hitchhiking as a feminist political act, seeking freedom from traditional sex and gender roles. For example, Reid argues: "Second wave feminists viewed uncompromising mobility as a critical component of their liberation. In this way, hitchhiking, long perceived as a male activity, became a politicized act among young women that presented opportunities for personal freedom, self-exploration, and romanticized adventure."[111] Contemporaneous accounts also linked female hitchhiking to women's liberation. Grimm argues, for example, that women's liberation inspires hitchhiking among women as a way for women to claim literal and figurative space.[112] Valian, who warns of the dangers of hitchhiking for women and views women as "the rub in the hitchhiking scene," argues that women are "caught between the crossfire of Madison Ave and women's liberation," both of which, she suggests, promulgate false fantasies of freedom. On the one hand, she links women's liberation to a "rejection of cherished sexual roles" that leads women to hitchhike and puts them in danger; on the other hand, she herself speaks from within feminist discourse when she notes the failure of the justice system regarding rape, in a tendency to blame the victim.[113]

While hitchhiking guidebooks promote hitchhiking among women and link it to women's liberation, they also acknowledge that hitchhiking still often subjects women to sexual harassment and rape. The discourse on female runaways from 1967 forward strongly views them as subject to sexual exploitation, trafficking, and prostitution.[114] Male drivers assumed that female hitchhikers were open to sexual advances owing to "sexism, long-held assumptions about lone women on the road, and misguided interpretations of hippie free love."[115] The famous slogan "Gas, Ass, or Grass: Nobody Rides for Free" marks a common currency for hitchhiking hippies; and, while both gay male cruising and gay sexual abuse exist on the road, the exchange of "ass," or sexual favors for rides, stereotypically targets women hitchers.

Underscoring the tension between the promise of liberation available to female hitchhikers and the discriminatory reality of rape and sexual harassment, contemporary accounts frame their discussions of women's abuse within feminist discourse. Lobo and Links, for example, somewhat surprisingly anchor their discussion of female hitchhikers with an epigraph from Emma Goldman's 1910 essay "The Traffic in Women," which had been reprinted in the volume *The Traffic in Women and Other Essays on Feminism* in 1970. Lobo and Links write that "in the face of a male-enforced social code rendering a single woman on the street fair game in an open season, women hitchhikers are clearly considered to be prostitutes by a significant number of Americans." Even with fellow hitchhikers, they claim, women have found that "survival in so-called 'hip' communities also involves 'paying with your ass,' for places to crash, for companionship, and for hitchhiking, too."[116] DiMaggio similarly views the vulnerability of women on the road through a feminist lens: "Many men take the attitude that any girl who gets on a highway with an extended thumb is making an implicit sexual proposition. The woman is either a tramp with nymphomaniac tendencies or a whore. The kind of mythology is rampant in slicker men's magazines and in the bars and locker rooms of America. A milder stereotype is that of the Adventurous Hippie Chick, also fair game for John Q. Public's secret lusts."[117] As counter to the pervasive threat of rape and harassment, Lobo and Links, along with virtually all hitchhiking guides, warn women not to hitch at night, to travel with a man, to avoid cars with multiple men, to stay on main roads, and to avoid sitting in the back seat of two-door cars.

HITCHHIKING FILMS AS YOUTH CINEMA

The complex and contradictory discourse around women's hitchhiking similarly frames hitchhiking films. The cycle of hitchhiking films roughly bracketed by *The Young Runaways* (Dreifuss 1968) and the TV movie *Diary of a Teenage Hitchhiker* (Post 1979) can be attributed to a cultural fascination with the runaway hippie girl that Pussycat invokes in *Once Upon a Time ... in Hollywood* and the moral panic effected by her presence on the streets and highways. The fascination with the hitchhiking hippie girl extends to literature in Kundera's 1974 short story "The Hitchhiking Game," where a couple's pretend role-play as hitchhiker and driver reveals the woman's true erotic desires, and Tom Robbins's famous 1976 novel *Even Cowgirls Get the Blues* (later made into a film), which links the female hitchhiker to free love, lesbianism, and a countercultural commune influenced by pseudo-Eastern thought. Hitchhiking also permeated pop charts in songs that celebrated hitchhiking as youth culture, such as Marvin Gaye's "Hitch Hike" from 1962, which created a dance craze; Vanity Fare's 1969 hit "Hitchin' a Ride"; Creedence Clearwater Revival's "Sweet Hitchhiker," from 1971; and the 1974 song "Riding Thumb" by Seals and Croft.

Here, I am more interested in the brief but intense cycle of films that form a cultural context for these other approaches. The film noir hitchhiking cycle focused on male hitchhikers placed in opposition to and threatening postwar ideals of hegemonic masculinity associated with marriage, domesticity, suburban life, breadwinning, and middle-class white-collar professional work. This 1970s cycle focuses on the young female hitchhiker as an emblem of quasi-feminist independence and countercultural nonconformity, largely understood as sexual liberation, and the concomitant risks of—

and punishments for—her freedom and mobility. This hitchhiking film cycle differs from earlier examples because, while they show female hitchhikers and align hitching with sexuality, they offer extended views of hitchhiking as a lifestyle, not an occasional activity. While both these and the film noir hitchhiking films can be considered exploitation pictures, this later cycle of female-centered hitchhiking films, as post–Hays Code films, are generally more sensationalist and risqué than the noirs. They have frequent scenes of sex and nudity, and some veer toward soft-core pornography. Unlike the noir films, they are not, in the main, pitched primarily as "educational."

The late 1960s and early 1970s cycle of hitchhiking films consists of a mixture of mainstream studio films, exploitation pictures, drive-in movies, skin-flicks, and TV movies of the week that, together, fit Jeffrey Sconce's category of "paracinema": "a most elastic textual category" that includes entries from "seemingly disparate subgenres ... of exploitation cinema from juvenile delinquency documentaries to soft core pornography."[118] Paracinema describes subcultural modes of spectatorship, as opposed to genre, and thus offers a way of understanding the ongoing cultural currency and availability of hitchhiking films through DVD distribution companies dedicated to exploitation, such as Video Beat, whose website, thevideobeat.com, advertises its specialties as rock 'n' roll movies and TV; beatniks, hippies, and dope; monsters, surf, and teens; hillbillies, mod, noir, and more.

As Pam Cook argued in 1976, exploitation films "present serious problems for feminists."[119] Certainly, by most 1970s views of feminism, exploitation films would not fit the desire articulated by Gloria Steinem at the First International Festival of Women's Films in 1972 for "a new kind of film in which women are shown as 'strong, compassionate, and beautiful—inside'" against "the stereotypes they saw in Hollywood movies—sex objects, bitches, aggressive castrators, passive idiots, masochists and losers."[120] Rather than work in opposition to the fetishized image of woman as sex object analyzed by Laura Mulvey and others, or offer "new images of women as active subjects in society and history," these films "have generally been seen as produced exclusively by men for the male market."[121] But as Cook argued, while certain "naturalist" or realist feminist films "represent an attempt to efface and suppress contradictions," the "overt manipulation of stereotypes and genre conventions" in exploitation can work "to produce contradictions, shifts in meaning which disturb the patriarchal myths of women on which the exploitation film itself rests."[122] While exploitation can serve conservative interests, as in film noir, Cook underscores the possibility for exploitation to operate as a kind of "working through" of feminism and hitchhiking alike.[123]

Rather than claim these films as wholeheartedly feminist or resistant, then, I suggest we view them as registering discontent in showing women running away from family and opting out of the stereotypical trajectory toward domesticity. Of course, moral panics marshal contradictory discourses—in this case, the promise of liberation vs. the threat of violence; freedom as autonomy vs. freedom as, to borrow from Janis Joplin, "nothin' left to lose"; and sexual liberation and free love vs. rape and assault. These films do not by any means resolve these contradictions but, instead, stockpile them in a way that, intentionally or not, denaturalizes the process of acquiescence to the mainstream and allows space for alternative paths.

My argument depends, in part, on understanding these films as youth films. Indeed, much of what constitutes paracinema could also be characterized as youth cinema insofar as many of the film categories of paracinema represent teens or target teen spectators. Rock 'n' roll movies, surf films, and mod and hippie films not only represent youth subcultures, but they and other paracinema subgenres are marketed to youth. Yannis Tzioumakis notes that, from the 1950s forward, both exploitation and independent cinema relied on the youth market, which comprised not only teenagers but also postadolescents and young adults, ranging from age twenty to thirty-five. Drive-in theaters became the main exhibition site for low-budget independent films, offering double-bills that catered to youth. While the low-budget cinema of the late 1960s and early 1970s was deemed "the cinema of counterculture," sixteen- to twenty-four-year-olds were responsible for almost half the ticket sales.[124]

In distinction from the film noir hitchhiking films, 1970s hitchhiking films are routinely described not only as exploitation but also as youth films, and they are slotted into drive-in theaters on double bills. For example, reviews of *The Young Runaways* describe it as "a lot more perceptive than most youth exploitation stories" and "pure exploitation thrills for the teenage crowd."[125] Suggesting how pliant the notion of "teenage crowd" was, that film ran primarily as the second half of a double bill at drive-ins alongside Alan Funt's movie length X-rated version of his hidden camera show *What Do You Say to a Naked Lady* (1970), which features a segment with naked women hitchhiking, as well as the R-rated *Rosemary's Baby* (Polanski 1968). *Variety* calls the R-rated *Thumb Tripping* (Masters 1972) a "youth-oriented programmer."[126] The PG *Pickup on 101* (Florea 1972) is described as "good stuff for the bottom half of a double bill."[127] The R-rated *The Hitchhikers,* described as an "exploitationer" with a "ready market," played at drive-ins on double-bills with the Mario Bava R-rated 1971 horror film *Twitch of the Death Nerve* (a.k.a. *Bay of Blood*) and the PG countercultural sex-farce *The Young Graduates* (Anderson 1971).[128]

Despite being characterized as youth films at the time, hitchhiking films of the late 1960s and early 1970s are not generally considered in academic discussions of youth film. In part, this relates to changing conceptions of what "counts" as teenage or youth. Now, we tend to think of teens as people between age thirteen and eighteen, but, as mentioned above, the category of youth in this period encompassed not only school-age youth but also young adults. In addition, as paracinema, hitchhiking films may seem too marginal or salacious to have been considered part of the youth film canon. More important, I think, hitchhiking films do not represent youth in ways that fit the typical teen film, which, as Barbara Brickman suggests, offers a "'straight' (in the broadest sense of that term) developmental narrative, wherein the acculturation of the adolescent into a compliant, gendered, heterosexual, middle-class contributor to society seems the foregone conclusion or desired good."[129] While juvenile delinquent films, rock 'n' roll films, or beach movies of the 1950s and early 1960s might fit this model, insofar as they at least represent hegemonic normativity as "the desired good," countercultural hippie hitchhiking films are more disruptive of those norms.

As Brickman suggests, the 1970s are generally viewed as a "clear nadir or empty period for the production of films aimed at youth" in large part because the youth in 1970s films do not fit later conceptions of teens related to high school, cliques, college aspirations, and heterosexual coupling.[130] Instead, they trouble the category of the teenager as well as the teen film. Brickman expands the category of youth films by considering "previously marginalized voices" that rework the largely white heterosexual story of youth film by examining slasher films, queer youth in films featuring Robbie Benson and Jodie Foster, and art cinema about deviant youth, like *Badlands* (Malick 1973), alongside more conventional and, not coincidentally, nostalgic narratives like *American Graffiti* and *Grease* (Kleiser 1978).[131] Accounting for hitchhiking films provides another point of entry to such marginalized voices: young women who reject and unsettle dominant conceptions of femininity and family, and films that are marginalized within scholarly and academic film discourse. The girls in these films and the films themselves are, likewise, marginal, insofar as they are distinct from and out of sync with the dominant; but they also exist in proximity to, and in conversation with, the dominant; and they provide an understanding of female youth and the broad and elastic category of youth film available at the time.

SHE'S LEAVING HOME

In the brief but intense cycle of films about hitchhiking women in the late 1960s and early 1970s, certain themes dominate that distinguish these films from film noir and underscore their youth focus. The majority of these films feature female protagonists who run away from home either because of parental abuse or because of the parents' oppression of the girl's sexuality. *The Young Runaways,* for example, begins with three scenarios of teens running away. In the first, we see Deanie (Patty McCormack of *The Bad Seed* fame), a blonde girl with long pigtails, enter her family home, shutting the door carefully to minimize noise. As she creeps across the living room, her mother appears and interrogates her about where she has been. Her mother nags her for having "relations" with a musician. Deanie counters the euphemism of *relations,* by saying she had sex; she then says that she is lying but doesn't trust that her mother would believe the truth. As Deanie accuses her mother of being "hung up" about sex, her mother slaps her repeatedly. In the next shot, we see Deanie by the side of the road hitching. The second scenario shows a high school boy, Dewey (Kevin Coughlin), with a girl. She tells him she is pregnant, seemingly entrapping him. Worried that his parents will be upset, he runs away. In the third scenario, two white men sit by a swimming pool at a posh house discussing advertising. One man, Raymond (Lloyd Bochner), tells the other that the "teenage problem" is "just another selling job," "the most important selling job we've ever tackled," selling "our way of life" to today's youth; and he brags that he has practiced selling it to his daughter. Dismayed as she overhears this, his daughter, Shelley (Brooke Bundy), packs a bag and flees. In both *The Hitchhikers* and *Ginger in the Morning* (Wiles 1974), Maggie (Misty Rowe) and Ginger (Sissy Spacek), respectively, each run away from home after getting pregnant by a boyfriend who refuses to marry her. *The Grasshopper* (Paris 1970) opens with Christine (Jacqueline Bisset) sneaking out of her house with two suitcases, leaving her parents a note; later we discover that she is leaving an abusive home. The TV movie-of-the-week *Maybe I'll Come Home in the Spring* (Sargent 1971) reverses the trope to have the runaway girl Denise (Sally Field) return home from running away at the start of the film, to then reveal the abusive and hypocritical behavior of her parents that led to her leaving in the first place.

In marked distinction to film noir, these films consistently give voice to the characters' subjectivity through nondiegetic pop theme songs that attempt to explain their reasons for running away. Unlike the square-up pronouncements at the start of *The Hitch-Hiker*, for example, which purports to be educational, these songs provide sympathetic understanding of why youth leave home, and they do so in pop idioms that relate to youth culture. In some cases, the songs describe the character's motivations in second- or third-person narration. The soulful theme song of *The Young Runaways*, for example, sung by African American male singer Arthur Prysock, addresses the runaways directly from the perspective of maturity:

> When you're young, you think you carry
> such a heavy load.
> You think to solve your problems,
> You just have to hit the road.

Later, at a club where Deanie dances, the diegetic band the Gordian Knot sing in "Ophelia's Dream" of a girl "longing to be on board a Greyhound bus that's California bound." In *The Grasshopper*, the crossover country star Bobby Russell's song "As Far as I'm Concerned" (later a hit for Glenn Campbell) offers an explanation for Christine's frustrations focused on the adolescent problem of growth and change:

> If the morning sun should rise and find that you are bored with living,
> And you've changed,
> And because you're not your used-to-be,
> Perhaps you ought to leave and rearrange.

These songs conform to a condition Catherine Driscoll has identified as central to youth film: "a modern idea of adolescence as personal and social crisis" and a narrative centered on "difficulty." She argues that the youth film is "less about growing up than about the expectation, difficulty and social organization of growing up."[132] These songs, with lyrics about having to solve problems and become a new person, situate the narratives as being about youth.

More typically, the hitchhiking youth films reflect the character's interiority through first-person pop songs. In some cases, the singer is male. At the start of *The Hitchhikers*, a male voice singing in a guitar-heavy folk-rock style expresses the first-person interior thoughts of Maggie as we see her run out of her parents' home:

> Running in the yard,
> I was breathing kind of hard,
> As I finally got in gear,
> I was wearing just a rag,
> In my hand was a bag.

The chorus then shifts to reflect the difficulty of her situation:

> I know where I wanna go,
> But you can't get there from here.

In *Dawn: Portrait of a Teenage Runaway* (Kleiser 1976), teen heartthrob Shaun Cassidy performs "Coming Home Again" to capture Dawn's (Eve Plumb) feelings about leaving her brother behind with their abusive mother:

> I've just begun to feel the pain of leaving you this way,
> Someday I hope you'll understand why I can't stay
> Please don't cry,
> You're not the reason I've got to go.

Some theme songs are sung by a female vocalist to better match the central female character. For example, Linda Ronstadt performs "Maybe I'll Come Home in the Spring," in the film of that name, to explain Denise's return home as evincing the lack of satisfaction she felt in running away:

> I've been gone so long, but I really haven't been gone.
> I've seen everything, yet I've seen nothing,
> As my life keeps moving on,
> And my thoughts keep wandering to more familiar things,
> So, maybe I'll come home in the spring.

In *Breezy* (Eastwood 1973), Shelby Flint sings the Michel Legrand theme song, with lyrics by Marilyn and Alan Bergman, in which Breezy offers her love to an unnamed other. In *Ginger in the Morning,* Sissy Spacek pens and sings her own theme song, a treacly song about her contentment:

> Got everything I need,
> Guitar and my favorite jeans,
> I've got a bad case of the sweetcheeks,
> And it's showing all over me.

These songs provide access to the character's feelings and provide an approximation of female voiceover that grants the woman narrative authority. As Kaja Silverman articulates, voiceover is often denied female characters and, when granted, their authority is often undermined, "associated with unreliable, thwarted, or acquiescent speech."[133] Here, we do not experience the woman speaking directly, but, especially when the singer is female, we have a relay of her thoughts and feelings via song.

The authority granted these songs as enunciating the woman's point of view is reinforced in the films through flashbacks that provide access to her subjectivity through image and sound. These flashbacks provide a further backstory to the girl's decision to run away, backstory that is largely absent from the midcentury hitchhiking films. For instance, in *The Young Runaways*, when Deanie visits a nightclub in Chicago and begins to dance, a dissolve shows us images of her dancing in her living room, where her mother scolds her for listening to "lewd" and "dirty" music and then breaks her 45 rpm record; and we see her father (Norman Fell) symbolically castrated and diminished by the mother.[134] In *Dawn: Portrait of a Teenage Runaway*, Dawn is similarly accused of being a "tramp" in a flashback where her drunken mother crashes a school dance to drag her home.

In contrast to the class divide that defines noir's hitchhiking films, each of these films marks out a generational divide. Where most films mark a conflict between youth and their parents as one of abuse or misunderstanding, *Maybe I'll Come Home in the Spring* also shows the alcoholism and hypocrisy of Denise's parents' generation. In one scene after Denise returns home, her parents host a party. As the women at the party admire Denise's emaciated, because starved, frame, the men leer at her and grab at her body. As Denise watches the adults who are cacophonous, drunk, and gross, a flashback shows us an idyllic scene of her and her boyfriend, Flack (David Caradine), kissing and hanging with their friends.

Many of these flashback scenes use jump cuts, repeated actions, mismatches of image and sound, and other techniques of the avant-garde that were absorbed by independent and exploitation cinemas in the late 1960s and early 1970s.[135] For example, when Maggie packs her bag in *The Hitchhikers*, we hear in voiceover a phone call in which she tells her boyfriend, who raped her, that she is pregnant, and we hear him laugh at her. While we listen to this sound from a different time and place, we also see quick disjointed images of Maggie having sex, a newspaper want ad for childcare, and a crucifix; all these sounds and images encapsulate a narrative about Maggie's decision to leave home. In *The Grasshopper*, after Christine's car breaks down and she hitches rides, we see a montage of rides in quick succession. As she rides in the back seat of a bickering couple's car, we hear the couple argue, and we also hear a voiceover of Christine's mom speaking, blended into the couple's fight. Her mother screams, then says, "I don't have to listen to you. I'm leaving and I'm taking Christine with me." A split-screen image shows Christine in the present on the left-hand side of the frame, filmed in color, and, in the lower right-hand corner, a smaller image of a house in black and white, presumably marking it as located in the past. We hear Christine's father threaten to "beat the tar" out of his wife and the sound of slaps as he demands that she undress Christine in what is presumably an incestuous pedophilic sexual assault that provides a darker backstory to Christine's home-leaving than the adolescent growth signaled by the film's theme song.

Maybe I'll Come Home in the Spring directly uses a female voiceover and provides the most extensive use of flashback. The film opens with a one-sided voiceover of a call between Denise and her parents in which she reassures her parents that she is happy and well. As we hear their conversation, we see a montage of Denise's life: Denise walking in traffic thumbing a ride, in alternation with her walking alone on a country road; Denise with her boyfriend, Flack, begging outside a grocery store; Denise getting in a truck with a leering driver. Interspersed with these images, we see very rapid images of Denise's mom, reacting with horror to something offscreen in one shot, and a shot of Flack crashing through a glass window. As Denise rides in the truck, we see more nostalgic images of her mom brushing her hair, a swimming pool, her dad lighting the barbecue, and shots of her empty bedroom at home and her toys. As Denise arrives home, the title of the film appears, the theme song begins, and we hear an internal subjective voiceover as Denise recalls her mother saying, "What's the matter with you?" A shot of a younger Denise kissing a boy appears, and we hear Denise's sister first saying in a child's voice that she loves Denise, nicknamed Dennie, then as a teen shouting that she hates her. We see a brief shot of Denise kissing the boy again as her father's voice intervenes to say, "We wouldn't have to do this if we could trust you"; and we briefly see the couple startled, caught in the act of having sex by Denise's mom, thus explaining the earlier reaction shot of her mother. This use of disjunctive images, rapid cuts, and sounds from other moments in time recurs across the film as we see more of the primal scene of her being caught having sex; hear Dennie's childhood voice as she recalls her previous life; and see images of her time as a runaway, including both romantic memories of her and Flack together and the trauma of seeing Flack, high on meth, crashing through glass.

To be sure, while sympathetically portraying the female runaway's subjectivity and reasons for being on the road, this film cycle also underscores both the risks of sexual assault and perceptions of the hitchhiker as sexually available. As in the logic of "Gas, Grass, or Ass," these films show sexual harassment and rape to be the unconditional currency of the road. In *The Young Runaways,* Shelley gets in a car with a middle-aged man who quickly suggests that they get a motel room and pulls her close to him. She struggles with him, which results in the car crashing; then she runs away without her suitcase. In *The Hitchhikers,* Maggie is first offered five dollars for sex by a truck driver; then she is raped when she tries to sneak out a diner window to escape. In *Breezy,* likewise, Breezy (Kay Lenz) catches a ride with a man who brags about paying another girl fifteen dollars for sex. He takes a deliberate wrong turn onto an isolated road and says how much he "digs you hippie dippies." He describes another girl who refused his offer of cash and threatened to call rape, telling Breezy, "I gave her something to yell about." Breezy's response indicates how taken-for-granted such dangerous situations are: "Another typical day in the life of Miss Dum Dum," she says, as she runs away. The sexploitation film *Teenage Hitchhikers* has a running "gag" about a serial rapist who attacks female runaways and whom the film's teen hitchhikers taunt and torture repeatedly. In *Thumb Tripping,* a truck driver offers the boy hitchhiker Gary (Michael Burns) money to let him have sex with Gary's companion, Shay (Meg Foster). Gary refuses, but the driver locks him in the back of the truck and rapes Shay anyway. *The Grasshopper* shows Christine being punched and raped by a businessman to whom she has appealed for help with her husband's career.

Most of the films assume the female hitchhikers are sexually promiscuous. In *Pickup on 101,* when college student Nicky (Lesley Ann Warren) decides to run away from school, her boyfriend accuses her of wanting to sleep with lots of men and blames her promiscuity on birth control, saying "the pill swallowed the girl." In *The Hitchhikers,* Maggie meets a handsome hippie named Benson (Nick Klar), who brings her back to a Manson-like free-love commune at a dilapidated ranch and announces to the various barely clad women already there that Maggie will be "one of our sisters now." After getting an abortion, Maggie begins an affair with Benson and joins him and the other women as they snare and rob unsuspecting male drivers by hitchhiking in skimpy clothes. *Thumb Tripping* shows Shay behaving flirtatiously and

FIGURE 3.4. Titillating shot of Maggie (Misty Rowe) hitchhiking in *The Hitchhikers*.

having sex with multiple men while traveling with Gary (even claiming to have enjoyed the rape!); while she asserts her freedom, he casts aspersions on the logic of free love by claiming that "being free isn't a lack of commitment but being able to love." *Teenage Hitchhikers* and *Little Miss Innocence* (Warfield 1973) make the young hitchhikers' sexuality their raison d'être. In the former, the two hitchhiking girls, Mouse (Chris Jordan) and Bird (Sandra Peabody), acknowledge that "in this economy, boobs and busts are legal tender." They try to seduce a waiter in a diner to get food, then strip and seduce a driver, and, later, participate in an orgy—all while proclaiming that they hitchhike for "freedom and excitement." More than just sexually promiscuous as characters, in this film, the women exist to be sexualized spectacles for the audience with frequent shots of them in wet T-shirts or nude (figs. 3.4, 3.5). *Little Miss Innocence* takes the sexual provocation further. In this film, two hitchhiking girls, Carol (Sandy Dempsey) and Judy (Terri Johnson), seduce a driver who picks them up; they then refuse to leave his home, having decided to see if they can kill a man with sex. Eventually, with the man tied up and nearly dead, we discover that Carol was pimped out by her father and experienced sexual abuse and rape from her brother and stepfather.

In some narratives that emphasize the dangers of hitchhiking, female hitchhikers are seen to be at risk of sliding into prostitution. In *The Young Runaways*, Shelley is trafficked by a female roommate. In *The Grasshopper*,

FIGURE 3.5. Mouse (Chris Jordan) and Bird (Sandra Peabody) flash their boobs to get a ride in *Teenage Hitchhikers.*

after a string of relationships that she flees because she avoids commitment, Christine finds herself with a junkie who pimps her out. *Dawn: Portrait of a Teenage Runaway* shows Dawn's slow descent into prostitution as she finds herself with no options for legitimate work and gets lured to a pimp who threatens her and forces her to work for him (an especially surprising and sensationalist twist for those who recognize Eve Plumb as Jan Brady of *The Brady Bunch*).

Getting at the allure of hitchhiking hippies like Pussycat from *Once Upon a Time . . . in Hollywood* for the older generation—and suggesting the complex web of envy and desire that is part and parcel of the generation gap—many hitchhiking films show older men not only as attracted to, and assaulting, young women but also as being transformed by the hitchhiking hippie. In these films, the hitchhikers' values of freedom, free love, and mobility are seen as authenticating. In films such as *Breezy, Ginger in the Morning,* and *Rafferty and the Gold Dust Twins* (Richards 1975), the hippie girl loosens up the staid middle-aged man. Rather than show her being acculturated into his world—the world of domesticity, marriage, breadwinning—these films show the man becoming unmoored from his life and made free. They, in effect, reverse the life cycle and the logic of social mobility as the older man is rejuvenated and exits the world of work. In *Breezy,* Breezy (a twenty-year-old who has been on the road since graduating high school) hitches a ride with divorced successful businessman Frank Harmon (William Holden, age fifty-five at the time of filming), then, inexplicably, shows up at his house—guitar in hand—and quickly declares her love for him. Frank sleeps with her but ditches her after he is embarrassed when his ex-wife and a male friend both see him with her. In the end, however, Frank leaves his comfortable existence and joins Breezy and her hippie friends in the park, greeting her with "Hello my love, hello my life." *Ginger in the Morning* has a remarkably similar trajectory as the successful, divorced, middle-aged man Joe (Monte Markham, who was forty-nine years old to Sissy Spacek's twenty-five) picks up Ginger, invites her home for what he plans as a sexual adventure, offends and rejects her, but then realizes he has fallen in love. At the end of this film, he leaves his home and joins her by the side of the road, thumbs out.

Rafferty and the Gold Dust Twins varies the formula somewhat, having Rafferty (Alan Arkin, age forty-one at the time) be himself a failure—a former gunnery sergeant now working as a driving instructor, barely able to pay his rent. Rafferty meets two girls in the park and agrees to give them a ride in his broken-down car; then, they force Rafferty at gunpoint to drive them across the country. Rafferty discovers that the gun is fake and escapes, but he decides to join them anyway as he has nothing worthwhile at home. He sleeps with McKinley, nicknamed Mac (Sally Kellerman, age thirty-eight but playing younger). When she ditches him for another male hitchhiker, he first returns Rita, nicknamed "Frisbee" (Mackenzie Phillips, aged sixteen), to the children's home but then helps her escape by posing as her father and heads off on the road with her.

As Brickman suggests, most youth films point toward "the acculturation of the adolescent into a compliant, gendered, heterosexual, middle-class contributor to society" through such things as the successful formation of a couple, scenes of the teen leaving for college, or otherwise indicating the teen's movement from a state of adolescent crisis into one of nascent maturity.[136] In the hitchhiking cycle, however, endings are unresolved; rather than assert a terminus, or arrival somewhere, the film ends with the girl still on the road, mobile and unmoored from home. These films proffer no resolution to the crisis of adolescence and, instead, mark youth as a period of perpetual motion. At the end of *The Hitchhikers,* for example, Benson and the girls buy a school bus and start driving to Los Angeles: we see a female hitchhiker by the side of the road, and they stop to let her in. In *Thumb Tripping,* Gary goes home, his hitchhiking only a short reprieve from college, but Shay remains on the side of the road, "just waiting for somebody." As I have suggested, in *Breezy, Ginger in the Morning,* and *Rafferty and the Gold Dust Twins,* even as a couple forms, the ending is irresolute, with the men joining the women to become mobile and placeless.

In some films, as one girl stops hitchhiking, she is replaced by a new girl, suggesting repetition or a sequential chain rather than conclusion. At the end of *The Young Runaways,* for example, Deanie is murdered, but Shelley and Dewey return home. But rather than end there, the film shows a new runaway girl getting a ride. Similarly, in *Maybe I'll Come Home in the Spring,* Denise acquiesces to middle-class domesticity. After Flack visits and tries to get her to rejoin him on the road, he tells her not to "settle for this. It's not enough." He asks, "Is all you want this swimming pool and a vacuum cleaner?" Sure enough, at film's end, we see Denise in her parents' living room running the vacuum cleaner. But her sister, Susie (Lane Bradbury), is gone, having run away, and we see her hitching a ride. Even in *Diary of a Teenage Hitchhiker,* after the film has shown at least four girls raped and murdered—and after the main character, Julie (Dominique Dunn), narrowly escapes the same—we see a montage of numerous girls hitching. Like *Maybe I'll Come Home in the Spring, Diary of a Teenage Hitchhiker* ends with a shot of Julie's little sister, Trish (Katie Kurtzman), hitchhiking in a bathing suit, a curious acknowledgment of the failure of the film's sensationalist discourse to stop girls from hitchhiking.

THE END OF THE ROAD

Hitchhiking's reign as a dominant practice among youth ended quickly. Most immediately, crime took on an outsized role in the public imagination. Valian's 1974 book, *Hitchhiking: The Road to Rape and Murder,* emphasizes this view. She creates distinct fictional narratives in which a woman is picked up by a sadistic rapist and murderer, a male driver is brutalized by hitchhikers, a young Black boy is raped by a homosexual predator, and so on. In particular, hitchhiking came to be viewed as especially risky for women. Stories of rape and sexual abuse had been part of the narrative of female hitchhiking from the start, taken largely as a given cost of the ride, but a series of murders in the early 1970s brought public attention, once again, to the risks of hitchhiking. While hitchhiking was still statistically no more dangerous than walking down the street, a few murders were highly publicized. Most notably, in 1972 and 1973, Ed Kemper killed six female hitchhikers in California and three other hitchhiking coeds were murdered in the Boston area.[137]

Newspapers roused fears of hitchhiking for women with headlines such as "Hitchhiking: Who Can Tell?," "Hitchhiking Girls: They Follow a Dangerous Road," "Hitchhiking: The Deadly New Odds," and "Lure of In-City Hitchhiking Growing Peril to Coeds."[138] As in the hitchhiking guides and sociological accounts, newspapers linked female hitchhiking to women's liberation. Emphasizing the "horror stories" of hitchhiking, a *Boston Globe* writer described the frequent site of women hitching in Boston and said, "This is not unusual in Boston or almost any place else these days because this is the permissive age of the Pill and Women's lib and all that. They call it freedom or something, and if the boys can do it, why can't we?"[139] An article in the *New York Times* claimed that female hitchhikers "follow and often support the women's liberation movement" and thus "resent any potential legal double standard against hitchhiking."[140] Newspapers described female hitchhikers in prurient terms—"attractive, tanned and scantily clad teen-age girls"—and suggested that they somehow invite or deserve rape. To a large degree, women's increased presence on the streets was taken as causal:[141] "Hitchhiking has taken a new—and perilous—turn. Once almost exclusively a male-dominated practice, more girls than ever before are hitting the roads, singly, in pairs and sometimes with boyfriends. Police and traffic safety officials estimate that girls now make up a fourth to half of all hitchers. As girls stream onto the avenues and highways, crimes have skyrocketed appallingly.[142] Not only did journalists attribute the rise in hitchhiking dangers to "the number of young people, particularly girls, who regularly use their thumbs to get around," but they suggested that women were "asking for it": "They placed themselves in the position where it could happen to them.... They 'practically invite rape.'"[143] Indeed, the court of appeals in Los Angeles overturned a rape conviction, ruling that "a lone female who hitchhikes in a metropolitan area must at least foresee the possibility that a man who picks her up will make sexual advances."[144]

The late entry *Diary of a Teenage Hitchhiker* heralded the end of the "hitchhiking craze" by emphasizing the danger inherent in hitching and focusing on fear rather than female subjectivity. Like its film noir counterparts, *Diary of a Teenage Hitchhiker* begins with a square-up that shows text crawling up the screen while a woman's voiceover reads the text detailing cases of sexual assault and murder that female hitchhikers have faced, warning that "young women continue to thumb rides." By the time of *The Hitcher* in 1986, hitchhiking is once again viewed through a masculine lens—the film's poster shows a man's eyes reflected in a rear-view mirror as he spies a male hitchhiker on the road—and reverts to a 1950s FBI logic in its tagline "never pick up a stranger," a tagline equally suited to 1980s fearmongering over "stranger danger."[145] With this film and *The Texas Chainsaw Massacre* (Hooper 1974), where teens traveling by van pick up a psychotic hitchhiker, hitching became the stuff of horror films.

In addition to fears of crime, hitchhiking's demise can be seen as happening in tandem with the diminishment of the counterculture, as the neoliberal emphasis on competition and wealth—which would lead in the 1980s to the rise of the yuppie—eclipsed hippie values of cooperation, encounter, ecology, spontaneity, and authenticity. Thus, unlike its resurgence after the FBI's anti-hitchhiking campaign following a similar spate of highly publicized crimes, hitchhiking never fully recovered, transforming instead to "rideshares" such as Uber and Lyft, which translated the values of hitchhiking into a commercial transaction in a gig economy.

Where we now think of rideshares as systems of local mobility akin to taxicabs, a means to get from place to place, this cycle of films about countercultural women hitchhikers shows a different conception of ride-sharing tied to being mobile, placeless, and deliberately unhomed.

. . .

If *Once Upon a Time . . . in Hollywood* gestures toward Pussycat's lineage, it also underlines the degree to which we have occluded the history of female hitchhiking in films and reality. As I hope to have shown here, hitchhiking was once upon a time a vital countercultural form that offered young women complex and contradictory forms of liberation. In recalling the figure of the hitchhiking "hippie chick" evoked by Pussycat, we deepen our understanding of countercultural representation, youth films, road films, and female-centered narratives; broaden our conception of ways in which women may have pushed back against conventional gender roles and domesticity; and can reimagine a world where hitchhiking was a form of resistance in which women could claim their right to the road with their thumbs.

To be sure, the hitchhiking woman's freedom in these films, and in reality, is, at best, ambivalent. While Pussycat and her foresisters represent a kind of freedom—from the expectations of family, domesticity, and rootedness—they are still bound by gendered expectations about their sexual availability. But if we return to Cook's assessment of exploitation's ability to "produce contradictions, shifts in meaning which disturb the patriarchal myths of women on which the exploitation film itself rests," we can see that these films cluster together discourses that both titillate and castigate; produce narratives of female adolescent development that challenge dominant norms and especially domesticity; and suggest, however tenuously, not only the dangers but also the pleasures of taking a detour and being adrift.

FOUR

Trash

THE HOMELESS AS URBAN WASTE

IN APRIL 1991, THE SINGER Crystal Waters released her debut album, *Surprise,* with the lead single "Gypsy Woman (She's Homeless)." The single was a huge commercial success, peaking at number 8 on *Billboard's Hot 100* and topping the charts in Belgium, Italy, the Netherlands, Spain, Switzerland, Germany, Ireland, Australia, France, and the United Kingdom. In 2020, *Slant Magazine* ranked it one of the ten best dance songs of all time, and *Mixmag* included it among its 2018 list of the best vocal house music anthems ever. It has been remixed numerous times.

"Gypsy Woman" is about an unnamed homeless woman singing on a street corner for money.[1] Waters claims to have written the song after witnessing a homeless woman who "didn't look homeless": "She looked *fine*. . . . She always had a full face of makeup and black clothes and she'd be singing these gospel songs."[2] Waters explains that learning more about the woman changed her view of homelessness: "I used to think, 'Well, why don't you go and get a job instead of asking me for money?' Then there was an article on her in the paper! It said she'd just lost her job in retail, and she said that she thought if she was going to ask people for money, then she should at least *look* presentable. And that changed my idea of homelessness. It could happen to anyone."[3] The lyrics of the song describe the homeless woman's beauty rituals:

> Just to do her hair now
> Because she cares you all
> Her day, oh, wouldn't be right
> Without her make up.

In addition, the song conveys Waters's transformed understanding of homelessness:

> She's just like you and me
> But she's homeless, she's homeless.

Rather than its message about the homeless being "just like you and me," however, "Gypsy Woman" is most famous for its frequently sampled keyboard riff and its refrain, "La da dee la dee da," meant to signify the homeless woman's song. The refrain dominates the song, which has very few lyrics beyond those quoted above. Waters asked the record company to add the parenthetical title "(She's Homeless)" because she felt that people were enjoying the song as a dance hit without listening to the lyrics about homelessness.[4]

Contributing to the song's "misreading," the official music video for "Gypsy Woman (She's Homeless)" (dir. Mark Pellington) employs MTV-style editing—discontinuity editing reliant on quick cuts, montage effects, sudden changes in scale and angle, and spectacle over narrative—that emphasizes the song's funky rhythm over its supposed message about homelessness. The video shows Waters with her hair pulled back tightly, wearing a black pantsuit with a large silver Egyptian ankh necklace and earrings, or, alternately, a white pantsuit with a black and white polka dot necktie, sometimes dancing in long shot against a white background and sometimes in extreme close-up, singing. Images of Waters singing and dancing are intercut with images of three young African American male dancers in brightly colored shirts, sometimes in infrared images, who dance singly, in pairs, or all together in the frame. Across the video, we see images of cash falling from the sky; floating mannequin hands; "la da dee la dee da" in spiral text superimposed over Waters or printed on a spinning umbrella; abstract spiral images that echo the "la da dee la dee da" shape; a drawing of a purple and red house; and, separately, a white toy brick house with a red roof and large green tree outside that is eventually shown in flames. The homeless woman is first introduced via a close-up of a gold lamé glove holding a bright pink lipstick; then we see the gloved hand holding a gold mirror and a pink hairbrush. The video cuts to a medium shot that shows the homeless woman's face framed with teased brown hair and covered with a bright white porcelain mask, with cherry red lips, green eyes, and drawn-on eyebrows and eyeliner. With her gold lamé gloves holding the gold mirror, the homeless woman gazes at herself and touches her face/mask (fig. 4.1). Later in the video, we see her in a loose-fitting black jumpsuit and hoodie, still wearing the mask and gloves, vaguely dancing with a black column, and, at one point, in a position of supplication. A pan from a red wire trash can to a shot of a green park bench

FIGURE 4.1. Homeless woman abstracted and dehumanized in the music video for "Gypsy Woman (She's Homeless)."

shows her lying down, perhaps asleep, but with her painted-on eyes remain wide open.

Rather than give a sense of the homeless woman as "just like you and me," the woman in the music video for "Gypsy Woman" is radically dehumanized (and deracialized). Hidden behind a porcelain mask and situated amid toy houses and mannequins, she seems more like a doll isolated from reality than a person experiencing homelessness. Where the unnamed woman in the newspaper story puts on makeup to be "presentable," and sings to get money rather than simply beg, the music video callously turns her into a narcissist with no voice: she preens and poses, obsessively gazing in the mirror, and does not sing her gospel songs or even have a working mouth. The video offers a mishmash of signifiers of wealth and superficiality—cash, mannequin hands, gold lamé—in tandem with vague signifiers of homelessness, such as the park bench and the trash can, with no clear logic or politics. Hilariously critiquing the song and video's superficiality, the sketch comedy show *In Living Color* (1990–94) lampooned "Gypsy Woman (She's Homeless)" with a video "My Songs Are Mindless" ("Krishna Cop" S3, EP9). The spot-on parody characterized Waters as a no-talent hack and underscored the song and video's insensitivity, with Kim Wayans as Waters wearing a tiara and mink coat singing, "Ha ha hee, ha ha ho / I'll be rich and you'll be po'."

160 • CHAPTER 4

If a dance hit about homelessness and a video representing the homeless in a kind of incoherent Kabuki theater seems like an outlier, consider the similarly perplexing opening track on David Bowie's 1987 album *Never Let Me Go*, "Day-In Day-Out." Like "Gypsy Woman," "Day-In Day-Out"—which also charted in *Billboard's Hot 100* (peaking at number 21), *Dance Club Songs* (number 10), and *Mainstream Rock* (number 3)—purports to offer a serious take on homelessness. According to a 1987 MTV interview with Bowie, the song assayed "some kind of statement or indictment of an uncaring society, particularly the response to what's happening in major cities in terms of the homeless, people who are totally uncared for."[5] This "statement," however, is, as Bowie admits, less didactic and more "impressionistic, almost surrealistic" in its approach. Bowie sings:

> What she lacks is a backup
> Nothing seems to make a dent
> Gonna find her some money honey
> Try to pay her rent
> That's the kind of protection that everyone is shouting about.

These lyrics are interspersed with the chorus:

> Day-in (day in), day-out (day out)
> Stay-in fade-out
> Day-in ooh-ooh
> Day-out ooh-ooh ooh.

The music video for "Day-In Day-Out," directed by Julian Temple and Bowie, presents more of a plot than "Gypsy Woman" does, but it is equally nonsensical. Here, an abandoned white baby is discovered by two angels, one white and one black, each carrying a video camera. A cut suggests that the baby grows up to be a gorgeous woman (Kathy Foy) with a biracial child. She passes by shop windows offering expensive gowns for sale, but she finds herself amid crazy people in a poor neighborhood. She shoplifts from a convenience store and later steals CDs with a white male boyfriend (Rick Burks), presumably seeking drug money ("Stealing for that one good rush"). Then, having fallen further into poverty, she wears a bright red wig and corset to work as a prostitute on the Sunset Strip. After a man tries to rape her in his car, she runs from the car in her white bra and panties, and we see her get arrested for loitering, her white-pantied rear-end framed in close-up as she is handcuffed. Then, we see the woman, man, and child walk through a homeless encampment that shows people sitting or sleeping in and among cardboard boxes and garbage. Next, inexplicably, the man, woman, and child are enjoying a meal and dancing at a seafood restaurant. They end up in a cute little house, where the child spells out "L-U-C-K" in blocks (the letter *F* is adjacent, and one version of the video has him spell "F-U-C-K"). A Los Angeles Police Department tank, with a battering ram and an ironic sign reading "Have a nice day," arrives and smashes the house to pieces. Interspersed with this narrative, we see Bowie performing with his band in what appears to be a hotel repurposed as a homeless squat or roller skating through the homeless encampment.

Both "Gypsy Woman (She's Homeless)" and "Day-In Day-Out" seem, in retrospect, facile, tone deaf, and exploitative. To be sure, they emerge in the context of other glib pop-music performances of righteous concern, such as U.S.A. for Africa's 1985 "We Are the World," or The Specials' 1984 "Free Nelson Mandela." But "Gypsy Woman (She's Homeless)" and "Day-In Day-Out" are particularly interesting because they emerged in the context of a larger cycle of films, TV shows, and news media attention to homelessness that treated it with a similar mix of earnestness and superficiality, sympathy and othering. These videos and the larger cycle of media texts respond to homelessness as a new crisis and, as with these hit songs, are unsure whether to indict the "uncaring society" or the homeless themselves, whether to dance or cry.

This chapter examines a cycle of films during the long 1980s—1980 to 1994—that take up what was then considered the "new" homelessness but that, from our perspective decades later, marks the beginnings of modern homelessness. While there are key films about the homeless after 1994, such as *The Pursuit of Happyness* (Muccino 2006) or *Shelter* (Bettany 2014), I focus on films that deal with homelessness as an emergent crisis rather than as a taken-for-granted dominant. Here, as in other chapters, I want to map a cycle of films that undertake what John Ellis calls "working through" the problem of homelessness by offering "multiple stories and frameworks of explanation which enable understanding and, in the very multiplicity of those frameworks ... enable(s) viewers to work through the major public and private concerns of their society."[6] This "working through" occurs before a narrative about a social problem coheres and settles; its multiplicity allows for contradiction, complexity, and incoherence of message, tone, and sympathies.

Previous chapters have dealt with the ways in which mainstream genres, social problem films, and exploitation films all "work through" moral panics about different unhomed, unhoused, placeless, and mobile figures such as tramps, World War II soldiers, and hitchhikers. The tramp, defined as ubiquitous across the nation, was similarly pervasive across widespread media and film genres, traversing comedies, dramas, melodrama, musicals, and ranging from short films to features, high budget to low, major mainstream films to obscurities. The World War II films I discussed fell under a broad category of social problem films, including comedic, musical, and dramatic treatments of the veteran problem and problems related to war-related mobility and housing. Hitchhiking films were, on the whole, linked to exploitation, with a midcentury cycle of mostly film noir B movies and an early 1970s cycle of exploitation youth films.

This 1980s cycle of films about homelessness includes a mixture of mainstream studio films, social problem films, and exploitation films, but the dominant modality is middlebrow. When we think of 1980s cinema, we tend to think, on the one hand, of blockbuster cinema consisting of high-concept films and sequels that "represented a consolidation of control by the Hollywood majors"—think, for example, of the *Rambo, Star Wars,* and *Indiana Jones* franchises —and, on the other, of independent auteurist cinema, such as the films of Spike Lee, Gus Van Sant, or Jim Jarmusch.[7] This leaves out many popular films that are neither "low" masculinist action films nor "high" auteurist darlings but mainstream middlebrow studio fare.[8] While middlebrow entertainment has historically been associated with female audiences, critics now view it more expansively. Anne Hornaday defines middlebrow cinema as consisting of "predictable stories, slick production values and interchangeable Q-rated movie stars. Pandering, undemanding, philosophically inert, these are the movies so desperate to be palatable that they wind up being the screen equivalent of a suburban strip mall: featureless, bland, efficient for commerce but deadening for the soul."[9] Fitting Hornaday's description, 1980s homeless films include a surprising number of comedies featuring well-known, Q-rated (i.e., familiar, likable, well-regarded) stars and directors such as Eddie Murphy and Dan Ackroyd in John Landis's *Trading Places* (1983); Richard Dreyfuss, Bette Midler, and Nick Nolte in Paul Mazursky's *Down and Out in Beverly Hills* (1986); Jeff Bridges and Robin Williams in Terry Gilliam's *The Fisher King* (1991); Jim Belushi and Kelly Lynch in John Hughes's *Curly Sue* (1991); and Mel Brooks in his film *Life Stinks* (1991). These light comedies feature homeless characters in individual narratives of redemption and even romance that dodge the darker truths of homelessness. Certainly, some homeless films are social problem films intended to draw attention to the problem of homelessness, such as *Where the Day Takes You* (Rocco 1992); the TV movie *Stone Pillow* (Schaefer 1985), starring Lucille Ball; and the TV movie *No Place like Home* (Grant 1989), starring Christine Lahti and Jeff Daniels. They, too, are middlebrow: earnest, conventional, and digestible. There are a few low-budget exploitative horror films, such as *C.H.U.D* (Cheek 1984), *Prince of Darkness* (Carpenter 1987), and *Street Trash* (Muro 1987), that make homelessness spectacle rather than subject. One film, Charles Lane's 1989 *Sidewalk Stories*, qualifies as auteurist art cinema, and it is the only film to focus exclusively on African American characters. Most films in the cycle, however, are Hollywood studio fare or TV movies, pitched as light entertainment. Although homelessness was viewed as a massive societal problem that needed to be solved, these films tend to make the crisis "palatable" by focusing primarily on white characters and personal backstories to favor individual-level explanations and solutions that elide larger intractable structural factors such as the housing market, policy, or gentrification.

To say that 1980s homeless films are middlebrow is not to dismiss them. Indeed, Hornaday notes that middlebrow films can be "generously humanistic," simple but not simplistic, accessible but not patronizing, earnest but not condescending. Sally Faulkner suggests that "middlebrow culture tends to be the culture that 'works through' after the event, or occasionally the culture that anticipates before the event, rather than the culture of the event itself."[10] Middlebrow cinema offers a space for "working through" homelessness; it negotiates massive cultural change as new forms of homelessness emerge. Crucially, these films make visible the emergent inequality of the 1980s—inequality that has only increased in the United States since then—as a period defined by extreme wealth and upward mobility for some and by deep poverty and downward mobility for others. While these films do not, for the most part, draw the lines between these different populations to show cause and effect, in which the rise of some causes the fall of others, the films do frequently juxtapose rich and poor in ways that expose the neoliberal fantasies that prop up wealth and render the poor disposable.

THE NEW HOMELESS

To understand the way in which middlebrow films work through the crisis of homelessness, it is important to consider how the facts and appearance of homelessness changed in the 1980s. Of course, as I have been discussing throughout this book, large populations of unhoused people existed well before the 1980s. But in that decade, a shift occurred in the numbers and demographics of the unhoused population. While counting the homeless is always difficult, given that many will not use shelters or double up with family and friends and thus remain "invisible," analysts agree that the numbers of homeless soared in the 1980s.[11] In 1984, the Department of Housing and Urban Development (HUD) estimated there were two to three hundred thousand homeless nationwide, and by 1987, the department reckoned that the homeless population had at least doubled to five or six hundred thousand. In 1992, some estimates counted two or three million homeless people.[12] In a watershed moment, on Thanksgiving Day 1981, activists in Washington, DC, drew attention to the rise of homelessness by setting up a tent encampment in Lafayette Park across from the White House that they dubbed "Reaganville," referencing the Hoovervilles of the Depression.[13] In early 1982, grassroots activists, mayors of big cities, and some members of Congress began to insist that homelessness was a national crisis.[14]

At the same time that the numbers of homeless increased markedly, the face of homelessness changed. As Marian Moser Jones puts it, "dwindling clusters of grizzled, single, white, older alcoholic men who had historically circulated between flophouses and missions in the nation's Skid Rows had seemingly been replaced by a more diverse population that included more women, more African Americans, more young people, and a substantial number of people suffering from serious mental illness."[15] To be sure, as I discussed in relation to the tramp, women had always existed among the homeless, but they had been largely invisible. Starting in the 1970s, however, homeless women became much more visible. According to the *Oxford English Dictionary*, the slang term *bag lady* emerged in 1972 to characterize an elderly, usually white, homeless woman who carries her possessions in shopping bags.[16] As homelessness increased among women, "bag ladies" began to encompass more racially diverse women made homeless by a variety of causes: they were widowed, divorced, mentally ill, victims of domestic abuse, alcoholics, chemically dependent, or women who worked jobs that did not accrue Social Security benefits. Owing to threats of rape and violence, these women tended to fear shelters and favored life on the streets.[17] In addition to including more women, the homeless population in the 1980s differed most from previous generations of unhoused people because it was composed substantially of minorities: the proportion of minorities among the homeless was much larger than the proportion of minorities among the general population, and homeless women and children were more likely than other homeless people to be minorities.[18] While noting the growth of Black homelessness, especially, the media also paid special attention to the smaller increase in the "new homeless," comprising two-parent families with stable work histories and no problems with mental illness or chemical dependency. This new demographic could be directly attributed to economic circumstance such as layoffs, plant closings, or unemployment and, as a *Washington Post* article put it in 1983, comprised "more whites, more families, more able-bodied young people, and more suburbanites."[19] Thus, where tramps and skid-row inhabitants had typically been single middle-aged white men—and single men, Black and white, still made up the majority of the homeless—the homeless population in the 1980s expanded noticeably to include more women and children, the majority of whom were Black, but also including a small percentage of white families.[20]

In addition to increasing numbers and changing demographics, the homeless seemed more prevalent in the 1980s and continuing until today, in part because they began to inhabit public spaces in new ways. Prior to the 1980s, and after the demise of the tramp, the homeless primarily lived in skid rows, sections of cities that were ceded to the transient. Skid rows were primarily "a place for placeless men";[21] women were part of the 1970s skid-row community but "considered themselves, and were considered, a group apart and different from the men."[22] Skid rows contained much of what transients needed to survive: flophouses, cheap hotels, and single-room-occupancy hotels (SROs); cheap or free food; thrift and pawn shops; and blood banks, barber colleges, and employment agencies that specialized in seasonal and temporary labor.[23] In the 1980s, as skid rows disappeared for reasons I will discuss below, the homeless began to share space with the sheltered and to occupy public urban spaces such as sidewalks, parks, underpasses, and abandoned lots across cities and towns.[24] Owing to concerns over safety and surveillance, they moved frequently among these spaces. They were as pervasive as the tramp, but their mobility was more circumscribed. Where tramps traversed the nation on foot and by rail, the new homeless "mark out for themselves particular neighborhoods, blocks, buildings, doorways" and "reduce their world to a small area" within a city.[25]

Marking this different way of inhabiting public space, the term *street people* was used more often than before to describe the unhoused.[26] More significantly, the word *homeless,* previously not much used, came to the fore as this new population of transients and their public visibility seemed to demand a new nomenclature. In particular, a 1981 report by the Community Service Society in New York used the word *homeless* as opposed to *bum* or *vagrant* to account for the more diverse population.[27] The media noted the shift in the size and demographics of the homeless population with stories such as "Record Number of Homeless Living in City Shelters," "Hard Times Breed New Homeless," "Homeless: More Join the Rolls," "Growing Problem of Homeless Families Attracts New Attention," and "Homeless Children on Increase, Study Shows."[28] In 1983, *homelessness* and *homeless person* were added to the *New York Times* index.[29]

REAGANVILLE

The causes behind the increase in number and changing demographics of the homeless are numerous. Many think that mental illness and drug use are causal. For the most part, news coverage in the 1980s helped foster this stereotype as media ignored the rise of minorities, families, and single mothers among the homeless and focused instead on single white men, particularly veterans and the mentally ill.[30] But in the 1980s, personal problems such as mental illness or chemical dependency made people more vulnerable to homelessness but were not generally causal.[31] To be sure, the rise in drug abuse, especially cocaine and crack, in the mid-to-late 1980s affected the risk of homelessness among the poor, but there is no evidence that there was more mental illness or drug abuse in the early 1980s than before; and prior to the 1980s those people who were mentally ill or addicted were not necessarily homeless.[32] Instead of being caused by mental illness and addiction, the rise of homelessness occurs during Ronald Reagan's two terms as US president, from 1981 to 1989; and increased homelessness correlates to the rise in poverty, changes in social policy, and changes in the housing market that are related to neoliberal government policies, including cuts in government spending, economic deregulation, and tax reduction.

The Reagan years witnessed a large increase in poverty that magnified a trend begun in the 1970s. From 1970 to 1980, the numbers of poor increased by 15 percent nationally, and the rate of poverty increased by 12 to 13 percent. From 1980 to 1983, these same demographics saw a 20 percent and 17 percent increase respectively.[33] Between 1980 and 1988, jobs that paid relatively well came to account for a smaller share of all American jobs, while those paying the least grew the most, in number and proportion.[34] High-wage industries moved to low-wage countries or countries with lax environmental laws, tax breaks, and other subsidies.[35] With deindustrialization and the shift to a service economy, high-wage jobs were replaced with jobs that offered low wages, no career advancement, and no upward mobility.[36] In the 1960s and 1970s, a full-time year-round worker earning minimum wage could raise a family of three above the poverty line. But between 1980 and 1988, the minimum wage lost 23 percent of its purchasing power (compared to a loss of 3 percent in the 1970s). By the end of the Reagan administration, the minimum wage was lower in real purchasing power than at any time since the 1950s.[37] The average middle-class American saw family income stagnate or decline in terms of real buying power, and the share of income going to the wealthiest 20 percent was the highest since the 1920s.[38]

As the number of people in poverty rose, social services decreased. In the 1970s, noncash food and housing benefit programs served more people, noncash benefits were worth more, and tax policy was less punitive to poor people than a decade later.[39] Reagan famously castigated the "Welfare Queen," a racist stereotype of a single Black mother living large on the taxpayer's dime, and he viewed public assistance as "waste and abuse" in the federal government budget.[40] As a waste-cutting effort, the Omnibus Budget Reconciliation Act (OBRA) of 1981 restricted eligibility for major benefit programs such as Aid to Families and Dependent Children (AFDC), a benefit created by the 1935 Social Security Act (SSA) that provided financial assistance to children whose families had low or no income; and this reduction in benefits coincided with the worst recession and highest unemployment since the Depression.[41] OBRA left fifty thousand families ineligible for AFDC benefits and reduced AFDC benefits for another three hundred thousand families. The number of children covered by AFDC shrank by one-fourth in the 1980s.[42] Eligibility requirements were also tightened for Supplemental Security Income (SSI), which served the aged as well as poor blind or poor mentally or physically disabled people. Legislative changes in 1981 and 1982 also reduced eligibility and cut benefit amounts for Food Stamps. In addition, the value and coverage of unemployment benefits were reduced beginning in 1984.

Most historians and analysts argue that when low-rent housing was available, people on the margins could find shelter. But the combined effects of the declining middle class, changes in federal housing policies, urban renewal, and gentrification eliminated most options for low-income housing. When Reagan's famous "Morning in America" presidential campaign ad aired in

1984, it claimed, "With interest rates at about half the record highs of 1980, nearly 2,000 families today will buy new homes, more than at any time in the past four years"; but, as Peter Dreier and Richard Applebaum have shown, 1980s America witnessed the worst housing crisis since the Depression, as the gap between what Americans could afford to pay for housing was outpaced by costs to build and maintain housing.[43] The rate of home ownership rose steadily from the 1940s through the 1970s but declined during the 1980s. Since the early 1970s, as household incomes fell, the size of required down payments and monthly mortgage payments had both increased significantly as a percentage of first-time-buyer income. In 1973, it took one-quarter of the median income of a young family to carry a new mortgage. In 1991, it took more than half. In 1988, homeownership rates for household heads aged forty-four and younger were at their lowest since 1973. The inability of even higher-income buyers to purchase homes put pressure on the rental market and raised rents, impacting both rich and poor renter households.[44] High rents made it very hard for the poor to save money for a down payment, as 85 percent of low-income renters were paying at least 30 percent of their income for housing, and two-thirds of the poor were paying at least half their income on rent, while the average poor single mother paid 70 percent of her income on housing.[45]

The number of poor renter households increased between 1974 and 1988, with single-parent families contributing disproportionately to this growth.[46] Between 1981 and 1989, however, by one estimate, the federal budget for subsidized housing decreased more than 80 percent, from $32 billion to somewhere between $6 billion and $9 billion.[47] In the 1970s, federal government programs represented 31 percent of the rental stock growth. In the 1980s, federal programs accounted for only 14 percent of the rental units added; and between 1982 and 1989, additions to rental stock from federal programs dropped 66 percent, so that the number of new federally subsidized apartments built plunged from more than two hundred thousand in the 1970s to just fifteen thousand in 1990.[48] At the same time, higher interest rates and new types of financing, such as variable rate mortgages, changed incentives to invest in rental housing. The Tax Reform Act of 1986 further reduced incentives, largely through the loss of tax shelters and low-income housing tax credits.[49] Housing choice vouchers to help low-income families secure affordable housing outside subsidized housing projects did not solve the problem, as low vacancy rates made it extremely difficult to find apartments that would take vouchers.[50]

While the building of new subsidized housing decreased, the ongoing effects of midcentury urban renewal and gentrification eliminated much of the existing stock of low-income housing. To a large degree, urban renewal and gentrification displaced Black and other poor minorities. Discrimination in housing markets against minorities had created residential racial and class segregation; and low-cost housing near ghettos was a prime target of urban renewal, disinvestment, conversion, and abandonment, including those buildings deliberately destroyed through arson and those warehoused until they could be converted to condos.[51] James Baldwin named urban renewal "Negro removal," since urban renewal so often depended on eliminating Black neighborhoods and populations from sight.[52]

In addition, urban renewal and gentrification displaced inhabitants of skid row. Many cities demolished skid rows altogether. New York and Los Angeles transformed them using changes in codes, redevelopment, and tax abatement programs that offered incentives to convert low-income properties to middle- and high-income properties.[53] From the 1960s forward, urban renewal targeted SROs, as well as accommodations in boarding or lodging houses. This displaced many people who lived precariously but were not homeless in the modern sense: in previous decades, *homeless* meant "detachment from a family type living arrangement," so a person might have had a low-rent room in a skid row SRO and been considered "homeless."[54]

The destruction of SROs is largely responsible for the rise in mentally ill persons among the homeless.[55] A common myth of 1980s homelessness is that it was caused by deinstitutionalization of the mentally ill, or "Greyhound therapy," in which mentally ill patients were put on a bus to California. But most deinstitutionalization occurred between 1964 and 1973. The Community Mental Health Act of 1963 was motivated in part by the advent of Medicaid, which shifted costs for the mentally ill from the federal government to states and specifically precluded dispersal to mental institutions. At the same time, deinstitutionalization also addressed the legitimate problem of asylums being used as dumping grounds for the mentally ill, the elderly, and even those with syphilis.[56] Deinstitutionalization was intended to provide better, more individualized, treatment and greater autonomy for mentally ill people who could function on medication; however, the comprehensive after-care and outpatient services that were supposed to be provided after deinstitutionalization were left to local municipalities and never materialized.[57] In the late 1970s, after deinstitutionalization, 20 to 25 percent of all people with chronic mental illnesses lived in SROs. Many of these mentally ill people relied on SSI benefits and were able to care for themselves in SROs. The destruction of SROs and loss of other low-cost rentals resulted in the mentally ill becoming unsheltered, while the loss of SSI benefits placed them in poverty. As Stephen Eide notes, "Housing reform and mental health reform intersected as governments sent more and more mentally ill adults into a housing market whose supply was dwindling."[58]

HOMELESS AS URBAN WASTE

At the same time that poverty and homelessness increased in the 1980s, the rich got richer, and America experienced widening income inequality.[59] This is the decade that produced popular TV shows that showcased the excesses of the wealthy, like *Dallas* (1978–91), *Dynasty* (1981–89), *Lifestyles of the Rich and Famous* (1984–18), and, later, the narratives of yuppie striving, such as *L.A. Law* (1986–94) and *thirtysomething* (1987–91). It is no accident that the stereotype of the yuppie, or young urban professional, is invented at the same time that homelessness increases. The parodic guidebook *The Yuppie Handbook* was published in 1984, the same year that *Newsweek* declared "The Year of the Yuppie." The yuppie—defined as a baby boomer who is upwardly mobile, not born to wealth, earning $40K or more from a professional or management job, and living in the city—became a symbol of the wealth gap in the 1980s. As *Newsweek* suggested, "the glamour of this group obscures a more significant trend toward *downward* mobility among their peers."[60]

The rise of yuppies, and especially their role in gentrifying neighborhoods, was viewed as correlative to the displacement of the homeless. Dreier and Applebaum note that "the spectacle of homeless Americans living literally in the shadow of luxury condos and yuppie boutiques symbolized the paradox of the decade: It was a period of both outrageous greed and outrageous suffering."[61] Yuppies helped spur gentrification and followed on the heels of artists to move into previously poor neighborhoods.[62] *The Yuppie Handbook* stated that "the yuppification of a neighborhood has been compared to termite infestation. Yuppies descend in swarms and leave nothing behind but dumpsters filled with discarded linoleum." The book joked that one sign of a neighborhood's yuppification was "disoriented bums trying to figure out why their favorite bar now has asparagus ferns in the window"; and it jested, "Many a bag lady has had nightmares about returning to her train station locker and finding an offering prospectus."[63] Emphasizing the degree to which yuppie relocation into a neighborhood was seen as displacing underserved communities, at a 1989 protest when radicals smashed the glass on the Tompkins Square Christadora House, which had been converted to condos after previously housing social services, they chanted, "Die yuppie scum."[64]

Just as Reagan's cuts to social services and entitlements were viewed as waste cutting, urban renewal and gentrification were also considered a kind of waste removal, clearing an unsightly unwanted population (poor, Black, mentally ill, alcoholic) out to make room for a more appealing, wealthier one (white yuppies). Katherine McKittrick terms the various strategies associated with urban renewal and gentrification, including "'cleaning up' of slums, the forceful displacement of economically disadvantaged communities, the deliberate destruction of buildings" as "urbicide." She argues that "while place annihilation certainly differs according to time and place, the devastations, so clearly pointed to in the term *urbicide*—the deliberate killing of the city—brings into sharp focus how violence functions to render specific human lives, and thus their communities, as waste."[65] As McKittrick suggests, not only were the social services they relied on and the areas where they lived considered waste, but the poor and homeless themselves were treated as a form of urban waste. Making a similar argument in a 1989 forum on homelessness in *Ebony* magazine, Reverend Willie Taplin Barrow, the executive director of Operation Push, decried the treatment of the homeless as garbage: "Homelessness may be the clearest evidence in a body politic that it has abandoned to the slag heap of worthlessness some of its less fortunate citizens. It is a way of institutionalizing third-tier citizenship and social nonpersonhood."[66] Pointedly, in a 1986 internal memo about handling the homeless in Penn Station, an Amtrak official asked, "Can't we get rid of this trash?" Shortly after, Penn Station and Grand Central Station each removed hundreds of lockers where homeless people stored their belongings, and they prohibited the use of washrooms for shaving, cleaning clothes, and forms of self-hygiene to "get rid" of the homeless who had previously used the bathrooms.[67] According to Jonathan Kozol, *Washington Post* columnist George Will argued that it was "simply a matter of public hygiene" to put the homeless out of sight.[68]

To a large degree, the homeless in the 1980s were viewed as not just disposable but disgusting. As anthropologists Margaret Boone and Thomas Weaver noted in their analysis of homelessness, homelessness frequently engenders a kind of disgust: "Many Americans find a fundamental moral fault in poverty itself—its filth, stench and disease ... invoke long-standing and well worn puritanical values in revulsion to the disorganization of homeless lifestyles."[69] In a mostly sympathetic analysis of homelessness, Peter Marin acknowledges that, "to put it as bluntly as I can, for many of us the homeless are shit. And our policies toward them, our spontaneous sense of disgust and horror, our wish to be rid of them—all of this has hidden in it, close to its heart, our feelings about excrement."[70]

In many ways, the homeless are seen as what Julia Kristeva characterizes as the abject, "a threat that seems to emanate from an exorbitant outside or inside, ejected beyond the scope of the possible, the tolerable, the thinkable." The abject is Other: "Not me. Not that." At the same time, the abject threatens because it upsets boundaries and reveals the porousness between "me" and "not me." As Kristeva writes, the abject "*show(s) me* what I permanently thrust aside in order to live." The abject, she writes, is not caused by the lack of cleanliness or health "but what disturbs identity, systems, order."[71] Kristeva's ideas about the abject dovetail with Mary Douglas's analysis of dirt and rubbish. Douglas notes that bits of rubbish are initially seen as "recognizably out of place, a threat to good order;" but at the same time, they have some identity, some link to "whatever it was they came from"; thus, "they are dangerous; their half identity still clings to them and the clarity of the scene in which they protrude is impaired by their presence." But, Douglas writes, as the bits of rubbish enter into the "mass of common rubbish," they lose identity: rubbish "clearly belongs in a defined place, a rubbish heap of one kind or another."[72] In this sense, the homeless are perceived as dangerous because they disturb order and ideas of systems of categorization, but the more the homeless are relegated to the status of rubbish or waste (or shit), the more they seem like rubbish and "not me."

Viewing the homeless as trash works to dehumanize and other them, but the feelings of horror and revulsion they engender also reveal our recognition of their humanity and their being "just like you and me." The equation of the homeless with trash works, on the one hand, to construct the homeless "as deviants: fortifying the boundaries between 'us' and 'them.'"[73] As Kozol argues, labeling the homeless as mentally ill, or "disordered," "helps to place them at a distance. It says they aren't quite like us—and more important that we could not be like them."[74] Similarly, Marin suggests that "the homeless, simply because they are homeless, are strangers, alien—and, therefore, a threat."[75] On the other hand, the homeless are never fully alien but always carry the contradictory possibility for identification. As Boone and Weaver state, the homeless "stand in opposition to American values of industriousness, involvement, progress, and a belief in each human being's inherent and unique potential," but, at the same time, they "arouse a deeply seated fear that 'there but for the grace of God, go I.'"[76]

The 1980s cycle of films about the homeless "works through" these contradictory feelings in various ways. Most of the films seek to create sympathy for this population by providing a backstory and explanation for their homelessness to emphasize the logic of "there but for the grace of God go I." Some of the films portray the homeless as martyrs who suffer at the hands of an uncaring society, similar to Bowie's "Day-In Day-Out." Others suggest that the homeless are "just like you and me" through narratives of redemption and transformation that show individual characters being lifted out of homelessness and even becoming wealthy, thus "proving" their worthiness. Virtually all the films highlight trash (trash cans, garbage bags, debris, etc.) in their mise-en-scène, simultaneously marking out urban space as impoverished "waste" and creating a visual equation between homelessness and trash. Whether tragic or comedic, emphasizing martyrdom or redemption, these films, like the social problem films about the veteran discussed in chapter 2, point to large-scale social problems but offer individual (re)solutions. Rather than critique the various neoliberal policies that inflated homelessness in the 1980s, by emphasizing free market capitalism and even a form of trickle-down economics in narratives of private benevolence, these films feed into the free-market logic Reagan promulgated when he described "the people who are sleeping on the grates, the homeless who are homeless, you might say, by choice."[77]

HOMELESS HORROR

While the majority of films in the 1980s cycle tend to humanize the homeless to some degree, a few films "work through" the homeless crisis by rendering the homeless not only abject but horrific. The title of the horror film *Street Trash* (Muro 1987) makes the homology between the homeless and trash explicit. The homeless here are cartoons, avatars of the abject. The film situates the homeless in and among garbage, starting with a chase that lands one homeless man, Fred (Mike Lackey), in a garbage truck and continuing to a junkyard where the homeless gather and are ruled over by the brutal tyrant Bronson (Vic Noto). The film hyperbolizes its investment in the disgusting in shots of severed heads, spewing guts, and even a game of keep-away with a detached penis. The narrative revolves around infighting among the homeless, on the one hand, and the murder of a gangster's girlfriend in the homeless encampment, on the other: two parallel insular worlds that are invisible to the public. The main thrust of the narrative, however, is the circulation of a mysterious old case of cheap toxic booze, Viper, discovered in a liquor store basement and sold by an unscrupulous salesman, that kills the homeless who drink it. Whenever a homeless person drinks Viper, he or she explodes, dissolves, or melts away in a shower of bright primary colors. Fred becomes aware of this, but the deaths are unnoticed by and seemingly without consequence to the general public.

The sci-fi horror film *C.H.U.D* (Cheek 1984), similarly, links the homeless to toxic waste. George (John Heard), a photographer doing a photojournalistic series on the homeless, especially "undergrounders" who live in the sewers and subway tunnels, learns that street people and "undergrounders" have been going missing. The police are mostly uncaring, but Captain Bosch (Christopher Curry) admits that many other people, including his wife, have gone missing. Initially, Bosch is told by higher-ups that there is a monster beneath the city labeled C.H.U.D. (for Cannibalistic Humanoid Underground Dweller), which grabs people from the sewers and drags them below. Exposed to radiation, it was "once human," he is told, and "dressed in the rags of a Bowery bum"; in other words, it is a homeless vagrant. As Bosch and George investigate further, with help from a reporter, Murphy (J. C. Quinn), and a social worker, A. J. "The Reverend" Shepard (Daniel Stern), they discover that rather than one monster, a community of monsters has developed as a result of government corruption: to avoid transporting toxic waste through the city, thus endangering the public, the Nuclear Regulatory Commission (NRC) has instead dumped the waste, labeled C.H.U.D. (Contamination Hazard Urban Disposal), in the subway tunnels where the homeless live, thus treating the homeless as themselves waste (not as "the public") and literally turning them into mutants. When Bosch confronts the bureaucrat from the NRC, he yells, "You're nothing but the government garbageman," highlighting the view of the homeless as trash. The film ends with A. J., George, and Bosch defeating the bureaucrat, exploding a truck that then seals a manhole cover, trapping the toxic menace below ground.

John Carpenter's film *Prince of Darkness* (1987) yokes the homeless to both a toxic biological agent and Satan. In the film, a Catholic priest (Donald Pleasance) invites a quantum physicist (Victor Wong) and his students to investigate a mysterious cylinder containing a swirling green liquid, located in a seemingly abandoned church linked to a mysterious cult. The scientists investigate the liquid, which is found to be a "self-organizing life form growing out of a probiotic liquid." As the scientists decipher the mysterious language of a sort of Bible found next to the liquid, they learn that the container is seven million years old, sentient, and the corporeal embodiment of Satan, worshipped by the cult. Before the scientists get contaminated and, in effect, hypnotized by the liquid, the homeless serve as spooky foreshadowing. The homeless, led by Alice Cooper, gather round the church and stare at the scientists, seemingly mesmerized. One woman approaches the priest and shows her begging cup, filled with maggots. When one of the students attempts to leave the church, the homeless swarm and attack him, turning him into a ghoulish spirit. Never given voice or names, the homeless lurk near the church throughout the film, serving as background minions to Satan.

These three films rely on and further an association between the homeless and waste for horrific effect. Although they are not social problem films, it is not hard to see an allegorical connection to the contemporary crisis of increased homelessness. *Street Trash* not only equates the homeless with garbage but underscores their insignificance as their melting and exploding bodies litter the streets in campily excessive colorful blasts that go unnoticed. *C.H.U.D* and *Prince of Darkness* relegate the homeless to an underworld—literally, in subway tunnels and, metaphysically, in a Satanic cult, respectively. The danger posed by the homeless in these two films relates to seepage, their toxic intrusion into and contamination of the public. Whatever modest critique of business, government, or the church these three films allow depends on a conservative view of the homeless as less than human and needing to be contained.

RESIDUAL MODELS OF HOMELESSNESS

While the films described above overstate the contemporary crisis of homelessness through horror, other films minimize the threat by displacing homeless narratives into more sentimental views. These films do not explicitly address the emergent model of homelessness but, instead, rely on residual models. Films of the 1980s sometimes represent more traditional skid row inhabitants. For example, *Ironweed* (Babenco 1987), based on William Kennedy's Pulitzer Prize–winning novel of the same name, hearkens back to Depression-era tramping and centers on alcoholic drifters Francis (Jack

Nicholson) and Helen (Meryl Streep), who circulate in a world of mission revivals, soup kitchens, SROs, and hobo camps. Francis, a former baseball pitcher, is haunted by two deaths: as a youth involved in a strike, he killed a scab, Harold Allen (Nathan Lane), whose ghost still haunts him; and as a young father, he accidentally dropped and killed his baby boy and then, devastated, abandoned his family. Helen is a former singer, her downfall not explained, her alcoholism defining. The film is more of a "chamber piece," as Roger Ebert says, a narrative about redemption, guilt, and love rather than homelessness per se. Still, the mise-en-scène of *Ironweed* works to render Francis as trash in ways similar to contemporary films. At the opening of the film, we see him sleeping, covered by a newspaper, with trash blowing around him. Ebert captures the way the film equates the homeless man and garbage: "At first the shape simply seems to be some old debris, blown up against the side of a building, but then the shape stirs and we see that it is a man."[78]

Rather than a period piece, *On the Nickel* (1980), directed by and starring Ralph Waite, offers a last-gasp view of Los Angeles skid row inhabitants. The film focuses on a recovering alcoholic, Sam (Donald Moffat), who misses his previous life among the skid row winos. The film shows mostly middle-aged homeless males, including one Black man, Paul (Hal Williams), who is introduced digging through a garbage can, and one white bag lady, Rose (Penelope Allen), who carefully guards her shopping cart full of debris. In many ways, the world portrayed in *On the Nickel* is a throwback to the tramp cycle: it includes a character who rides the rails, emphasizes the drunken camaraderie among bums, and depicts homelessness as a rejection of false society. Sam decries the "game" of ordinary life, where you "have to pretend that things are important." "You can get the wine out of your system," he says, "but, damn, it's hard to get the life out of your system. It's boring out there." Emphasizing its ties to an older model of tramping, the film concludes with a rousing rendition of the 1895 Australian anthem "Waltzing Mathilda"—a tramp slang song that conveyed the grim realities of itinerant workers in Australia in the 1890s but was revised in a lighter version in 1903 and became a popular anthem of Australian character over the years—about an itinerant worker pursued by the police after he steals a sheep (jumbuck) to eat, who travels by foot (waltzing) with his belongings slung over his back in a swag bag (mathilda).

In a different kind of throwback, *On the Right Track* (Philips 1981) features Gary Coleman as a plucky orphan who lives in Union Station in Chicago. Set in contemporary times, and featuring Maureen Stapleton as

Mary the bag lady, this TV movie is nonetheless akin to 1930s movies about orphans, such as those starring Shirley Temple or Jane Withers, that show the urban environment as a space of fortuitous encounter and family formation.[79] In this film, the orphan Lester fears "up there" in the world because he is called "incorrigible," "runaway," and "juvenile delinquent," while down below he runs a shoeshine business, has friends among all the workers in the train station's arcade, and is valued for his ability to predict the winners of horse races. Mary also rejects the world "up there." Having "dropped out of society" twelve years prior, Mary wins $54K from one of Lester's racetrack tips, but after a trip to the beauty salon and to a department store to buy a new designer outfit, she returns to the station to live in her trash can, albeit with a new Gucci shopping bag. Lester proves his worthiness not only by picking horses but also by helping the city solve its fiscal crisis through gambling. Because of his financial worth, the mayor (Norman Fell) declares Lester "a human being, not something to be thrown away." As in films starring Temple and Withers, Lester helps connect two single people, singer Jill (Lisa Eilbacher), who works in the train station and has befriended Lester, and social worker Frank (Michael Lembeck), who is sent to remove Lester from the station. They quickly fall in love, decide to marry, and adopt Lester. At film's end, the three exit the station together, the scary "up there" now rendered in streaming heavenly light.

While these films speak to the contemporary moment by invoking homelessness, they seem to exist out of time. In *Ironweed*, homelessness is mixed with nostalgia, in scenes invoking old-time baseball, live singing performances on radio, Victrolas, and ragpicker wagons. *On the Nickel* seems wistful for a bygone time, as evidenced by its invocation of the bush ballad "Waltzing Mathilda" and its skid row mise-en-scène. *On the Right Track* relies on cuteness and familiar tropes of movie childhood to soften its tale. Together, they all displace attention from the immediate crisis of homelessness into the past.

HOMELESSNESS AS SUBCULTURE

Where *On the Right Track* has resonances with 1930s films, many other films connect to the trope of the runaway in 1970s films. But where the 1970s runaway was seen as mobile and connected to hitchhiking, 1980s runaway films more often show homeless runaways clustered in cities, caught in bureaucratic circuits of juvenile justice and social services, on the one hand, and drug dealing and prostitution, on the other. Rather than traversing the nation, these runaways inhabit street corners and squats, often not far from where they grew up, their movements largely limited to a small circle of spaces. As with the 1970s hitchhiking films, adults are represented as inadequate or abusive; but instead of a generational *counter*culture, the runaways form a multicultural urban *sub*culture defined by life on the street, nondomestic forms of family, and negative relations to expectations around teen life such as school and family.

Where the Day Takes You (Rocco 1992) approaches runaway youth as a social problem. The screenplay was written by actor Michael Hitchcock, based on his work as a volunteer in homeless shelters. It includes a closing crawl text announcing, "Every 26 seconds a child runs away from home;" and it is framed as an interview by an earnest social worker (Laura San Giacamo) seeking to understand homeless youth. *Where the Day Takes You* has a mainly white cast, aside from a bit part with a young Will Smith as a paraplegic teen. The narrative is largely told through interviews with King (Dermot Mulroney), just released from a two-month stint in jail. The film aims for realism and shows teens in Los Angeles working as prostitutes, dealing and taking drugs, involved in petty crimes such as stealing CDs from cars and dine-and-dash meals, train-hopping, and panhandling or "spare changing"—territory also covered in the gritty documentary *Streetwise* (Bell 1984) about Seattle homeless youth. The kids in *Where the Day Takes You* live in "the Hole," a space under the freeway overpass. Some work as prostitutes in motels, and King admits to sometimes sleeping with girls just to have a bed.

Similar to the youth in 1970s hitchhiking films, the kids in *Where the Day Takes You* come from dysfunctional and abusive homes. King's father was a drug addict. Greg (Sean Astin), a drug addict himself, has a cruel stepmother who refuses him shelter. The gay hustler Lil J (Balthazar Getty) was abused by his uncle at age ten. When King asserts that his girlfriend, Heather (Lara Flynn Boyle), likely left home because her father or stepfather molested her, she corrects him and says it was her brother who did. King describes the community of homeless youth as his chosen family, and he helps other kids hide from the police so they will not get sent home, the family home thus seen as a worse option than homelessness. Along with familial causes of homelessness, *Where the Day Takes You* also projects blame onto other adults. The narrative includes a sinister drug pusher, Ted (Kyle MacLachlan), who nudges Greg from meth to heroin, eventually leading to the latter's death. *Where the Day Takes You* also shows the failure of the juvenile justice system and social services, as we see Greg arrested after robbing his stepmother, then in rehab, then back on the streets robbing a liquor store to get drugs.

The end of *Where the Day Takes You* underscores the intractable ongoingness of homelessness among youth. After Greg's death, King, Heather, and Lil J attempt an escape from the city, even as King warns that a new city will be the same for them, just "another city, another freeway." They get stopped by the cops at the bus station. Lil J pulls a gun. In a slow-motion shot, we see King push Lil J out of the way as the cops shoot. At the end of the film, nine months later, the Interviewer shows Heather a videotape of the now-dead King talking about his love for her; then Heather joins Lil J as he is released from prison. They head back to the streets and immediately start panhandling. This ending resembles the endings of youth hitchhiking films that refuse closure and emphasize the cyclical replenishment of new homeless youth.

Where the Day Takes You and *Streetwise* portray homeless youth as a subculture with their own distinctive practices, ideas, and way of life—including, as I have mentioned, panhandling, prostitution, train-hopping, petty theft, and the creation of alternate families. Other films about homeless teens stitch teen homelessness to artistic subcultures, making homelessness seem even more of a lifestyle choice. In Robert Wise's film *Rooftops* (1989), for example, an inferior sort of bookend to his *West Wide Story* (1961), homeless teens live in a subcultural world, largely invisible to the mainstream, in rooftop dwellings on top of abandoned buildings. The teens participate in two other subcultural activities: graffiti, which marks their status as fugitive urban dwellers, and what they call "combat," a dance competition that takes place in a graffiti-covered alley with burning trash cans, in which the victor forces the loser off a platform without touching him. The white teen T (Jason Gedrick), a top combat player, learns from Squeak (Alexis Cruz), a Puerto Rican graffiti artist, about capoeira, a Brazilian form that combines elements of dance with martial arts. Squeak describes it as something developed by slaves to conceal their knowledge of martial arts from their masters.

As in *Where the Day Takes You*, each of the teens in *Rooftops* has a backstory of parental failure that leads them away from home. As a sympathetic cop says, "Kids leave bad homes." T, who lives in a rooftop water tower, is an orphan. When he was six years old, his father threw his mother out of the house after a drunken argument. She drunkenly tried to climb a rain gutter, slipped, got electrocuted, and died. T's father killed himself shortly after. Squeak is thrown out of his mother's apartment by her abusive boyfriend.

The mother of Amber (Tisha Campbell), a Black card hustler, is a prostitute and junkie whose pimp tries to force her to work the streets. Another Black homeless teen, Kadim (Allen Payne), cares for his father, a former boxer with dementia, who lives in a sleazy rundown hotel. The one housed teen, Elana (Troy Byer), lives with her father and sisters in a building where her father is superintendent. When her father's health fails, she falls prey to her cousin Lobo (Eddie Velez), a Puerto Rican gangster, and is forced to serve as lookout for his drug dealing.

In *Rooftops,* the homeless teens contend with the gangsters who want to use abandoned buildings for drug dealing and thus push the teens out of their makeshift homes. The gangsters become convenient foils that displace the larger social issues that shape the teens' lives. Near the end of the film, after the gangsters kill Squeak, T uses his capoeira training to battle Lobo on a garbage-strewn rooftop and defeats him when Lobo falls to his death through a large hole in the roof. In the final scene, T, Kadim, and others perform capoeira on the combat platform; then all the teens join together in a dance party while Jeffrey Osborne's theme song "Rooftops" plays. The lyrics of the song, along with the utopian mood of the party, celebrate the status quo and make the teens' homelessness seem to be about freedom rather than poverty:

> You want somebody in your life
> This could be the perfect time
> People gonna say we got no money
> I say we don't need a dime . . .
> You want some action in your life
> This could be the perfect time . . .
> Hear the people say, won't go spending our lives in chains . . .
> I'm gonna climb right out of here
> And scream from the rooftops
> yeah yeah yeah yeah
> On the rooftops of New York City.

Where *Rooftops* invents the subcultural "combat," *Smithereens* (Seidelman 1982) situates its narrative of teen homelessness in New York's punk scene. Paul (Brad Rijn) lives in a van, having left Montana seeking the excitement and adventure of New York. He is on a road trip and is still in contact with his family, not homeless. He meets Wren (Susan Berman), a runaway from New Jersey and would-be punk musician seeking fame. Wren has a part-time job at a copy shop but mainly uses her time there making flyers of herself with the headline "WHO IS THIS?"—an attempt to garner fame. When Wren is evicted from her apartment, she travels to her sister's house in New Jersey to borrow money. Her sister offers her a home, but Wren refuses. When Wren says "I'm not setting foot in New Jersey again. Ever," we take it be about her desire to be part of the punk scene and the cool of New York City, and away from her sister's suburban lifestyle, as opposed to an escape from abuse. Wren chooses to squat in Paul's van until she opportunistically latches onto Eric (played by Richard Hell of the bands "Television" and "Richard Hell and the Voidoids"), a one-hit-wonder punk star whom Wren thinks will be her ticket to stardom. At film's end, Eric tricks Wren into thinking he will take her to Los Angeles but robs and abandons her; and Paul sells his van and travels to New Hampshire. Wren ends up alone, walking the highway and, faced with little choice, gets into the convertible of a man who propositions her. Rather than a narrative about homelessness as a social problem, Wren's story is seen as one of female striving and drift, more akin to *Wanda* (Loden 1970) or *Vagabond* (Varda 1985) than to *Where the Day Takes You*.

Similar to *Smithereens*, *Times Square* (Moyle 1980), in part, links homeless runaway teen girls Pamela Pearl (Trini Alvarado) and Nicky Marotta (Robin Johnson) to a punk subculture. The film was produced by Robert Stigwood, the producer and music industry entrepreneur who made films such as *Grease* (Kleiser 1978) and *Saturday Night Fever* (Badham 1977), projects that made the synergistic marketing of soundtrack albums equally important to the film. The soundtrack for *Times Square* includes such pop punk and New Wave artists as The Pretenders, Suzi Quatro, the Ramones, Joe Jackson, Patti Smith, Lou Reed, The Cure, and The Cars; and Nicky performs two punk songs in the film. The girls label their band the Sleez Sisters, taking ownership of the public perception of them as sordid and disgusting. They find an audience through a talk radio DJ, Johnny LaGuardia (Tim Curry), who realizes that Pamela is the daughter of a political leader behind a campaign to clean up Times Square, "Reclaim the ♥ of the City," echoing the famous 1977 "I ♥ NY" slogan. Johnny reads on the air a letter from Pamela in which she describes herself as a "zombie girl," neglected by her father and treated as mentally ill for being unhappy. Then, he broadcasts the girls' music on the air, and celebrates their rebellious act of throwing TV sets off rooftops across the city.

Ultimately, Pamela and Nicky elicit a subculture of teen girls who dress in garbage bags, parodying their dismissal as "garbage." As Nicky becomes depressed and angry, Pamela plans a concert to showcase Nicky's talent. A

FIGURE 4.2. Punk "Sleez Bags" throng to see Nicky (Robin Johnson) in concert in *Times Square*.

promo for the concert says, "Nicky Moratta says, 'If they treat you like garbage, put your body in a garbage bag. If they treat you like a criminal, black out your eyes.'" In a montage sequence, we see thousands of girls all over the city leaving their homes and flocking to Times Square in garbage bags and bandit raccoon-eye makeup (fig. 4.2). Sidewalk vendors sell "Sleez Bags." Here, a discourse associating the homeless with garbage is given a feminist twist, as Nicky's message resonates with Sleez Sisters fans, none of whom are homeless but all of whom feel they have been treated as garbage, presumably just for being girls. But they masquerade as garbage without giving up the comforts of home: homelessness is a costume and a punk posture. The film's ending further cements the view that homelessness is a lifestyle choice. As the police arrive to stop the concert, Nicky triumphantly stage dives from the rooftop and then disappears into the crowd; but Pamela gets ready to return home, having reconnected with her father, and wanting to be "normal."

These teen films mostly show runaway youth in the city, but they are isolated from other homeless people. In one scene in *Where the Day Takes You*, after "spare changing," King gives an older homeless woman money, distinguishing himself from her and suggesting that she is more needy than he. Because homelessness in these films is largely viewed as a teen problem, it does not rise to the status of a broadly representative social problem. Unlike the countercultural youth of the hitchhiking cycle of films, however, the runaway teens in these films form a subculture that is unique and separate from the dominant culture but does not challenge it.

UN/SHELTERED HOMELESSNESS

While teen homeless films tend to place the blame for homelessness on bad family situations, or, in other words, a failure of home, other social problem films look more squarely at poverty and displacement and consider institutional failures, particularly the failure of the shelter system. Lee Grant's documentary *Down and Out in America* (1986) sets a template for representations of the new homeless, especially white families. Grant's opening voiceover narration announces that there are thirty-four million people living in poverty, twenty million who don't have enough food, eight million unemployed, and two million homeless. Her voiceover describes the "new street people" as "people who did everything right," people who "were riding high on the American dream," people whose newfound poverty can be blamed on deindustrialization, loss of jobs to foreign competition, and corporate takeovers of farms. The documentary tracks different communities of homeless people and the indifference and violence they face from an uncaring government. In Los Angeles, Grant films "Justiceville," a well-organized encampment on a vacant lot where homeless people—"just people down on their luck"—try to find work, get an education, and get off drugs. The police evict residents and bulldoze the camp. In New York's Lower East Side, she meets mostly Latinx people who have taken over abandoned buildings and offered to buy them from the city, but they are refused. In particular, Grant focuses on one white family of five that lost their Coney Island home to a fire and ended up in a residential hotel in Manhattan. Despite the fact that the hotel charges the government $3,000 a month for rooms—while residents are offered only tiny below-market subsidies to rent apartments—the hotel does not provide cooking facilities or hot water, and rooms are filthy and rat-infested. Residents are caught in a bureaucratic nightmare: stuck on years-long waiting lists for housing projects, unable to get jobs because they cannot secure childcare, and thus unable to pay rent, they cannot escape the hotel.

Grants' made-for-TV film *No Place like Home* (1989), similarly, details the travails of a white family that falls on hard times and shows them as martyrs to the economy, social services, and an uncaring society. When the film begins, family dad Mike Cooper (Jeff Daniels) has already lost his job at "the plant" and is taking classes to pivot from factory work and become an electrician. Then, as in the documentary, the family loses their home to fire, and they move in with Mike's wealthy brother, Eddie (Scott Marlowe). When Eddie discovers that Mike's wife, Zan (Christine Lahti), is using food stamps, both he and Mike are angry—Eddie because it is an insult to his hospitality and Mike because it is an insult to his masculine identity. "I'm a worker," he says, "the plant quit me." When the Coopers and their two children leave Eddie's, they fall further and further into poverty and precarity. They live in their car for a week until they find a welcoming campground, but the campground limits visits to ten days. They stay briefly in a shelter and then are moved to a residential hotel, like the one in *Down and Out in America*. Mike spirals further into self-pity, declaring "I'm not a welfare bum." He briefly gets a job but is fired when his boss moves to Florida, so he goes South to seek work, leaving Zan and the kids behind. Mile's son David (Lantz Landry) falls in with criminally minded homeless kids and starts working for a drug dealer. A hotel guard who discovers David's activity blackmails and attempts to rape Zan. Zan and the kids flee and live on the streets. When they attempt to return to Eddie's home, Eddie and his wife are away, so Zan and the kids break in, but the police come and kick them out. After trying shelters and the train station, they eventually find an abandoned house. Mike returns, dejected—"Nobody wants people like me anymore"—and soon after, the house becomes vulnerable to carousing thugs. At film's end, the family walks away from the house on the street, a la *Modern Times* (Chaplin 1936), and a crawl reminds us that "there are three million homeless, families the largest growing population."

The TV movie *God Bless the Child* (Elikann 1988) likewise details the frustrations, humiliations, and hazards of homelessness, in this case focusing on a white mother and child. Rather than a recent fall into poverty, single mother Theresa Johnson (Mare Winningham) describes herself as coming from a poor background and describes poverty as "like a disease" that "grabs hold of you and won't let you go." Theresa is pushed out of her modest apartment as a result of gentrification. She asks to stay with a woman for whom she worked as a cleaner, but the woman, in a palatial house, says she has no room. She can't stay with her mom, who already shares a trailer with Theresa's two sisters. After being evicted, she stays at a church shelter, but, owing to rules about how long you can stay, she has to move from shelter to shelter. She loses her job in a hotel laundry because she leaves work early to sign up at one shelter. Unable to get a place without a job, or a job without a place, and unable to get AFDC benefits for a month, she and her child, Hilary (Grace Johnston), end up sleeping on the street. Eventually an African American social worker, Calvin (Dorian Harewood), helps her secure a small filthy home. Theresa cleans it up and makes it palatable, but after rats invade

Hilary's bed, she reports the landlord, who then evicts her. Back at a shelter, Hilary gets lead poisoning and ends up in hospital, which she says is the best place she's ever lived. Ultimately, after telling the social worker that "people look at us like we're trash," Theresa abandons Hilary so that the child can be adopted. As with *No Place like Home,* the film ends with a crawl declaring that thirteen million children live in poverty.

While *No Place like Home* and *God Bless the Child* both focus on white families, and especially white women, both films show these women relying for support on Black people. In *No Place like Home,* at the residential hotel, Zan meets Prue (CCH Pounder), a victim of domestic abuse who has been in the hotel for thirteen months. Prue teaches Zan the ropes, showing her how to cook in her room, despite the rules, and how to navigate the system. When Prue leaves, having secured public housing, Zan suddenly becomes vulnerable to the predatory guards. In *God Bless the Child,* Theresa not only receives help from Calvin but also gets advice about shelters from Black female coworkers at the laundry, and she becomes friends with a Black family who live next door to her. The Watkins family's story in some ways parallels Theresa's. Single mother Althea (L. Scott Caldwell) struggles to maintain her family of three children. Like Theresa, she has been deserted by her husband, Raymond (Obba Batatundé), who does not pay child support. They go hungry the fourth week of every month, when food stamps run out. Althea's son Richard (Yasiin Bey, a.k.a. Mos Def) is smart and about to graduate eighth grade, but his mother can't afford to get him graduation clothes. In a deux ex machina, however, Richard's father, Raymond, provides money for the clothing, and the family joins together to celebrate the graduation.

In both films, the Black family's story of poverty is treated as more natural and expected than the white family's. In both films, the Black family is also ultimately more successful than the white family. Prue's family exits the residential hotel, whereas Zan slips further down the social ladder; and the Watkins enjoy a scene of restored patriarchy and potential social mobility at Richard's graduation, while Theresa is forced to abandon her child. In part, these films juxtapose white and Black families to underscore the "new" crisis of white homelessness, showing white poverty as a fall into the underclass, stereotypically assumed to be Black. At the same time, in showing Black characters as more successfully navigating poverty and homelessness, these films privilege whiteness by making homelessness seem worse for white people.

In a different vein, *The Saint of Fort Washington* (Hunter 1993) situates its white homeless character as a martyred saint for its Black costar. The opening of the film shows mentally ill Matthew (Matt Dillon) evicted from his SRO as demolition crews arrive to tear it down, an instance of mentally ill persons unmoored through urban renewal. As Matthew wanders the streets, taking photos with an empty camera, a diegetic voiceover by Danny Glover's character, a Vietnam vet named Jerry, begins. "This here's the story of that little Black boy goin' to the jungle. What's his name? Sambo. Little Black Sambo." The voiceover explains that this Sambo is "not particularly Black," however, because "this here's the honest-to-God, up-to-date, unexpurgated version." In this version, as in Helen Bannerman's original racist 1899 children's book *The Story of Little Black Sambo,* Sambo enters the jungle with bright fancy clothes and an umbrella, but the tigers take all his clothing. But where the tigers in the book destroy themselves by becoming vain over their clothes and fighting each other, in this version, Jerry says that white Sambo walks out of the jungle with the precious gift of "his own naked self," and "no one goin' to take that away from him."

The Saint of Fort Washington is an earnest film that wants to paint a sensitive portrait of modern homelessness. The *Los Angeles Times* review described it as "so well-meaning that it makes you want to go out and make a donation to your favorite charity."[80] The film's vision of homelessness seems to depend on "draping a cloak of nobility over its characters."[81] Disturbingly, this nobility depends on elevating to the status of a deity the white homeless character; "a pathetic White boy thrown in, hoping to draw some people to the theater," according to one review.[82] That the film allegorizes its narrative of homelessness through a children's book generally regarded as racist, and does so in a Black-voiced frame narration that makes Sambo a white hero, is bizarre enough. But the film goes further. After Jerry and Matthew meet at a shelter where Jerry schools Matthew in how to protect himself and his goods, they become friends (fig. 4.3). Jerry teaches Matthew how to get money by squeegeeing car windshields and collecting cans; he supplies film to help Matthew take real photos; and they make plans to rent an apartment together when they get a down payment because the shelter is too dangerous. When Matthew tells Jerry that he is schizophrenic and hears voices, Jerry dismisses the diagnosis and suggests that Matthew is perhaps, instead, a saint.

The film's privileging of whiteness assumes a postracial logic and erasure of difference. When Matthew is hassled by shelter bully Little Leroy (Ving Rhames), Jerry claims that Matthew is his son, emphasizing Jerry's paternal role and denying Matthew's whiteness. To Leroy's argument that Matthew is white, Jerry replies, "Skin tone mean shit, Leroy. He's blacker than you."

FIGURE 4.3. Matthew (Matt Dillon) and Jerry (Danny Glover) seek shelter together in *The Saint of Fort Washington*.

Then, when Matthew asks why he claimed him as his son, Jerry tells him he had a dream the night before that they were together in Africa hundreds of years ago when slave traders came; the slave traders tried to take Matthew away from Jerry; and Matthew died in his arms—an odd vision of white sacrifice amid historical violence against Blacks. Eventually, Matthew does die at Leroy's hands. Jerry follows his casket to Potter's Field and mourns his "son." At the end, as Jerry cleans windshields, we hear his voiceover, now addressed to Matthew's spirit: "I'm startin' over now boy. Nothin' gonna stop me, man or God. I get by cause you with me. So long I be, you be. And that our story." Despite Jerry's greater experience and knowledge in the way of the streets, Matthew is rendered Jerry's spiritual protector—Sambo, saint, and vaguely Christological.

PHILANTHROPIC SOLUTIONS

Most social problem films about homelessness, whether about teens or families, show homelessness to be an unending problem. Characters either continue being homeless or end in tragedy. In these films, characters mainly interact with other homeless people or social services. When they interact with wealthy people, such as brother Eddie in *No Place Like Home* or Theresa's former employer in *God Bless the Child*, the wealthy are unsympathetic and unhelpful. In contrast, the made-for-TV movie *Stone Pillow* (Schaefer 1985) shows the rich as beneficent, thus celebrating philanthropy over structural change.

Stone Pillow begins with a stark visual metaphor of the figure of the bag lady. An aerial shot establishes the city setting; then a cut brings us to ground level, and we track in to a sidewalk grate where we find a black garbage bag. The bag stirs, and the camera moves into a close-up to reveal Lucille Ball's

FIGURE 4.4. Flora (Lucille Ball) emerges from a trash bag, a hieroglyph of the "bag lady" in *Stone Pillow*.

face emerging from the bag (fig. 4.4). Ball, playing Flora the bag lady, peels off the garbage bag and unwraps her shopping cart, which is also covered in a garage bag. After meeting Flora, we cut to Carrie (Daphne Zuniga), a worker in the Delano Women's Shelter. Unable to understand or sympathize with shelter clients, Carrie is told by her white male boss to go learn about life or lose her job. Carrie is counseled by a Black female coworker, a security guard named Collins (Anna Maria Horsford), to go out and talk to the homeless. Sure enough, Carrie meets Flora, and because Carrie has had her purse stolen, Flora mistakenly assumes she is a homeless runaway. Interested in learning about homelessness, Carrie allows the misconception.

As in other social problem films, the white homeless character requires a backstory to justify her status. Flora explains to Carrie that she had a husband and child but got sick and was sent to the hospital. When she returned, her husband and son were gone, and she could never find them. She worked in the wartime defense industry and other jobs but then got welfare. She got evicted from her home and, without an address, could no longer get benefits; without benefits, she could not get a home. Now she wanders the streets calling "Sonny" and carries her child's toys and mementos in the hopes of one day seeing him again.

Similar to *The Saint of Fort Washington*, the more experienced homeless person, Flora, takes the younger Carrie under her wing. Flora teaches Carrie how to dumpster-dive for food and warns her about the shelters, making clear that she doesn't want to go to one because they take your belongings, force you to be scrubbed, and put you in a room with "screaming Mimis." With Flora, Carrie learns to navigate spaces such as the Port Authority Bus Terminal, where they wash themselves, and hidden tunnels under Grand Central, where they huddle with other homeless. Undercutting somewhat the perception of mental illness among the homeless, Flora teaches Carrie that rape and sexual assault are inevitable for women but can be avoided if one acts crazy. When the homeless are rousted from Grand Central, Flora, trying to rescue Carrie, ends up in the women's shelter against her will. There her worst nightmare comes true: her cart is taken away, she is scrubbed and changed, and she is housed with crazy women. Most hurtfully, she discovers Carrie's deception.

The film shows the failures and insensitivities of the shelter system. Instead of suggesting ways to improve it, however, the film proffers individual solutions as more effective than institutional ones. Carrie goes back to the Delano Shelter and discusses her worry about Flora with Collins. When Carrie asks why the shelters treat Flora as a criminal, Collins, a shelter employee whose job is presumably to help the homeless, answers in a way that negates any promise of help from social services: "It's such a big problem, people don't know how to handle it. Mostly we just do what we can." She advises Carrie that one-on-one interventions are best. This leads to a deux ex machina happy ending in which, through rich friends on Long Island who have a cottage, Carrie finds Flora a house with a picket fence and garden where she can collect Social Security checks.

REVERSALS OF FORTUNES

The philanthropic rich friends in *Stone Pillow* remain offscreen: they exist only to provide a happy ending to Flora's story. By comparison, in comedic narratives about the homeless, the interactions between rich people and the homeless are central to the narrative. In certain ways, the interactions between the homeless and the wealthy echo the relationship in tramp films discussed in chapter 1: the male homeless character seems more authentic and manly than the feminized male elite. In this vein, Angela Stukator reads *The Fisher King* in relation to Robert Bly's best-selling book *Iron John* as a "guide to how men can rescue 'true masculinity,' repressed and denied in modern culture." But where the tramp provided a counter to hegemonic ideals of masculinity, these 1980s films "in fact reclaim a conservative vision of masculinity."[83] In a marked difference from tramp films, these comedies about homelessness can be characterized as romantic comedies. Not only does the wealthy person learn from the homeless one, but the homeless person effects a personal change in status, moving up the social ladder and into marriage and domesticity. While the films flirt with a model of masculinity that veers away from breadwinning and domesticity, ultimately, they reaffirm the values of hegemonic masculinity, including material success.

In part, the interactions between rich housed characters and poor unhoused ones in 1980s films partake of what Jane Feuer describes as "yuppie envy and yuppie guilt" in 1980s TV. Feuer argues that guilt is a constitutive part of yuppie values; unlike those born to wealth, yuppies, children of the 1960s, feel guilt over "their material and financial success, their compromised ideals, and, for women, their lost opportunities for love and children."[84] While TV shows like *L.A. Law* (1986–94) and *thirtysomething* create envy for the characters' lifestyles at the level of mise-en-scène (nice apartments, designer clothes, fancy cars, upscale restaurants), Feuer claims that they simultaneously embed guilt into their narratives, making the characters seem despicable (greedy, amoral, mean, etc.).

Homeless films similarly explore yuppie guilt in narratives that force a questioning of the yuppie lifestyle and its values. As David Levinson and Marcy Ross argue, the "romanticized homeless protagonists help the housed characters discover what is truly important in life. The homeless condition is used as a critique of the materialistic and competitive aspects of American culture."[85] But even as the spectacle of yuppie wealth is critiqued, even mocked, the films ultimately promote envy, not in the sense the *OED* describes as feeling "displeasure or ill-will at the superiority of (another person) in happiness . . . or the possession of anything desirable" but in the "less unfavorable sense" of wishing oneself "on a level with (another) in happiness or the possession of something desirable." In films such as *Father Steps Out* (Yarbrough 1941) or *It Happened on Fifth Avenue* (del Ruth 1947), when the tramp transformed the wealthy elite, he was not himself transformed but proved resistant to and critical of the niceties of wealth. In contrast, in 1980s films, despite the elite's attraction toward the homeless person's authenticity, the pull of the narrative is ultimately to absorb the poor person into the rich world, with no deep critique of or structural change to the system. In an opposition between "a life of material comfort and security, or a life of freedom, risk and adventure," 1980s films pick the life of comfort.[86]

The Mel Brooks film *Life Stinks* sets out the contrast between rich and poor and the callousness of the rich from the start. As the film opens, we see a sign for Beverly Hills and hear an offscreen radio announcer discussing the problem of unemployment benefits and rising jobless claims. Then we see a white limousine drive past a row of homeless "bums" on the sidewalk. The radio shifts to announce that stock in the company Bolt Enterprises is rising as Bolt purchases real estate. The company's CEO, Goddard Bolt (Brooks), then emerges from the limousine and enters the Bolt Enterprises skyscraper headquarters. As he discusses his plans for redevelopment—a large-scale development project that will eradicate a slum—he is untroubled when his staff tell him that his plans will decimate the Brazilian rain forest and members of a lost tribe, as well as a local nursing home (fig. 4.5a). A business competitor, Vance Craswell (Jeffrey Tambor), owns half the slum land Bolt wants to develop. Craswell grew up in the neighborhood and wants to rebuild it. He makes a bet with Bolt that if Bolt can survive in the neighborhood for thirty days—with no money, no credit cards, no identification—he will give him the property. In a reverse makeover, similar to that in *Sullivan's Travels,* we see Bolt stripped of his jewelry, money, even his toupee. Driven to the slum in a limousine, as soon as Bolt exits the car, he stands under a sign painted on a wall that has been graffitied with the word "trash," affirming his new status (fig. 4.5b). By nightfall, he is already mysteriously filthy, his suit ragged.

Life Stinks offers a transformation narrative in which Bolt gains authenticity through his encounter with homelessness. The business magnate initially suffers numerous misfortunes. He is unable to secure a room in an SRO, so he tries to bed down in a large drainage pipe, but mice crawl all over it. He knocks at a church door but is turned away. He attempts to sleep on a loading dock but gets garbage dumped on him. In the morning, a homeless man pees on him as he sleeps. When two guys grab him and steal his shoes—another echo of *Sullivan's Travels*—he is rescued by Molly (Lesley Ann Warren) in a meet-cute reversal of stereotypical gender and class roles. At first wary of Bolt, Molly eventually warms and shows him the location of the mission soup kitchen, and she teaches him how to survive. Molly tells Bolt her backstory: she was a dancer who gave up dancing to get married but was dumped and had a nervous breakdown that has left her still "troublesome" among people. We learn that Bolt, too, was married, but his wife left him because she felt he focused too much on making money. Of course, Molly and Bolt fall in love and share an evening together in a cardboard box under the overpass.

But Bolt's newfound humanity does not entail a wholesale rejection of his previous status. Bolt nearly loses his wealth and standing altogether: Craswell bribes Bolt's lawyers to declare Bolt *non compos mentis* and deny the existence of the bet, thus preventing him from regaining his place in the business or his fortune. At the opening ceremony for "Craswell City," however, Bolt urges

FIGURE 4.5A AND 4.5B. Bolt is stripped of his phallic power and becomes "trash," as the graffiti above him indicates, when he enters the world of the homeless in *Life Stinks*.

the homeless who are being chased from the land: "Let's fight for our rights, take our homes back." When Molly joins his call, the homeless, most of whom are Black, join the fight. Bolt hoists Craswell into the air with a demolition crane and forces him to admit to the bet. An epilogue shows that two weeks later, Bolt has decided to clean the slum, build a park, and offer no-cost housing and free medical care to the homeless. He and Molly marry in a mission church and then drive off in the white limousine. Bolt has been transformed from a greedy man to a more caring one, but his station in life is the same: only now, Molly has risen to his level.

Whereas *Life Stinks* pits the authenticity of the homeless against yuppie greed and the forces of gentrification, *Curly Sue* focuses on the other side of yuppie guilt: the successful woman's guilt over not having a family. Like *On the Right Track,* this film hearkens back to the glut of adorable orphan films that populated screens in the early twentieth century but is especially reminiscent of Chaplin's *The Kid* (1921). Much like Chaplin's character, Jim Belushi's Bill is the de facto parent of orphan Sue (Alison Porter), whose mother died and whom Bill barely knew. Bill takes care of Sue to avoid having her be a ward of the state. Together, Bill and Sue work cons with a moral code of their own: "We don't steal," Bill says, and, "We don't break any laws, not the good ones." After a sepia-toned introduction in which we see Bill and Sue hitchhiking and riding atop a freight train, we meet Grey (Kelly Lynch), a heartless divorce attorney who views divorce as a war and aims to destroy her client's husband. Bill, Sue, and Grey meet-cute when Bill and Sue perform a scam in which Grey is made to think she ran her car over Bill. When Grey takes them to a conciliatory dinner, Bill tells Sue, "She's the kind of lady you should be praying for as a mom." Their initial scam is thwarted when Grey's boyfriend, Walker (John Getz), pulls Grey away from the dinner, but then Grey actually accidentally hits Bill with her car. Grey invites Bill and Sue into her enormous high-end apartment. Inevitably, Bill and Grey fall in love, and Bill begins to better himself by getting a job. Grey is transformed by their influence, too, and we see her at the office, hair now down and loose rather than pulled tight back, as she asks her client if she'd like to *save* her marriage.

As Levinson and Ross note in their discussion of 1980s homeless films, "Many contemporary narratives have a pivotal transformation scene, in which the homeless character bathes and dresses like a 'regular' person, symbolically moving out of the homeless condition."[87] For Morgan, these transformation scenes indicate "an America obsessed with makeovers, second chances, and overnight success."[88] In *Curly Sue,* both Bill and Sue get a makeover courtesy of Grey, who buys them clothing for a night out at a fancy restaurant. Despite proclaiming that he feels like an idiot, Bill wears a nice suit, and Sue wears a girly dress and dress shoes, not sneakers, departing from her usual tomboy attire. While the makeover transforms Bill and Sue in the eyes of others, including a snooty maître d' who previously refused Bill service, the two resist somewhat their absorption into Grey's world. Sue, feeling uncomfortable, wisely declares, "It's no fun being someone else's toy, and that's what we are." To fully restore their authenticity and his masculinity,

Bill suggests that they should take Grey to dinner, their way, "no need for money." The three of them hitch a ride on a garbage truck (of course), and Grey discovers her own aptitude for a playful scam as they crash a wedding party and sneak into a movie. Following this, Grey asks to be bought out of her law firm partnership, opting for what her boss dismissively refers to as "quality of life." Rather than end here with Grey transformed, however, the film reaffirms the superiority of Grey's way of life. Her boyfriend, Walker, reports Bill to the DCFS: Bill is arrested and Sue taken into custody. Grey then blackmails her client's husband, a politician, employing her brutal tactics after all, and gets him to drop the charges against Bill. Then Grey begins the process of adopting Sue, as Bill is legally unable to do so. Just as we and Sue think Bill has run off, having secured a mother for Sue, he turns up in Grey's living room, a domesticated patriarch in an easy chair.

BROMANCING THE YUPPIE

As romantic comedies, *Life Stinks* and *Curly Sue* both focus on the formation of the couple. In Raymond Bellour's famous formulation, the Classical Hollywood film proceeds through a series of paired oppositions—for example male/female, rebellious/conformist, night/day, or, here, housed/unhoused, rich/poor—that are resolved by a solution that "in the majority of cases takes the form of a marriage."[89] In *Trading Places, Down and Out in Beverly Hills, The Fisher King,* and *With Honors* (Keshishian 1994), the formation of the couple operates as a secondary parallel plot to a bromance between rich/housed and poor/unhoused men. As Michael DeAngelis notes: "'Bromance' has come to denote an emotionally intense bond between presumably straight males who demonstrate an openness to intimacy that they neither regard, acknowledge, avow, nor express sexually, and this definition already begins to point to some of the paradoxes and contradictions inherent in the phenomenon: bromance involves something that must happen (the demonstration of intimacy itself) on the condition that other things not happen (the avowal or expression of sexual desire between straight males)."[90] As DeAngelis suggests, the bromance points toward the possibility of a romance between men but averts that possibility and the characters' potential homosexuality.

The bromance is similar to the "buddy film," which, as Robin Wood argues, can be seen as a "male love story" that subverts the classical Hollywood cinema's narrative trajectory toward a union of the heterosexual couple and the integration of the nuclear family.[91] But the buddy film marginalizes female characters, who exist mainly to relieve the male characters' sexual tensions and prove their heterosexuality, and is absent any identifiable "home" to anchor the male protagonists, who usually undertake a journey together. In contrast, DeAngelis claims that women and home alike remain central to the generic structure of the bromance as a motivating force that regulates male protagonists' actions in often stereotypical ways.[92] Wood writes, "the background to the 70s buddy movies was . . . the collapse of the concept of home, with all its complex associations," whereas "80s gay movies" seek the "restoration and reaffirmation" of home.[93] In contrast to this aspect of buddy films, however, the bromance "requires home to become a defining, stabilizing space. And whether or not bromance's male characters spend much time there, domestic space figures as a conspicuous narrative presence."[94] In emphasizing the influence of women and the "the firm ideological grounding of the protagonists in the institution of home," the homeless bromance thus not only skirts the potential queerness of its cross-class homosocial intimacies but also affirms hegemonic ideals of domesticity and marriage.[95]

Trading Places, Down and Out in Beverly Hills, The Fisher King, and *With Honors* all initiate the relationship between a rich man and a homeless man through a fortuitous meet-cute. In *Trading Places,* the wealthy Duke brothers (Ralph Bellamy and Don Ameche) callously make a nature vs. nurture bet to see if they can transform Black homeless con man Billy Ray Valentine (Eddie Murphy) into a rich investment banker while making rich white investment banker Louis Winthorpe III (Dan Akroyd) homeless and unemployed, a reversal-of-fortune narrative like *Life Stinks* (figs. 4.6a, 4.6b). Billy Ray and Louis meet when Louis crashes the company Christmas party (in a mysteriously obtained filthy Santa suit) and attempts to frame Billy Ray for drug use just as the Dukes framed *him*. Shortly after, Billy Ray learns of the bet and hears the Dukes making racist comments, and he decides to partner with Louis in opposition to the Dukes. In *Down and Out in Beverly Hills,* a reworking of Jean Renoir's *Boudu Saved from Drowning* (1932), the aptly named wealthy Dave Whiteman (Richard Dreyfuss) meets and rescues homeless Jerry Baskin (Nick Nolte) when, despondent over the loss of his dog Kerouac, who runs off with a pretty yuppie jogger, Jerry attempts to commit suicide in Whiteman's pool. While Dave's wife, Barbara (Bette Midler), is disgusted by Jerry, Dave reminds her that "there but for the grace of God go

FIGURE 4.6A AND 4.6B. Billy Ray (Eddie Murphy) goes from homeless street hustler to Wall Street tycoon via a makeover and bromance with Louis (Dan Akroyd) in *Trading Places*.

you or I." In *The Fisher King*, formerly rich Jack (Jeff Bridges) meets homeless mentally unstable Parry (Robin Williams) when Parry, along with a band of other homeless men, rescues a drunken Jack after he wanders into a homeless camp and is attacked by thugs. Their meeting is a second chance encounter as Jack is a former shock jock DJ whose glib goading of antiyuppie sentiment led a disturbed young man to commit mass murder in a restaurant and kill Parry's wife, sending both men into a downward spiral. In *With Honors*, wealthy college student Monty (Brendan Fraser) drops the only copy of his thesis down a sidewalk grate. When he goes into the library basement to secure it, he meets squatter Simon (Joe Pesci), who ransoms it one page at a time for food. "What do you see when you look at me?" Simon asks Monty. When Monty says he sees a man, Simon counters, "No, you see a piece of shit, Harvard."

In each of these films, as the unhoused man is brought into the rich man's home, he undergoes a makeover. In *Trading Places*, the Duke brothers move Billy Ray into Louis's house, complete with servant, and make him over with a new wardrobe and lessons in table manners. In *Down and Out in Beverly Hills*, Dave invites Jerry to stay at his house until he "straightens out," then takes him to a fancy salon for a haircut and shave and then to Rodeo Drive on a shopping spree. In *The Fisher King*, Jack makes Parry over for a date with a woman, Lydia (Amanda Plummer), he has been admiring on the street. We see Jack applying a mud mask to Parry's face, then dressing him in a white pinstripe suit. In *With Honors*, after Monty exposes Simon's squatting and gets him kicked out of the library, he invites him to stay first in a broken van in his yard and then in an empty room in his apartment, where Simon cleans up and becomes an ideal roommate.

While the rich man transforms the poor man's appearance and habitat, the poor man brings authenticity and wisdom to the rich man's life. Levinson and Ross observe that the homeless character in the 1980s is "predominantly characterized as a sage, imparting his wisdom to the wealthy in exchange for a place to sleep. In this view, the homeless are happy and resourceful teachers, catalysts for the growth of members of the upper class."[96] In *Trading Places*, Louis, like Bolt in *Life Stinks*, is transformed partly through his experience of poverty and homelessness and partly through his relationship with a woman. After the Dukes hire prostitute Ophelia (Jamie Lee Curtis) to compromise Louis's reputation, she takes pity on him and lets him stay at her apartment, teaching him both street smarts and empathy. At the same time, Billy Ray is discovered to be an intuitive market genius, and he and Louis together engineer a market killing that ruins the Dukes. Billy Ray declares that "the best way to hurt rich people is to turn them into poor people," and the film results in a reversal of fortunes, with the poor and homeless displacing the wealthy.

In *Down and Out in Beverly Hills*, Jerry's presence brings authenticity to each member of the family. Jerry introduces Dave to the homeless at Venice Beach, where he becomes enamored of what he perceives as the homeless men's greater authenticity and freedom. Dave drinks booze from a bottle in a paper bag and then joins the homeless crew to drunkenly sing, "We are the bums, We are the homeless" to the tune of "We Are the World." After this scene, Dave claims that the homeless "live like animals" but "have a great capacity for joy." He excitedly reports to his wife, "I ate garbage, and I loved it!" Finding in Jerry a model of freedom and lack of constraint, not only Dave but the entire rich family is transformed. Dave's masculinity is restored through his affiliation with Jerry, and he has sex with his wife for the first time in ages. Jerry sleeps with both mother and daughter, saving the one from frigidity and the other from anorexia; he gives the son permission to be gender fluid; and he gives the maid lessons in Marxism. But Jerry is transformed, too, and admits to being a fraud, no more sagacious or truly free than the yuppies.

In *The Fisher King,* Parry, a former history professor, is the sagacious fool. He sees Jack as an "errant knight" who can help him find the holy grail. While his quest is linked to his madness following his wife's murder, it is only when Jack accedes to Parry's fantasy and tries to secure the grail—a trophy cup in a rich man's home—that he does good in the world, saving a man who accidentally overdosed. This action frees Jack of his guilt and enables him to move forward, professionally and romantically. Whereas before he was a cynical shock jock, now he rejects the lucrative opportunity to appear in a wacky comedy about homeless men called "Home Free." When Jack brings the grail to Parry, who is suffering a nervous breakdown, Parry rallies and can honestly discuss his sadness about his wife.

In *With Honors,* Simon has a transformative effect on all the roommates, especially Monty. Simon's intelligence is marked from the start as he squats in the basement of the Harvard library surrounded by books he has secreted from upstairs and tells Monty he had been reading Zola's novel *Germinal* before he got evicted. Simon reads Monty's thesis and rejects it as "pessimistic junk" (perhaps opting for Zola's optimism regarding the seeds of revolution). Attending a class in government with Monty, when the professor (Gore Vidal) tries to humiliate Simon by suggesting he is an alcoholic, Simon addresses a question the professor had asked about the president's powers. Simon argues that the strength of the Constitution is its ability to be changed and corrected. He argues that the president is "not a king but a servant of the people, a bum" searching for freedom and justice. Following this, Monty throws out his first draft and writes an entirely new thesis that is optimistic about government.

While the main engine of these films is the bromance between the rich man and the poor man, each film affirms the value of heterosexual coupling and domesticity. In *Trading Places*, not only do Ophelia and Louis become a couple, but Billy Ray is given a deux ex machina girlfriend (Shelly Chee Chee Hall), as the film ends with three couples, including the servant Coleman and his girlfriend, at an island paradise. In *Down and Out in Beverly Hills*, Jerry quarrels with the Whitemans and decides to leave and return to his former life, seeking "freedom." In the end, however, Jerry's way of life is seen as disgusting, unable to compete with yuppie comforts: leaving the Whiteman home with their dog, Matisse, in tow, Jerry attempts to eat dog food from a garbage can, but his now-refined palate can't take it. The family follows him to the alley, and he is welcomed back into the home. Even as the Talking Heads song on the soundtrack questions the value of "a beautiful house, with a beautiful wife" and the lyric "Well, how did I get here?" matches Dave's slightly perplexed look, the film ultimately opts to restore the family and absorb the seemingly countercultural figure into it. In the *Fisher King*, Jack finally admits his love and need for girlfriend Anne (Mercedes Ruehl), and Parry is joined by Lydia as he finally deals with his trauma. *With Honors* shows Simon helping Monty to finally form a relationship with his longtime crush roommate, Courtney (Moira Kelly), though the students' efforts to reunite Simon with his son fail as the son rejects his efforts to apologize.

As in the romantic comedies discussed above, the homeless bromances navigate yuppie guilt and envy, and, by extension, the audience's guilt and envy, through narratives that enable individual homeless people to be uplifted by and absorbed into the rich person's world. The homeless character serves to judge, but not condemn, the yuppie lifestyle. Rather than address inequality itself as a problem, these films offer the homeless person the opportunity to gain access to a life of comfort and security. The homeless characters are usually disconnected from the larger world of homelessness; they are mostly lone men. To the degree that the homeless person is seen as part of a community—as in *Life Stinks* when Bolt finds a community through Molly, or with Parry's comrades in *The Fisher King*, or Jerry's friends at Venice Beach in *Down and Out in Beverly Hills*—that community is left behind as the poor man joins the rich.

GIVING VOICE TO THE HOMELESS

Charles Lane's film *Sidewalk Stories* is an outlier in a number of ways. It is the only film in this cycle that could be considered an art film; it is the only film to center exclusively on an African American homeless man; and it resists the easy resolution of the romance plots above. *Sidewalk Stories* is usually compared to Chaplin's *The Kid*, as a black-and-white film shot almost entirely without synced dialogue. It shows a homeless man temporarily taking custody of a small child (Nicole Alysia) who has been left destitute when her father gets stabbed to death; the homeless man manages to care for her reasonably well, despite his very limited resources. Like other films in this cycle, *Sidewalk Stories* can be characterized as a romantic comedy, in part, because it shows a growing relationship between the homeless man, called the Artist (Charles Lane), and a rich young woman listed only as the Young Woman (Sandye Wilson), who invites him to her fancy penthouse apartment for a dinner date.

Unlike other homeless comedies, however, this film resists the easy solution of philanthropic or romantic generosity. Over the course of the film, the Artist goes from living in an abandoned building to having his building reduced to rubble. He and the Child try shelters but end up sleeping in cardboard boxes on the street. After caring for the Child for some weeks, the Artist finds her mother and restores her to her home. With nowhere to go himself (against the Chaplinesque fantasy of the mother welcoming him into her home), he ends up sitting on a park bench amid other homeless people, surrounded by trash and near a burning trash can. The Young Woman finds him there and, rather than taking him back to her world, sits with him in the world of the homeless, not seeking authenticity but listening, as the film gives voice to the homeless in the film's only spoken dialogue. As we see the Artist and Young Woman quietly eat the sandwiches she has brought, we begin to hear the voices and see the images of individual homeless people calling out to wealthy passers-by (fig. 4.7). A woman asks for change to feed her family. A man asks for a cigarette or change. One homeless man babbles about a conspiracy involving Abraham Lincoln, fast food, and the space program, and another speaks in Spanish. Initially, we cut between these characters and the Artist and Young Woman, but eventually the film decenters the romantic couple and focuses on the crowd, as we hear a cacophony of voices asking for change, with a shot of a throng of homeless people in the center of the park and a few wealthy people walking around them on the edges. The film ends as the voice of a man wearing a trash bag comes to the fore and asks, "Hey, do you know what it's like to be homeless?"

While the 1980s cycle of films about homelessness seems to be "working through" the new crisis of homelessness from a variety of perspectives

FIGURE 4.7. The Artist (Charles Lane) and Young Woman (Sandye Wilson) listen to the voices of the homeless in *Sidewalk Stories*.

ranging from viewing the homeless as horrific and abject to figures of nostalgia to sympathetic characters who are "just like you and me," overall they approach homelessness via the modality of the middlebrow. The films are frictionless in the way Hornaday describes: they allow film spectators to feel sympathy for the homeless but do not question the status quo. If 1980s films show homeless characters opting for "a life of material comfort and security" as opposed to "a life of freedom, risk and adventure," the films also aim for the comfort of a broadly humanistic appeal.[97] They turn the encounter between rich and poor into the stuff of (b)romance rather than the conditions for insurgency, and they proffer individual solutions reliant on the benevolence of the rich. In capturing the voices of the homeless asking for "change," and ending with a question that shows the limits of imagining the homeless to be "just like you and me," *Sidewalk Stories* reminds us of the power of *dis*comfort as an artistic device and a spur to action.

. . .

Of course, the problem of unhoused people persists today. One conservative estimate, based on a point-in-time (PIT) head count of people sleeping on streets and in shelters, "found 582,462 people were experiencing homelessness on a single night in January 2022," down from 759,101 unhoused persons in January 2006.[98] Of those, roughly a third (173,800) are in California, which saw a 22 percent increase in numbers of unhoused people between 2020 and 2022.[99] As the National Coalition for the Homeless outlines in its assessment of PIT counts, these estimates are likely low given that they are done by minimally trained volunteers; they offer a snapshot of a single night that does not account for variables such as weather or the temporary changes in circumstance for unhoused people; they do not account for people who "double up" with relatives or friends, or people who stay in motels, or other temporary shelters; and they work with a narrow definition of *homelessness*.

Despite this ongoing crisis, and the large numbers of homeless in Hollywood itself, including encampments along the Hollywood Walk of Fame, filmic attention to the problem of homelessness in this century has been only intermittent. There has been some increased attention, with notable films like *Nomadland* (Zhao 2020) and the TV miniseries *Maid* (2021), but there has been no sustained attention since the 1980s cycle of films. As homelessness has become a fact of life and not an emergent crisis, the media has shifted its attention. Rather than working through the ongoing dilemma of the unhoused, and unable anymore to imagine homelessness as the stuff of romance, Hollywood has engaged in a kind of NIMBY denial of the discomfort close to home.

Of course, cinematic representation will not solve the crisis of homelessness in the United States today. But as we saw with World War II representations of the "veteran problem," responses to social problems can be transformative. During World War II, Hollywood films joined a shared ideological project that not only provided extensive and multidimensional attention to the veteran problem but also became part of a larger discourse that motivated real-world policy solutions. Today, rather than offer a "working through" to the very real crisis facing the unhoused—a crisis that is palpable in Los Angeles and every other major city, as well as small towns in the United States—Hollywood has turned increasingly to comic book superheroes such as Spiderman, Batman, and the Avengers, who exist in a CGI world of fantasy; or televisual avatars of the apocalypse who roam dystopic posturban landscapes such as the unhomed characters in *The Walking Dead* (2010–22), *Station Eleven* (2021–22), or *The Last of Us* (2023–); and, in diverting our attention to futuristic worlds, they have neglected the reality of the present-day "trash" gathering at their front door.

EPILOGUE

Stuck

PRECARITY AND PERPETUAL MOTION
AS SLOW DEATH

OVER THE COURSE OF THIS BOOK, I have analyzed cycles of films managing and transmuting moral panics about different unhomed, mobile, and placeless figures. Each form of mobility correlates to a specific cinematic cycle with its own modality suited to the topic: the ubiquity of the tramp found an analogous diversity in mainstream Hollywood pictures that widely traversed genres; social problem films of various moods grappled with the anxieties around unhomed and returning veterans and civilians during World War II; countercultural hitchhikers and runaways were rendered both dangerous and titillating in exploitation pictures; and a surprising combination of earnest social problem films and (b)romantic comedies worked through the emergent crisis of unhoused street people.

Here, by way of an epilogue, I consider a recent cycle of films that take up a different population and mode of mobility in a distinct cinematic mode. This cycle focuses on what has come to be called the precariat, an intersectional class of people who lack labor security and have unstable sources of income, people who have "no ladders of mobility to climb," people who live with anxiety.[1] The precariat consists of factions that may or may not interconnect and may or may not feel a class affinity, including those from the traditional working or lower middle class, migrants and ethnic minorities, and youth.[2] The reasons for the growth of the precariat are the many and various effects of neoliberalism and globalization. In particular, the reliance on temporary and contractual labor, the gig labor economy, dead end deskilled jobs, and other transformations have created weak employment security.[3] The world's youth, the largest youth cohort in history, make up the core of the precariat[4] as "a generation of young people struggling to secure livelihoods in the most dismal labor market since The Great Depression."[5] In the context of weak employment security, nearly forty-five million young people carry an average of $32,000 in student debt; most millennials have little to no savings and no clear path to homeownership; and there is little possibility of social mobility.[6]

The film cycle related to the precariat is a subset of what has been described as the new American realism or neo-neorealism.[7] The films in this chapter are mainly from the midteens of this century, but a few films from the aughts can be seen as what A. O. Scott described as "a quiet harbinger ... not so much a premonition of hard times ahead as a confirmation that they had arrived."[8] In particular, Scott identifies Kelly Reichardt's film *Wendy and Lucy* (2008), as well as Rahmin Bahrani's films *Chop Shop* (2007) and *Man Push Cart* (2005), as bellwether films for a timely reinvestment in realism. Scott lists certain aesthetic features of the films, including the use of nonprofessional actors, location shooting, long shots, and attention to frequently marginalized characters such as migrants and the poor. Linking the films to the aesthetics of postwar Italian neorealism, Scott claims neo-neorealism as "less a style or genre than as an ethic that finds expression [in] various places at critical times." Interviewed by Scott, Bahrani identifies a crucial aspect of that ethic as he connects neorealist films to the myth of Sisyphus insofar as the characters "push the stone up to the top, and it will come back down again." These are not "dramas of adversity followed by third-act redemption" but narratives of frustration, blockage, and terminus without resolution.

Underscoring the particularities of this specific historical context, as opposed to other times and places when neorealism has come to the fore, such as postwar Italy, I am characterizing these films as slow death cinema. I take the term "slow death" from Lauren Berlant, who describes slow death as "the physical wearing out of a population and the deterioration of people in a population that is very nearly a defining condition of their experience and historical existence ... the phenomenon of mass physical attenuation under global/national regimes of capitalist structural subordination and governmentality." It is a way to characterize experience that "is simultaneously at an extreme and in a zone of ordinariness, where life building and the attrition of human life are indistinguishable, and where it is hard to distinguish modes of incoherence, distractedness and habituation from deliberate and deliberative activity, as they are all involved in the reproduction of predictable life."[9] Berlant's notion of slow death captures an ongoing experience of difficulty, feelings of exhaustion, and the lack of futurity, "where life building and the attrition of human life are indistinguishable." Slow death ironically gets at the sense of hypermobility and perpetual motion—"distractedness and habituation" as opposed to "deliberative activity"—that describes both the actions of characters in these films and the aesthetic of the films themselves.[10]

The films under consideration include *The Last Black Man in San Francisco* (Talbot 2019), *The Florida Project* (Baker 2017), *Lean on Pete* (Haigh 2017), *Good Time* (Safdie Brothers 2017), *American Honey* (Arnold 2016), *Tramps* (Leon 2016), *Tangerine* (Baker 2015), *Heaven Knows What* (Safdie Brothers 2014), and *Gimme the Loot* (Leon 2012), as well as *Wendy and Lucy*, *Chop Shop*, and *Man Push Cart*.[11] These films are auteurist and independent. They are conducted in a minor key, understated and stylistically out of sync with dominant Hollywood films, critically well-regarded but largely existing under the radar in the mainstream marketplace.

As an indicator of how small these films are, we can consider their circulation in theaters. For example, *Wendy and Lucy* opened in only two theaters and made less than $20,000 its opening weekend; in its widest release, it reached forty theaters.[12] *Man Push Cart* was only in one theater during its entire original release. A relative hit in 2017, *The Florida Project* made just under $160,000 its first weekend and moved from four theaters to 229. By comparison, the top ranked box office film in 2017, *Star Wars Episode VIII: The Last Jedi* (Johnson), ran in 4,232 theaters and made over $220,000,000 its first weekend; and the film that was ranked two hundredth in box office grosses for 2017, a Christian film called *In Our Hands: Battle for Jerusalem* (Zimmerman), played in 733 theaters and made $1.6 million on its opening day. It is not the case that nobody saw more minor films such as *Wendy and Lucy* or *The Florida Project:* they circulated at festivals, on DVD, and via streaming; and many have been written about in academic circles and taught on college campuses.[13] But they are niche films that thrive in the independent recesses of American film culture. Like the precariat itself, the film cycle is bubbling under the surface but easily ignored. In this sense, this cycle differs from previous ones that *managed* a discourse about a moral panic: attending to this cycle of films *discloses* cultural anxiety.

Like the precariat, the films encompass but are not limited to youth, yet the films about older characters—*The Last Black Man in San Francisco, Tangerine, Good Time, Wendy and Lucy, Man Push Cart*—emphasize an ongoing sense of difficulty that marks the characters as not fully inhabiting stereotypical expectations of adulthood, such as jobs, child-rearing, home ownership, or other markers of having transitioned out of adolescence. This is in keeping with Guy Standing's claim that one feature of precariousness is a prolonged adolescence.[14] But these films do not fit with stereotypical models for films about youth. One strong tendency of stereotypical teen films has been to orient teens toward a normative and hopeful conception of adulthood that links geographic mobility to social mobility—the idea of moving away from one's childhood home and up the social ladder. Other youth films I have discussed, such as the tramp film *Wild Boys of the Road* (Wellman 1933); hitchhiking films, such as *The Hitchhikers* (Sebastians 1972) or *Maybe I'll Come Home in the Spring* (Sargent 1971); and films about homeless teens, such as *Rooftops* (Wise 1989) or *Where the Day Takes You* (Rocco 1992), show youth who are nonnormative in relation to expectations around teen life such as high school, leisure, and family; but those youth are perceived as deviant, resistant, failures, or victims, exceptions to the rule. In recent years, however, as the certainty of moving up has diminished, slow death cinema has revealed the normative orientation itself—the assumptions about social mobility and the ability to successfully enter adulthood—as having been bent, distorted, or derailed. As mobility has been refigured as and through precarity, geographic and social mobility themselves no longer seem the norm: they are exceptional.

Slow death differs from the focus on death in some teen cinema, such as *The Fault in our Stars* (Boone 2014) or *Me and Earl and the Dying Girl* (Gomez-Rejon 2015), because where those films mark death as a tragedy in which an individual is denied the future, slow death cinema lacks faith in the future and represents what characters in the Broadway musical *Spring Awakening* describe as the more draining "bitch of living," rather than the melodrama of mortality.[15] Slow death cinema is also distinguished from slow cinema, which is defined by stillness and static shots: it is in many ways its opposite, as the films generally have relatively fast-paced editing and elliptical action; and, when there are long takes, they often show characters moving in extended tracking shots. Slow death is signified here ironically through hypermobility as opposed to stasis.[16]

YOUTH FILMS AND FANTASIES OF MOBILITY

To understand slow death cinema, it is necessary to contrast it to more optimistic representations of youth and mobility, such as *American Graffiti* (Lucas 1973). That film situates white middle-class adolescence in relation to a kind of mobility in place, the often overlooked "everyday mobility on the streets and public spaces of neighborhoods," as teenagers cruise the streets of Modesto, California, and drag-race, less with an idea of getting somewhere than simply moving—to flirt, connect, and party.[17] This mobility exists in opposition to an idea of fixity, associated with adulthood, insofar as the teenagers are never shown at home. Instead, along with frequent shots of the characters driving aimlessly around Modesto, they are seen in parking lots, Mel's diner, a dance at the school gym, an airport, and other transitory spaces. They project ideas of mobility onto the super cool DJ Wolfman Jack, rumored to play records from "Mexico someplace" or a "plane that just flies around in circles," resistant to the more mundane reality that he broadcasts from a small station outside the town.

Of course, the film also positions this mobility as a liminal and ideally temporary state. The film is set on the final night of summer before two characters, Steve (Ron Howard) and Curt (Richard Dreyfuss), are supposed to leave for college. At the end of the film, however, Steve opts to stay in Modesto so as not to leave his girlfriend, Laurie (Cindy Williams). John Milner (Paul LeMat), the twentysomething drag racer who still hangs with high schoolers, and Terry, or Toad (Charles Martin Smith), the loser, are also left behind. Curt leaves on an airplane to go to college. We discover in the end titles that Steve never leaves but becomes an insurance salesman, marrying Laurie, and presumably never going to college, while Milner dies in a car crash, and Toad disappears in Vietnam. Only Curt escapes and survives, a writer in Canada.[18] The film suggests that, for its middle-class characters, mobility in place is fine as long as you do not get stuck spinning your wheels, like John; it posits forced mobility, like that of the military, as deadly; and it suggests that staying, opting for the safety of fixity—the girl, the job—is its own kind of death. Curt, the artist who escapes Modesto and Vietnam both, is the success story. Thus, the film suggests that growing up and being socially mobile entails voluntary geographic mobility.

American Graffiti's positioning of mobility is typical of many teen films. *Dazed and Confused* (Linklater 1993) similarly shows white middle-class teens engaged in a kind of mobility in place—driving around the small Texas town and partying on a similar night of transition: the last day of school as juniors cycle up to being seniors in high school and eighth graders are ritually hazed and eventually accepted into high school social circles. As in *American Graffiti,* those in *Dazed and Confused* who linger too long and fail to exit the teen world are viewed as failures. For example, O'Bannion (Ben Affleck) fails to graduate and thus overinvests in his second year of participating in the ritual hazing of new freshman, and Wooderson (Matthew McConaughey), in his early twenties, still hangs with teens and dates teen girls, stating, "I get older, they stay the same age."

We can think of the fixation on cars and other forms of mobility in youth films as linked to an idea of restlessness and nervous energy, a temporary state of crisis and movement prior to the real transition to adulthood, a moment frequently marked by leaving. A condition for the teen film, according to Catherine Driscoll, is "a modern idea of adolescence as personal and social crisis" and a narrative centered on "difficulty."[19] Mobility in place is not the only way this feeling of crisis is expressed. Some films, such as *Paper Towns* (Schreier 2015) or *The Fault in Our Stars,* show white middle-class teens on road trips or traveling for other reasons; and some are situated more in the domestic or school setting, like the John Hughes films that define the 1980s teen genre. But those films, too, often suggest that the successful transition to adulthood and social mobility will be tied to some form of leaving, as in, for example, films that end with a lower-class character heading to college, such as *Lady Bird* (Gerwig 2017), *Boyhood* (Linklater 2014), or *Real Women Have Curves* (Cardosos 2002); or with a presumably successful college application, as in *Dope* (Famuyiwa 2015) or *Me and Earl and the Dying Girl.* In films such as *American Graffiti* or *Dazed and Confused,* characters who do not orient themselves toward the future via geographic and social mobility can be seen as deviant, resistant, failures, or exceptional in some way. This model rules even many films that show the attainment of that dream as difficult, as with *Real Women Have Curves, Boyhood,* or *Lady Bird*. But the recent cycle of slow death cinema marks the orientation toward the future as always already difficult and, in most cases, unattainable. These characters are constantly moving but stuck, spinning in place.

SLOW DEATH CINEMA

Considered as a cycle, slow death cinema shares many hallmarks of neo-neorealism. The films feature characters who are marginalized by some combination of youth, class, race, nationality, ethnicity, and sexuality or who operate on the fringes of society as sex workers, gamblers, graffiti artists, hustlers, drug dealers, and itinerant workers. They are shot on location in sections of the city associated with poor, ethnic, underclass communities, including public parks, laundromats, cheap diners, streets, buses, and subways or landscapes riddled with cheap motels, fast food restaurants, racetracks, auto repair shops, and strip malls. They are often shot using digital handheld cameras or even an iPhone (for *Tangerine*). *Man Push Cart, Chop Shop, Heaven Knows What, Tangerine, American Honey,* and *The Florida Project* all employ nonactors, and the rest use mainly unknown or emerging actors, not stars. When present, stars such as Michelle Williams in *Wendy and Lucy* or Willem Defoe in *The Florida Project* are subsumed into character roles and play against type. The narratives tend to be compressed—one night and day for *Gimme the Loot, Tangerine, Tramps,* and *Good Time,* days or weeks for the remainder. The narratives are loosely organized, elliptical, and episodic, picaresque in structure but neither first-person nor comedic.[20]

Each film has different degrees and kinds of mobility. *The Florida Project* is about a young poor white mother raising her daughter by hustling money however she can, including selling stolen goods and prostitution. The story takes place entirely within a small circuit of trashy motels and abandoned homes adjacent to the Disney theme park in Orlando. Consisting largely of single mothers and their children, the motels' populations live hand-to-mouth in crowded rooms, the children playing in empty lots, parking lots, and motel walkways. The characters live rootless unstable lives in the space of the motel. They are forced to move from one room to the next on a regular basis to avoid claiming residence.

While mobility in *The Florida Project* is presented mainly as a lack of stability, in other films, characters are more explicitly on the move. In a variant of the road movie, *American Honey* crisscrosses the Midwest on the premise that a racially diverse group of teens has been hired to sell magazine subscriptions door-to-door, including not only in suburban developments but also at oilrigs and truck stops—a near perfect caricature of low-paying, outmoded, and itinerant work. They travel in a van, getting drunk and high, and stay at a series of motels, never stopping for more than a night. In *Lean on Pete,* teenage Charley (Charlie Plummer) moves to Portland with his dad and gets a part-time job at a racetrack, where he becomes attached to a horse named Lean on Pete. Before the boxes are even unpacked in their new home, his dad is badly beaten and sent to hospital, so Charlie secretly moves to the racetrack. When the horse is going to be sent to the glue factory, Charlie steals a truck and the horse and leaves, first in the truck and then walking from Portland to Laramie, Wyoming, to find his estranged aunt. Charlie is shown on long runs in Portland, then extended sequences when he first drives, then walks, the horse across deserted landscapes.

FIGURE E.1. Ale (Alejandro Pelanco) hustles for an auto repair shop at Willet's Point, Queens, in *Chop Shop*.

Many films show urban peregrinations. Some of these emphasize everyday movements. The narrative of *Man Push Cart* largely consists of Pakistani immigrant and former pop star Ahmad (Ahmad Razvi) journeying to and from his job selling breakfast from a pushcart. Time and again, we see him taking the subway from Brooklyn at the crack of dawn, walking to the warehouse where the pushcarts are stored, dragging his pushcart through the streets to his corner, and then reversing the journey each evening. In *Chop Shop,* twelve-year-old Puerto Rican orphan Alejandro (Alejandro Pelanco), nicknamed Ale, runs all over the city, selling candy bars on the subway, selling bootleg DVDs, working illegally at an auto repair shop in Willets Point Queens, and doing pickup work stripping stolen cars for anther repair shop (fig. E.1). In *Heaven Knows What,* a group of junkies navigate New York, moving between temporary shelters and squats, sidewalks where they beg for money, parks and benches where they get high, and such public spaces as the library, diners, and drugstores. In *Gimme the Loot,* an African American teen boy and girl, Malcolm (Ty Hickson) and Sophia (Tashiana Washington), are seeking cash to bribe their way in to graffiti-bomb Met Stadium, and thus traverse the city by subway, bicycle, and on foot, visiting parks, playgrounds, fast-food joints, trailers, and squats. In *The Last Black Man in San Francisco,* Jimmie (Jimmie Fails) and Mont (Jonathan Majors) repeatedly travel back and forth between Mont's father's home in the historically Black Bayview-Hunters Point district and the house Jimmie claims was built by his grandfather in the gentrified Fillmore district of San Francisco so that Jimmie can tend to and eventually squat in his family's former home.

Other films show characters moving because of a moment of crisis. On her way to Alaska to get a job in the fisheries, Wendy (Michelle Williams) in *Wendy and Lucy* gets stuck in Portland when her car breaks down: she wanders the city seeking a car repair and shelter and then searching for her lost dog, Lucy. *Tangerine* focuses on Sin-Dee (Kitana Kiki Rodriguez), a trans prostitute who tries to track down the cisgender prostitute Dinah (Mickey O'Hagan), who has been sleeping with Sin-Dee's pimp boyfriend. Sin-Dee chases Dinah down, forces her to attend a concert by her friend Alexandra (Mya Taylor), who is also a trans prostitute, and drags her across Los Angeles on foot and by bus to confront her boyfriend, Chester (James Ransone). In an intersecting plot, Armenian immigrant Razmik (Karren Karagulian) drives his taxi all over the city seeking a date with Sin-Dee. In *Tramps,* the characters move among various neighborhoods in New York and the suburbs of Connecticut, as they initially engage in a mysterious briefcase exchange that goes wrong; they then try to find the right case to deliver it and get paid. In *Good Time,* after a bank heist goes ridiculously wrong, Connie Nikas (Robert Pattinson) spends a long night trying to free his mentally challenged brother, Nick (Bennie Safdie), from jail. Connie travels around Queens, Brooklyn, and East Farmingdale, New York, in botched efforts to secure bail for his brother and rescue him from the hospital.

These films all emphasize mobility by showing extended tracking shots or sequences of characters walking, as well as shots on trains, buses, vans, and even skateboards. While some are shot with languorous long tracking shots, most have very short shots, with frequent discontinuous edits. These scenes dominate the narratives—in a very real sense, mobility is the plot—and emphasize the characters' restlessness and rootlessness.

Unlike suburban teen narratives, these films rarely feature cars. Most often, characters walk or use public transportation, and the films have frequent shots on trains and buses, especially. In *Man Push Cart,* the pushcart is dragged along city streets with cars, taxis, and buses whizzing by, but Ahmad has no transportation other than walking and the train. In *Chop Shop,* Ale purchases a van so that his sister can operate a food truck, but the van doesn't work and is ultimately stripped for parts. In *Wendy and Lucy,* Wendy's car breaks down, and she cannot afford to fix it so abandons it. In *Gimme the Loot,* the characters spend the night in a friend's car staking out an apartment, but we never see the car move, and they treat it as a home, even setting up a TV inside. The only cars in *Tangerine* are taxis, which emphasizes transitory transactional mobility and lack of ownership. In *Tramps,*

Ellie (Grace van Patten) drives a borrowed car for the drop only. Otherwise, she walks or takes trains. In *American Honey,* only the boss, Krystal (Riley Keough), travels by car, letting her favorite employee, Jake (Shia LaBeouf), ride along. *Good Time* and *Lean on Pete* both have characters drive stolen vehicles. In *The Florida Project,* despite living in a motel, most of the characters do not have cars.

The narratives range in tone from relatively light, quasi-romantic comedies, in *Tramps* and *Gimme the Loot,* to very dark and bleak. The bleakest films, such as *Wendy and Lucy, Man Push Cart, Heaven Knows What,* and *The Florida Project* are not moralistic or seeking pathos: both they and the lighter films are observational, almost like cinema verité, embedded in the world of the characters but distant from it. Unlike cinema verité, however, the films employ a variety of techniques—including long takes, but more often rapid editing, dramatic changes in scale, and particularly creative sound, especially electronic music—to capture the instability and anxiety of the characters' lives. In the relatively light film *Tramps,* for example, Danny (Callum Turner), enlisted by his brother to make a handoff to a woman with a green purse, realizes he has taken the wrong briefcase from the wrong woman. We see his reaction as we crosscut to Ellie, his partner in the crime. Underscored with the tropical punk of "El Tigeraso" by Maluca, the frantic sounds of the nondiegetic score work with discontinuous editing, performance, and cinematography to focalize the character's tension and produce a similar anxiety in the film spectator.

While *Tramps* adheres to scoring conventions by dropping dialogue to maintain the integrity of the song, other films use sound in less conventional and more discordant ways. For example, in *Heaven Knows What,* as the junky Harley (Arielle Holmes) discovers that her boyfriend, Ilya (Caleb Landry Jones), has ditched her on an interstate bus, we hear "Phaedra" by the electronic band Tangerine Dream in a complex layered sound mix that submerses but does not block the dialogue. Harley paces the bus, screaming at the driver and passengers and demanding to be let out, trying to smash windows and doors. This scene, excruciating in its intensity and duration, underscores the feelings of energy and instability typical of slow death cinema. That feeling is heightened when you know that the actress Arielle Holmes is playing herself, in a film based on her own memoir of being a junkie.

In *The Last Black Man in San Francisco,* an extended montage shows Jimmie and Mont skating from Bayview-Hunters Point to the Fillmore. The sequence combines normal and slow-motion tracking shots that show both

FIGURE E.2. Mont (Jonathan Majors) and Jimmie (Jimmie Falls) skateboard past new construction in *The Last Black Man in San Francisco*.

men riding the board, passing construction sites, moving through Black neighborhoods, past white yuppies whose freeze-frame stares meet Mont's gaze, through the Mission, and, comedically, past a white man stripping naked who wants to join them. As they skate, Michael Nyman's "MGV (Musique à grande Vitesse)" plays, its stirring vigorous tempo a counterpoint to the slow motion.[21] At the same time, the words of a soapbox preacher (Willie Hen), present at the start of the journey, carry over in voiceover. The preacher complains of encroaching gentrification in Bayview-Hunters Point, describing it as the "final frontier in Manifest Destiny." His words sync with the sites we see, as he describes the city being taken away from Black people and urges them to "fight for your city." Near the end, as Mont and Jimmie arrive at the Fillmore and Jimmie's supposed ancestral home amid the gorgeous Victorians, the voice proclaims, "Look at them look at you, look down at you. But we built them, we *are* these homes. . . . This is *our* home, *our* home, *our* home." Against standard scoring practices of having music creep in and out "inaudibly" to smooth scene transitions, as Claudia Gorbman describes, the soundtrack here abruptly stops as Jimmie and Mont gaze up at Jimmie's would-be home (fig. E.2).[22]

The quotidian mobility of the characters in these films is explicitly opposed to travel or tourism. *The Florida Project* makes the contrast between everyday mobility and tourism evident in housing the characters on the outskirts of the Disney tourist attraction, a site they have never visited. Similarly, in *Chop Shop*, Willets Point in Queens is close enough to LaGuardia to hear and see the planes all day but with no suggestion that anyone in the film would go to the airport. Ale's sister, Isamar (Isamar Gonzales), talks of moving to Florida but has no means to do so. In *Gimme the Loot,* the character's relatively limited sphere of travel is contrasted with that of the rich white girl Malcolm meets when dealing drugs. The white girl, Ginnie (Zoë Lescaze), blithely lists all her travels—"India, Costa Rica, Mexico, Paris, Italy... three times in Italy, Spain, elsewhere in France"—and does not seem to recognize her own privilege or understand that Malcolm's limited travel to only Florida is not a question of taste, as she avers, "I'm sure you'd like it."

In *Heaven Knows What,* Harley and Ilya hatch some sort of plan to leave New York, but both force the bus to make unplanned stops, and both return to the city. In *Tramps,* Danny has never traveled farther than Providence, Rhode Island. Ellie has traveled to Italy but only with her criminal boyfriend. Indicating her inability to escape her situation through travel, she says, "Italy has a lot of shady people once you get past all the tourist stuff."

Mobility is also contrasted to the fixity of home. In *Chop Shop,* Ale and Isamar have permission to sleep above the auto repair shop, where they have one room with a microwave and mini-fridge. In *Heaven Knows What,* Harley spends time in a psychiatric institution, then has to move her things out of a shelter and stays in shooting galleries and an empty apartment that is being renovated. Her boyfriend, Ilya, dies in a fire when he stays in an abandoned building. *Lean on Pete* shows Charley with an unstable homelife, then homeless, and temporarily in a trailer. When he stops briefly at one house of military veterans, he has to remind himself and the horse, "We just gotta keep going. This isn't our home." In *The Florida Project,* the transitory space of a motel substitutes for home. The children play in abandoned condos, the closest approximation of a real home they ever see. Projecting themselves into these abandoned homes, the children picture typical children's rooms, imagining where beds, books, and toys would go, but ultimately view the homes through their own distorted sense of normal as they chant "Party with beer!"

In *The Last Black Man in San Francisco,* the false promise of home is central to the plot. Jimmie clings to the idea that his family built and owned a gorgeous painted lady in the Fillmore. His belief leads him to sneak onto the grounds, tend the garden, touch up paint, and do other repairs, annoying the white couple who live there. When the white owners of the house lose it owing to a contested will, Jimmie and Mont move in and squat. But Jimmie's fantasy of home ownership is illusory. Having believed his whole life that the house was built by his grandfather after World War II, Jimmie discovers that the house was built in 1857, and his father lost the deed to the house in the 1990s. At film's end, Jimmie is unmoored from both the Fillmore home and Mont's father's home.

Some of these films show the characters' uncomfortable encounters with stable homes. *Gimme the Loot* shows Malcolm return to a home he shares with his mother only in the last seconds of the film; otherwise, he and Sophia are never shown in nor refer to home. The first time Malcolm visits Ginnie in her clean and spare apartment, she is friendly and flirtatious. The second time, with her friends present, she treats him as a member of the underclass. Referring to him only as "the drug dealer," her friend tells Malcolm to remove his socks so as not to "bring the street inside" with him. In *Tramps,* Ellie is in New York to escape her Pittsburgh boyfriend; Danny shares an apartment with his Polish mother and brother, but it is used as an illegal offtrack betting site. When they go to the suburbs looking for the lost briefcase, they are viewed suspiciously as intruders, and a neighbor threatens to call the police. Once they sneak into the suburban home, they view it as strange and distant, a place where the "living situation" is ideal, unlike either of theirs. *American Honey* shows Starr (Sasha Lane) fleeing an abusive home where her foster dad sexually abuses her. When the teens visit suburban homes to sell magazine subscriptions, the teens' presence is marked as odd and unwelcome in those homes. In each case, the characters' encounter with home marks their distance from ever being able to inhabit such a space. Through the gaze of the characters, these homes seem *unheimlich*—unhomelike, strange, uncanny.

Ultimately, these films show the characters' mobility to be without terminus and interminable. Their mobility becomes a kind of dwelling, "through intricate repeated, and habitual movements of people performing 'place-ballets.'"[23] Rather than move from point A to point B, they move in circles or dead-end with narratives that resist happy endings and closure.

Many of these films simply stop rather than conclude. In *Wendy and Lucy,* after finding her dog happily adopted at a nice man's home, Wendy leaves her there and wanders off, heading toward a freight train, but we never see her arrive at a destination. *Tangerine* places Sin-Dee and Alexandra at a laundromat, where they wait for their laundry. *Heaven Knows What* ends with Harley returning from the bus, entering a Dunkin Donuts, and joining her junkie friends, who note neither her absence nor her return. The credits roll while the action continues, refusing closure (fig. E.3). *Tramps* allows its characters the possibility of escape as Ellie and Danny leave New York together

FIGURE E.3. *Heaven Knows What* refuses closure as Harley (Arielle Holmes) returns unnoticed, and her junkie friends continue talking underneath the credits.

to go to Providence—but neither has a job or purpose there, and the narrative resists the romantic closure it teases by having Ellie refuse Danny's kiss. In *Gimme the Loot,* Malcolm and Sophia never get the money, and their connection at the stadium never shows up: this film also teases, then thwarts, a romantic ending. At the end of *American Honey,* as the teens party at a lake, Star walks into the water, dunks, disappears, and then emerges in a kind of rebirth, seeming resilient but not renewed. *Good Time* similarly resists closure as we watch Nick, institutionalized after all, play a game with other patients that involves walking back and forth across the room repeatedly. In *Lean on Pete,* what should be a happy ending—the orphaned Charley reunited with his loving single aunt—is troubled by Charley's nightmares. He has lost both his father and the horse he tried to rescue in separate violent episodes. At film's end, Charley is shown running in an extended tracking shot from behind; he then stops and looks at the viewer in a shot that echoes the famous end of *The 400 Blows* (Truffaut 1959). But where Antoine's gaze in the earlier film seems defiant, Charley seems lost and weary.

The Florida Project devolves into the imaginary as the child Moonee (Brooklynn Prince), being taken away from her mother by child services, fantasizes that she escapes into Disneyland with her best friend, Jancey (Valeria Cotto), in the film's only digital sequence. We see the girls running through the Disney gates, past crowds of tourists, through the park. Even here, rather than allowing us the satisfaction of seeing the characters arrive and achieve their dream of escape, they disappear into the crowd, still running, and the scene stops as they disappear from view.

TERMINUS

I am ending this book with an epilogue rather than a conclusion because the cyclical problems of mobility and placelessness in American culture continue. Slow death cinema relates to earlier cycles of films in what I have called "the long arc of genres of precarity," but it reflects a sea change in conceptions of mobility.[24] Slow death cinema portrays forms of mobility that do not have hope of social mobility, wherein a kind of hypermobility stems from insecurity and does not have an end point. These films show characters as unhomed and disoriented toward the future; taken together, they point to a suddenly large and mobile populace whose stories underscore the limits of social mobility.

Slow death cinema differs most sharply from earlier film cycles I have discussed in that these films are less about a temporary crisis or moral panic than a new reality. As Means argues, the stagnation of social mobility "is, in fact, *the normal state* of mature capitalist economies," where capitalism has reached an "overripe state in which workers are suffering slow-motion but inexorable obsolescence."[25] Berlant suggests that crisis rhetoric belies the point that slow death is neither exceptional nor banal but "a domain of revelation where an upsetting scene of living that has been muffled in ordinary consciousness is revealed to be interwoven with ordinary life after all, like ants scurrying under a thoughtlessly lifted rock." Rather than a temporary crisis, these recent films capture features of "slow death," which she describes as "the long-term conditions of privation" that are not "traumatic events" but "discrete time-framed phenomena"—that is, "episodes . . . that make experience while not changing much of anything."[26] More than simply describing the populations represented, slow death captures the films' aesthetics as episodic, resistant to closure, filled with drama but not raised to the status of tragedy or exceptionality.

Previous chapters dealt with cycles of films about characters perceived as marginal, such as tramps, hitchhikers, and the unhoused or, in the case of World War II, a cycle of films that reflected on a massive national problem and generated broad-based societal acknowledgment and care. Slow death cinema points to a population that is simultaneously marginalized and representative of an underacknowledged dominant. In this sense, the characters in these films might be the ants Berlant describes, which signify the upsetting scene of living that we have so far avoided seeing. With a future of "increasing precariousness defined by a vulgar race to the bottom for ever more scarce resources and degraded livelihoods for the majority of workers," where "those who make very little money in their first jobs will probably still be making very little decades later," youth today have no clear means to imagine "the promise of flourishing" that previous generations did, and they have lost faith in "a fantasy world to which generations have become accustomed."[27]

As Cresswell writes in relation to the figure of the tramp: "The story of mobility in America needs to include less central stories, often untold: tales of marginality and exclusion, which cast a different light on the grand narratives of nationhood, of progress, of democracy, and of modernity."[28] What I have tried to do across this book is to flip the narrative and recognize that those stories are not marginal at all. If we link slow death cinema to earlier film cycles, we can see that there have been genres of precarity all along, and confident, future-oriented narratives like *American Graffiti* may be the exception rather than the rule (indeed, *that* narrative was always already nostalgic for a lost moment of innocence).

In a world in which, as a recent *Atlantic* article put it, "Poor at 20" means "Poor for Life"; in a world in which 1 percent of the global population holds 82 percent of the wealth;[29] and in a world where economic inequality "reflects and exacerbates deeply rooted and expanding class and race inequalities across societies" and "young people are facing a future of great uncertainty," we need to (re)consider what fantasies we are selling ourselves about youth and the arc of futurity.[30] If instead of leaving on a jet plane, youth are stuck spinning their wheels, can we hold any longer to a fantasy of some magic kingdom that promises happily ever after?

Mobility means "the ability to move or be moved; capacity for movement and change of place; moveableness, portability"; but the *OED* identifies a second historical and rare, and, it notes, *contemptuous,* meaning as "the mob, the rabble, the common people, the working class." Throughout this book, I have been attending to both meanings of mobility by considering large populations who have been unhomed, mobile, and placeless in very different ways and contexts. Some of those populations, such as tramps and hitchhikers, have mostly disappeared; others, like the civilians and servicemen unhomed by war, were rehomed. But far too many others, including both the unhoused and the precariat, are unhomed, mobile and placeless, with no hope of social mobility, security, or stability. The question now is how we escape slow death and convert mobility, in both senses, to mobilization, to turn those spinning wheels into a revolution.

NOTES

INTRODUCTION

1. Jessica Bruder, *Nomadland: Surviving America in the Twenty-First Century* (New York: Norton, 2017), 204.
2. Bruder, 38.
3. Richard Brody, "*Nomadland* Reviewed: Chloé Zhao's Nostalgic Portrait of Itinerant America," *New Yorker,* Feb. 19, 2021, https://www.newyorker.com/culture/the-front-row/nomadland-reviewed-chloe-zhaos-nostalgic-portrait-of-itinerant-america.
4. Joshua Keating, "*Nomadland* Is the Oscar Front-Runner, but It's Missing a Big Piece of the Picture," *Slate,* March 17, 2021, https://slate.com/culture/2021/03/nomadland-oscars-road-movies-amazon.html.
5. Brian Tallerico, "*Nomadland,*" RogerEbert.com, Feb. 19, 2021, https://www.rogerebert.com/reviews/nomadland-movie-review-2020.
6. A. O. Scott, "*Nomadland* Review: The Unsettled Americans," *New York Times,* Feb. 18, 2021, https://www.nytimes.com/2021/02/18/movies/nomadland-review.html.
7. Keating, "*Nomadland.*"
8. Chris Moody, "The Agony and Ecstasy of Living Nowhere," *New Republic,* March 30, 2021, https://www.escapees.com/wp-content/uploads/2021/04/Agony-Ecstasy-of-Living-Nowhere-TNR.pdf.
9. Rachel Monroe, "#Van Life: The Bohemian Social-Media Movement," *New Yorker,* April 17, 2017, https://www.newyorker.com/magazine/2017/04/24/vanlife-the-bohemian-social-media-movement.
10. Caity Weaver, "I Lived the #VanLife: It Wasn't Pretty," *New York Times,* April 20, 2022, https://www.nytimes.com/2022/04/20/magazine/van-life-dwelling.html. Vanlife images are collected in books like Foster Huntington's *Van Life: Your Home on the Road* (New York: Black Dog and Leventhal, 2017).
11. Monroe, "#Van Life."
12. Monroe.

13. Jodi Pallidini and Beverly Dubin, *Roll Your Own: The Complete Guide to Living in a Truck, Bus, Van or Camper* (New York: Collier Books, 1974).

14. Rob McGraw, "My Old Truckee Home," *Boston Globe*, July 15, 1973, C9.

15. McGraw.

16. Richard H. Foster Jr., "Wartime Trailer Housing in the San Francisco Bay Area," *Geographical Review* 70, no. 3 (July 1980): 276.

17. Homi Bhabha, "The World and the Home" *Social Text*, no. 31/32 (1992): 142.

18. Elisenda Masgrau-Peya, "Towards a Poetics of the 'Unhomed': The House in Katherine Mansfield's 'Prelude' and Barbara Hanrahan's *The Scent of Eucalyptus*," *Antipodes* 18, no. 1 (June 2004): 60.

19. Masgrau-Peya, 60.

20. Bhabha, "The World and the Home," 141.

21. Sigmund Freud, "The Uncanny," in *The Complete Psychological Works: Standard Edition*, vol. 17 (London: Hogarth, 1955), 220.

22. Dwayne Avery, *Unhomely Cinema: Home and Place in Global Cinema* (London: Anthem Press, 2014), 3.

23. Avery, 5.

24. Edward C. Relph, *Place and Placelessness* (London: Pion, 1976), 51.

25. I will, however, specifically invoke Bhabha when describing the unhoming, rehoming, and global movements of servicemen and women during World War II.

26. Elisabeth Bronfen, *Home in Hollywood: The Imaginary Geography of Cinema* (New York: Columbia University Press, 2004), 21.

27. Bronfen, 21.

28. John David Rhodes, *The Spectacle of Property: The House in American Film* (Minneapolis: University of Minnesota Press, 2017), viii.

29. John David Rhodes, "'Concentrated Ground': *Grey Gardens* and the Cinema of the Domestic," *Framework: The Journal of Cinema and Media* 47, no. 1 (Spring 2006): 85.

30. Kevin Hannam, Mimi Sheller, and John Urry, "Editorial: Mobilities, Immobilities and Moorings," *Mobilities* 1, no. 1 (March 2006): 1.

31. Tim Cresswell, *On the Move: Mobility in the Modern Western World* (New York: Routledge, 2006), 1–2.

32. Cresswell, 2.

33. Timothy Shortell and Evrick Brown, "Introduction: Walking in the European City," in *Walking in the European City: Quotidian Mobility and Urban Ethnography*, ed. Timothy Shortell and Evrick Brown (Burlington, VT: Ashgate, 2014), 5.

34. For more on the pandemic and mobility, see Paula J. Massood and Pamela Wojcik, "Notes from the Editors: Precarious Mobilities," in "Precarious Mobilities," special issue, *Feminist Media Histories: An International Journal* 7, no. 3 (Summer 2021): 1–2.

35. Siegfried Kracauer, *Theory of Film: The Redemption of Physical Reality* (Princeton, NJ: Princeton University Press, 1997), 158.

36. Kracauer, 71, 62.

37. Relph, paraphrased in Tim Cresswell, *Place: A Short Introduction* (Malden, MA: Blackwell, 2004), 43.

38. Augé, paraphrased in Cresswell, 46.

39. Lucy Lippard, *The Lure of the Local: Senses of Place in a Multicentered Society* (New York: New Press, 1997), quoted in Cresswell, *Place,* 49.

40. Lippard, quoted in Cresswell, *Place,* 49.

41. On *Wanda* and drifting, see Pamela Robertson Wojcik, "*Wanda* (1970)," in *Screening American Independent Film,* ed. Justin Wyatt and Wyatt Phillips (New York: Routledge, 2023), 140–48.

42. Amanda Klein, *American Film Cycles: Reframing Genres, Screening Social Problems, and Defining Subcultures* (Austin: University of Texas Press, 2011), 6.

43. Klein, 6.

44. John Ellis, *Seeing Things: Television in an Age of Uncertainty* (London: I. B. Tauris, 2000), 74.

45. Klein, *American Film Cycles,* 6, 9.

46. Peter Marin argues that people need margins as an escape from and counter to the dominant: "A society needs its margins as much as it needs art and literature. It needs holes and gaps, breathing spaces, let us say, into which men and women can escape and live, when necessary, in ways otherwise denied them.... When margins vanish, society becomes too rigid, too oppressive by far, and therefore inimical to life." Peter Marin, "Helping and Hating the Homeless: The Struggle at the Margins of America," *Harper's Magazine,* Jan. 1987, 49.

47. Lauren Berlant, "Slow Death (Sovereignty, Obesity, Lateral Agency)," *Critical Inquiry* 33, no. 4 (Summer 2007): 754.

CHAPTER 1

1. Epes Winthrop Sargent, *The Technique of the Photoplay,* 2nd ed. (New York: Moving Picture World; Chalmers Publishing, 1913), 85, https://archive.org/details/techniqueofphotoo0sargrich.

2. I will use the pronoun *he* to describe the tramp unless a tramp is specifically marked as a woman. The tramp is stereotypically masculine and female tramping much less visible.

3. Sargent, *Technique of the Photoplay,* 86.

4. Frederick Palmer, *Palmer Handbook of Scenario Construction,* vol. 1, *An Elementary Treatise on the Theory and Practice of Photoplay Scenario Writing,* 2nd ed. (Hollywood, CA: Palmer Photoplay, 1922), 54, https://lantern.mediahist.org/catalog/elementarytreatioopalm_0001.

5. J. P. Lawrie, *The Home Cinema* (London: Chapman and Hall, 1933), 51–53, https://lantern.mediahist.org/catalog/homecinemaoolawr_0038.

6. In his 1929 *Film Technique and Film Acting,* V. I. Pudovkin also relies on the figure of the tramp to explain scenario writing. Describing a brief scene in *Tolable David* (King 1921) in which we see a shot of the tramp, his offscreen glance at a

kitten, and then the tramp picking up a rock, Pudovkin states, "We have found here a kitten, a tramp, a stone.... Each constitutes a visual image requiring no explanation and yet carrying a clear and definite meaning." V. I. Pudovkin, *Film Technique and Film Acting* (1929; repr., London: CreateSpace Independent Publishing Platform, 2015), 30. The claim here about the tramp's transparent meaning, and his equivalence to a kitten and a stone in his obviousness as an image, underscores the typicality and convenience of the tramp as a type.

7. Most historians claim that at the end of World War II, the figure of the tramp falls out of favor in discourse and representation, and the migrant replaces him, as both the rise of the automobile and Depression-era Dust Bowl migration highlight images of families on the move in cars and trucks rather than lone men traveling by rail. See Tim Cresswell, *The Tramp in America* (London: Reaktion, 2001), 44. That said, vestiges of tramp culture continue well past World War II in hobo songs, hobo conventions, and ongoing practices of riding the rails, scavenging, and begging. On contemporary practices of "the intertwined endeavors of train hopping, Dumpster diving, and flying a sign" among "gutter punks," see Jeff Ferrell, *Drift: Illicit Mobility and Uncertain Knowledge* (Oakland: University of California Press, 2018), 131. Alison Murray's documentary *Train on the Brain* (2000) provides an immersive view of contemporary train-hoppers, including their attendance at the 99th annual Hobo Convention.

8. Miriam Hansen, "Tracking Cinema on a Global Scale," in *The Oxford Handbook of Global Modernisms,* ed. Mark Wollaeger, with Matt Eatough (New York: Oxford University Press, 2012), 608.

9. Alex Woloch, *The One vs. the Many: Minor Characters and the Space of the Protagonist in the Novel* (Princeton, NJ: Princeton University Press, 2003), 11.

10. Cresswell, *The Tramp in America,* 11.

11. Woloch, *One vs. the Many,* 25.

12. Michelle Granshaw, "Inventing the Tramp: The Early Comic on the Variety Stage," *Theatre History Studies* 38, no.1 (2019): 203.

13. Todd DePastino, *Citizen Hobo: How a Century of Homelessness Shaped America* (Chicago: University of Chicago Press, 2003), 5, 8.

14. Kenneth L. Kusmer, *Down and Out, on the Road: The Homeless in American History* (New York: Oxford University Press, 2002), 7.

15. Cresswell, *The Tramp in America,* 9.

16. Cresswell, 50–55.

17. Overnight lodgings were one of the first functions of newly organized police stations in the 1850s, and by the 1870s, police stations were the primary source of public lodging for indigent men. DePastino, *Citizen Hobo,* 12.

18. Cresswell, *The Tramp in America,* 23.

19. DePastino, *Citizen Hobo,* 17–18.

20. Kusmer, *Down and Out,* 132.

21. DePastino, *Citizen Hobo,* 6.

22. Cresswell, *The Tramp in America,* 36.

23. Charles Musser, *Before the Nickelodeon: Edwin S. Porter and the Edison Manufacturing Company* (Berkeley: University of California Press, 1991), 311.

24. Said to have been written by Leon Ray Livingston, this was one of twelve books published under the moniker of A-No. 1. The other titles in the series were *Hobo Camp Fire Tales by A-No. 1, America's Most Famous Tramp Who Traveled 500,000 miles on $7.61* (1911); *The Curse of Tramp Life* (1912); *The Trail of the Tramp* (1913); *The Adventures of a Female Tramp* (1914); *The Ways of the Hobo* (1914); *The Snare of the Road* (1916); *From Coast to Coast with Jack London* (1917); *Mother Delcassee of the Hoboes: And Other Stories* (1918); *The Wife I Won* (1919); *Traveling with Tramps* (1920); and *Here and There with A-No. 1, America's Most Famous Tramp* (1921).

25. Sociologist Reitman wrote about prostitution and homosexual subcultures in Chicago. Reitman was nicknamed "King of the Hobos" when he opened a Chicago branch of the Hobo College, which became the largest of the International Brotherhood Welfare Centers for migrant education, political organizing, and social services. According to DePastino, *Sister of the Road* is really Reitman's own autobiography, and he adopted the persona of a woman to conceal his homosexual encounters on the road. See DePastino, *Citizen Hobo*, 90. Jim Elledge describes Reitman as "non-queer" but details some of Reitman's homosexual encounters as a "lamb" who was kidnapped and raped by an older tramp. See Jim Elledge, *The Boys of Fairy Town: Sodomites, Female Impersonators, Third-Sexers, Pansies, Queers, and Sex Morons in Chicago's First Century* (Chicago: Chicago Review Press, 2018), 70, 92.

26. Kusmer, *Down and Out*, 170.

27. See Cresswell, *The Tramp in America*, 62–70.

28. Stephen Pimpare, *Ghettos, Tramps, and Welfare Queens: Down and Out on the Silver Screen* (New York: Oxford University Press, 2017), 149–50; Kusmer, *Down and Out*, 185–88; Cresswell, *The Tramp in America*, 134; DePastino, *Citizen Hobo*, 156–58; Trav S.D., "Ten Tramp Comedians," *Travalanche*, August 11, 2017, https://travsd.wordpress.com/2017/08/11/ten-tramp-comedians/.

29. See Pamela Robertson Wojcik, *Fantasies of Neglect: Imagining the Urban Child in American Film and Fiction* (New Brunswick, NJ: Rutgers University Press, 2016), 86.

30. George Milburn, *The Hobo's Hornbook: A Repertory for a Gutter Jongleur* (New York: Ives Washburn, 1930). For more on the history of hobo songs, see Richard Phelps, "Songs of the American Hobo," *Journal of Popular Culture* 17, no. 2 (Fall 1983): 1–21. Iain McIntyre includes numerous hobo songs and poems in his collection *On the Fly! Hobo Literature and Songs, 1879–1941* (Oakland, CA: PM Press, 2018).

31. Rob King, "'A Purely American Product': Tramp Comedy and White Working-Class Formation in the 1910s," in *Early Cinema and the "National,"* ed. Richard Abel, Giorgio Bertellini, and Rob King (Bloomington: Indiana University Press, 2008), 237.

32. The terms *tramp* and *hobo* are used as largely interchangeable terms of homeless men and beggars in most films and books. But homeless men themselves

differentiated between a tramp, as one who travels but does not work; a hobo, as one who travels seeking work (possibly from his role as hoe-boy on the farm); and a bum, as one who does not travel and does not work. See Cresswell, *The Tramp in America*, 48; and DePastino, *Citizen Hobo*, 65. I will mainly use the word *tramp* to cover all three categories but *hobo* as the generic term in songs about tramps and hoboes.

33. Wojcik, *Fantasies of Neglect*, 82, 93.
34. Cresswell, *The Tramp in America*, 133.
35. DePastino, *Citizen Hobo*, 159.
36. Bettina Lerner, "Seriality and Modernity: *L'almanach des Mystères des Paris*," *L'Esprit Créator* 55, no. 3 (Fall 2015): 128.
37. Miriam Hansen, "The Mass Production of the Senses: Classical Cinema as Vernacular Modernism," *Modernism/Modernity* 6, no. 2 (1999): 59–77 (repr. in *Reinventing Film Studies*, ed. Christine Gledhill and Linda Williams [New York: Oxford University Press, 2000], 332–50); Hansen, "Tracking Cinema," 601–26.
38. Amanda Klein, *American Film Cycles: Reframing Genres, Screening Social Problems, and Defining Subcultures* (Austin: University of Texas Press, 2011), 102.
39. In Altman's formulation, genre functions like a language. The semantics consist of the mise-en-scène, characters, visual style, and music, or the specific "lexical choices" that make up the film and are typical of the genre. The syntax is the grammar, or patterns of formation of those things—in other words, the narrative meaning or ideology. Rick Altman, *Film/Genre* (London: British Film Institute, 1999).
40. Elaine S. Abelson, "'Women Who Have No Men to Work for Them': Gender and Homelessness in the Great Depression," *Feminist Studies* 29, no. 1 (Spring 2003): 105.
41. Michael Kimmel, *Manhood in America: A Cultural History*, 3rd ed. (New York: Oxford University Press, 2012), 62.
42. Steven Cohan, *Masked Men: Masculinity and Movies in the Fifties* (Bloomington: Indiana University Press, 1997), 35.
43. Kusmer, *Down and Out*, 35–49.
44. Miriam Hansen, *Babel and Babylon: Spectatorship in American Silent Film* (Cambridge, MA: Harvard University Press, 1991), 58.
45. Musser, *Before the Nickelodeon*, 311.
46. Musser, 311.
47. See Pamela Robertson Wojcik, "The Cop and the Kid in 1930s American Film," *The Oxford Handbook of Children's Film*, ed. by Noel Brown (New York: Oxford University Press, 2022), 169–87.
48. Chaplin's *Easy Street* (1917) is the exception. In this film, Chaplin's Tramp takes a job as a policeman. Where previously, the neighbors in a poor urban neighborhood ironically located on Easy Street have harassed and beaten the police, thus creating the job opening at the police station, the Tramp manages to subdue the Bully (Eric Campbell) through a combination of scrappiness and luck. After multiple fights and chases between the Tramp policeman and the bully, the Tramp and his love interest, a missionary (Edna Purviance) somehow reform the working-class

neighborhood, and in a cut forward in time, we see the newly scrubbed and well-mannered neighbors all streaming into a new popular mission house, respectfully waving to the Tramp. For Charles Maland, this film is evidence not only of Chaplin's increasing emphasis on romance in his Mutual films but also "demonstrate(s) that it is nearly impossible to find a consistent political and social perspective in the Chaplin Mutual films." Charles Maland, *Chaplin and American Culture: The Evolution of a Star Image* (Princeton, NJ: Princeton University Press, 1989), 32.

49. Kusmer, *Down and Out,* 177.

50. Kusmer, 137, 184; Ferrell, *Drift,* 92.

51. Kusmer, *Down and Out,* 9, 58, 202–4; John Allen, *Homelessness in American Literature: Romanticism, Realism, and Testimony* (New York: Routledge, 2004), 98; DePastino, *Citizen Hobo,* 195.

52. Maland, *Chaplin and American Culture,* 143–58.

53. Cohan, *Masked Men,* 56.

54. Cohan, 35.

55. Cresswell, *The Tramp in America,* 39.

56. Cresswell, 40.

57. In 1906, in Chicago, the tramp population was 85 percent native-born while the population of native-born among all adult males was only 46.5 percent. Cresswell, *The Tramp in America,* 39–40.

58. Kusmer, *Down and Out,* 114–15.

59. Kusmer, 138–39.

60. Kusmer, 10.

61. DePastino, *Citizen Hobo,* 14.

62. DePastino, 82–83; see also Stephen Eide, *Homelessness in America: The History and Tragedy of an Intractable Social Problem* (Lanham, MD: Rowman & Littlefield, 2022), 22.

63. Ferrell, *Drift,* 78; McIntyre, *On the Fly!,* 461.

64. Paul Garon and Gene Tomko, *What's the Use of Walking If There's a Freight Train Going Your Way? Black Hoboes and Their Songs* (Chicago: Charles H. Kerr, 2006), 1–5.

65. Granshaw, "Inventing the Tramp," 202.

66. Cresswell, *The Tramp in America,* 134–35.

67. Granshaw, "Inventing the Tramp," 200.

68. Michelle Granshaw, *Irish on the Move: Performing Mobility in American Variety Theatre* (Iowa City: University of Iowa Press, 2019), 17–18.

69. Granshaw, "Inventing the Tramp," 200.

70. Granshaw, 205.

71. Granshaw, 205; This disentangling of Black poverty from mobility may also explain the preponderance of Black blues hobo songs that are often overlooked in discussions of Black tramps. Among hobo songs, McIntyre includes African American blues songs such as "Frisco Whistle Blues," by Ed Bell; "Hobo Blues," by Peg Leg Howell; "I.C. Moan Blues," by Tampa Red; and "Hobo Jungle Blues," by Bumble Bee Slim, among others. McIntyre, *On the Fly!*.

72. King, "'A Purely American Product,'" 242, 239.

73. Josiah Flynt denigrates the tomato-can tramp as "the lowest type" in his hierarchy of tramps: "They live in boxes, barrels, cellars, and nooks and corners of all sorts, where they can curl up and have a 'doss' (sleep). They get their food, if it can be called that, by picking over the refuse in the slop-barrels and tomato-cans of dirty alleys." Josiah Flynt, *Tramping with Tramps* (1899; repr., New York: Okitoks Press, 2018), 45.

74. "Silent Film Makeup: What Was It Really Like?," *Silent-Ology* (Feb. 22, 2016), https://silentology.wordpress.com/2016/02/22/silent-film-makeup-what-was-it-really-like/.

75. Granshaw, *Irish on the Move*, 23–24.

76. King, "'A Purely American Product,'" 244.

77. King, 244.

78. Hobo jungles were ideally somewhere near rail lines and proximate to a stream, hidden from view, and out of town but close enough to walk to. See Kusmer, *Down and Out*, 135; and Cresswell, *The Tramp in America*, 42.

79. Originally titled *Marching On*, sometime in the 1950s the film was recut with additional musical performance footage and rereleased as *Where's My Man To-nite*. Elizabeth Reich, "A Broader Nationalism: Reconstructing Memory, National Narratives and Spectatorship in World War II Black Audience Propaganda," *Screen* 54, no. 2 (Summer 2013): 175.

80. For a history of debates over racial classification and the significance of blood "color" in American racialist and nationalist discourses from the 1890s to 1930s, see Heidi Ardizzone, "Red Blooded Americans: Mulattoes and the Melting Pot in United States Racialist and Nationalist Discourse, 1890–1930" (PhD diss., University of Michigan, 1997).

81. Reich, "Broader Nationalism," 191.

82. Reich, 185.

83. Cresswell cites an 1897 law in Iowa that claims, "Any male person, sixteen years of age or over, physically able to perform manual labor, who is wandering about, practicing common begging, or having no visible calling or business to maintain himself, and is unable to show reasonable efforts in good faith to secure employment, is a tramp." Another law from Connecticut in 1902 delimits tramp laws to exclude all but able-bodied adult males, making clear the distinction between tramping and other forms of nonmobile begging as well: "These provisions shall not apply to any female, or minor under the age of 16 years, nor to any blind person, nor to any beggar roving within the limits of the town in which he resides." Cresswell, *The Tramp in America*, 88, 92.

84. Lynn Weiner, "Sisters of the Road: Women Transients and Tramps," in *Walking to Work: Tramps in America, 1790–1935*, ed. Eric H. Mokkonen (Lincoln: University of Nebraska Press, 1984), 174.

85. Weiner, 182.

86. Abelson, "'Women Who Have No Men,'" 106.

87. Cresswell claims that the contemporary use of the word *tramp* to describe a woman was used for prostitutes in the nineteenth century, but *The Oxford English Dictionary* notes the first use of the word *tramp* to denote a sexually promiscuous woman in 1922.

88. Weiner, "Sisters of the Road," 178.

89. Abelson, "Women Who Have No Men," 117.

90. In this sense, the woman tramp resembles the *flaneuse*. Janet Wolff argues that the literature of modernity is epitomized through such masculine figures as "the dandy, the *flaneur*, the hero, the stranger," and "occurred mainly in the public sphere" and was thus unavailable to women, "who could not stroll alone in the city." Janet Wolff, "The Invisible *Flaneuse:* Women and the Literature of Modernity," in *Feminine Sentences* (Berkeley: University of California Press, 1990), 35, 41. Other feminists have shown that nineteenth-century women of all classes did traverse public spaces, such as department stores and restaurants; that the city was populated by prostitutes, shopgirls, political "platform women," charity workers, and others; and that women's use of certain public spaces, such as the department store, the cinema, and the culture of amusements, opened up alternative public spheres for women. See Elizabeth Wilson, "The Invisible *Flaneur*," in *The Contradictions of Culture: Cities, Culture, Women* (London: Sage, 2001), 72–89; Anne Friedberg, *Window Shopping: Cinema and the Postmodern* (Berkeley: University of California Press, 1993); Hansen, *Babel and Babylon;* and Kathy Peiss, *Cheap Amusements: Working Women and Leisure in Turn-of-the-Century New York* (Philadelphia: Temple University Press, 1986). Akin to these other figures, the female tramp signals the presence of women in the public sphere and the ideological work required to keep her hidden from view.

91. Cresswell, *The Tramp in America,* 102. While tramp laws excluded women, in some places, there were laws against dressing as a man that would criminalize female tramps who cross-dressed. See Weiner, "Sisters of the Road," 176.

92. Cresswell, *The Tramp in America,* 105.

93. Weiner, "Sisters of the Road," 176, 172.

94. DePastino, *Citizen Hobo,* 83.

95. The *main stem* is the term tramps gave to urban skid rows, which developed in marginal urban areas already experiencing residential and commercial decline. The main stem was downtown and not far from railroad stations. It had lodging houses, soup kitchens, employment agencies, saloons, secondhand stores, pawn shops, storage rental facilities, billiards, bookstores, burlesque shows, and gambling. See Kusmer, *Down and Out,* 145, 154–56, 160; and Cresswell, *The Tramp in America,* 42.

96. Cresswell, *The Tramp in America,* 93–94.

97. DePastino, *Citizen Hobo,* 27, 84.

98. Cresswell, *The Tramp in America,* 13, 97.

99. *The Oxford English Dictionary* lists the first such use in 1872.

100. An odd variant has the tramp intrude into a woman's space and replace a baby. In *A Tramp's Dinner* (American Mutoscope 1897), *The Tramp and the Nursing*

Bottle (Edison Manufacturing 1901), *On a Milk Diet* (American Mutoscope 1902), and *While Strolling in the Park* (American Mutoscope and Biograph 1904), an attractive nursemaid neglects her infant charge while she flirts with a policeman. A tramp, proximate and opportunistic, takes the baby's bottle and drinks the milk from it. The nurse discovers the loss and the policeman chases or punishes the tramp. These films place less emphasis on the tramp's sexuality than on his perverse refusal of societal or familial norms, as I will discuss with the similar plot in *Wandering Willies* (Lord 1926).

101. Maland, *Chaplin and American Culture*, 6.

102. Leana Hirschfeld-Kroen, "Weavers of Film: The Girl Operator Mends the Cut," *Feminist Media Histories* 7, no. 3 (Summer 2021): 105–6.

103. Susan Fraiman, *Extreme Domesticity: A View from the Margins* (New York: Columbia University Press, 2017), 159.

104. Shelley Stamp, *Lois Weber in Early Hollywood* (Berkeley: University of California Press, 2015), 42.

105. While *wolf* and *lamb* clearly suggest a predatory relationship, *jocker* derives from a term for penis, and, like wolf, assumes that the adult male uses his penis to penetrate or for interfemoral (between the thighs) activity. *Punk* is a term used to describe any young male in turn-of-the-century transient culture. The origin of *prushun* is unclear. See Peter Boag, *Same-Sex Affairs: Constructing and Controlling Homosexuality in the Pacific Northwest* (Berkeley: University of California Press, 2003), 25–26; and Elledge, *The Boys of Fairy Town*, 87.

106. DePastino, *Citizen Hobo*, 88.

107. Boag, *Same-Sex Affairs*, 32.

108. Elledge, *The Boys of Fairy Town*, 90–93.

109. George Chauncey, *Gay New York: Gender, Urban Culture, and the Making of the Gay Male World, 1890–1940* (New York: Basic Books, 1994).

110. Boag, *Same-Sex Affairs*, 29.

111. Lynne Kirby, *Parallel Tracks: The Railroad and Silent Cinema* (Durham, NC: Duke University Press, 1997), 89–90.

112. Kirby, 90.

113. As George Chauncey indicates, "the sailor, seen as young and manly, unattached, and unconstrained by conventional morality, epitomized the bachelor subculture in the gay cultural imagination. . . . He was a central figure in the subculture, and his haunts became the haunts of gay men as well." Chauncey, *Gay New York*, 78.

114. Alexander Doty, *Making Things Perfectly Queer: Interpreting Mass Culture* (Minneapolis: University of Minnesota Press, 1993), 3.

115. John Belton characterizes certain film noir characters—Frank Chambers (John Garfield) in *The Postman Always Rings Twice* (Garnett 1946) and Al Roberts (Tom Neal) in *Detour* (Ulmer 1945)—as tramps. See John Belton, "Film Noir's Knights of the Road," *Bright Lights* 12 (1994): 5–15. But these characters, whom I will discuss in chapter 3, are more properly understood as drifters and hitchhikers. Instead of the tramp, the primary representative of the homeless in the 1950s became

the more localized skid-row derelict or bum, who was viewed as an alcoholic, maladjusted deviant with no interest in employment, even in a booming economy. See Kusmer, *Down and Out,* 229–30.

116. James Harvey, *Romantic Comedy in Hollywood: From Lubitsch to Sturges* (New York: Alfred A. Knopf, 1987), 591.

117. Harvey, 592.

118. Kelli Fuery, "The Two Textures of Invisibility: Shoes as Liminal Questionings in *Sullivan's Travels,*" in *Shoe Reels: The History and Philosophy of Footwear in Film,* ed. Elizabeth Ezra and Catherine Wheatley (Edinburgh: Edinburgh University Press, 2020), 79.

119. Harvey, *Romantic Comedy in Hollywood,* 593.

120. See Brandi Neal, "13 'Funny' Halloween Costumes That Are Actually Quite Offensive," *Bustle,* Oct. 5, 2017, https://www.bustle.com/p/13-funny-halloween-costumes-that-are-actually-really-offensive-2482167; and Sam Escobar and Marci Robin, "15 Offensive Halloween Costumes That Shouldn't Exist," *Good Housekeeping,* Oct. 5, 2020, https://www.goodhousekeeping.com/holidays/halloween-ideas/a40778/most-offensive-halloween-costumes/.

CHAPTER 2

1. Willard Walter Waller, *The Veteran Comes Back* (New York: Dryden Press, 1944), 13.

2. For the sake of simplicity, I will alternately refer to soldiers and servicemen to cover all branches and genders of the armed forces, unless I specify women.

3. Waller, *The Veteran,* 81.

4. Waller, 15.

5. Waller, 259.

6. Waller, 130.

7. Dixon Wecter, *When Johnny Comes Marching Home* (Boston: Houghton Mifflin, 1944), 3.

8. Sonya Michel, "Danger on the Homefront: Motherhood, Sexuality, and Disabled Veterans in American Postwar Films," *Gendering War Talk,* ed. Marian G. Cooke and Angela Woollacott (Princeton, NJ: Princeton University Press, 1993), 261.

9. Wanger, quoted in "Wanger Agenda?," *Motion Picture Herald,* May-June 24, 1944, https://lantern.mediahist.org/catalog/motionpictureher155unse_0593.

10. National World War II Museum, "Research Starters: The Draft and World War II," accessed Jan. 8, 2022, https://www.nationalww2museum.org/students-teachers/student-resources/research-starters/draft-and-wwii.

11. Mark D. Van Ells, *To Hear Only Thunder Again: America's World War II Veterans Come Home* (Lanham, MD: Lexington Books, 2001); National World War II Museum, "Research Starters."

12. National World War II Museum, "Research Starters"; Kara Dixon Vuic, *The Girls Next Door: Bringing the Home Front to the Front Lines* (Cambridge, MA: Harvard University Press, 2019), 60.

13. Richard Polenberg, *War and Society: The United States, 1941–1945* (Philadelphia: J. B. Lippincott, 1972), 138; Frank Krutnik, "Critical Accommodations: Washington, Hollywood, and the World War II Housing Shortage," *Journal of American Culture* 30, no. 4 (2007): 419; Emily Yellin, *Our Mother's War: American Women at Home and at the Front during World War II* (New York: Free Press, 2004), 16–19.

14. Ken Coates and W. R. Morrison, "The American Rampant: Reflections on the Impact of United States Troops in Allied Countries during World War II," *Journal of World History* 2, no. 2 (1991): 206. Of course, there have been large-scale mass migrations and refugee crises since World War II. The 1947 Partition of the Indian subcontinent into the independent nations of Hindu-majority India and Muslim-majority Pakistan was accompanied by one of the largest mass migrations in human history; approximately seven million Hindus and Sikhs and seven million Muslims had to relocate to a different country. The migrations due to Russia's recent war on Ukraine certainly rivals that of US World War II mobilization in percentage of the population uprooted. As of August 2022, out of a population of forty-four million, approximately 6.6 million refugees had left Ukraine, while an estimated seven million people had been displaced within the country, and another thirteen million are stranded and unable to escape contested ground.

15. Homi Bhabha, "The World and the Home," *Social Text*, no. 31/32 (1992): 141.

16. Tim Cresswell, *Place: A Short Introduction* (Malden, MA: Blackwell, 2004), 43. See also Carol Anderson, "Accidental Tourists: Yanks in Rome, 1944–1945," *Journal of Tourism History* 11, no. 1 (2019): 22–45; Andrew Buchanan, "'I Felt like a Tourist Instead of a Soldier': The Occupying Gaze—War and Tourism in Italy, 1943–1945," *American Quarterly* 68, no. 3 (2016): 593–615; Beth Bailey and David Farber, *The First Strange Place: The Alchemy of Race and Sex in World War II Hawaii* (New York: Free Press, 1992).

17. Alfred Schuetz, "The Homecomer," *American Journal of Sociology* 50, no. 5 (March 1945): 369, 375.

18. Edward Humes, *Over Here: How the G. I. Bill Transformed the American Dream* (Orlando, FL: Harcourt, 2006), 8. Initially, the letters *G* and *I* were stamped on military trash cans to indicate they were made of galvanized iron. Later, the broader terms *government issue* and *general issue* were taken up by soldiers who viewed themselves sarcastically as similarly mass-produced by the government. See Elizabeth Nix, "Why Are American Soldiers Called GIs?," *History.com*, August 22, 2018, https://www.history.com/news/why-are-american-soldiers-called-gis#. The term's popularity extended when cartoonist Dave Breger began publishing the cartoon "G. I. Joe" in *Yank* magazine in 1942. Hasbro created an action doll for boys named G. I. Joe in 1964.

19. Van Ells, *To Hear Only Thunder*, 25–29.

20. Humes, *Over Here*, 12.

21. American Revolution Institute, "America's First Veterans," Nov. 8, 2019–Jan. 31, 2022, https://www.americanrevolutioninstitute.org/exhibition/americas-first-veterans/.

22. Humes, *Over Here,* 13.

23. National Archives and Records Administration, "Confederate Pension Records," last reviewed Sept. 13, 2022, https://www.archives.gov/research/military/civil-war/confederate-pension-records.

24. Humes, *Over Here,* 14. The musical number "Remember My Forgotten Man" from *Gold Digger of 1933* (Berkeley 1933) explicitly links World War I veterans and tramps. In an extraordinary montage sequence, we see large groups of men marching off to war with cheering crowds; then as soldiers, marching in the rain; then returning from the war—wounded, scarred, limping, carried on stretchers; and finally in breadlines.

25. Humes, *Over Here,* 16.

26. Humes, 52, 99.

27. As Edward Humes explains, while the GI Bill was "on its face race and gender neutral," it contained a provision that deliberately limited benefits for African American soldiers. The bill required that soldiers receiving benefits had honorable discharges; but the military, still rigidly segregated, had an unofficial policy of granting dishonorable discharges to Black servicemen in "disproportionately high numbers." Humes, *Over Here,* 36. Moreover, while many veterans got housing loans through the GI Bill and the Federal Housing Authority, the government and private banks alike "redlined" or refused loans to Black veterans, and restrictive covenants in many new suburban developments banned the sale of homes to minorities. See Van Ells, *To Hear Only Thunder,* 237. For more on the unequal and prejudiced treatment of Black soldiers and veterans, see also Mary Pennick Motley, ed., *The Invisible Soldier: The Experience of the Black Soldier, World War II* (Detroit, MI: Wayne State University Press, 1975).

28. Steven Doles, "Social Problem Films," *Oxford Bibliographies in Cinema and Media Studies,* last modified March 30, 2015, https://www.oxfordbibliographies.com/view/document/obo-9780199791286/obo-9780199791286-0161.xml.

29. Doles.

30. Doles.

31. See Janet Bergstrom, "Alternation, Segmentation, Hypnosis: Interview with Raymond Bellour," *Camera Obscura* 1–2, no. 3/4 (1979): 88.

32. Susan Fraiman, *Extreme Domesticity: A View from the Margins* (New York: Columbia University Press, 2017), 14, 25.

33. Elisabeth Bronfen, *Home in Hollywood: The Imaginary Geography of Cinema* (New York: Columbia University Press, 2004), 21.

34. My thinking on the tension between film "middles" and their happy endings are informed by Altman, Doty, and Modleski and are discussed more fully in my book *Gidget: Origins of a Teen Girl Transmedia Franchise* (New York: Routledge, 2020), 39–49. See also Rick Altman, "From Homosocial to Heterosexual: The Musical's Two Projects," in *The Sound of Musicals,* ed. Steven Cohan (London: Palgrave

Macmillan, 2010), 19–29; Alexander Doty, *Making Things Perfectly Queer: Interpreting Mass Culture* (Minneapolis: University of Minnesota Press, 1993); and Tania Modleski, *The Women Who Knew Too Much: Hitchcock and Feminist Theory* (New York: Methuen, 1988).

35. Frank Krutnik lists nine films just about the housing crisis in Washington, DC, alone and another ten about the housing crisis elsewhere. See Krutnik, "Critical Accommodations."

36. Michelle Granshaw, "Inventing the Tramp: The Early Comic on the Variety Stage," *Theatre History Studies* 38, no.1 (2019): 203.

37. National Railroad Museum, "Wartime Restrictions on Passenger Travel," last updated March 21, 2021, http://www.railpage.com.au/news/s/wartime-restrictions-on-passenger-travel.

38. Kaja Silverman, *Male Subjectivity at the Margins* (New York: Routledge, 1992), 55.

39. Krutnik, "Critical Accommodations," 430.

40. Wecter, *When Johnny Comes Marching Home*, 11.

41. William L. Fleming, "The Venereal Disease Problem in the United States in World War II," *Journal of the Elisha Mitchell Scientific Society* 61, no. 1/2 (1945): 199.

42. Amanda H. Littauer, *Bad Girls: Young Women, Sex, and Rebellion before the Sixties* (Chapel Hill: University of North Carolina Press, 2015), 21.

43. Waller, *The Veteran*, 83.

44. In line with Richard Dyer's argument in "Entertainment and Utopia," *Anchors Aweigh* sets up a tension between the utopian ideal of transparency and the negative impulse of capitalism, manipulation. See Richard Dyer, "Entertainment and Utopia," in *Only Entertainment* (London: Routledge, 1992), 19–35. Where naive Clarence moves easily into sincere and transparent ballads such as "I Fall in Love Too Easily," the more cynical Joe is wary and only declares his love for Susie at the last minute.

45. Allison McCracken, "Real Men Don't Sing Ballads: The Radio Crooner in Hollywood, 1929 to 1933," in *Soundtrack Available: Essays on Film and Popular Music*, ed. Arthur Knight and Pamela Robertson Wojcik (Durham, NC: Duke University Press, 2001), 105–33; Karen McNally, *When Frankie Went to Hollywood: Frank Sinatra and American Male Identity* (Urbana: University of Illinois Press, 2008), 135–41.

46. A wartime job in the original Broadway production, cab driving is explained in this postwar film as a job Hildy continued after the war because she likes it.

47. Of course, the films do not show the couples having sex. As Linda Williams discusses, by cutting from a kiss to an unspecified later time, Classical Hollywood films operating under the Production Code discreetly deny what they simultaneously indicate. An ellipsis "is as close as a Code film can get to otherwise unmentionable sexual contacts." Linda Williams, *Screening Sex* (Durham, NC: Duke University Press, 2008), 40.

48. Beth Genné, "'Freedom Incarnate': Jerome Robbins, Gene Kelly, and the Dancing Sailor as an Icon of American Values in World War II," *Dance Chronicle* 24, no. 1 (2001): 90.

49. Marilyn E. Hegarty, "Patriot or Prostitute: Sexual Discourse, Print Media, and American Women during World War II," *Journal of Women's History* 10, no. 2 (1998): 113.

50. For a more complete reading of *The Miracle of Morgan's Creek*, see James Harvey, *Romantic Comedy in Hollywood: From Lubitsch to Sturges* (New York: Alfred A. Knopf, 1987), 617–31.

51. Waller, *The Veteran*, 130; Krutnik, "Critical Accommodations," 425.

52. Emily Yellin, "Lining Up for Wartime Weddings," *New York Times*, Feb. 2, 2017, https://www.nytimes.com/interactive/projects/cp/weddings/165-years-of-wedding-announcements/world-war-two-weddings.

53. Willard Walter Waller, "What You Can Do to Help the Returning Veteran," *Ladies Home Journal* 62, no. 2 (Feb. 1945): 94.

54. Krutnik, "Critical Accommodations," 419; Van Ells, *To Hear Only Thunder*, 211.

55. Van Ells, *To Hear Only Thunder*, 211.

56. Richard H. Foster, "Wartime Trailer Housing in the San Francisco Bay Area," *Geographical Review* 70, no. 3 (1980): 280.

57. Van Ells, *To Hear Only Thunder*, 211; Foster, "Wartime Trailer Housing," 280.

58. Van Ells, *To Hear Only Thunder*, 216.

59. L. B. Wheildon, "National Housing Emergency, 1946–1947," *Editorial Research Reports 1946*, vol. 2, accessed July 8, 2022, https://cqpress.sagepub.com/cqresearcher/report/national-housing-emergency-1946-1947-cqresrre1946121700; Barton J. Bernstein, "Reluctance and Resistance: Wilson Wyatt and Veterans' Housing in the Truman Administration," *The Register—Kentucky Historical Society* 65, no. 1 (1967): 47–66.

60. Margaret Mead, "What's the Matter with the Family?," *Harper's Magazine*, April 1945, 393.

61. Mead, 399, 395.

62. Krutnik, "Critical Accommodations," 426.

63. Krutnik, 430.

64. Thornton Delahanty, "Tender Comrade," *Redbook* 82, no. 4 (Feb. 1944): 6.

65. Thomas Doherty, *Projections of War: Hollywood, American Culture, and World War II* (New York: Columbia University Press, 1993), 153.

66. Waller, "What You Can Do," 27, 26.

67. Beth Linker and Whitney Laemmli, "Half a Man: The Symbolism and Science of Paraplegic Impotence in World War II America," *Osiris* 30, no. 2 (2015): 229; see also Martin Halliwell, "Going Home: World War II and Demobilization," in *Therapeutic Revolutions: Medicine, Psychiatry, and American Culture, 1945 to 1970* (New Brunswick, NJ: Rutgers University Press, 2013), 17–47.

68. Martin F. Norden, "Bitterness, Rage, and Redemption: Hollywood Constructs the Disabled Vietnam Veteran," in *Disabled Veterans in History*, ed. David Gerber (Ann Arbor: University of Michigan Press, 2012), 105.

69. Van Ells, *To Hear Only Thunder*, 73.

70. Michel, "Danger on the Homefront," 261.

71. Mona Gardner, "Has Your Husband Come Home to the Right Woman?," *Ladies Home Journal* 62, no. 2 (Dec. 1945): 41.

72. Jessica Brockmole, "Pink Cars and Pocketbooks: How American Women Bought Their Way into the Driver's Seat" (PhD diss., University of Notre Dame, 2022), 193.

73. Brockmole, 145.

74. Brockmole, 193.

75. Silverman, *Male Subjectivity*, 53.

76. Linker and Laemmli, "Half a Man," 229.

77. David Gerber, "Heroes and Misfits: The Troubled Social Reintegration of Disabled Veterans in *The Best Years of Our Lives*," in *Disabled Veterans in History*, ed. David Gerber (Ann Arbor: University of Michigan Press, 2012), 73.

78. Hans Pols, "War Neurosis, Adjustment Problems in Veterans, and an Ill Nation: The Disciplinary Project of American Psychiatry during and after World War II," *Osiris* 22, no. 1 (2007): 76–77.

79. Halliwell, "Going Home," 30.

80. Dana Polan, "Blind Insights and Dark Passages: The Problem of Placement in Forties Film," *Velvet Light Trap* (Summer 1983): 28; Dana Polan, *Power and Paranoia: History, Narrative, and the American Cinema, 1940 to 1950* (New York: Columbia University Press, 1986), 87–96.

81. Polan, "Blind Insights," 29.

82. Van Ells, *To Hear Only Thunder*, 61.

83. Franklin M. Reck, "Will He Be Changed?," *Better Homes and Gardens*, Dec. 1944, 15.

84. Waller, *The Veteran*, 93.

85. Kaja Silverman and Sarah Kozloff, among others, have provided excellent in-depth readings of *The Best Years of Our Lives*, including the adjustments faced by Al and Fred as they rediscover class hierarchies, Homer's inability to let Wilma accept him, and especially the role played by women in ministering to the men. See Silverman, *Male Subjectivity*, 65–90; and Sarah Kozloff, *The Best Years of Our Lives* (London: Palgrave MacMillan, 2011).

86. For example, at the beginning of *Living in a Big Way*, when Leo and his friend Schultz (William "Bill" Phillips) are first discharged, we see them in a clothing store, fighting with other servicemen for suits made scarce by war rations. Once they secure suits, both Leo and Schultz find them comical, because they are unaccustomed to being out of uniform, the strangeness of civilian clothing marking their feeling of not belonging. In *The Blue Dahlia* (Marshall 1946), when ex-bomber Johnny Morrison (Alan Ladd) returns home only to find his unfaithful wife, Helen (Doris Dowling), partying, he changes into his civilian clothes, and his wife complains because he is no longer attractive, making clear she loves the uniform and not the man.

87. Silverman, *Male Subjectivity*, 78.

88. Silverman, *Male Subjectivity*, 87.

89. Kozloff notes that these scenes led the Right to view *The Best Years of Our Lives* as communist, whereas the Left complained that the film's tendency to treat social problems as personal was overly conservative. See Kozloff, *The Best Years*, 56–57.

90. Richard Dyer, "White," in *The Matter of Images: Essays on Representation* (London: Routledge, 1993), 141.

91. Dyer, 141.

92. Christine Goding, "White Event Horizon," *Monday Journal* 4, accessed April 2, 2022, https://monday-journal.com/white-event-horizon/.

93. Kevin M. Kruse and Stephen Tuck, "The Second World War and the Civil Rights Movement," in *Fog of War: The Second World War and the Civil Rights Movement,* ed. Kevin M. Kruse and Stephen Tuck (New York: Oxford University Press, 2012), 3–14.

94. Waller, *The Veteran,* 13.

95. Dante A. Ciampaglia, "Why Were Vietnam War Vets Treated Poorly When They Returned?," *History.com,* March 29, 2019, https://www.history.com/news/vietnam-war-veterans-treatment. Vietnam veterans returned to an America sliding into recession and a VA system unable to adequately help them, and GI benefits were much less adequate to meet their demands than were those provided to vets from World War II. See Jeb Wyman, "The Battle after the War," *Humanities Washington Blog,* Nov. 10, 2020, https://www.humanities.org/blog/the-battle-after-the-war/.

96. Charles Champlin, "'Coming Home': A Reminder of the Costs of War," *Los Angeles Times,* Feb. 12, 1978; Ciampaglia, "Why Were Vietnam War Vets Treated Poorly?"

CHAPTER 3

1. E. J. Dickson, "18 Details *Once Upon a Time . . . in Hollywood* Got Right about the Manson Murders," *Rolling Stone,* August 7, 2019, https://www.rollingstone.com/culture/culture-features/manson-murders-once-upon-time-hollywood-tarantino-ending-868192/. Notably, Beach Boys drummer Dennis Wilson picked up Patricia Krenwinkel and Ella Jo Bailey on Sunset Boulevard and became enthralled with Manson and his followers, who then briefly moved into his home. Wilson wanted the Beach Boys to join Manson's family and tried to help Manson with his music career. Gwen Gowen and Alexa Valiente, "'Beach Boys' Mike Love Recalls Meeting Charles Manson through Bandmate Dennis Wilson for the 1st Time," *ABC News,* March 15, 2017, https://abcnews.go.com/US/beach-boys-mike-love-recalls-meeting-charles-manson/.

2. Yeoman Lowbrow, "The Hitchhiking Craze: When Women Thumbed a Ride," *Flashbak,* Dec. 10, 2017, https://flashbak.com/hitchhiking-craze.

3. Jeremy Fuster, "Tarantino Slid a Classics Grindhouse Film into *Once Upon a Time . . . in Hollywood,*" *The Wrap,* July 26, 2019, https://www.thewrap.com/tarantino-namath-once-upon-a-time-in-hollywood/; Brian Tallerico, "All the

Movies and Shows Referenced in *Once Upon a Time... in Hollywood*," *Vulture*, July 31, 2019, https://www.vulture.com/article/once-upon-a-time-in-hollywood-influences-references.html; Bruce Fretts, "A Pop Culture Glossary for *Once Upon a Time... in Hollywood*," *New York Times*, July 30, 2019, https://www.nytimes.com/2019/07/30/movies/once-upon-a-time-in-hollywood-glossary.html.

4. "A Retro Look... with a Twist: Robert Richardson, ASC, Employed Panavision Anamorphic Optics for Writer-Director Quentin Tarantino's *Once Upon a Time... in Hollywood*," Panavision.com, https://panavision.com/highlights/highlights-detail/richardson-creates-a-retro-look-with-a-twist-for-once-upon-a-time-in-hollywood.

5. Alci Rengifo, "The Aesthetic of Nostalgia in *Once Upon a Time... in Hollywood*," *Riot Material*, August 1, 2019, https://cvonhassett.medium.com/the-aesthetic-of-nostalgia-in-once-upon-a-time-in-hollywood; Adrienne Westenfeld, "Sharon Tate Never Wanted to Be an Object. That's Exactly What Happened in *Once Upon a Time... in Hollywood*," *Esquire*, July 31, 2019, https://www.esquire.com/entertainment/movies/a28538449/quentin-tarantino-once-upon-a-time-in-hollywood-fails-sharon-tate-female-characters/; Caspar Salmon, "Tarantino's Revenge Fantasies Are Growing More Puerile and Misogynistic," *The Guardian*, August 23, 2019, https://www.theguardian.com/film/2019/aug/23/quentin-tarantino-gruesome-revenge-fantasies-once-upon-a-time-in-hollywood; Richard Brody, "Quentin Tarantino's Obscenely Regressive Vision of the Sixties in *Once Upon a Time... in Hollywood*," *New Yorker*, July 27, 2019, https://www.newyorker.com/culture/the-front-row/review-quentin-tarantinos-obscenely-regressive-vision-of-the-sixties-in-once-upon-a-time-in-hollywood.

6. Zack Sharf, "Quentin Tarantino Picks 10 Films to See before *Once upon a Time... in Hollywood*," *IndieWire*, July 17, 2019, https://www.indiewire.com/gallery/quentin-tarantino-movies-influenced-once-upon-a-time-in-hollywood/.

7. Tallerico, "All the Movies and Shows"; Sharf, "Quentin Tarantino Picks 10 Films."

8. As I will discuss, Barbara Jane Brickman does expand the category of 1970s youth film in ways that are compatible with my project; however, she does not acknowledge this cycle of female hitchhiker films or the trope of the runaway in her analysis. See Barbara Jane Brickman, *New American Teenagers: The Lost Generation of Youth in 1970s Film* (New York: Bloomsbury, 2012).

9. Parul Sehgal, "The Bright, Brief Flame of an Impatient Writer," *New York Times*, April 15, 2021.

10. Hitchhiking, alternately known as *autostop* or *trampen*, has its own rich history in other nations, including but not limited to its role in US tourism abroad. This broader history is outside the scope of my project but discussed in Laviolette, Brazil, and Buryn. See Patrick Laviolette, *Hitchhiking: Cultural Inroads* (London: Palgrave Macmillan, 2020); Benjamin D. Brazil, "Wandering Spirits: Youth Travel and Spiritual Seeking, 1964 to 1980" (PhD diss., Emory University, 2015); and Ed Buryn, *Vagabonding in Europe and North Africa* (New York: Random House, 1971).

11. Jeremy Packer, *Mobility without Mayhem: Safety, Cars, and Citizenship* (Durham, NC: Duke University Press, 2008), 78.

12. Patricia Valian, *Hitchhiking: The Road to Rape and Murder* (Chatsworth, CA: Brandon, 1974).

13. Ben Lobo and Sara Links, *Side of the Road: A Hitchhiker's Guide to the United States* (New York: Simon and Schuster, 1972), 19.

14. Jack Reid, *Roadside Americans: The Rise and Fall of Hitchhiking in a Changing Nation* (Chapel Hill: University of North Carolina Press, 2020), 6; Packer, *Mobility without Mayhem*, 10.

15. Packer, *Mobility without Mayhem*, 9.

16. *Oxford English Dictionary*, s.v. "hitch-hike," https://www.oed.com/search/dictionary/?scope=Entries&q=hitch-hike.

17. Reid, *Roadside Americans*, 16.

18. Reid, 18.

19. Reid, 10; John T. Schlebecker, "An Informal History of Hitchhiking," *The Historian* 20, no. 3 (May 1958): 309.

20. Reid, *Roadside Americans*, 18–19.

21. Packer, *Mobility without Mayhem*, 83. A series of short stories by Booth Jameson in the *Saturday Evening Post* used the characters of two hitchhiking women, Elise and Zula, to cast a class-based critical eye on certain forms of privileged and frivolous masculinity. Booth Jameson, "Charles V and the Hitch-Hikers," *Saturday Evening Post*, May 26, 1928; Booth Jameson, "Hitchhikers by Night Light," *Saturday Evening Post*, May 5, 1928; Booth Jameson, "Just Students," *Saturday Evening Post*, Oct. 15, 1928.

22. Reid, *Roadside Americans*, 25; Schlebecker, "Informal History of Hitchhiking," 313; Packer, *Mobility without Mayhem*, 80.

23. Reid, *Roadside Americans*, 24.

24. Reid, 35–37.

25. Reid, 26–27.

26. Reid, 39.

27. Mia Bay, *Traveling Black: A Story of Race and Resistance* (Cambridge, MA: Belknap Press of Harvard University Press, 2021), 124.

28. Bay, 125–29.

29. Bay, 128–35.

30. Reid, *Roadside Americans*, 27.

31. Reid, 40.

32. Reid, 40–41.

33. See Schlebecker, "Informal History of Hitchhiking," 318; see also National Park Service, "Sacrificing for the Common Good: Rationing in World War II," last updated June 3, 2016, https://www.nps.gov/articles/rationing-in-wwii.htm; and National World War II Museum, "Rationing," accessed June 22, 2021, https://www.nationalww2museum.org/war/articles/rationing.

34. Reid, *Roadside Americans*, 65–66, 62.

35. Reid, 55.

36. "Emily Post Gives Nod to Hitch-Hiking and Frames Rules for 'Defense Debutantes,'" *New York Times*, Dec. 23, 1942.

37. Reid, *Roadside Americans*, 90–101.

38. Ginger Strand, *Killer on the Road: Violence and the American Interstate* (Austin: University of Texas Press, 2012), 66.

39. Reid, *Roadside Americans*, 77–78.

40. Packer, *Mobility without Mayhem*.

41. Strand, Reid, and Packer all describe this as a mid-to-late 1950s campaign. See Strand, *Killer on the Road;* Reid, *Roadside Americans;* and Packer, *Mobility without Mayhem*. An article by Richard Frey in *Cosmopolitan*, "Don't Let Death Hitch a Ride with You!," opens with a quote from Hoover—"When the motorist is asked 'How about a lift, buddy?,' the hitchhiker may be a serviceman returning to his sick wife—or he may be death in disguise"—and seems to be promoting the FBI's antihitchhiking campaign, thus dating it more precisely to 1953. Richard L. Frey, "Don't Let Death Hitch a Ride with You!," *Cosmopolitan*, August 2, 1953.

42. Mark Osteen, *"Noir's Cars:* Automobility and Amoral Space in American Film Noir," *Journal of Popular Film and Television* 35, no. 4 (2008): 185.

43. My thinking about postwar masculinity is strongly informed by Steven Cohan. See Steven Cohan, *Masked Men: Masculinity and Movies in the Fifties* (Bloomington: Indiana University Press, 1997).

44. At the same time, however, filmic representations reinforce the association between whiteness and mobility. As Eric Lott has argued, film noir can be seen, in part, as a reaction to racial unrest, "a sort of whiteface dream-work of social anxieties with explicitly racial sources, condensed on film into the criminal undertakings of abjected whites." White film noir hitchhikers conjure "dark" fears about subordinate masculinities but redirect fears about race onto white men. Eric Lott, "The Whiteness of Film Noir," *American Literary History* 9, no. 3 (Autumn 1997): 551.

45. Vivian Sobchack, *"Detour:* Driving in a Back Projection, or Forestalled by Film *Noir,"* in *Kiss the Blood Off My Hands: On Classic Film Noir,* ed. Robert Miklitsch (Urbana: University of Illinois Press, 2014) 113–14.

46. Noah Isenberg, *Detour* (Basingstoke, Hampshire: British Film Institute, 2008), 11.

47. Isenberg, 45–46.

48. Robert Polito, "Some Detours to *Detour,"* Criterion.com, March 21, 2019, https://www.criterion.com/current/posts/6257-some-detours-to-detour.

49. Isenberg, *Detour,* 23.

50. "Review of *Detour,"* *Variety,* Jan. 23, 1946.

51. Isenberg, *Detour,* 71 (Isenberg's translation). See also Stefan Grissemann, *Mann im Schatten: Der Filmemacher Edgar G. Ulmer* (Vienna: Zsolnay, 2003), 222.

52. Dana Polan, *Power and Paranoia: History, Narrative, and the American Cinema, 1940 to 1950* (New York: Columbia University Press, 1986), 232.

53. *Dark Passage* (Daves 1947) also plays off the fear of "Death in Disguise," as Vincent Parry (Humphrey Bogart) hitches a ride after escaping from prison. In this film, however, it's the driver who proves a danger as he attempts to blackmail Parry.

Furthermore, Parry has been framed and wrongly convicted and thus his prison garb provides the real "disguise."

54. Amanda Klein, *American Film Cycles: Reframing Genres, Screening Social Problems, and Defining Subcultures* (Austin: University of Texas Press, 2011), 102.

55. Klein, 103.

56. Howard Barnes, "On the Screen: *The Postman Always Rings Twice*—Capitol," *New York Herald Tribune*, May 3, 1946; "'Postman Rings Twice' Sexy," *Hollywood Reporter*, Jan. 30, 1946.

57. Isenberg, *Detour*, 10.

58. Isenberg, 16.

59. Brog, "Film Reviews: *The Night Holds Terror*," *Variety*, July 13, 1955; Jack Moffitt, "'Night Holds Terror' Fine: Andrew Stone Does Expert Triple Job," *Hollywood Reporter*, July 13, 1955.

60. Brog, "Film Reviews: *The Devil Thumbs a Ride*," *Variety*, Feb. 26, 1946; Irving Hoffman, "Thumbs Up on 'Devil' but 3 Critics Take It for a Ride: RKO Thriller Has Plenty BO Draw," *Hollywood Reporter*, March 26, 1947; Toronto Film Society, "*The Devil Thumbs a Ride* (1947)," July 12, 2018, http://torontofilmsociety.com/film-notes/the-devil-thumbs-a-ride-1947-2/.

61. Guy Barefoot, *Trash Cinema: The Lure of the Low* (New York: Wallflower, 2017), 46.

62. Barefoot, 35–37.

63. In 1960, both the *Twilight Zone* and *Alfred Hitchcock Presents* had episodes about hitchhiking—still leaning on the associations with menace.

64. See Reid, *Roadside Americans*, 103.

65. Gwyneth Cravens, "Hitching Nowhere: The Aging Youth on the Endless Road," *Harper's Magazine*, Sept. 1972, 67. The Zen poet Japhy—Kerouac's stand-in for Gary Snyder—says, "Think of millions of guys all over the world with rucksacks on their back tramping around the back country and hitchhiking and bringing the world down to everybody." Jack Kerouac, *The Dharma Bums* (1958; repr., New York: Penguin, 2006), 155. Kerouac's character Ray is less sanguine about hitchhiking: he describes a stint of hitchhiking as "harder than ever and more like hell than ever," comprising boiling hot roads, torrential rainstorms, drunken and aggressive drivers, and other mishaps that lead him to say "to hell with hitchhiking" and take a bus instead. Kerouac, *The Dharma Bums*, 114.

66. Karen M. Staller, *Runaways: How the Sixties Counterculture Shaped Today's Practices and Policies* (New York: Columbia University Press, 2006), 68.

67. Reid, *Roadside Americans*, 113.

68. Packer, *Mobility without Mayhem*, 89.

69. Abraham Miller, "On the Road: Hitchhiking on the Highway," *Society* 10, no. 5 (1973): 15–16.

70. Miller, 17.

71. Miller, 16.

72. Damon R. Bach, *The American Counterculture: A History of Hippies and Cultural Dissent* (Lawrence: University Press of Kansas, 2020), xii.

73. Cravens, "Hitching Nowhere," 69.

74. Brazil, "Wandering Spirits," 1, 5.

75. Bach, *The American Counterculture*, 225 (quoting Susan Sands, "Backpacking: 'I Go to the Wilderness to Kick the Man-World Out of Me," *New York Times*, May 9, 1971, 7); Tom Grimm, *Hitchhiker's Handbook* (New York: Plume, 1972), 23.

76. Brazil, "Wandering Spirits," 151.

77. Ed Buryn, *Vagabonding in America: The People's Guide to the U.S.A.*, 2nd ed. (New York: Random House Bookworks, 1977), 2.

78. Brazil, "Wandering Spirits," 6.

79. Buryn, *Vagabonding in America*, 31.

80. Phil Wernig, *The Hitchhikers* (Millbrae: Celestial Arts, 1972), 9.

81. Miller, "On the Road," 15.

82. Lobo and Links, *Side of the Road*, 8–9.

83. Grimm, *Hitchhiker's Handbook*, 84.

84. Reid, *Roadside Americans*, 136.

85. Walter F. Weiss, *America's Wandering Youth: A Sociological Study of Young Hitchhikers in the United States* (Jericho: Exposition, 1974), 75.

86. Weiss, *America's Wandering Youth*, 79.

87. Lobo and Links, *Side of the Road*, 11, 7.

88. Reid, *Roadside Americans*, 133, 142–43; see also Bach, *The American Counterculture*, 191; Grimm, *Hitchhiker's Handbook*, 84; and Lobo and Links, *Side of the Road*, 14.

89. Paul DiMaggio, *The Hitchhiker's Field Manual* (London: Collier, 1973), 4.

90. Lobo and Links, *Side of the Road*, 113.

91. Lobo and Links, 123.

92. Reid, *Roadside Americans*, 134; see also Packer, *Mobility without Mayhem*, 100.

93. Packer, *Mobility without Mayhem*, 93.

94. Schlebecker, "Informal History of Hitchhiking," 308.

95. Brazil, "Wandering Spirits," 113.

96. Grimm, *Hitchhiker's Handbook*, 66.

97. DiMaggio, *The Hitchhiker's Field Manual*, 16.

98. Reid, *Roadside Americans*, 133.

99. Staller, *Runaways*, 17–20.

100. Staller, 30–34.

101. Staller, 48.

102. Lillian Ambrosino, *Runaways* (Boston: Beacon, 1971), 3.

103. Bach, *The American Counterculture*, 247.

104. Staller, *Runaways*, 38–39, 88.

105. Staller, 39.

106. Bach, *The American Counterculture*, xviii.

107. Ambrosino, *Runaways*, 3.

108. Ambrosino, 4.

109. Staller, *Runaways*, 74.

110. Lobo and Links, *Side of the Road*, 130–31.
111. Reid, *Roadside Americans*, 139; see also Packer, *Mobility without Mayhem*, 95.
112. Grimm, *Hitchhiker's Handbook*, 84.
113. Valian, *Hitchhiking*, 68, 90–91.
114. Staller, *Runaways*, 46.
115. Reid, *Roadside Americans*, 146.
116. Lobo and Links, *Side of the Road*, 94–95; see also Reid, *Roadside Americans*, 140.
117. DiMaggio, *The Hitchhiker's Field Manual*, 58.
118. Jeffrey Sconce, "'Trashing' the Academy: Taste, Excess, and an Emerging Politics of Style," *Screen* 35, no. 4 (Winter 1995): 372.
119. Pam Cook, "Film Culture: 'Exploitation' Films and Feminism," *Screen* 17, no. 2 (1976): 123.
120. Elenore Lester, "At Last: A Festival of Women's Films," *Ms. Magazine*, Oct. 1972 (a reprint of "Every Day Was Ladies Day," *New York Times*, July 2, 1972).
121. Cook, "Film Culture," 123.
122. Cook, "Film Culture," 124, 127.
123. I discuss the idea of "working through" in my introduction. See also John Ellis, *Seeing Things: Television in an Age of Uncertainty* (London: I. B. Tauris, 2000), 74.
124. Yannis Tzioumakis, *American Independent Cinema*, 2nd ed. (Edinburgh: Edinburgh University Press, 2017), 125–26, 130–31, 166, 169.
125. Murf, "The Young Runaways," *Variety*, Sept. 11, 1968; "Current Film Reviews: The Young Runaways," *Independent Film Journal* 62, no. 8 (Sept. 17, 1968): 865.
126. Murf, "Thumb Tripping," *Variety*, Oct. 4, 1972.
127. "Pickup on 101," *Independent Film Journal* 70, no. 9 (Oct. 2, 1972): 56. In 1968, the modern voluntary ratings system was born, and movies were rated X, R, M for mature, or G for general public. GP, for parental guidance, was introduced in 1972 and later changed to PG. PG-13, specifically designating more intense content for teens and not children, was introduced in 1984. Here, I use the contemporary designation PG for films that were marked M or GP.
128. Diane White, "Lure of In-City Hitchhiking Growing Peril to Coeds," *Boston Globe*, Nov. 21, 1969.
129. Brickman, *New American Teenagers*, 3.
130. Brickman, 1.
131. Brickman, 3.
132. Catherine Driscoll, *Teen Film: An Introduction* (Oxford: Berg, 2011), 11–12, 66.
133. Kaja Silverman, "Dis-embodying the Female Voice," in *Issues in Feminist Film Criticism*, ed. Patricia Erens (Bloomington: Indiana University Press, 1990), 309.
134. This scene fits the common twentieth-century trope of female use of the phonograph being marked as sexually transgressive. See Pamela Robertson Wojcik, "The Girl and the Phonograph, or the Vamp and the Machine Revisited," in *Soundtrack Available: Essays on Film and Popular Music*, ed. Pamela Robertson Wojcik and Arthur Knight (Durham, NC: Duke University Press, 2001), 433–54.

135. Tzioumakis, *American Independent Cinema*, 167.
136. Brickman, *New American Teenagers*, 3.
137. Strand, *Killer on the Road*, 81; Reid, *Roadside Americans*, 133.
138. Jeremiah Murphy, "Hitchhiking: Who Can Tell?," *Boston Globe*, Nov. 16, 1972; Norma Meyer, "Hitchhiking Girls: They Follow a Dangerous Road," *Los Angeles Times*, July 28, 1977; Lester David, "Hitchhiking: The Deadly New Odds," *Good Housekeeping*, July 1973; White, "Lure of In-City Hitchhiking."
139. Murphy, "Hitchhiking: Who Can Tell?"
140. George Vecsey, "More Women Defy Risks of Hitchhiking," *New York Times*, Dec. 26, 1972.
141. Meyer, "Hitchhiking Girls."
142. David, "Hitchhiking: The Deadly New Odds."
143. White, "Lure of In-City Hitchhiking"; Vecsey, "More Women Defy Risks."
144. *Los Angeles Times*, "Hitchhiking Women Must Expect Sexual Advances, Calif. Court Says," *Boston Globe*, July 21, 1977.
145. For more on "stranger danger" and 1980s hysteria over child safety, see Pamela Robertson Wojcik, *Fantasies of Neglect: Imagining the Urban Child in American Film and Fiction* (New Brunswick, NJ: Rutgers University Press, 2016), 172–73.

CHAPTER 4

1. I refer to the "homeless" throughout this chapter, rather than using the now-preferred term *unhoused*, because the term *homeless* was newly in use at the time, meant to capture a new demographic and new visibility. As I am talking about the discourse and moral panic related to the cultural moment, the term *unhoused* would be anachronistic.
2. Crystal Waters, "The Story of Crystal Waters' 'Gypsy Woman (She's Homeless),'" Vice.com, April 8, 2016, https://www.vice.com/en/article/jp4gkp/crystal-waters-gypsy-woman-interview.
3. Waters, "The Story of Crystal Waters."
4. "Crystal Waters—Stockton Welcomes a True Music Legend and 'International Dance Diva!,'" *Caravan News*, August 24, 2016, https://www.caravannews.com/News/crystal-waters-stockton-welcomes-a-true-music-legend-and-international-dance-diva.
5. TheBestOfVoxPop, "David Bowie: The Raw and Uncut Interview," MTV, 1987, https://www.youtube.com/watch?v=IhaRvqIonHk.
6. Ellis speaks particularly about the multiplicity of TV—stories told across sitcoms, reality shows, news, and other formats. John Ellis, *Seeing Things: Television in an Age of Uncertainty* (London: I. B. Tauris, 2000), 74. I am considering the cycle of films about homelessness to be a form of multiplicity.
7. Stephen Prince, "Introduction: Movies and the 1980s," in *American Cinema of the 1980s: Themes and Variations*, ed. Stephen Prince (New Brunswick, NJ: Rutgers University Press, 2007), 4.

8. I am grateful to Michael Kackman, who spurred me to think about 1980s films as middlebrow.

9. Ann Hornaday, "'Middlebrow' Doesn't Have to Be Bad," *Washington Post*, April 18, 2013, https://www.washingtonpost.com/lifestyle/style/middlebrow-doesnt-have-to-be-bad-a-reappraisal-of-likable-movies/2013/04/18/9e9a7df2-a789-11e2-8302-3c7e0ea97057_story.html.

10. Sally Faulkner, "Introduction: Approaching the Middlebrow," in *Middlebrow Cinema*, ed. Sally Faulkner (London: Routledge, 2016), 2.

11. See, e.g., Kim Hopper, "The New Urban Niche of Homelessness: New York City in the Late 1980s," *Bulletin of the New York Academy of Medicine* 66, no. 4 (Sept.-Oct. 1990): 442; and Jonathan Kozol, *Rachel and Her Children: Homeless Families in America* (New York: Three Rivers, 1988), 13. Even now, shelter counts can be inadequate because they often count only those shelters run by the Department of Homeless Services and not shelters for runaway kids, shelters for victims of domestic violence, shelters for those with HIV-AIDs, and disaster relief shelters. Eric Lach, "Why Thousands of People Are Left Out of New York City's Daily Homeless Census," *New Yorker*, July 30, 2022, https://www.newyorker.com/news/our-local-correspondents/why-thousands-of-people-are-left-out-of-new-york-citys-daily-homeless-census.

12. Martha R. Burt, *Over the Edge: The Growth of Homelessness in the 1980s* (New York: Russell Sage Foundation, 1992), 3.

13. Marian Moser Jones, "Creating a Science of Homelessness during the Reagan Era," *Milbank Quarterly* 93, no. 1 (March 2015): 150.

14. Jones, 141.

15. Jones, 141.

16. *Oxford English Dictionary*, s.v. "bag lady," https://www.oed.com/search/dictionary/?scope=Entries&q=bag+lady.

17. Ella Howard, *Homeless: Poverty and Place in Urban America* (Philadelphia: University of Pennsylvania Press, 2013), 185–86.

18. Burt, *Over the Edge*, 17.

19. Burt, *Over the Edge*, 12; Sandra Evans Teeley, "Hard Times Breed New Homeless," *Washington Post*, Jan. 23, 1983. Analysts differ on the significance of the "new homeless." Burt claims that "new homeless" made up only 1 percent of the homeless population in 1987 and that families are typically overcounted among the homeless because they stay in shelters more than single people do (Burt, 13, 16). She claims that adult single men made up more than 70 percent of the homeless population in 1987 (Burt, 13). In 1988, Kozol argued that families were the fastest growing sector of the homeless population. Jonathan Kozol, "Distancing the Homeless," *Yale Review* 77, no. 2 (1988): 159.

20. Burt, *Over the Edge*, 13, 17.

21. Stephen Eide, *Homelessness in America: The History and Tragedy of an Intractable Social Problem* (Lanham, MD: Rowman & Littlefield, 2022), 26.

22. Judith A. Strasser, "Urban Transient Women," *American Journal of Nursing* 78, no. 12 (Dec. 1978): 2077.

23. Peter Marin, "Helping and Hating the Homeless: The Struggle at the Margins of America," *Harper's Magazine,* Jan. 1987, 43; Eide, *Homelessness in America,* 19.

24. Howard, *Homeless: Poverty and Place,* 187.

25. Marin, "Helping and Hating," 42.

26. According to the *Oxford English Dictionary,* use of the term *street people* to describe "people who live or work on the street, or habitually occupy the streets; (now *esp.*) homeless or vagrant people" and use of *street person* to define "a person living on the streets; a homeless person, a vagrant" exist from the early nineteenth century but become more common from the 1970s forward. *Oxford English Dictionary,* s.v. "street people," https://www.oed.com/search/dictionary/?scope=Entries&q=street+people; *Oxford English Dictionary,* s.v. "street person," https://www.oed.com/search/dictionary/?scope=Entries&q=street+person.

27. Jones, "Creating a Science of Homelessness," 148.

28. Peter Perl, "Record Number of Homeless Living in City Shelters," *Washington Post,* Oct. 21, 1982; Teeley, "Hard Times Breed New Homeless"; Sandra Gardner, "Homeless: More Join the Rolls," *New York Times,* Jan. 22, 1984; Paul Bass, "Growing Problem of Homeless Families Attracts New Attention," *New York Times,* March 16, 1986; Leo H. Carney, "Homeless Children on Increase, Study Shows," *New York Times,* August 17, 1986, https://www.nytimes.com/1986/08/17/nyregion/homeless-children-onincrease-study-shows.html.

29. Todd G. Shields, "Network News Construction of Homelessness: 1980–1993," *Communication Review* 4, no. 2 (2001): 197.

30. According to Shields, one-third of homeless men were veterans, but veterans represented 44 percent of the homeless on the news. Shields, "Network News Construction," 203.

31. Burt, *Over the Edge,* 11; Hopper, "The New Urban Niche," 437; Kozol, *Rachel and Her Children,* 14.

32. Burt, *Over the Edge,* 11, 112.

33. Burt, 60–62.

34. Burt, 73–78.

35. Peter Dreier and Richard Applebaum, "American Nightmare: Homelessness," *Challenge* 34, no. 2 (1991): 47.

36. Dreier and Applebaum, 48.

37. Burt, *Over the Edge,* 73–78.

38. Dreier and Applebaum, "American Nightmare," 48.

39. Burt, *Over the Edge,* 63.

40. Gillian Brockell, "She Was Stereotyped as 'The Welfare Queen.' The Truth Was More Disturbing, a New Book Says," *Washington Post,* May 21, 2019, https://www.washingtonpost.com/history/2019/05/21/she-was-stereotyped-welfare-queen-truth-was-more-disturbing-new-book-says/.

41. Burt, *Over the Edge,* 63.

42. Burt, 63; Kozol, "Distancing the Homeless," 166.

43. Dreier and Applebaum, "American Nightmare," 47; Burt, *Over the Edge,* 6.

44. Burt, *Over the Edge,* 38–39.

45. Dreier and Applebaum, "American Nightmare," 47.

46. Burt, *Over the Edge*, 36.

47. Burt, 49. This exact figure varies in different reports. Kozol says the federal budget for subsidized housing dropped from $30 billion to $9 billion. Kozol, "Distancing the Homeless," 153. Dreier and Applebaum claim a drop from $33 billion to $8 billion. Dreier and Applebaum, "American Nightmare," 49.

48. Burt, *Over the Edge*, 32–33; Dreier and Applebaum, "American Nightmare," 49.

49. Burt, *Over the Edge*, 48–53; Dreier and Applebaum, "American Nightmare," 48.

50. Dreier and Applebaum, "American Nightmare," 50.

51. Burt, *Over the Edge*, 48.

52. Baldwin made this comment on "The Negro and the American Promise," a TV show produced by Henry Morgenthau III. It first aired in 1963 on the Boston Public Television Station WGBH.

53. Howard, *Homeless: Poverty and Place*, 182–83; Eide, *Homelessness in America*, 26.

54. Burt, *Over the Edge*, 107.

55. The claim about the prevalence of mentally ill people among the homeless is common but disputed. Burt says that, overall, more people who were chemically dependent or mentally ill became homeless in the 1980s than ever before, without being deeply correlated to similar increases in the general population. Burt, *Over the Edge*, 12. Eide argues that modern homelessness is defined by a greater number of mentally ill homeless. Eide, *Homelessness in America*, 37. But Jones notes that a research program begun in 1982 by the National Institute of Mental Health (NIMH) showed that the majority of homeless persons were not mentally ill; she says that even in a study that referred to "Greyhound therapy," in which mental patients were discharged with a bus ticket to California, the data did not support the notion that the homeless were predominantly mentally ill. Jones, "Creating a Science of Homelessness," 142, 156.

56. Eide, *Homelessness in America*, 29.

57. Howard, *Homeless: Poverty and Place*, 181.

58. Eide, *Homelessness in America*, 30. Similarly, progressive policies for the chemically dependent backfired as the decriminalization of public drunkenness, vagrancy, and loitering in the 1960s—although positive in many ways—eliminated the use of the drunk tank as an alternative form of shelter. Burt, *Over the Edge*, 123.

59. James Risen, "Only the Rich Got Richer in '80s, Fed Concludes During Reagan Era, Poor Lost Ground," *Baltimore Sun*, January 7, 1992, https://www.baltimoresun.com/news/bs-xpm-1992-01-07-1992007010-story.html.

60. "The Year of the Yuppie," *Newsweek*, Dec. 31, 1984, 16.

61. Dreier and Applebaum, "American Nightmare," 46.

62. "The Year of the Yuppie," 24.

63. Marissa Piesman and Marilee Hartley, *The Yuppie Handbook* (New York: Long Shadow, 1984), 33.

64. Howard, *Homeless: Poverty and Place*, 212.

65. Katherine McKittrick, "On Plantations, Prisons, and a Black Sense of Place," *Social and Cultural Geography* 12, no. 8 (2011): 952.

66. Quoted in Charles Whitaker, "What Can We Do about the Homeless?," *Ebony,* June 1989, 99.

67. Kozol, "Distancing the Homeless," 163; Barbara Basler, "Citing Safety Issue, Two Depots Begin Removing Lockers," *New York Times,* April 3, 1986.

68. Kozol, "Distancing the Homeless," 157.

69. Margaret S. Boone and Thomas Weaver, "Public Policy Issues Affecting the Homeless in America," *Practicing Anthropology* 11, no. 1 (1989): 4.

70. Marin, "Helping and Hating," 47.

71. Julia Kristeva, *Powers of Horror: An Essay on Abjection,* trans. Leon S. Roudiez (New York: Columbia University Press, 1982), 1–4.

72. Mary Douglas, *Purity and Danger: An Analysis of Concept of Pollution and Taboo* (London: Routledge, 2002), 197–98.

73. Shields, "Network News Construction," 194.

74. Kozol, "Distancing the Homeless," 155.

75. Marin, "Helping and Hating," 44.

76. Boone and Weaver, "Public Policy Issues," 4.

77. Reagan said this in an interview on *ABC World News Tonight* on January 30, 1984. See Ronald Reagan, "Interview with David Hartman of ABC News on the 1984 Presidential Election," by David Hartman, *ABC World News Tonight,* Jan. 30, 1984; repr., Ronald Reagan Presidential Library & Museum, https://www.reaganlibrary.gov/archives/speech/interview-david-hartman-abc-news-1984-presidential-election.

78. Roger Ebert, "Ironweed," Feb. 12, 1988, https://www.rogerebert.com/reviews/ironweed-1988.

79. For more on Temple and Withers in urban films, see Pamela Robertson Wojcik, *Fantasies of Neglect: Imagining the Urban Child in American Film and Fiction* (New Brunswick, NJ: Rutgers University Press, 2016), 62–100.

80. Peter Rainer, "The Review: Tim Hunter's Film about a Pair of Homeless Souls in New York Has Its Heart in the Right Place, but It Loses Its Bite in the Fairy-Tale Presentation," *Los Angeles Times,* Nov. 17, 1993.

81. Janet Maslin, "Homeless, Helpless and Holy, in One Kind of Hell," *New York Times,* Nov. 17, 1993.

82. Abiola Sinclair, "Review: The Saint of Fort Washington," *New York Amsterdam News,* Nov. 27, 1993.

83. Angela Stukator, "'Soft Males,' 'Flying Boys,' and 'White Knights': New Masculinity in *The Fisher King,*" *Literature/Film Quarterly* 25, no 3 (1997): 215.

84. Jane Feuer, "Yuppie Envy and Yuppie Guilt," in *Seeing through the Eighties: Television and Reaganism* (Durham, NC: Duke University Press, 1995), 60–61.

85. David Levinson and Marcy Ross, "How Others See the Homeless," in *Homelessness Handbook* (Great Barrington, MA: Berkshire, 2007), 236–37.

86. Janice Morgan, "From Clochards to Cappuccinos: Renoir's Boudu is 'Down and Out' in Beverly Hills," *Cinema Journal* 29, no. 2 (Winter 1990): 28.

87. Levinson and Ross, "How Others See the Homeless," 237.

88. Morgan, "From Clochards to Cappuccinos," 29.

89. Janet Bergstrom, "Alternation, Segmentation, Hypnosis: Interview with Raymond Bellour," *Camera Obscura* 1–2, no. 3/4 (1979): 88.

90. Michael DeAngelis, introduction to *Reading the Bromance: Homosocial Relationships in Film and Television,* ed. Michael DeAngelis (Detroit: Wayne State University Press, 2014), 1.

91. Robin Wood, *Hollywood from Vietnam to Reagan . . . and Beyond* (New York: Columbia University Press, 2003), 203–4.

92. DeAngelis, introduction, 12.

93. Wood, *Hollywood from Vietnam,* 213.

94. DeAngelis, introduction, 11.

95. DeAngelis, 14.

96. Levinson and Ross, "How Others See the Homeless," 236.

97. Morgan, "From Clochards to Cappuccinos," 28.

98. United States Department of Housing and Urban Development (HUD), "HUD Releases 2022 Annual Homeless Assessment Report," press release no. 22-253, Dec. 19, 2022, https://www.hud.gov/press/press_releases_media_advisories/HUD_No_22_253; "Homeless Population," USA Facts, accessed Dec. 19, 2022, https://usafacts.org/data/topics/people-society/poverty/public-housing/homeless-population/.

99. Manuela Tobias, "California Homeless Population Grew by 22,000 over Pandemic," *CalMatters,* Oct. 6, 2022, https://calmatters.org/housing/2022/10/california-homeless-crisis-latinos/.

EPILOGUE

1. See Guy Standing, *The Precariat: The New Dangerous Class* (New York: Bloomsbury, 2016), 22–23.

2. Guy Standing, "The Precariat," *Contexts* 13, no. 4 (2014): 11.

3. Standing, *The Precariat,* 31–56.

4. Standing, 76–77.

5. Alexander J. Means, "Generational Precarity, Education, and the Crisis of Capitalism: Conventional, Neo-Keynesian, and Marxian Perspectives," *Critical Sociology* 43, no. 3 (2017): 339.

6. Zack Friedman, "Student Loan Debt Statistics in 2020: A Record $1.6 Trillion," *Forbes,* Feb. 3, 2020, https://www.inkl.com/news/student-loan-debt-statistics-in-2020-1-6-trillion-total-student-loan-debt. According to Chris Moody, "In 2019, when the median age for millennials was 31, members of the generation owned just 4 percent of the nation's real estate value, according to data compiled by the Federal Reserve. In 1990, when the median age of Baby Boomers was just four years older, their generation owned more than 30 percent." Chris Moody, "The Agony and the Ecstasy of Living Nowhere," *New Republic,* March 30, 2021, https://www.escapees.com/wp-content/uploads/2021/04/Agony-Ecstasy-of-Living-Nowhere-TNR.pdf.

7. See Manohla Dargis, "New American Realism Emerges amid Grousing and Hummers," *New York Times,* Jan. 25, 2008, https://www.nytimes.com/2008/01/25/movies/25sund.html?searchResultPosition=1; see also A. O. Scott, "Neo-Neo Realism," *New York Times,* March 17, 2009, https://archive.nytimes.com/www.nytimes.com/2009/03/22/magazine/22neorealism-t.html. Linda Badley links this tendency particularly to contemporary American women's filmmaking. Linda Badley, "Down to the Bone: Neo-neorealism and Genre in Contemporary Women's Indies," in *Indie Reframed: Women's Filmmaking and Contemporary American Independent Cinema,* ed. Linda Badley, Claire Perkins, and Michele Schreiber (Edinburgh: Edinburgh University Press), 123 passim.

8. Scott, "Neo-Neo Realism."

9. Lauren Berlant, "Slow Death (Sovereignty, Obesity, Lateral Agency)," *Critical Inquiry* 33, no. 4 (Summer 2007): 754.

10. Slow death relates to what Rob Nixon has described as "slow violence": "a violence that occurs gradually and out of sight, a violence of delayed destruction that is dispersed across time and space, an attritional violence that is typically not viewed as violence at all." Rob Nixon, *Slow Violence and the Environmentalism of the Poor* (Cambridge, MA: Harvard University Press, 2011), 2. Nixon links slow violence especially to environmental violence, though he also links it to certain patterns of abuse. *Slow death* seems a somewhat more apt term for the films I am discussing because of its sense of the grind of everyday life, which may encompass violence but is not limited to it.

11. It might make sense to include *Nomadland* (Zhao 2020), *Captain Fantastic* (Ross 2016), *Leave No Trace* (Granik 2018), *Kajillionaire* (July 2020), and other films about characters living off the grid. I bracketed these because the radical lifestyle in these films differs from the more mundane suffering in other films, but their stories of characters opting out of normative modes of living certainly respond to similar anxieties as the films I discuss. I am sure there are many other films I inadvertently left out. Tom Zaniello's book *The Cinema of the Precariat: The Exploited, Underemployed, and Temp Workers of the World* (New York: Bloomsbury Academic, 2020) examines films about similar populations; however, among his corpus of roughly two hundred films, the only film in common with mine is *Chop Shop.* Cynthia Baron identifies six films she describes as "naturalistic" that examine "outsiders." She includes *Man Push Cart* and *Wendy and Lucy.* See Cynthia Baron, "Independent Films in an Age of Crisis: Illuminating the Lives of Outsiders in Neoliberal America," in *Screening the Crisis: US Cinema and Social Change in the Wake of the 2008 Crash,* ed. Juan A. Tarancón and Hilaria Loyo (New York: Bloomsbury Academic, 2022), 31–50.

12. All figures are from boxofficemojo.com.

13. Timothy Corrigan argues that the shift in patterns of moviegoing toward home viewing can "better accommodate the edginess of those crucially alternative visions." Timothy Corrigan, "Foreword: Crisis and Critique," in *Screening the Crisis: US Cinema and Social Change in the Wake of the 2008 Crash,* ed. Juan A. Tarancón and Hilaria Loyo (New York: Bloomsbury Academic, 2022), ix.

14. Standing, *The Precariat*, 74.

15. "The B*tch of Living," Audio CD, track 4 on Duncan Shiek and Steven Sater, *Spring Awakening: A New Musical*, Verve, 2006.

16. While my analysis focuses on hypermobility, its opposite—stasis and endless waiting—is another equally important feature of life under late capitalism. In Scott Bukatman's gloss of a talk given by Dana Polan, "the traumatic can become banal" through both "endless waiting" and "ineffectual movement." Scott Bukatman, "A Day in New York: *On the Town* and *The Clock*," in *City That Never Sleeps: New York and the Filmic Imagination*, ed. Murray Pomerance (New Brunswick, NJ: Rutgers University Press, 2007), 40. See also Dana Polan, "Urban Trauma and the Metropolitan Imagination" (lecture delivered at Stanford University, Stanford, CA, May 5–7, 2005). *Wendy and Lucy* combines hypermobility—long tracking shots, a sense of placelessness—with slow scenes of waiting and long takes.

17. Timothy Shortell and Evrick Brown, "Introduction: Walking in the European City," in *Walking in the European City: Quotidian Mobility and Urban Ethnography*, ed. Timothy Shortell and Evrick Brown (Burlington, VT: Ashgate, 2014), 1.

18. Laurie and other female characters' destinies are not noted, a misogynistic absence noted in Barbara Brickman, *New American Teenagers: The Lost Generation of Youth in 1970s Film* (New York: Bloomsbury, 2014), 42–70.

19. Catherine Driscoll, *Teen Film: A Critical Introduction* (New York: Berg, 2011), 11, 12.

20. As Rob Nixon reminds us, picaros, the heroes of the picaresque, are typically "canny, scheming social outliers ... drawn from polite society's vast impoverished margins, [who] survive by parasitism and by their wits. ... The picaro embodies everything the socially remote privileged classes ... seek to contain, repress, and eject." Nixon, *Slow Violence*, 55.

21. Translated as "High Speed Music," this composition was commissioned by the Festival de Lille for the inauguration of the TGV LGV Nord train line between Paris and Lille and was conceived as an abstract imaginary journey. "MGV (Musique a Grande Vitesse)," Wise Music Classical, accessed Jan. 15, 2023, https://www.wisemusicclassical.com/work/8623/MGV-Musique-a-Grande-Vitesse—Michael-Nyman/.

22. Claudia Gorbman, *Unheard Melodies: Narrative Film Music* (Bloomington: Indiana University Press, 1987), 78.

23. Tim Cresswell, *On the Move: Mobility in the Modern Western World* (New York: Routledge, 2006), 45–46.

24. Pamela Robertson Wojcik, "Is the Home Ever Not Precarious? The Long Arc of Genres of Precarity," *Mediapolis: A Journal of Cities and Culture* 6, no. 5 (Nov. 12, 2021): https://www.mediapolisjournal.com/2021/11/is-the-home-ever-not-precarious/.

25. Means, "Generational Precarity," 350. See also Alana Semuels, "Poor at 20, Poor for Life," *The Atlantic*, July 14, 2016, www.theatlantic.com/business/archive/2016/07/social-mobility-america/491240/.

26. Berlant, "Slow Death," 761, 760.

27. Means, "Generational Precarity," 351; Semuels, "Poor at 20"; Jasbir Puar, ed., "Precarity Talk: A Virtual Roundtable with Lauren Berlant, Judith Butler, Bojana Cvejić, Isabell Lorey, Jasbir Puar, and Ana Vujanović," *TDR: The Drama Review* 56, no. 4 (Winter 2012): 166.

28. Tim Cresswell, *The Tramp in America* (London: Reaktion, 2001), 20.

29. Semuels, "Poor at 20"; "Richest 1 Percent Bagged 82 Percent of Wealth Created Last Year—Poorest Half of Humanity Got Nothing," OxFam International, Jan. 22, 2018, https://www.oxfam.org/en/pressroom/pressreleases/2018-01-22/richest-1-percent-bagged-82-percent-wealth-created-last-year.

30. Means, "Generational Precarity," 341.

WORKS CITED

Abelson, Elaine S. "'Women Who Have No Men to Work for Them': Gender and Homelessness in the Great Depression." *Feminist Studies* 29, no. 1 (Spring 2003): 104–27.
Allen, John. *Homelessness in American Literature: Romanticism, Realism, and Testimony.* New York: Routledge, 2004.
Altman, Rick. *Film/Genre.* London: British Film Institute, 1999.
———. "From Homosocial to Heterosexual: The Musical's Two Projects." In *The Sound of Musicals,* edited by Steven Cohan, 19–29. London: Palgrave Macmillan, 2010.
Ambrosino, Lillian. *Runaways.* Boston: Beacon, 1971.
American Revolution Institute. "America's First Veterans." Nov. 8, 2019–Jan. 31, 2022. https://www.americanrevolutioninstitute.org/exhibition/americas-first-veterans/.
Anderson, Carol. "Accidental Tourists: Yanks in Rome, 1944–1945." *Journal of Tourism History* 11, no. 1 (2019): 22–45.
Ardizzone, Heidi. "Red Blooded Americans: Mulattoes and the Melting Pot in United States Racialist and Nationalist Discourse, 1890–1930." PhD diss., University of Michigan, 1997.
Avery, Dwayne. *Unhomely Cinema: Home and Place in Global Cinema.* London: Anthem, 2014.
Bach, Damon R. *The American Counterculture: A History of Hippies and Cultural Dissent.* Lawrence: University Press of Kansas, 2020.
Badley, Linda. "Down to the Bone: Neo-neorealism and Genre in Contemporary Women's Indies." In *Indie Reframed: Women's Filmmaking and Contemporary American Independent Cinema,* edited by Linda Badley, Claire Perkins, and Michele Schreiber, 121–37. Edinburgh: Edinburgh University Press, 2016.
Bailey, Beth, and David Farber. *The First Strange Place: The Alchemy of Race and Sex in World War II Hawaii.* New York: Free Press, 1992.
Barefoot, Guy. *Trash Cinema: The Lure of the Low.* New York: Wallflower, 2017.

Barnes, Howard. "On the Screen: *The Postman Always Rings Twice*—Capitol." *New York Herald Tribune,* May 3, 1946.

Baron, Cynthia. "Independent Films in an Age of Crisis: Illuminating the Lives of Outsiders in Neoliberal America." In *Screening the Crisis: US Cinema and Social Change in the Wake of the 2008 Crash,* edited by Juan A. Tarancón and Hilaria Loyo, 31–50. New York: Bloomsbury Academic, 2022.

Basler, Barbara. "Citing Safety Issue, Two Depots Begin Removing Lockers." *New York Times,* April 3, 1986.

Bass, Paul. "Growing Problem of Homeless Families Attracts New Attention." *New York Times,* March 16, 1986.

Bay, Mia. *Traveling Black: A Story of Race and Resistance.* Cambridge, MA: Belknap Press of Harvard University Press, 2021.

Belton, John. "Film Noir's Knights of the Road." *Bright Lights* 12 (1994): 5–15.

Bergstrom, Janet. "Alternation, Segmentation, Hypnosis: Interview with Raymond Bellour." *Camera Obscura* 1–2, no. 3/4 (1979): 71–103.

Berlant, Lauren. "Slow Death (Sovereignty, Obesity, Lateral Agency)." *Critical Inquiry* 33, no. 4 (Summer 2007): 754–80.

Bernstein, Barton J. "Reluctance and Resistance: Wilson Wyatt and Veterans' Housing in the Truman Administration." *The Register—Kentucky Historical Society* 65, no. 1 (1967): 47–66.

The Best of Vox Pop. "David Bowie: Raw & Uncut Interview." *MTV,* 1987. https://www.youtube.com/watch?v=IhaRvqIonHk.

Bhabha, Homi. "The World and the Home." *Social Text,* no. 31/32 (1992): 141–53.

Boag, Peter. *Same-Sex Affairs: Constructing and Controlling Homosexuality in the Pacific Northwest.* Berkeley: University of California Press, 2003.

Boone, Margaret S., and Thomas Weaver. "Public Policy Issues Affecting the Homeless in America." *Practicing Anthropology* 11, no. 1 (1989): 4–5, 21.

Brazil, Benjamin D. "Wandering Spirits: Youth Travel and Spiritual Seeking, 1964 to 1980." PhD diss., Emory University, 2015.

Brickman, Barbara Jane. *New American Teenagers: The Lost Generation of Youth in 1970s Film.* New York: Bloomsbury, 2012.

Brockell, Gillian. "She Was Stereotyped as 'The Welfare Queen.' The Truth Was More Disturbing, a New Book Says." *Washington Post,* May 21, 2019. https://www.washingtonpost.com/history/2019/05/21/she-was-stereotyped-welfare-queen-truth-was-more-disturbing-new-book-says/.

Brockmole, Jessica. "Pink Cars and Pocketbooks: How American Women Bought Their Way into the Driver's Seat." PhD diss., University of Notre Dame, 2022.

Brody, Richard. "*Nomadland,* Reviewed: Chloé Zhao's Nostalgic Portrait of Itinerant America." *New Yorker,* Feb. 19, 2021. https://www.newyorker.com/culture/the-front-row/nomadland-reviewed-chloe-zhaos-nostalgic-portrait-of-itinerant-america.

———. "Quentin Tarantino's Obscenely Regressive Vision of the Sixties in *Once Upon a Time . . . in Hollywood.*" *New Yorker,* July 27, 2019. https://www

.newyorker.com/culture/the-front-row/review-quentin-tarantinos-obscenely-regressive-vision-of-the-sixties-in-once-upon-a-time-in-hollywood.

Brog. "Film Reviews: *The Devil Thumbs a Ride*." *Variety*, Feb. 26, 1946.

———. "Film Reviews: *The Night Holds Terror*." *Variety*, July 13, 1955.

Bronfen, Elisabeth. *Home in Hollywood: The Imaginary Geography of Cinema*. New York: Columbia University Press, 2004.

Bruder, Jessica. *Nomadland: Surviving America in the Twenty-First Century*. New York: Norton, 2017.

Buchanan, Andrew. "'I Felt like a Tourist Instead of a Soldier': The Occupying Gaze—War and Tourism in Italy, 1943–1945." *American Quarterly* 68, no. 3 (2016): 593–615.

Bukatman, Scott. "A Day in New York: *On the Town* and *The Clock*." *City That Never Sleeps: New York and the Filmic Imagination*, edited by Murray Pomerance, 33–48. New Brunswick, NJ: Rutgers University Press, 2007.

Burt, Martha R. *Over the Edge: The Growth of Homelessness in the 1980s*. New York: Russell Sage Foundation, 1992.

Buryn, Ed. *Vagabonding in America: The People's Guide to the U.S.A*. 2nd ed. New York: Random House Bookworks, 1977.

———. *Vagabonding in Europe and North Africa*. New York: Random House, 1971.

Carney, Leo H. "Homeless Children on Increase, Study Shows." *New York Times*, August 17, 1986. https://www.nytimes.com/1986/08/17/nyregion/homeless-children-onincrease-study-shows.html.

Champlin, Charles. "'Coming Home': A Reminder of the Costs of War." *Los Angeles Times*, Feb. 12, 1978.

Chauncey, George. *Gay New York: Gender, Urban Culture, and the Making of the Gay Male World, 1890–1940*. New York: Basic Books, 1994.

Ciampaglia, Dante A. "Why Were Vietnam War Vets Treated Poorly When They Returned?" History.com, March 29, 2019. https://www.history.com/news/vietnam-war-veterans-treatment.

Coates, Ken, and W. R. Morrison. "The American Rampant: Reflections on the Impact of United States Troops in Allied Countries during World War II." *Journal of World History* 2, no. 2 (1991): 201–21.

Cohan, Steven. *Masked Men: Masculinity and Movies in the Fifties*. Bloomington: Indiana University Press, 1997.

Cook, Pam. "Film Culture: 'Exploitation' Films and Feminism." *Screen* 17, no. 2 (1976): 122–27.

Corrigan, Timothy. "Foreword: Crisis and Critique." In *Screening the Crisis: US Cinema and Social Change in the Wake of the 2008 Crash*, edited by Juan A. Tarancón and Hilaria Loyo, viii–x. New York: Bloomsbury Academic, 2022.

Cravens, Gwyneth. "Hitching Nowhere: The Aging Youth on the Endless Road." *Harpers Magazine*, Sept. 1972.

Cresswell, Tim. *On the Move: Mobility in the Modern Western World*. New York: Routledge, 2006.

———. *Place: A Short Introduction*. Malden, MA: Blackwell, 2004.

———. *The Tramp in America*. London: Reaktion, 2001.

"Crystal Waters—Stockton Welcomes a True Music Legend and 'International Dance Diva!'" *Caravan News,* August 24, 2016. https://www.caravannews.com/News/crystal-waters-stockton-welcomes-a-true-music-legend-and-international-dance-diva.

"Current Film Reviews: *The Young Runaways.*" *Independent Film Journal* 62, no. 8 (Sept. 17, 1968): 865.

Dargis, Manohla. "New American Realism Emerges amid Grousing and Hummers." *New York Times,* Jan. 25, 2008. https://www.nytimes.com/2008/01/25/movies/25sund.html?searchResultPosition = 1.

David, Lester. "Hitchhiking: The Deadly New Odds." *Good Housekeeping,* July 1973.

DeAngelis, Michael. Introduction to *Reading the Bromance: Homosocial Relationships in Film and Television,* edited by Michael DeAngelis, 1–27. Detroit: Wayne State University Press, 2014.

Delahanty, Thornton. "Tender Comrade." *Redbook* 82, no. 4 (Feb. 1944): 6, 8.

DePastino, Todd. *Citizen Hobo: How a Century of Homelessness Shaped America*. Chicago: University of Chicago Press, 2003.

Dickson, E.J. "18 Details *Once Upon a Time . . . in Hollywood* Got Right about the Manson Murders." *Rolling Stone,* August 7, 2019. https://www.rollingstone.com/culture/culture-features/manson-murders-once-upon-time-hollywood-tarantino-ending-868192/.

DiMaggio, Paul. *The Hitchhiker's Field Manual*. London: Collier, 1973.

Doherty, Thomas. *Projections of War: Hollywood, American Culture, and World War II*. New York: Columbia University Press, 1993.

Doles, Steven. "Social Problem Films." *Oxford Bibliographies in Cinema and Media Studies*. Last modified March 30, 2015. https://www.oxfordbibliographies.com/view/document/obo-9780199791286/obo-9780199791286-0161.xml.

Doty, Alexander. *Making Things Perfectly Queer: Interpreting Mass Culture*. Minneapolis: University of Minnesota Press, 1993.

Douglas, Mary. *Purity and Danger: An Analysis of Concept of Pollution and Taboo*. London: Routledge, 2002.

Dreier, Peter, and Richard Applebaum. "American Nightmare: Homelessness." *Challenge* 34, no. 2 (1991): 46–52.

Driscoll, Catherine. *Teen Film: An Introduction*. Oxford: Berg, 2011.

Dyer, Richard. "Entertainment and Utopia." In *Only Entertainment,* 19–35. London: Routledge, 1992.

———. "White." In *The Matter of Images: Essays on Representation,* 141–63. London: Routledge, 1993.

Ebert, Roger. "Ironweed." Feb. 12, 1988. https://www.rogerebert.com/reviews/ironweed-1988.

Eide, Stephen. *Homelessness in America: The History and Tragedy of an Intractable Social Problem*. Lanham, MD: Rowman & Littlefield, 2022.

Elledge, Jim. *The Boys of Fairy Town: Sodomites, Female Impersonators, Third-Sexers, Pansies, Queers, and Sex Morons in Chicago's First Century.* Chicago: Chicago Review Press, 2018.

Ellis, John. *Seeing Things: Television in an Age of Uncertainty.* London: I. B. Tauris, 2000.

"Emily Post Gives Nod to Hitch-Hiking and Frames Rules for 'Defense Debutantes.'" *New York Times,* Dec. 23, 1942.

Escobar, Sam, and Marci Robin. "15 Offensive Halloween Costumes That Shouldn't Exist." *Good Housekeeping,* Oct. 5, 2020. https://www.goodhousekeeping.com/holidays/halloween-ideas/a40778/most-offensive-halloween-costumes/.

Faulkner, Sally. "Introduction: Approaching the Middlebrow." In *Middlebrow Cinema,* edited by Sally Faulkner, 1–12. London: Routledge, 2016.

Ferrell, Jeff. *Drift: Illicit Mobility and Uncertain Knowledge.* Oakland: University of California Press, 2018.

Feuer, Jane. "Yuppie Envy and Yuppie Guilt." In *Seeing through the Eighties: Television and Reaganism,* 60–81. Durham, NC: Duke University Press, 1995.

Fleming, William L. "The Venereal Disease Problem in the United States in World War II." *Journal of the Elisha Mitchell Scientific Society* 61, no. 1/2 (1945): 195–200.

Flynt, Josiah. *Tramping with Tramps.* 1899. Reprint, New York: Okitoks, 2018.

Foster, Richard H. "Wartime Trailer Housing in the San Francisco Bay Area." *Geographical Review* 70, no. 3 (1980): 276–90.

Fraiman, Susan. *Extreme Domesticity: A View from the Margins.* New York: Columbia University Press, 2017.

Fretts, Bruce. "A Pop Culture Glossary for *Once Upon a Time . . . in Hollywood.*" *New York Times,* July 30, 2019. https://www.nytimes.com/2019/07/30/movies/once-upon-a-time-in-hollywood-glossary.html.

Freud, Sigmund. "The Uncanny." In *Complete Psychological Works: Standard Edition.* Vol. 17, 219–52. London: Hogarth, 1955.

Frey, Richard L. "Don't Let Death Hitch a Ride with You!" *Cosmopolitan,* August 2, 1953.

Friedberg, Anne. *Window Shopping: Cinema and the Postmodern.* Berkeley: University of California Press, 1993.

Friedman, Zack. "Student Loan Debt Statistics in 2020: A record $1.6 Trillion." *Forbes,* Feb. 3, 2020. https://www.forbes.com/sites/zackfriedman/2020/02/03/student-loan-debt-statistics/?sh=4f017070281f.

Fuery, Kelli. "The Two Textures of Invisibility: Shoes as Liminal Questionings in *Sullivan's Travels.*" In *Shoe Reels: The History and Philosophy of Footwear in Film,* edited by Elizabeth Ezra and Catherine Wheatley, 78–93. Edinburgh: Edinburgh University Press, 2020.

Fuster, Jeremy. "Tarantino Slid a Classics Grindhouse Film into *Once Upon a Time . . . in Hollywood.*" *The Wrap,* July 26, 2019. https://www.thewrap.com/tarantino-namath-once-upon-a-time-in-hollywood/.

Gardner, Mona. "Has Your Husband Come Home to the Right Woman?" *Ladies Home Journal*, Dec. 1945, 41.

Gardner, Sandra. "Homeless: More Join the Rolls." *New York Times*, Jan. 22, 1984.

Garon, Paul, and Gene Tomko. *What's the Use of Walking If There's a Freight Train Going Your Way? Black Hoboes and Their Songs*. Chicago: Charles H. Kerr, 2006.

Genné, Beth. "'Freedom Incarnate': Jerome Robbins, Gene Kelly, and the Dancing Sailor as an Icon of American Values in World War II." *Dance Chronicle* 24, no. 1 (2001): 83–103.

Gerber, David. "Heroes and Misfits: The Troubled Social Reintegration of Disabled Veterans in *The Best Years of Our Lives*." In *Disabled Veterans in History*, edited by David Gerber, 70–95. Ann Arbor: University of Michigan Press, 2012.

Goding, Christine. "White Event Horizon." *Monday Journal* 4. Accessed April 2, 2022. https://monday-journal.com/white-event-horizon/.

Gorbman, Claudia. *Unheard Melodies: Narrative Film Music*. Bloomington: Indiana University Press, 1987.

Gowen, Gwen, and Alexa Valiente. "'Beach Boys' Mike Love Recalls Meeting Charles Manson through Bandmate Dennis Wilson for the 1st Time." *ABC News*, March 15, 2017. https://abcnews.go.com/US/beach-boys-mike-love-recalls-meeting-charles-manson/.

Granshaw, Michelle. "Inventing the Tramp: The Early Comic on the Variety Stage." *Theatre History Studies* 38, no.1 (2019): 199–208.

———. *Irish on the Move: Performing Mobility in American Variety Theatre*. Iowa City: University of Iowa Press, 2019.

Grimm, Tom. *Hitchhiker's Handbook*. New York: Plume, 1972.

Halliwell, Martin. "Going Home: World War II and Demobilization." In *Therapeutic Revolutions: Medicine, Psychiatry, and American Culture, 1945 to 1970*, 17–47. New Brunswick, NJ: Rutgers University Press, 2013.

Hannam, Kevin, Mimi Sheller, and John Urry. "Editorial: Mobilities, Immobilities and Moorings." *Mobilities* 1, no. 1 (March 2006): 1–22.

Hansen, Miriam. *Babel and Babylon: Spectatorship in American Silent Film*. Cambridge, MA: Harvard University Press, 1991.

———. "The Mass Production of the Senses: Classical Cinema as Vernacular Modernism." *Modernism/Modernity* 6, no. 2 (1999): 59–77. Reprinted in *Reinventing Film Studies*, edited by Christine Gledhill and Linda Williams, 332–50. New York: Oxford University Press, 2000.

———. "Tracking Cinema on a Global Scale." In *The Oxford Handbook of Global Modernisms*, edited by Mark Wollaeger, with Matt Eatough, 601–26. New York: Oxford University Press, 2012.

Harvey, James. *Romantic Comedy in Hollywood: From Lubitsch to Sturges*. New York: Alfred A. Knopf, 1987.

Hegarty, Marilyn E. "Patriot or Prostitute: Sexual Discourse, Print Media, and American Women during World War II." *Journal of Women's History* 10, no. 2 (1998): 112–36.

Hirschfeld-Kroen, Leana. "Weavers of Film: The Girl Operator Mends the Cut." *Feminist Media Histories* 7, no. 3 (Summer 2021): 104–34.

Hoffman, Irving. "Thumbs Up on 'Devil' but 3 Critics Take It for a Ride: RKO Thriller Has Plenty BO Draw." *Hollywood Reporter,* March 26, 1947.

"Homeless Population." USA Facts. Accessed Dec. 19, 2022. https://usafacts.org/data/topics/people-society/poverty/public-housing/homeless-population/.

Hopper, Kim. "The New Urban Niche of Homelessness: New York City in the Late 1980s." *Bulletin of the New York Academy of Medicine* 66, no. 4 (Sept.-Oct. 1990): 435–50.

Hornaday, Ann. "'Middlebrow' Doesn't Have to Be Bad." *Washington Post,* April 18, 2013. https://www.washingtonpost.com/lifestyle/style/middlebrow-doesnt-have-to-be-bad-a-reappraisal-of-likable-movies/2013/04/18/9e9a7df2-a789-11e2-8302-3c7e0ea97057_story.html.

Howard, Ella. *Homeless: Poverty and Place in Urban America.* Philadelphia: University of Pennsylvania Press, 2013.

Humes, Edward. *Over Here: How the G. I. Bill Transformed the American Dream.* Orlando, FL: Harcourt, 2006.

Huntington, Foster. *Van Life: Your Home on the Road.* New York: Black Dog and Leventhal, 2017.

Isenberg, Noah. *Detour.* Basingstoke, Hampshire: British Film Institute, 2008.

Jameson, Booth. "Charles V and the Hitch-Hikers." *Saturday Evening Post,* May 26, 1928.

———. "Hitchhikers by Night Light." *Saturday Evening Post,* May 5, 1928.

———. "Just Students." *Saturday Evening Post,* Oct. 15, 1928.

Jones, Marian Moser. "Creating a Science of Homelessness during the Reagan Era." *Milbank Quarterly* 93, no. 1 (March 2015): 139–78.

Keating, Joshua. "*Nomadland* Is the Oscar Front-Runner, but It's Missing a Big Piece of the Picture." *Slate,* March 17, 2021. https://slate.com/culture/2021/03/nomadland-oscars-road-movies-amazon.html.

Kerouac, Jack. *The Dharma Bums.* 1958. Reprint, New York: Penguin, 2006.

———. *On the Road.* 1957. Reprint, New York: Penguin, 1999.

Kimmel, Michael. *Manhood in America: A Cultural History.* 3rd ed. New York: Oxford University Press, 2012.

King, Rob. "'A Purely American Product': Tramp Comedy and White Working-Class Formation in the 1910s." In *Early Cinema and the "National,"* edited by Richard Abel, Giorgio Bertellini, and Rob King, 236–47. Bloomington: Indiana University Press, 2008.

Kirby, Lynne. *Parallel Tracks: The Railroad and Silent Cinema.* Durham, NC: Duke University Press, 1997.

Klein, Amanda. *American Film Cycles: Reframing Genres, Screening Social Problems, and Defining Subcultures.* Austin: University of Texas Press, 2011.

Kozloff, Sarah. *The Best Years of Our Lives.* London: Palgrave MacMillan, 2011.

Kozol, Jonathan. "Distancing the Homeless." *Yale Review* 77, no. 2 (1988): 153–67.

———. *Rachel and Her Children: Homeless Families in America.* New York: Three Rivers, 1988.

Kracauer, Siegfried. *Theory of Film: The Redemption of Physical Reality.* Princeton, NJ: Princeton University Press, 1997.

Kristeva, Julia. *Powers of Horror: An Essay on Abjection.* Translated by Leon S. Roudiez. New York: Columbia University Press, 1982.

Kruse, Kevin M., and Stephen Tuck. "The Second World War and the Civil Rights Movement." In *Fog of War: The Second World War and the Civil Rights Movement,* edited by Kevin M. Kruse and Stephen Tuck, 3–14. New York: Oxford University Press, 2012.

Krutnik, Frank. "Critical Accommodations: Washington, Hollywood, and the World War II Housing Shortage." *Journal of American Culture* 30, no. 4 (2007): 417–33.

Kundera, Milan. "The Hitchhiking Game." 1974. Translated by Suzanne Rappaport. Reprint, *London Magazine,* May 1978.

Kusmer, Kenneth L. *Down and Out, on the Road: The Homeless in American History.* New York: Oxford University Press, 2002.

Lach, Eric. "Why Thousands of People Are Left Out of New York City's Daily Homeless Census." *New Yorker,* July 30, 2022. https://www.newyorker.com/news/our-local-correspondents/why-thousands-of-people-are-left-out-of-new-york-citys-daily-homeless-census.

Laviolette, Patrick. *Hitchhiking: Cultural Inroads.* London: Palgrave Macmillan, 2020.

Lawrie, J. P. *The Home Cinema.* London: Chapman and Hall, 1933. https://lantern.mediahist.org/catalog/homecinema00lawr_0038.

Lerner, Bettina. "Seriality and Modernity: *L'almanach des Mystères des Paris.*" *L'Esprit Créator* 55, no. 3 (Fall 2015): 127–39.

Lester, Elenore. "At Last: A Festival of Women's Films." *Ms. Magazine,* Oct. 1972. A reprint of "Every Day Was Ladies Day," *New York Times,* July 2, 1972.

Levinson, David, and Marcy Ross. "How Others See the Homeless." In *Homelessness Handbook,* edited by David Levinson and Marcy Ross, 221–44. Great Barrington, MA: Berkshire, 2007.

Linker, Beth, and Whitney Laemmli. "Half a Man: The Symbolism and Science of Paraplegic Impotence in World War II America." *Osiris* 30, no. 2 (2015): 228–49.

Lippard, Lucy. *The Lure of the Local: Senses of Place in a Multicentered Society.* New York: New Press, 1997.

Littauer, Amanda H. *Bad Girls: Young Women, Sex, and Rebellion before the Sixties.* Chapel Hill: University of North Carolina Press, 2015.

Lobo, Ben, and Sara Links. *Side of the Road: A Hitchhiker's Guide to the United States.* New York: Simon and Schuster, 1972.

Los Angeles Times. "Hitchhiking Women Must Expect Sexual Advances, Calif. Court Says." *Boston Globe,* July 21, 1977.

Lott, Eric. "The Whiteness of Film Noir." *American Literary History* 9, no. 3 (Autumn 1997): 542–66.

Lowbrow, Yeoman. "The Hitchhiking Craze: When Women Thumbed a Ride." *Flashbak,* Dec. 10, 2017. https://flashbak.com/hitchhiking-craze-girls-thumbed-ride-1960s-70s-390854/.

Maland, Charles. *Chaplin and American Culture: The Evolution of a Star Image.* Princeton, NJ: Princeton University Press, 1989.

Marin, Peter. "Helping and Hating the Homeless: The Struggle at the Margins of America." *Harper's Magazine,* Jan. 1987.

Masgrau-Peya, Elisenda. "Towards a Poetics of the 'Unhomed': The House in Katherine Mansfield's 'Prelude' and Barbara Hanrahan's *The Scent of Eucalyptus.*" *Antipodes* 18, no.1 (June 2004): 60–66.

Maslin, Janet. "Homeless, Helpless and Holy, in One Kind of Hell." *New York Times,* Nov. 17, 1993.

Massood, Paula J., and Pamela Wojcik. "Notes from the Editors: Precarious Mobilities." In "Precarious Mobilities." Special issue, *Feminist Media Histories: An International Journal* 7, no. 3 (Summer 2021): 1–18.

McCracken, Allison. "Real Men Don't Sing Ballads: The Radio Crooner in Hollywood, 1929 to 1933." In *Soundtrack Available: Essays on Film and Popular Music,* edited by Pamela Robertson Wojcik and Arthur Knight, 105–33. Durham, NC: Duke University Press, 2001.

McGraw, Rob. "My Old Truckee Home." *Boston Globe,* July 15, 1973, C9.

McIntyre, Iain, ed. *On the Fly! Hobo Literature and Songs, 1879–1941.* Oakland: PM Press, 2018.

McKittrick, Katherine. "On Plantations, Prisons, and a Black Sense of Place." *Social and Cultural Geography* 12, no. 8 (2011): 947–63.

McNally, Karen. *When Frankie Went to Hollywood: Frank Sinatra and American Male Identity.* Urbana: University of Illinois Press, 2008.

Mead, Margaret. "What's the Matter with the Family?" *Harper's Magazine,* April 1945.

Means, Alexander J. "Generational Precarity, Education, and the Crisis of Capitalism: Conventional, Neo-Keynesian, and Marxian Perspectives." *Critical Sociology* 43, no. 3 (2017): 339–54.

Meyer, Norma. "Hitchhiking Girls: They Follow a Dangerous Road." *Los Angeles Times,* July 28, 1977.

"MGV (Musique a Grande Vitesse)." Wise Music Classical. Accessed Jan. 15, 2023. https://www.wisemusicclassical.com/work/8623/MGV-Musique-a-Grande-Vitesse—Michael-Nyman/.

Michel, Sonya. "Danger on the Homefront: Motherhood, Sexuality, and Disabled Veterans in American Postwar Films." In *Gendering War Talk,* edited by Marian G. Cooke and Angela Woollacott, 260–79. Princeton, NJ: Princeton University Press, 1993.

Milburn, George. *The Hobo's Hornbook: A Repertory for a Gutter Jongleur.* New York: Ives Washburn, 1930.

Miller, Abraham. "On the Road: Hitchhiking on the Highway." *Society* 10, no. 5 (1973): 14–21.

Modleski, Tania. *The Women Who Knew Too Much: Hitchcock and Feminist Theory*. New York: Methuen, 1988.

Monroe, Rachel. "#Van Life: The Bohemian Social-Media Movement." *New Yorker*, April 17, 2017. https://www.newyorker.com/magazine/2017/04/24/vanlife-the-bohemian-social-media-movement.

Moody, Chris. "The Agony and Ecstasy of Living Nowhere." *New Republic*, March 30, 2021. https://www.escapees.com/wp-content/uploads/2021/04/Agony-Ecstasy-of-Living-Nowhere-TNR.pdf.

Morgan, Janice. "From Clochards to Cappuccinos: Renoir's Boudu is 'Down and Out' in Beverly Hills." *Cinema Journal* 29, no. 2 (Winter 1990): 22–35.

Motley, Mary Pennick, ed. *The Invisible Soldier: The Experience of the Black Soldier, World War II*. Detroit: Wayne State University Press, 1975.

Murf. "Thumb Tripping." *Variety*, Oct. 4, 1972.

———. "The Young Runaways." *Variety*, Sept. 11, 1968.

Murphy, Jeremiah. "Hitchhiking: Who Can Tell?" *Boston Globe*, Nov. 16, 1972.

Musser, Charles. *Before the Nickelodeon: Edwin S. Porter and the Edison Manufacturing Company*. Berkeley: University of California Press, 1991.

National Archives and Records Administration. "Confederate Pension Records." Last reviewed Sept. 13, 2022. https://www.archives.gov/research/military/civil-war/confederate-pension-records.

National Park Service. "Sacrificing for the Common Good: Rationing in World War II." Last updated June 3, 2016. https://www.nps.gov/articles/rationing-in-wwii.htm.

National Railroad Museum. "Wartime Restrictions on Passenger Travel." Last updated March 21, 2021. https://www.railpage.com.au/news/s/wartime-restrictions-on-passenger-travel.

National World War II Museum. "Rationing." Accessed June 22, 2021. https://www.nationalww2museum.org/war/articles/rationing.

———. "Research Starters: The Draft and World War II." Accessed Jan. 8, 2022. https://www.nationalww2museum.org/students-teachers/student-resources/research-starters/draft-and-wwii.

———. "Research Starters: US Military by the Numbers." Accessed Jan. 8, 2022. https://www.nationalww2museum.org/students-teachers/student-resources/research-starters/research-starters-us-military-numbers.

Neal, Brandi. "13 'Funny' Halloween Costumes That Are Actually Quite Offensive." *Bustle*, Oct. 5, 2017. https://www.bustle.com/p/13-funny-halloween-costumes-that-are-actually-really-offensive-2482167.

Nix, Elizabeth. "Why Are American Soldiers Called GIs?" History.com, August 22, 2018. https://www.history.com/news/why-are-american-soldiers-called-gis#:.

Nixon, Rob. *Slow Violence and the Environmentalism of the Poor*. Cambridge, MA: Harvard University Press, 2011.

Norden, Martin F. "Bitterness, Rage, and Redemption: Hollywood Constructs the Disabled Vietnam Veteran." In *Disabled Veterans in History*, edited by David Gerber, 96–114. Ann Arbor: University of Michigan Press, 2012.

Osteen, Mark. "Noir's Cars: Automobility and Amoral Space in American Film Noir." *Journal of Popular Film and Television* 35, no. 4 (2008): 183–92.
Packer, Jerome. *Mobility without Mayhem: Safety, Cars, and Citizenship.* Durham, NC: Duke University Press, 2008.
Pallidini, Jodi, and Beverly Dubin. *Roll Your Own: The Complete Guide to Living in a Truck, Bus, Van or Camper.* New York: Collier, 1974.
Palmer, Frederick. *Palmer Handbook of Scenario Construction.* Vol. 1, *An Elementary Treatise on the Theory and Practice of Photoplay Scenario Writing.* 2nd ed. Hollywood, CA: Palmer Photoplay Corporation, 1922. https://lantern.mediahist.org/catalog/elementarytreatioopalm_0001.
Peiss, Kathy. *Cheap Amusements: Working Women and Leisure in Turn-of-the-Century New York.* Philadelphia: Temple University Press, 1986.
Perl, Peter. "Record Number of Homeless Living in City Shelters." *Washington Post,* Oct. 21, 1982.
Phelps, Richard. "Songs of the American Hobo." *Journal of Popular Culture* 17, no. 2 (Fall 1983): 1–21.
"Pickup on 101." *Independent Film Journal* 70, no. 9 (Oct. 2, 1972): 56.
Piesman, Marissa, and Marilee Hartley. *The Yuppie Handbook.* New York: Long Shadow, 1984.
Pimpare, Stephen. *Ghettos, Tramps, and Welfare Queens: Down and Out on the Silver Screen.* New York: Oxford University Press, 2017.
Polan, Dana. "Blind Insights and Dark Passages: The Problem of Placement in Forties Film." *Velvet Light Trap* 20 (Summer 1983): 27–33.
———. *Power and Paranoia: History, Narrative, and the American Cinema, 1940 to 1950.* New York: Columbia University Press, 1986.
———. "Urban Trauma and the Metropolitan Imagination." Lecture delivered at Stanford University, Stanford, CA, May 5–7, 2005.
Polenberg, Richard. *War and Society: The United States 1941–1945.* Philadelphia: J.B. Lippincott, 1972.
Polito, Robert. "Some Detours to *Detour.*" Criterion.com, March 21, 2019. https://www.criterion.com/current/posts/6257-some-detours-to-detour.
Pols, Hans. "War Neurosis, Adjustment Problems in Veterans, and an Ill Nation: The Disciplinary Project of American Psychiatry during and after World War II." *Osiris* 22, no. 1 (2007): 72–92.
"'Postman Rings Twice' Sexy." *Hollywood Reporter,* Jan. 30, 1946.
Prince, Stephen. "Introduction: Movies and the 1980s." In *American Cinema of the 1980s: Themes and Variations,* edited by Stephen Prince, 1–21. New Brunswick, NJ: Rutgers University Press, 2007.
Puar, Jasbir, ed. "Precarity Talk: A Virtual Roundtable with Lauren Berlant, Judith Butler, Bojana Cvejić, Isabell Lorey, Jasbir Puar, and Ana Vujanović." *TDR: The Drama Review* 56, no. 4 (Winter 2012): 163–77.
Pudovkin, V.I. *Film Technique and Film Acting.* 1929. Reprint, London: CreateSpace Independent Publishing Platform, 2015.

Rainer, Peter. "The Review: Tim Hunter's Film about a Pair of Homeless Souls in New York Has Its Heart in the Right Place, but It Loses Its Bite in the Fairy-Tale Presentation." *Los Angeles Times,* Nov. 17, 1993.

Reagan, Ronald. "Interview with David Hartman of ABC News on the 1984 Presidential Election." *ABC World News Tonight,* Jan. 30, 1984. Reprint. Ronald Reagan Presidential Library & Museum. https://www.reaganlibrary.gov/archives/speech/interview-david-hartman-abc-news-1984-presidential-election.

Reck, Franklin M. "Will He Be Changed?" *Better Homes and Gardens,* Dec. 1944.

Reich, Elizabeth. "A Broader Nationalism: Reconstructing Memory, National Narratives and Spectatorship in World War II Black Audience Propaganda." *Screen* 54, no. 2 (Summer 2013): 174–93.

Reid, Jack. *Roadside Americans: The Rise and Fall of Hitchhiking in a Changing Nation.* Chapel Hill, NC: University of North Carolina Press, 2020.

Relph, Edward C. *Place and Placelessness.* London: Pion, 1976.

Rengifo, Alci. "The Aesthetic of Nostalgia in *Once Upon a Time . . . in Hollywood.*" *Riot Material,* August 1, 2019. https://cvonhassett.medium.com/the-aesthetic-of-nostalgia-in-once-upon-a-time-in-hollywood.

"Review of *Detour.*" *Variety,* Jan. 23, 1946.

Rhodes, John David. "'Concentrated Ground': *Grey Gardens* and the Cinema of the Domestic." *Framework: The Journal of Cinema and Media* 47, no. 1 (Spring 2006): 83–105.

———. *Spectacle of Property: The House in American Film.* Minneapolis: University of Minnesota Press, 2017.

"A Retro Look . . . with a Twist: Robert Richardson, ASC, Employed Panavision Anamorphic Optics for Writer-Director Quentin Tarantino's *Once Upon a Time . . . in Hollywood.*" Panavision.com. Accessed June 1, 2021. https://panavision.com/highlights/highlights-detail/richardson-creates-a-retro-look-with-a-twist-for-once-upon-a-time-in-hollywood.

"Richest 1 Percent Bagged 82 Percent of Wealth Created Last Year—Poorest Half of Humanity Got Nothing." OxFam International. Jan. 22, 2018. https://www.oxfam.org/en/pressroom/pressreleases/2018-01-22/richest-1-percent-bagged-82-percent-wealth-created-last-year.

Risen, James. "Only the Rich Got Richer in '80s, Fed Concludes during Reagan Era, Poor Lost Ground." *Baltimore Sun,* Jan. 7, 1992. https://www.baltimoresun.com/news/bs-xpm-1992-01-07-1992007010-story.html.

Salmon, Caspar. "Tarantino's Revenge Fantasies Are Growing more Puerile and Misogynistic." *The Guardian,* August 23, 2019. https://www.theguardian.com/film/2019/aug/23/quentin-tarantino-gruesome-revenge-fantasies-once-upon-a-time-in-hollywood.

Sands, Susan. "Backpacking: 'I Go to the Wilderness to Kick the Man-World Out of Me." *New York Times,* May 9, 1971.

Sargent, Epes Winthrop. *The Technique of the Photoplay.* 2nd ed. New York: Moving Picture World; Chalmers Publishing, 1913. https://archive.org/details/techniqueofphotooosargrich.

Sehgal, Parul. "The Bright, Brief Flame of an Impatient Writer." *New York Times,* April 15, 2021.

Schlebecker, John T. "An Informal History of Hitchhiking." *The Historian* 20, no. 3 (May 1958): 305–27.

Schuetz, Alfred. "The Homecomer." *American Journal of Sociology* 50, no. 5 (March 1945): 369–76.

Sconce, Jeffrey. "'Trashing' the Academy: Taste, Excess, and an Emerging Politics of Style." *Screen* 35, no. 4 (Winter 1995): 371–93.

Scott, A. O. "Neo-Neo Realism." *New York Times,* March 17, 2009. https://archive.nytimes.com/www.nytimes.com/2009/03/22/magazine/22neorealism-t.html.

———. "*Nomadland* Review: The Unsettled Americans." *New York Times,* Feb. 18, 2021. https://www.nytimes.com/2021/02/18/movies/nomadland-review.html.

S. D., Trav. "Ten Tramp Comedians." *Travalanche.* August 11, 2017. https://travsd.wordpress.com/2017/08/11/ten-tramp-comedians/.

Semuels, Alana. "Poor at 20, Poor for Life." *The Atlantic,* July 14, 2016. www.theatlantic.com/business/archive/2016/07/social-mobility-america/491240/.

Sharf, Zack. "Quentin Tarantino Picks 10 Films to See before *Once Upon a Time in Hollywood.*" IndieWire, July 17, 2019. https://www.indiewire.com/gallery/quentin-tarantino-movies-influenced-once-upon-a-time-in-hollywood/.

Shields, Todd G. "Network News Construction of Homelessness: 1980–1993." *Communication Review* 4, no. 2 (2001): 193–218.

Shiek, Duncan, and Steven Sater. "The B*tch of Living." Track 4 on *Spring Awakening: A New Musical.* Verve, 2006, compact disc.

Shortell, Timothy, and Evrick Brown. "Introduction: Walking in the European City." In *Walking in the European City: Quotidian Mobility and Urban Ethnography,* edited by Timothy Shortell and Evrick Brown, 1–18. Burlington, VT: Ashgate, 2014.

"Silent Film Makeup: What Was It Really Like?" *Silent-Ology,* Feb. 22, 2016. https://silentology.wordpress.com/2016/02/22/silent-film-makeup-what-was-it-really-like/.

Silverman, Kaja. "Dis-embodying the Female Voice." In *Issues in Feminist Film Criticism,* edited by Patricia Erens, 309–27. Bloomington: Indiana University Press, 1990.

———. *Male Subjectivity at the Margins.* New York: Routledge, 1992.

Sinclair, Abiola. "Review: *The Saint of Fort Washington.*" *New York Amsterdam News,* Nov. 27, 1993.

Sobchack, Vivian. "*Detour:* Driving in a Back Projection, or Forestalled by Film Noir." In *Kiss the Blood off My Hands: On Classic Film Noir,* edited by Robert Miklitsch, 113–29. Urbana: University of Illinois Press, 2014.

Staller, Karen M. *Runaways: How the Sixties Counterculture Shaped Today's Practices and Policies.* New York: Columbia University Press, 2006.

Stamp, Shelley. *Lois Weber in Early Hollywood.* Berkeley: University of California Press, 2015. http://www.jstor.org/stable/10.1525/j.ctt13x1gnm.

Standing, Guy. "The Precariat." *Contexts* 12, no. 4 (Fall 2014): 10–12.

———. *The Precariat: The New Dangerous Class.* New York: Bloomsbury, 2016.

Strand, Ginger. *Killer on the Road: Violence and the American Interstate.* Austin: University of Texas Press, 2012.

Strasser, Judith A. "Urban Transient Women." *American Journal of Nursing* 78, no. 12 (Dec. 1978): 2076–79.

Stukator, Angela. "'Soft Males,' 'Flying Boys,' and 'White Knights': New Masculinity in *The Fisher King*." *Literature/Film Quarterly* 25, no. 3 (1997): 214–21.

Tallerico, Brian. "All the Movies and Shows Referenced in *Once Upon a Time . . . in Hollywood*." *Vulture*, July 31, 2019. https://www.vulture.com/article/once-upon-a-time-in-hollywood-influences-references.html.

———. "*Nomadland*." RogerEbert.com. Feb. 19, 2021. https://www.rogerebert.com/reviews/nomadland-movie-review-2020.

Teeley, Sandra Evans. "Hard Times Breed New Homeless." *Washington Post*, Jan. 23, 1983.

Tobias, Manuela. "California Homeless Population Grew by 22,000 over Pandemic." *CalMatters*, Oct. 6, 2022. https://calmatters.org/housing/2022/10/california-homeless-crisis-latinos/.

Toronto Film Society. "*The Devil Thumbs a Ride* (1947)." July 12, 2018. https://torontofilmsociety.com/film-notes/the-devil-thumbs-a-ride-1947-2/.

Tzioumakis, Yannis. *American Independent Cinema.* 2nd ed. Edinburgh: Edinburgh University Press, 2017.

United States Department of Housing and Urban Development (HUD). "HUD Releases 2022 Annual Homeless Assessment Report." Press release no. 22-253, Dec. 19, 2022. https://www.hud.gov/press/press_releases_media_advisories/HUD_No_22_253.

Valian, Patricia. *Hitchhiking: The Road to Rape and Murder.* Chatsworth, CA: Brandon, 1974.

Van Ells, Mark D. *To Hear Only Thunder Again: America's World War II Veterans Come Home.* Lanham, MD: Lexington Books, 2001.

Vecsey, George. "More Women Defy Risks of Hitchhiking." *New York Times*, Dec. 26, 1972.

Vuic, Kara Dixon. *The Girls Next Door: Bringing the Home Front to the Front Lines.* Cambridge, MA: Harvard University Press, 2019.

Waller, Willard Walter. *The Veteran Comes Back.* New York: Dryden, 1944.

———. "What You Can Do to Help the Returning Veteran." *Ladies Home Journal*, Feb. 1945, 26–27.

"Wanger Agenda?" *Motion Picture Herald*, June 24, 1944.

Waters, Crystal. "The Story of Crystal Waters' 'Gypsy Woman (She's Homeless).'" Vice.com, April 8, 2016. https://www.vice.com/en/article/jp4gkp/crystal-waters-gypsy-woman-interview.

Weaver, Caity, "I Lived the #VanLife: It Wasn't Pretty." *New York Times*, April 20, 2022. https://www.nytimes.com/2022/04/20/magazine/van-life-dwelling.html.

Wecter, Dixon. *When Johnny Comes Marching Home.* Boston: Houghton Mifflin, 1944.

Weiner, Lynn. "Sisters of the Road: Women Transients and Tramps." In *Walking to Work: Tramps in America, 1790–1935*, edited by Eric H. Mokkonen, 171–88. Lincoln: University of Nebraska Press, 1984.

Weiss, Walter F. *America's Wandering Youth: A Sociological Study of Young Hitchhikers in the United States.* Jericho: Exposition, 1974.

Wernig, Phil. *The Hitchhikers.* Millbrae, CA: Celestial Arts, 1972.

Westenfeld, Adrienne. "Sharon Tate Never Wanted to Be an Object. That's Exactly What Happened in *Once Upon a Time... in Hollywood.*" *Esquire*, July 31, 2019. https://www.esquire.com/entertainment/movies/a28538449/quentin-tarantino-once-upon-a-time-in-hollywood-fails-sharon-tate-female-characters/.

Wheildon, L. B. "National Housing Emergency, 1946–1947." Editorial Research Reports 1946. Vol. 2. Accessed July 8, 2022. https://cqpress.sagepub.com/cqresearcher/report/national-housing-emergency-1946-1947-cqresrre1946121700.

Whitaker, Charles. "What Can We Do about the Homeless?" *Ebony*, June 1989.

White, Diane. "Lure of In-City Hitchhiking Growing Peril to Coeds." *Boston Globe*, Nov. 21, 1969.

Williams, Linda. *Screening Sex.* Durham, NC: Duke University Press, 2008.

Wilson, Elizabeth. "The Invisible *Flaneur.*" In *The Contradictions of Culture: Cities, Culture, Women*, 72–89. London: Sage, 2001.

Wojcik, Pamela Robertson. *The Apartment Plot: Urban Living in American Film and Popular Culture, 1945 to 1975.* Durham, NC: Duke University Press, 2010.

———. "The Cop and the Kid in 1930s American Film." *The Oxford Handbook of Children's Film*, edited by Noel Brown, 169–87. New York: Oxford University Press, 2022.

———. *Fantasies of Neglect: Imagining the Urban Child in American Film and Fiction.* New Brunswick, NJ: Rutgers University Press, 2016.

———. *Gidget: Origins of a Teen Girl Transmedia Franchise.* New York: Routledge, 2020.

———. "The Girl and the Phonograph, or the Vamp and the Machine Revisited." In *Soundtrack Available: Essays on Film and Popular Music*, edited by Pamela Robertson Wojcik and Arthur Knight, 433–54. Durham, NC: Duke University Press, 2001.

———. "Is the Home Ever Not Precarious? The Long Arc of Genres of Precarity." *Mediapolis: A Journal of Cities and Culture* 6, no. 5 (Nov. 12, 2021). https://www.mediapolisjournal.com/2021/11/is-the-home-ever-not-precarious/.

———. "*Wanda* (1970)." In *Screening American Independent Film*, edited by Justin Wyatt and Wyatt Phillips, 140–48. New York: Routledge, 2023.

Wolff, Janet. "The Invisible *Flaneuse:* Women and the Literature of Modernity." In *Feminine Sentences*, 34–50. Berkeley: University of California Press, 1990.

Woloch, Alex. *The One vs. the Many: Minor Characters and the Space of the Protagonist in the Novel.* Princeton, NJ: Princeton University Press, 2003.

Wood, Robin. *Hollywood from Vietnam to Reagan ... and Beyond.* New York: Columbia University Press, 2003.

Wyman, Jeb. "The Battle after the War." *Humanities Washington Blog,* Nov. 10, 2020. https://www.humanities.org/blog/the-battle-after-the-war/.

"The Year of the Yuppie." *Newsweek,* Dec. 31, 1984.

Yellin, Emily. "Lining Up for Wartime Weddings." *New York Times,* Feb. 2, 2017. https://www.nytimes.com/interactive/projects/cp/weddings/165-years-of-wedding-announcements/world-war-two-weddings.

———. *Our Mother's War: American Women at Home and at the Front during World War II.* New York: Free Press, 2004.

Zaniello. Tom. *The Cinema of the Precariat: The Exploited, Underemployed, and Temp Workers of the World.* New York: Bloomsbury Academic, 2020.

INDEX

Abelson, Elaine S., 42
Ackroyd, Dan, 163
Allotment Wives, 82
Ambrosino, Lillian, 140
American Graffiti, 114, 145, 207–209, 219
American Honey, 206, 210, 213, 216, 217
American Pluck, 39–40
Anchors Aweigh, 76–78
Anderson, Nels, 24, 46, 54
A-Noi (books), 24, 225n24
Apartment for Peggy, 89–90
Applebaum, Richard, 169, 171
Arbuckle, Fatty, 26
Arkin, Alan, 154
Augé, Marc, 13
Austen, Albert, 36
Avery, Dwayne, 9

Bach, Damon, 135
Badlands, 145
bag lady, 165, 171, 177, 178, 188–189
Bahrani, Rahmin, 205
Baldwin, James, 170
Ball, Lucille, 164, 188–189
Bannerman, Helen, 187
Barefoot, Guy, 133
Barrow, Reverend Willie Taplin, 172
Battle of the Coral Sea, 114
Bava, Mario, 145
Bay, Mia, 119
beggar(s), 23, 225n32, 228n83
Beggars of Life, 44–45, 51
Bellour, Raymond, 70

Belushi, Jim, 163, 194
Bergman, Alan, 148
Bergman, Marilyn, 148
Berlant, Lauren, 17, 205–206, 218
Best Years of Our Lives, The, 71, 92, 98–103
Bhaba, Homi, 9–10, 67
blacks, blackness, 34–36, 38–42, 62, 69, 75, 85, 102–108, 118–119, 121, 166, 168, 170, 172, 186–188, 189, 193, 196, 211, 214, 227n71
  blackface, 35–36, 39, 40
Bloom, Lew, 24–25
Bly, Robert, 190
Boag, Peter, 54
Bonus Marchers, 31, 69, 96
Boone, Margaret, 172, 173
Born on the Fourth of July, 109
Boudu Saved from Drowning, 196
Bowie, David, 161, 174
Boyhood, 209
Brazil, Benjamin, 135, 138
Breezy, 113, 148, 151, 153, 154
Brickman, Barbara, 145, 154, 238n8
Bridges, Jeff, 163
Bright Victory, 92–93, 96–98, 104–105, 106, 107, 108
Brockmole, Jessica, 93
Brody, Richard, 2
bromance, 195–200, 202
Bronfen, Elisabeth, 10, 71
Brooks, Mel, 163, 191
Brown, Evrick, 11

Brown, Tom, 25
Bruder, Jessica, 1–3
bum(s), 32, 167, 175, 185, 199, 230–232n115
　distinction from tramps and hoboes, 225–226n32
Buryn, Ed, 135–136

Cabin in the Sky, 104
Cain, James M., 132
Capra, Frank, 26, 58, 60, 104
Carpenter, John, 175
cars, 84, 117, 224n7
　and hitchhiking, 114, 117, 118, 119, 124, 137, 142
　and precarity, 212–213
　and rationing, 121, 122
　rideshares, 157
　women driving, 92–94, 123
　and youth films, 209, 212–213
Cassidy, Shaun, 148
Caught in a Cabaret, 32
C. C. & Company, 113
Chaplin, Charlie, 24, 25, 26, 31, 32, 36, 48, 51–52, 61, 194, 201, 226n48
Chauncey, George, 55, 230n113
Chop Shop, 205–206, 210, 211, 212, 214–215, 250n11
C. H. U. D., 164, 175–176
Clock, The, 74, 82–83, 91
Coates, Ken, 66, 103
Cohan, Steven, 28
Colbert, Claudette, 119
Coleman, Gary, 177
Colmery, Harry, 68
Coming Home, 109
Cook, Pam, 143, 144, 157
Cooper, Alice, 176
counterculture, 115
　hippie truckees, 6–7
　hitchhikers, 16, 116, 134–140, 142, 157
　runaways, 16, 138–140, 179
Coxey's Army, 31
Clubs are Trump, 30, 57
Crane, Stephen, 24
Cravens, Gwyneth, 133, 135
Creedence Clearwater Revival, 142
Cresswell, Tim, 11, 21, 22, 23, 42, 43, 219
Curly Sue, 163, 194–195

Dallas, 171
Daniels, Jeff, 164
Davies, W. H., 24
Dawn: Portrait of a Teenage Runaway, 148, 149, 153
"Day-In, Day-Out," 161–162
Dazed and Confused, 208–209
DeAngelis, Michael, 195, 196
Death Proof, 113
Deer Hunter, The, 109
Defoe, Willem, 210
DePastino, Todd, 23, 35
Detour, 4, 115, 125–128, 132, 133
Devil Thumbs a Ride, The, 128–132
Dharma Bums, 133, 134
Diary of a Teenage Hitchhiker, 142, 155, 156
DiMaggio, Paul, 136, 137, 138, 141
Dimples, 26
Dmytryk, Edward, 89
Donleavy, Brian, 81
Dope, 209
Doty, Alexander, 58
Double Indemnity, 132
Douglas, Mary, 173
Down and Out in America, 184, 185
Down and Out in Beverly Hills, 163, 195–196, 198–199, 200
Dreier, Peter, 169, 171
Dreiser, Theodore, 24
Dreyfuss, Richard, 163
Driscoll, Catherine, 147, 209
Duel, 4
Dynasty, 171

Easy Rider, 113, 114
Easy Street, 226n48
Ebert, Roger, 177
Ellis, John, 14, 162
Evel Knievel, 114
Exorcist, The, 114
exploitation films, 129, 132–133, 142–144, 157, 162, 163

Farmer's Daughter, The, 132
Father Steps Out, 32–34, 191
Faulkner, Sally, 164
Fault in Our Stars, The, 207, 209
Feuer, Jane, 191

Fields, W. C., 25
film cycles, defined, 13–15
   about hitchhiking, 113–115, 124–133, 142–157, 163, 204
   about homelessness, 162–164, 174–203, 204
   moral panics and, 14, 27, 144, 155–157, 204
   about precariat, 204–218
   about tramps, 19–63, 163, 177, 204
   about veterans, 64–110, 163, 204
film noir, 16, 115, 123–133, 142, 144
Fisher King, The, 163, 190, 195–200
Flagg, James Montgomery, 25
Flint, Shelby, 148
Florida Project, The, 206, 210, 213, 214, 215, 217
Flynt, Josiah, 24, 228n73
Ford, Henry, 117
Ford, John, 119
Foster, Richard, 7
Fraiman, Susan, 50, 70, 83
Freud, Sigmund, 9
From Here to Eternity, 76
Funt, Alan, 144

Gable, Clark, 120
Gabriel Over the White House, 31, 32
Garon, Paul, 35
Gaye, Marvin, 142
Genné, Beth, 79–80
gentrification, 170–172
Getting Straight, 114
G. I. Bill of Rights, 68–69, 85, 96, 102, 233n27
Gilliam, Terry, 163
Gilman, Charlotte Perkins, 89
Gimme the Loot, 206, 210, 211, 212, 213, 215, 216, 217
Ginger in the Morning, 113, 146, 153–154
Girl and Her Trust, A, 49–50
Girls of the Road, 43–44, 46, 119
Glover, Danny, 187
God Bless the Child, 185–186, 188
Goldman, Emma, 141
Good Time, 206, 210, 212, 213, 217
Gorbman, Claudia, 215
Gordian Knot, 147

Granshaw, Michelle, 22, 35–36
Grant, Lee, 184
Grapes of Wrath, The, 119, 131
Grasshopper, The, 146, 147, 150, 151, 152
Grease, 145, 182
Great Escape, The, 113
Griffith, D. W., 49, 50, 61
Grimm, Tom, 136, 138, 141
Gun Crazy, 124
Gunman's Walk, 114
Guy-Blaché, Alice, 37
"Gypsy Woman (She's Homeless)," 158–160, 162

Hallelujah I'm a Bum, 32, 38
"Hallelujah I'm a Bum," 30–31
Ham's Whirlwind Finish, 38
Hansen, Miriam, 21, 27, 29, 36
Happy Hooligan (comic), 25
Happy Hooligan (film), 36–37
Happy Hooligan: The Spider and the Fly, 29
Harvey, James, 60
Heaven Knows What, 206, 210, 211, 213, 215, 216
Hegarty, Mary, 75, 80
Hell, Richard, 182
Heroes, 109
Highway Hell, 114, 120–121
Hirschfeld-Kroen, Leana, 49
Hitchcock, Michael, 179
Hitcher, The, 115, 156
hitchhiking, hitchhikers, 16, 111–157
   black, 118–119, 121
   female, 111–116, 117–118, 119–120, 122, 124, 139–155
   and feminism, 140–142, 143, 144
   film cycles, 113–114, 123–133, 142–157, 163
   in film noir, 123–133, 142, 144
   history of, 116–119, 121–123, 133–142
   and masculinity, 123–133
   moral panics and, 16, 116, 144, 155–157
   and police, 119, 120, 122, 128, 131, 138, 156, 138
   pop songs, 142, 147–149
   and race, 118–119, 123
   sexual assault, 141, 151
   versus tramping and vagrancy, 118, 138

hitchhiking, hitchhikers *(continued)*
   whiteness, 113, 117, 118–119, 134
   young, 116, 117, 133–138
   and youth film, 114–116, 142–155
Hitch-Hiker, The, 115, 128–133, 147
Hitchhikers, The, 113, 145, 146, 147–148, 149, 151, 154, 207
hobo(es), 24, 25–26, 61, 225*n*25
   camps (or jungles), 12, 27, 33, 40, 45, 177, 228*n*78
   conventions, 42, 224*n*7
   distinction from tramps and bums, 225–226*n*32
   songs, 25, 27, 30–31, 35, 224*n*7, 225*n*30, 227*n*71
home, 7, 8, 9–10, 16, 17, 20, 28, 37, 43, 47, 50–55, 58, 64–65, 67, 69, 70, 71, 72, 83–84, 85, 91–92, 95, 96, 97, 98, 99–100, 105, 106, 107, 108–109, 183, 184, 196, 198–200, 208, 214, 215, 216
   building, 53, 85, 90–91, 101, 170
   fantasy of, 51–52, 70, 71, 83–84, 95, 98, 201, 215–216
   front, 64–68, 69, 75, 84, 85, 91, 93, 121
   leaving, 116, 130, 131, 135, 137, 139, 140, 146–155, 178–179, 207
   ownership, 65, 68, 169, 206
Homecoming, The, 75, 91
homeless, homelessness, 16, 166–167
   black, 166, 168, 170, 172, 186–188
   bromances, 195–200, 202
   comedic films, 190–202
   and disgust, 172–173
   film cycle, 162–164, 174–203
      as middlebrow, 163–164
   heterosexual coupling, 195–200
   history and causes, 165–173
   horror films, 174–176
   and masculinity, 190–191, 194–200
   and mental illness, 167, 170, 190, 247*n*55
   minorities, 165–166
   moral panic and, 16
   social problem films, 184–188, 189
   versus unhoused, 244*n*1
   youth films, 178–184
   and whiteness, 164, 165–166, 167, 179, 184–188, 189
   women, 165

Home of the Brave, 107–108
Hoover, J. Edgar, 123, 240*n*41
Hornaday, Anne, 163, 164, 202
housing, 7, 11, 65, 67, 68, 74, 84–91, 164, 167, 168–171
   loans, 233*n*27
   shortage, 7, 16, 66, 67, 69, 70, 71, 84–91, 101, 103, 104, 109, 163, 234*n*35
   subsidized, 247*n*47
Howells, William Dean, 24
Hubby to the Rescue, 48
Hughes, John, 163, 209

I'll Be Seeing You, 73–74, 94–95
Immigrant, The, 36
Impatient Years, The, 84, 88, 92
In Living Color, 160
In Our Hands: Battle for Jerusalem, 206
In the Meantime, Darling, 74, 86–87, 88–89
In Search of America, 6
Ironweed, 176–178
Isenberg, Noah, 126, 127, 128
It Happened in Brooklyn, 89, 92
It Happened One Night, 115, 119–120, 131
It Happened on Fifth Avenue, 52–53, 58, 90, 191

Jazz Singer, The, 38
Johnny Doesn't Live Here Anymore, 86, 88
Jolsen, Al, 32, 38
Jones, Marian Moser, 165
Jubilo, 29, 38–39
Jurado, Arthur, 96

Keating, Joshua, 2, 4
Kellerman, Sally, 154
Kelley, Emmett, 25
Kelly, Gene, 76, 77
Kemper, Ed, 155
Kennedy, William, 176
Kerouac, Jack, 133, 134–135
Kid, The, 52, 194, 201
Kid Auto Races, 25
Kimmel, Michael, 28
King, Rob, 25, 36, 37–38
Kings Go Forth, 106, 107, 108
Kirby, Lynne, 55–56

272 · INDEX

Kiss Me Deadly, 124
Klein, Amanda, 13–15, 27, 129
Kozol, Jonathan, 172, 173
Kracauer, Siegfried, 12, 13
Kristeva, Julia, 173
Kromer, Tom, 24
Kruse, Kevin, 103
Krutnik, Frank, 75, 87
Kundera, Milan, 111, 116, 142
Kusmer, Kenneth, 23, 35

La Cava, Gregory, 26
Lady Bird, 209
Laemmli, Whitney, 94
Lahti, Christine, 164
L. A. Law, 171, 191
Lancer, 113
Landis, John, 163
Lane, Charles, 164, 195–202
Last Black Man in San Francisco, The, 206, 211, 213–214, 215–216
Last of Us, The, 203
Lean on Pete, 206, 210, 213, 215, 217
Legrand, Michel, 148
Levinson, David, 191, 194, 198
Life Stinks, 163, 191–193, 194, 195, 196, 198, 200
Lifestyles of the Rich and Famous, 171
Linker, Beth, 94
Links, Sara, 136, 137, 138, 140, 141
Lippard, Lucy, 13
Littauer, Amanda, 75
Little Miss Innocence, 113, 152
Little Orphan Annie (comic), 25
Live Fast Die Young, 114
Living in a Big Way, 84, 90–91
Lloyd, Harold, 26, 30, 57
Lobo, Ben, 136, 137, 138, 140, 141
Lonedale Operator, The, 49–50
Lonely Villa, The,^#-^$ 50
London, Jack, 24
Love Laughs at Andy Hardy, 132
Lupino, Ida, 130, 132
Lynch, Kelly, 163

Mabel's Strange Predicament, 25, 48
Maid, 203
Maluca, 213

Man Push Cart, 205–206, 210, 211, 212, 213, 250n11
Man's Castle, 44
Manson family, 112, 113, 237n1
Marching On, 40–42, 58, 228n79
Marin, Peter, 173
marriage, 70, 81–84, 101
masculinity
    film noir, 123–133
    and hitchhiking, 123–133
    and homelessness, 190–191, 194, 195–200
    and servicemen, 72, 77, 94, 97–98
    and tramps, 28–58, 190
Masgrau-Peya, Elisenda, 9
Maybe I'll Come Home in the Spring, 146, 148, 149, 150, 155, 207
Mazursky, Paul, 163
McCormack, Patty, 146
McDormand, Frances, 1
McGraw, Rob, 6
McGuire, Dorothy, 83
McKittrick, Katherine, 172
McManus, John T., 132
Mead, Margaret, 87
Means, Alexander J., 218
Me and Earl and the Dying Girl, 207, 209
Meet John Doe, 58–60, 62
Meet Me in St. Louis, 62–63
Men, The, 93, 96–98, 106
Michel, Sonya, 92
middlebrow, 163–164
Midler, Bette, 163
Miller, Abraham, 134, 136
Miracle of Morgan's Creek, The, 80–81
mobility, 4, 5, 7, 8, 9, 10, 13, 14, 15, 17, 18, 21, 66, 69, 71, 72, 108, 116, 124, 125, 153, 157, 163, 164, 168, 171, 218–219
    auto, 116–117, 122
    black, 35, 36, 42, 118–119, 227n71
    countercultural, 114, 115, 134, 137–138
    defined, 11–12
    and feminism, 140, 143
    and homeless, 166
    and precariat, 204–205, 206, 207, 210–216
    and tramp, 23, 24, 28, 29, 34, 47, 165
    women's, 43–43, 66, 114, 115, 116, 120
    and youth, 16, 133–138, 207–209

Modern Times, 31, 51–52, 185
Monroe, Rachel, 5
Moody, Chris, 4–5
moral panics
   film cycles and, 14, 129
   hitchhikers and, 16, 116, 144
   homeless and, 16
   tramps and, 16, 27, 177
   veterans and, 66–67
More the Merrier, The, 86, 88
Morgan, Janice, 194
Morrison, W. R., 66, 103
Mulvey, Laura, 143
Munshin, Jules, 76
Murphy, Eddie, 163
Musser, Charles, 29–30
My Foolish Heart, 74
My Man Godfrey, 53–54

Neal, Tom, 126
Negro Soldier, The, 104
neo-neorealism, 17, 205, 209–210
Nervy Nat Kisses the Bride, 29, 48
Night Holds Terror, The, 128–133
Nolte, Nick, 163
Nomadland, 1–5, 203
No Place Like Home, 164, 184–186, 188
Norden, Martin, 92
Nyman, Michael, 214

Once Upon a Time . . . in Hollywood, 111–114, 142, 153, 157
On the Benches in the Park, 47
On the Nickel, 177–178
On the Right Track, 177–178, 194
On the Road, 133
On the Town, 71, 76, 78–80
Only a Hobo, 26
Opper, Frederick Burr, 25
Osborne, Jeffrey, 181
Osteen, Mark, 124

Packer, Jeremy, 117, 118, 133
Palmer, Frederick, 19–20
Paper Towns, 209
paracinema, 15, 143
Phillips, Mackenzie, 154
Pickup on 101, 144, 151

Pickup on South Street, 132
Pollard, "Snub," 30, 57
placeless, placelessness, 8, 10, 13, 14, 15, 17, 18, 21, 22, 35, 54, 66, 67, 71, 72, 114, 115, 138, 154, 157, 162, 166, 204, 218, 219, 251*n*16
   defined, 12–13
Polan, Dana, 95, 128
Polito, Robert, 127
Post, Emily, 122
Postman Always Rings Twice, The, 124–126, 128, 132, 133
Plumb, Eve, 153
precariat, 17, 204–205
Pride of the Marines, 72–73, 74–75, 93, 96–98
Prince of Darkness, 164, 175–176
Prysock, Arthur, 147
Pudovkin, V. I., 223*n*6
Pursuit of Happyness, The, 162

Rafferty and the Gold Dust Twins, 153, 154
Reagan, Ronald, 167–169, 172, 174
Real Women Have Curves, 209
Reich, Elizabeth, 40
Reichardt, Kelly, 205
Reid, Jack, 117, 137, 139, 140
Reitman, Ben L., 24, 225*n*25
Relph, Edward, 10, 12, 13, 67
Renoir, Jean, 196
Rhodes, John David, 10
Richardson, Robert, 114
Road, The, 4
Robbie, Margot, 112
Robbins, Tom, 142
Rogers, Will, 29, 38
Romance of the Rail, A, 55–56
Rondstadt, Linda, 148
Rooftops, 180–181, 207
Roosevelt, Franklin Delano, 68, 69, 121
Rosemary's Baby, 144
Rosie the Riveter, 86, 87–88
Ross, Marcy, 191, 194, 198
runaways, 16, 113, 138–140, 178–179
Russell, Bobby, 147
Russell, Harold, 99

Saint of Fort Washington, The, 186–188, 189
Sargent, Epes Winthrop, 19, 20

Saturday Night Fever, 182
Savage Gringo, 113
Scarecrow, The, 29
Schlebecker, John T., 138
Schuetz, Alfred, 67
Sconce, Jeffrey, 143
Scott, A. O., 3, 205
Seals and Croft, 142
Sehgal, Parul, 111, 116
servicemen, 64–110
    black, 75, 102–108, 233*n*27
    heterosexual coupling, 70, 75, 79, 81–84
    hitchhiking, 121
    mobility of, 66, 69, 72–74, 108
    mobilization, 65–66
    moral panic, 81
    and sexual promiscuity, 75–81
Shelter, 162
Shortell, Timothy, 11
Sidewalk Stories, 164, 200–202
Silverman, Kaja, 74, 94, 101, 149
Sinatra, Frank, 76, 77, 89, 106
Since You Went Away, 73, 74, 89
skid row(s), 35, 47, 61, 165, 166, 170, 176, 177, 178, 229*n*95, 229*n*95, 230*n*115
Skirts Ahoy, 73
slow death, 205
    slow death cinema, 205–207, 209–218
    versus slow cinema, 207
Smalley, Phillips, 50
Smith, Will, 179
Smithereens, 181–182
Sobchack, Vivian, 126
social problem films, 69–70, 104, 162, 163, 184, 189, 203
Something for the Boys, 90
South Pacific, 105–106, 107
Spacek, Sissy, 148
Spring Awakening, 207
Square Shoulders, 29
Staller, Karen, 133, 139
Stamp, Shelley, 50
Standing, Guy, 207
Stapleton, Maureen, 177
Star Wars Episode VIII: The Last Jedi, 206
Station Eleven, 203
Steinem, Gloria, 143
Stigwood, Robert, 182

Stone Pillow, 164, 188–190
Story of Little Black Sambo, The, 187
Street Trash, 164, 174–176
Streetwise, 179
Stukator, Angela, 190
Sturges, Preston, 26, 58, 60, 61, 80
subculture, 179–183
Sullivan's Travels, 58, 59, 60–62, 192
Sunrise, 83
Suspense, 50–51

Tallerico, Brian, 3
Tangerine, 206, 210, 212, 216
Tangerine Dream, 213
Tarantino, Quentin, 111–114
Tate, Sharon, 112, 113
Teenage Hitchhikers, 113, 151, 152
Temple, Julian, 161
Temple, Shirley, 26, 178
Tender Comrade, 72, 75, 89
Texas Chainsaw Massacre, The, 156
thirtysomething, 171, 191
This is the Life, 26
Thumb Tripping, 144, 151, 154
Till the End of Time, 83–84, 92, 98–103
Times Square, 182–183
Tolable David, 223*n*6
Tomko, Gene, 35
Too Busy to Work, 29, 38–19
Trading Places, 163, 195, 196, 198, 200
train, 72–74, 123, 212
tramp(s), 15–16, 19–63, 118, 163, 191
    autobiographies, 24
    black, 34–36, 38–42, 227*n*71
    comics, 25, 27
    demise of, 224*n*7
    distinction from hoboes and bums, 225–226*n*32
    female, 42–46, 223*n*2, 228*n*83, 229*n*90, 229*n*91
    and femininity, 46–54
    in filmmaking manuals, 19–20
    films, 25–26
    Halloween costume, 62–63
    and home, 10, 37, 47, 50–55
    Irish, 35–36, 37
    masculinity, 28–58, 190, 223*n*2
    as masher, 47–48

tramp(s) *(continued)*
  mobility, 23–24, 28, 47, 72, 165
  modernity and, 21–22, 24, 26–27
  moral panics and, 16, 23, 27, 29
  origins of, 23–24
  and police, 23, 30, 31, 36, 40, 42, 45, 46, 49, 51, 52, 57, 224n17, 226n48
  queer, 54–58, 225n25, 230n105, 230n113
  songs, 25, 27, 30–31, 35, 224n7, 225n30, 227n71
  stock character, 20
  vaudeville, 24–25, 26, 34–36
  versus hitchhiking, 118, 138
  whiteness, 34–42, 227n57
  work/working class, 28–34
Tramp and the Dog, The, 25
Tramps, 206, 210, 212, 213, 215, 216
Tramp's First Bath, The, 47
Tramp's Story, The, 26
Tramp Strategy, The, 37
Troop Train, 72
Truman, Harry, 85
Trumbo, Dalton, 89
Tuck, Stephen, 103
Tully, Jim, 24
Twenty Minutes of Love, 48–49
Twitch of the Death Nerve, 145
Two-Lane Blacktop, 114
Tzioumakis, Yannis, 144

Ulmer, Edgar, 132
unhomed, 95, 106–107, 128, 216
  defined, 9–10
  unhomeliness, 9–10, 67
urban renewal, 170–172

Vagabond, 182
vagrant, 23, 26, 167, 175, 246n26
  differentiated from hitchhikers, 138
Valian, Patricia, 136, 141, 155
Valley of the Dolls, 113
Van Ells, Mark, 92, 98
Vanishing Point, 114
Vanity Fare, 142
#vanlife, 4–6, 115
veterans, 64–110
  alienation, 67
  black, 69, 85, 233n27

  conversion narratives, 95–98
  mental illness, 94–103
  and moral panic, 66–67
  racism, 103–108
  rehabilitation and reintegration, 64–65, 94–103
    women's role, 91–94, 97–98, 100–101
  veteran problem, 64–66, 108–110
  Vietnam, 109
  whiteness, 103–108

Waite, Ralph, 177
Waller, Willard Walter, 64–65, 76, 84
Walking Dead, The, 203
"Waltzing Mathilda," 177
Wanda, 13, 182
Wandering Willies, 30, 57
Wanger, Walter, 65, 103
Waters, Crystal, 158–160
Wayans, Kim, 160
Weary Willie Kisses the Bride, 48
Weaver, Caity, 5
Weaver, Thomas, 172, 173
Weber, Lois, 50
Wecter, Dixon, 65, 75–76
Weiner, Lynn, 42, 43
Weiss, Walter F., 137
Wendy and Lucy, 205–206, 210, 212, 213, 216, 250n11
Wernig, Phil, 136
West Side Story, 180
What Do You Say to a Naked Lady, 144
When We Were Twenty-One, 47
Where the Day Takes You, 164, 179–180, 183, 207
whiteness, 5–6, 34–42, 69, 75, 103–108, 113, 117, 119, 145, 164, 165–166, 167, 179, 184–190, 207–209, 215, 240n44
Wild Boys of the Road, 44, 45–46, 207
Williams, Michelle, 210
Williams, Robin, 163
Williams, Spencer, 40
Wills, Nat, 25
Wise, Robert, 180
Withers, Jane, 26, 178
With Honors, 195, 196, 197, 198, 199, 200
Woloch, Alex, 21, 22, 59

women's liberation, 116, 141, 143, 155
Wood, Robin, 195, 196
World War II, 16, 163
    housing shortage, 7, 16, 65, 66, 67, 69, 70, 71, 84–91, 101, 103, 104, 109, 163, 234*n*35
    marriage boom, 81–82
    and mobilization, 65–66
    veteran problem, 64–66
World's Most Beautiful Girls, The, 132
Wrecking Crew, The, 113
Wyatt, Wilson, 85

"Year of Jubilo, The", 38
Young, Loretta, 132

Young Graduates, The, 145
Young Runaways, The, 142, 144, 146, 147, 149, 151, 152, 154–155
youth, 16
    audience, 15,
    films, 114–116, 144–155, 157, 163, 178–184
    and precarity, 204–207
    runaway, 138–140
    travel, 6, 133–138
yuppies, 17, 157, 171–172, 196
    guilt, 191, 194
Yuppie Handbook, The, 171

Zhao, Chloé, 1

Founded in 1893,
UNIVERSITY OF CALIFORNIA PRESS
publishes bold, progressive books and journals
on topics in the arts, humanities, social sciences,
and natural sciences—with a focus on social
justice issues—that inspire thought and action
among readers worldwide.

The UC PRESS FOUNDATION
raises funds to uphold the press's vital role
as an independent, nonprofit publisher, and
receives philanthropic support from a wide
range of individuals and institutions—and from
committed readers like you. To learn more, visit
ucpress.edu/supportus.

www.ingramcontent.com/pod-product-compliance
Lightning Source LLC
Chambersburg PA
CBHW021340230426
43666CB00006B/354